ICONS OF R&B AND SOUL

ICONS OF R&B AND SOUL

An Encyclopedia of the Artists Who Revolutionized Rhythm

VOLUME 2

Bob Gulla

Greenwood Icons

GREENWOOD PRESS
Westport, Connecticut · London

Library of Congress Cataloging-in-Publication Data

Gulla, Bob.
   Icons of R&B and soul: an encyclopedia of the artists who revolutionized rhythm /
Bob Gulla.
      p.   cm.—(Greenwood icons)
   Includes bibliographical references and index.
   ISBN 978-0-313-34044-4 (set: alk. paper)—ISBN   978-0-313-34045-1 (vol. 1: alk.
paper)—ISBN 978-0-313-34046-8 (vol. 2: alk. paper)
   1. African Americans—Music—History and criticism.   2. Rhythm and blues music—
United States—History and criticism.   3. Soul music—United States—History and
criticism.   4. Rhythm and blues musicians—United States.   5. Soul musicians—United
States. I. Title.
   ML3479.G85   2008
   781.643092′396073—dc22
   [B]   2007040518

British Library Cataloguing in Publication Data is available.

Library of Congress Catalog Card Number: 2007040518
ISBN: 978-0-313-34044-4 (set)
      978-0-313-34045-1 (vol. 1)
      978-0-313-34046-8 (vol. 2)

First published in 2008

Greenwood Press, 88 Post Road West, Westport, CT 06881
An imprint of Greenwood Publishing Group, Inc.
www.greenwood.com

Printed in the United States of America

The paper used in this book complies with the
Permanent Paper Standard issued by the National
Information Standards Organization (Z39.48–1984).

10   9   8   7   6   5   4   3   2   1

Contents

Photos

Ray Charles (page 1). 1973. Courtesty of Photofest.

Richard Wayne Penniman; aka Little Richard (page 27). ca. 1950s. Courtesy of Photofest.

Fats Domino (as himself) (page 47). In Roy Lockwoods's 1957 film, *Jamboree*. Courtesy of Warner Bros./Photofest.

Ruth Brown (page 69). Performing at Michael's Pub in New York City, 1988. Courtesy of Photofest.

LaVern Baker (page 91). ca. 1950s. Courtesy of Photofest.

Sam Cooke (page 107). ca. 1960s. Courtesy of Photofest.

Jackie Wilson (page 129). ca. 1960. Courtesy of Photofest.

Etta James (page 147). ca. 1970. Michael Ochs Archives/Getty Images.

Ike and Tina Turner (page 167). ca. 1960s. Courtesy of Photofest.

The Isley Brothers (page 191). ca. 1973. Courtesy of Photofest.

James Brown (page 211). Undated picture. Courtesy of Photofest.

Curtis Mayfield (page 233). Undated picture. AP Photo/Curtom Records.

Smokey Robinson and The Miracles (page 249). Courtesy of Photofest.

The Temptations (page 267). Shown from the left: Eddie Kendricks, David Ruffin, Otis Williams, Melvin Franklin, and Paul Williams. Courtesy of Photofest.

The Supremes (page 289). Late 1960s. Shown from left: Mary Wilson, Florence Ballard, and Diana Ross. Pictorial Press Ltd./Alamy.

Stevie Wonder (page 309). ca. 1970s. Courtesy of Photofest.

Marvin Gaye (page 329). 1974. Courtesy of Photofest.

Dusty Springfield (page 355). 1969. AP Photo.

Aretha Franklin (page 377). Undated picture. Pictorial Press Ltd./Alamy.

Otis Redding (page 395). 1967. Courtesy of Photofest.

Sly and the Family Stone (page 417). 1969. Shown clockwise from top: Larry Graham, Freddie Stone, Gregg Errico, Sly Stone, Rose Stone, Cynthia Robinson, and Jerry Martini. Courtesy of Photofest.

George Clinton (page 439). Performs with Parliament-Funkadelic, c. late 1970s. Courtesy of Photofest.

Gamble & Huff (page 459). Leon Huff and Kenny Gamble pose for this 1970 photo. Michael Ochs Archives/Getty Images.

Prince (page 481). Starring as The Kid in Albert Magnoli's 1984 film, *Purple Rain*. Courtesy of Photofest.

Preface

We are inundated with information. On the Web, in the bookstores, over the airwaves, our daily lives are saturated with data—new, old, reliable, not so reliable. We possess so much information at our fingertips that we as a people feel compelled to collate it as a community into encyclopedic Web pages (i.e., Wikipedia) so as not to lose track of all the knowledge we're amassing as a culture.

So it comes as a bit of a surprise when we stumble collectively on an idea that is more or less unexplored. Not that we haven't read about the personalities collected herein or that the R&B and soul genres are under-represented in the marketplace of ideas. It just hasn't been collected, packaged, and presented like the collection now in your hands.

There is a handful of books on the market right now that address the racial, political, and social repercussions of R&B and Soul. In the late 1940s, and through the 1950s and 1960s, the seminal acts were remarkable in that they functioned as both "uniters" and dividers. Influential performers like Ruth Brown and Fats Domino brought young black and white audiences together (when venues allowed it), but they also caused racial tension among the older guard. Many older Americans saw these talented artists, and their fame, wealth, and power as a source of resentment, deepening the racial divide. This divisiveness has provided fertile turf for sociologically minded authors, in particular Peter Guralnick, Nelson George, and Craig Werner, all of whom have written eloquently on the subject.

While the *Icons* series understands that the racial ramification is central to the story of soul and R&B, it also understands it is not the only tale to tell. The artists themselves—many who've made such an incredible impact on pop and popular culture—had imposing obstacles to overcome. Sam Cooke's storied transition from sacred to secular, Otis Redding's brief but soaring career as R&B's great hope, and Etta James's endless battles with the demons of drug addiction. Some of these stories have been told in cradle-to-grave biographies or autobiographies. Many have been compiled in encyclopedic fashion; their stories told hastily with only the most salient details.

A few of the artists presented here have been written about prodigiously, like James Brown and Little Richard. David Ritz, a reputable author specializing in R&B and Soul artists, has written biographies and ghost-written with a handful of artists included in these pages: Aretha Franklin, Ray Charles, Marvin Gaye, and Etta James to name a few. His work was helpful throughout the research process. Another author, R&B scholar Rick Coleman, recently dusted off the remarkable story of the legendary Fats Domino. His book *Blue Monday: Fats Domino and the Lost Dawn of Rock and Roll*, added insight and information to the Fat Man saga.

An equal handful, however, don't have many words at all dedicated to their lives and work. George Clinton, the Isley Brothers, LaVern Baker, and Stevie Wonder, for example, have had luminous careers, but minimal coverage. Digging up the information to execute these stories required consulting a variety of sources, then piecing those sources together as an archaeologist would piece together bones.

The result is a chronological excursion through R&B and soul, as envisioned through the eyes of its most significant contributors, from its incipient hit makers through its controversial popularization in the 1950s, its world domination in the 1960s, and its ultimate demise at the hands of disco and dance music, unofficially known as the R&B death knell, in the late 1970s.

Because the original, classic wave of R&B and soul suffered a miserable extinction at the hands of disco, I've ended this set with the last true soul legend, Prince, the one man brave enough to soldier on in soul despite the poor odds. Sure, there were many popular artists throughout the 1980s that also mined the genre, but none qualify as legends along the lines of the chosen few presented here. Much of the latest generation's so-called neo-soul music is fleeting, ephemeral, and so many of the artists responsible for it have been so derivative, it was hard to rationalize including anyone after Prince. Michael Jackson, arguably, was the only other consideration, but ultimately he ranks as a pop artist, despite his important early work for Motown with his brothers in the Jackson 5.

Anyone interested in the major personalities of the genres should find the work featured here useful, whether it be for student research or just to enhance one's appreciation of the idiom's most accomplished purveyors. Appended to each essay is a complementary sidebar, an element designed to add color and dimension to the subject's life story, whether it be the history of a studio, an instrument, or an executive integral to the star's life and work. Further Reading and Selected Discography suggestions can also be found at the end of each essay. These are not definitive, but good jumping-off points for lengthier explorations.

More complete, but still not definitive is the ending Bibliography, and complete listening section, which taken together provide a good indication of the breadth of sources used in executing these essays. A timeline is also included; it takes a look at the years through the prism of R&B and soul music's epic moments.

To execute the various essays included in this book, I consulted both traditional and new media sources, from books and magazines to Web sites, blogs, and Internet video sites. I traced the path of each subject's career in a linear way, beginning with childhood, family life, and musical beginnings, and then ending with either their death or the present day. Along the way, each one's salient moments receive coverage; peak and post-peak activities are pointed out. Most subjects experienced down periods of creativity and artistic misguidance at one time or another, resulting in unanimously maligned work. Critics recognize these phases, so when this happens, I make sure to say so. I did not intend to cast these artists in nothing but a positive light. On the other hand, editorializing is kept to a minimum.

Incidentally, the artists are represented chronologically, in part because so much of what happened throughout the history of R&B had so much to do with what came before it, or its antecedents. This kind of evolution is critical to the study of popular music. Having a foundation is an integral part of any study, especially in the arts, not only for critics looking for antecedents and precedents, but for casual listeners looking to optimize their appreciation and enjoyment of the music they already love.

DEFINING MOMENT

"Rhythm and blues" was a term used to describe a number of postwar American popular music forms, like boogie-woogie, 12-bar blues, and jump blues. All of these forms possessed a backbeat, an element that would later become fundamental to rock and roll. Where Delta blues is often seen as music of resignation, R&B, despite its common name, is actually more antithetical to it. It is seen as dance music, erotic music, escapist music, and spiritual music. It also expressed hope, pride, defiance, solidarity, and rebirth. These qualities can be found in all the best R&B, from early examples like Duke Ellington's "Black, Brown, and Beige" to Chuck Berry's "Brown-Eyed Handsome Man," the Impressions' "Keep on Pushing," Sam Cooke's "A Change Is Gonna Come," and John Coltrane's "A Love Supreme."

The early center of rhythm and blues was Los Angeles, which hosted a number of small independent labels that arose after the war. Specialty, Duke/Peacock, King/Federal, Chess, Sun, Modern, RPM, Vee-Jay, and Atlantic all formed to take advantage of, among other audiences, the new population of urban blacks. Their success foreshadowed the later rise of Motown a decade later, the most successful of all black-owned businesses.

The major labels at the time had been slipping in their attention on what had been going on in popular music. Most had applied their efforts to bland big band and vocal pop. In 1948, RCA Victor began marketing black music under the name "Blues and Rhythm," a term that replaced the original "race music," a moniker deemed offensive in traditional, conservative postwar America. At the time, a *Billboard* journalist named Jerry Wexler was editing the charts for his magazine and he simply reversed the words. The term was used then in the chart listings from 1949 onward and the charts in question encompassed a number of contemporary forms that emerged around that time. *Billboard* even called it the "Harlem Hit Parade" in 1949.

Based on the exciting progress it saw with acts like Wynonie Harris and Roy Brown, Atlantic Records, an independent label owned by Ahmet Ertegun, Herb Abramson, and later Wexler, began assembling a roster of artists of its own in 1947. They signed Ruth Brown and LaVern Baker, along with Tiny Grimes, Sticks McGhee, and the Clovers. Atlantic's grouping of these like-minded artists proved instrumental in shifting R&B as an art form over to a wider audience. Suddenly, a movement was born. As the sound evolved Atlantic and others, including Specialty, Modern, and RPM began ramping up their output. Ray Charles, Chuck Willis, Fats Domino, Hank Ballard, Clyde McPhatter, Jackie Wilson, and others bridged the gap between blues, big band, R&B, and rock and roll.

When Billy Haley and rock and roll surged in 1954, R&B also gained traction, as an Afro-American companion to the predominantly white sounds of rock.

A few years later, by the early 1960s, rock and roll had nearly completely usurped R&B and the genre in its narrowest sense waned. Rock and roll dominated record sales, and many of the genre's biggest sellers had already passed their peak creative years. An offshoot of R&B, soul music, took its place at center stage thanks to the able hands of Charles, Sam Cooke, and the acts of Berry Gordy's Detroit label, Motown.

Soul music redefined R&B and brought it into the 1970s and beyond. Many of the greatest soul performers of the age—Cooke, Curtis Mayfield, Smokey Robinson—radically reinterpreted R&B and turned it into popular music, in many cases for both whites and blacks. R&B on its own rarely sold to white audiences; white record stores did not carry it, white radio stations did not play it (rather, they played whitewashed versions of R&B tunes), and the white-owned television stations did not invite R&B acts to perform. Early on, due to segregated booking policies, black acts were not even booked to play at the better hotels and casinos. But soul music, with its ability to attract white audiences, changed all that. The demand had become too great to ignore.

By the 1970s, R&B had again returned to favor as a term, only with different connotations. It was used as an umbrella phrase to describe the various splinters of R&B, soul, disco, and funk.

SUBJECT MATTERS

Part of the fun and a good source of deliberation involved in putting this *Icons* project together had to do with deciding which artists would make the final list. In many instances, of course, the choices were what we'd refer to as no-brainers: Ray Charles, James Brown, Aretha Franklin, Otis Redding, Sam Cooke. These are names synonymous with the topic. Elsewhere, though, shades of gray arose.

One feverish debate had to do with whether Fats Domino and Little Richard were considered "R&B" or "rock and roll." In many sources, they are referred to as nothing short of "rock and roll royalty." But in others, they are described as seminal R&B artists. So which is it? Well, the short answer is they were, in fact, both. They played rock and roll before the term was invented, when all musicians in that rhythmic style were referred to as R&B acts. Fats and Little Richard were front and center during the bumpy transition from R&B to rock and roll between the years of 1949 and 1954. But because rock and roll stemmed from R&B, it hadn't emerged as a distinct art form. And so, during the transition, artists like LaVern Baker, Jackie Wilson, Domino, and Little Richard all resided at the intersection of the two. This is why there is so much confusion.

Clearly, Little Richard and Fats Domino, with their piano pounding techniques and rollicking rhythms, represented the future of rock and roll style. But their music, written by legends like "Bumps" Blackwell and Dave Bartholomew, was pure R&B. Fats Domino, Bartholomew's early charge, articulated the confusion in an interview: "When we played a slow number they called it 'Rhythm & Blues.' When we played a fast number, they called it 'rock and roll.'" In case you were wondering, Chuck Berry also received serious consideration. But because his instrument of choice was the guitar rather than the more conventional, R&B-accepted piano, he fit more squarely into rock and roll, which truly came of age when he, Billy Haley, and Ike Turner began making their guitars featured instruments within their bands.

I also felt that the incredible story of blue-eyed soul queen Dusty Springfield, a white woman from Britain, was more significant than say, Roberta Flack, Mary Wells, Martha Reeves, or a number of other women who made brief but important contributions to the soul canon of the 1960s. Springfield's masterful *In Memphis* is reason enough for inclusion in this book. But Dusty also served as a soul ambassador to many outside the States, not to mention she had a riveting tale to tell.

I also made the 11th-hour decision to write on the life and times of LaVern Baker, a woman often called the "first female rock and roller," and an essential artist whose contributions to popular music have been tragically overlooked. She became one of seven women presented in this set. My only regret is that I had to omit the most excellent Drifters, with Clyde McPhatter and, later, Ben E. King. They remain the first act on my virtual waiting list.

These decisions are all arguable, of course, and have provided fodder for lively debate. Please don't feel, though, that the results of my decisions, the topics of my essays, have not been thought through thoroughly.

I also had to draw a couple of other lines: Motown is well represented here with essays on the Supremes, the Temptations, Smokey Robinson and the

Miracles, Stevie Wonder, and Marvin Gaye. The label dominated the 1960s soul scene and helped define the genre. Because they were so well represented, I had to exclude deserving acts like the Four Tops, Martha Reeves and the Vandellas, and the Jackson 5.

And speaking of Motown, attentive readers might pick up on the fact that there is no chapter on Berry Gordy himself, but there is one on Kenny Gamble, Leon Huff, and Thom Bell, the men responsible for creating the Sounds of Phildelphia. Just as Gordy created the Motown Sound, Gamble, Huff, and Bell created Philly soul. The reason for this is simple. The Motown story is told here from many different angles, through the artists that are represented with essays. But the Philly soul story—with its brilliant bands—the O'Jays, Harold Melvin and the Blue Notes, the Spinners, and others—was not. Telling that story through the eyes of the men who popularized it provided me with an easy way out. Besides, I feel Philly soul at its best is one of the genre's picture perfect offshoots.

And speaking of groups, another line was drawn concerning which ones to include. There were many vocal and instrumental acts throughout the classic R&B and soul period running from the mid-1950s to the mid-1970s and I did include a handful: the Temptations, Sly and the Family Stone, George Clinton's Parliament-Funkadelic, and the Isley Brothers. But there were so many more excellent and important bands we did not have the space to include, especially from the decade of the 1970s when soul turned to funk and slick pop in the hands of War; Kool and the Gang; Earth, Wind and Fire; and the Commodores. Chic, led by Bernard Edwards and Nile Rodgers, dominated the late 1970s with its funk-R&B fusion.

IN CLOSING

There is a tremendous amount to be learned from these life stories. An important aspect of presenting this collection is discovering the common elements from the lives and careers of these artists. For example, many if not all had to overcome a daunting and mean-spirited racial climate. In the South this meant dealing with Jim Crow laws and intimidating, bigoted law enforcement officials. Because entertainers kept late hours and did so much traveling, they frequented risky and unsavory areas populated by police and trouble.

Also, most of the men and women in these pages dealt with unscrupulous businessmen. Some of the artists, Ruth Brown, for example, Sam Cooke, and Ray Charles, were able to fight the inequity of the system and gain some respect, not to mention financial justice, by starting their own business, or taking their profiteering bosses to task. Most were not.

Virtually all of these legends had their indulgences—a symptom of fame and circumstance—from money to sex and drugs, and most coped with addictions of one form or another. But back when these artists were active, media coverage and press scrutiny was only a fraction of what it is today, so the private lives of these musicians remained, for the most part, private. For example, when Etta James disappeared for a couple of years, few but those who knew her personally had any idea of her whereabouts. It was only until she told her own story in her book *Rage to Survive* that we found out the hell she'd gone through. And what a story it is. That she is alive today is a miracle.

I also delved deeper into the critically important role music played in integration. In many cities and towns across America music served as something that united white with black, men with women, young with old. Often, because of racial conflicts, that unity never materialized. In the worst of times, audiences were segregated with white fans in the ground-level seats and blacks looking on from the balcony. In the best of times, generally in the North, these important acts would play to sophisticated, open-minded multiracial audiences. Still, music united as much as it divided.

In the 1950s, many labels set a precedent by featuring white and black collaborations, with white urbanites establishing the companies and black artists making products for them to sell. This partnership continued through the 1960s. These labels—Stax, Atlantic, Curtis Mayfield's Curtom, Ray Charles's Tangerine, and others—were at the forefront of a social revolution. Without the integrative foundation established by these collaborations, racial barriers would have stayed up longer, and remained stronger.

In the 1960s, the music itself played a revolutionary role in the civil rights movement. Artists like Sam Cooke, Curtis Mayfield, Sly Stone, the Tempations, Stevie Wonder, Marvin Gaye, and others wrote eloquently of racial inequality and the turbulent socio-cultural climate. Their albums made massive national impact and helped pave the way for better race relations if not outright civil rights legislation.

And last—perhaps best of all—is that the story of a good number of these brilliant artists embodies the archetypal narrative arc that runs from rags to riches. It is a distinctly American concept, and the tremendous success, creative accomplishment, and social impact of these performers have remained a template for aspiring young black artists ever since. In Detroit in the 1950s for example, every teenager on every street corner, inspired by the work of the Drifters, Hank Ballard, Ruth Brown, Clyde McPhatter, Jackie Wilson, and Billy Ward, wanted to be a pop star. It is a testament to the life and work of these pioneers.

Courtesy of Photofest.

Smokey Robinson and The Miracles

MOTOWN'S MAIN MEN

The numbers speak for themselves. The Miracles, with Smokey Robinson at the helm, had 46 Hot 100 hits between 1959 and 1975 and 29 of those landed in the Top 40. On the list of the hundred greatest songs of the 1960s, at least 10 of them would have Smokey Robinson's byline on it, including "Tracks of My Tears," "My Girl," "Since I Lost My Baby," and "Ain't That Peculiar." The material is indelibly etched into the pantheon of popular music. If there were a contest to name the all-time number one songwriter of mainstream soul, Smokey Robinson would win hands down, in the face of some towering competition.

As a songsmith, few have matched Robinson's craft, his melodic grace, and his mastery of arranging. As a singer, he communicated innocence and devotion better than any other, via a flexible tenor that soared effortlessly into falsetto.

He and the Miracles explored the sweeter side of soul with a string of exquisite ballads sung in that satiny falsetto.

As a lyricist, Robinson's words mingled sincerity and eloquence, often describing love with unique metaphors. Even Bob Dylan recognized him as one of America's greatest living poets.

The Miracles used to headline the famous Motortown Revues, which says an awful lot when two other giants, the Supremes and the Temptations, were also on the bill. The Supremes may have had bigger hits and the Temptations could sure slay them with dance steps. The Miracles weren't fancy dancers, or huge hitmakers. They worked their magic with nothing more than great songs and solid performances.

The early turning point in Smokey Robinson's career came fortuitously, when he met another Detroit native, Berry Gordy, at an audition in New York City in 1957. Gordy suggested when they returned to Detroit that they might work together. That meeting would change both of their lives forever.

More than a decade his senior, Gordy and Robinson were close from the start. Berry tutored Smokey in songwriting, taking him under his wing, and grooming him as a well rounded musical talent. "Every song should have an idea, tell a story, mean something," he told him (Charlie Gillett, "The Miracle of Smokey Robinson," *Record Mirror*; September 25, 1971). He employed Gordy's advice. Songs had to mean something. In time, Robinson's songs would mean quite a lot, financially as well as musically. Gordy, looking for acts to sign to his new management company, contracted Smokey's vocal group the Miracles. Along with Eddie Holland, they formed the nucleus of Gordy's upstart venture.

Gordy licensed the first Miracles record, "Got a Job," to End Records (owned by a man named George Goldner in New York) and the second, "Bad Girl," to Chess (owned by Leonard Chess in Chicago). But Gordy hadn't been remunerated very generously for his work, and that's when he decided to make a move, establish his own label. Eventually they'd call it Tamla. If Gordy had been properly compensated for the work he did for End and Chess, he might never have been driven to start his own company.

In 1960, Gordy signed the Miracles to Tamla and he soon began grooming Smokey as his second in command. The grooming paid off. Robinson served as vice president until the company's sale to MCA in 1988. Early on, Gordy initially allowed Robinson to oversee the work of his own band, the Miracles, as songwriter, arranger, and producer. But once he proved himself in that project, he allowed him to develop the talents of Mary Wells and the Supremes. Wells hit it big first, and so Robinson focused his efforts on her. One measure of Robinson's superb work is the fact that once Wells left Motown in 1964, she never again had the same success.

Many more acts benefited from Robinson's golden touch, and his tale is one of pop's great success stories. He wrote and produced for numerous Motown artists, including Marvin Gaye ("Ain't That Peculiar," "I'll Be Doggone"), the Temptations ("Get Ready," "The Way You Do the Things You Do," "My

Girl"), Mary Wells ("My Guy," "You Beat Me to the Punch"), and the Mar-velettes ("Don't Mess with Bill," "The Hunter Gets Captured by the Game").

In July 1972, Robinson parted ways with the Miracles, and both parties enjoyed a further phase of continued success. Robinson's biggest solo hits, "Cruisin'" and "Being with You," came in the late 1970s and early 1980s.

Legend has it that audience members would break into tears when Robin-son and the Miracles sang "The Tracks of My Tears." Even the notoriously hard-to-please Berry Gordy proclaimed the song a masterpiece. It also fore-shadowed another melancholy classic, "The Tears of a Clown," which in 1970 became the Miracles' first number one pop hit. Excluding compilations, Smokey Robinson and the Miracles released 15 albums for Motown. On his own Robinson recorded another 16 albums for Tamla and Motown. But he was responsible for so much more than music at Motown. He was one of the chief architects of the label's campaign to capture the "Sound of Young America," which is exactly what they did.

EARLY YEARS

He was born William Robinson Jr. in Detroit in 1940. An uncle had nick-named him "Smokey" in reference to his skin tone. He had light-brown skin and blue eyes; his uncle didn't ever want him to forget he was black. They grew up in a working-class home in Detroit, comfortable enough to get by.

Junior's mom sang and played piano in church, but not professionally. There was a piano in the house that Smokey sat at frequently, but he didn't take lessons or learn to read music. Some of the first songs Smokey recalls hearing were his mother's church hymns, which he sang aloud around the house, much to the chagrin of his sisters.

At 10, life at home changed dramatically for Robinson. His mom died, and considering his father, a municipal truck driver nicknamed "Five," was away from home for extended periods, he became the legal ward of his older sister Geraldine. Fortunately for Smokey, Gerry was a music enthusiast, and his life was filled, if not with the nurturing of his natural parents, at least with the sounds of Sarah Vaughan and Billie Holiday.

"Long before I heard rock and roll," Smokey remembers, "Sarah was a part of my household. Man, I worshipped her sound and I emulated her lush licks and tasty turns. Her range thrilled me. I loved the way she cried with her voice. I was awestruck by her subtlety and sensitivity" (David Ritz, liner notes, *Smokey Robinson and the Miracles: The 35th Anniversary Collection*, Motown, 1994, p. 9).

As a student at Northern High, Smokey and a couple of his best friends were studying to be electrical engineers. On the side, they had formed a doo-wop group; they sang on the street corners for the neighborhood. Smokey was gifted and ambitious, and his skills as a songwriter had already surfaced.

Detroit at the time was a jumping metropolis. The automobile manufacturing revolution had hit a peak, pumping out ever longer-finned luxury vehicles and employing the city's population. Coming of age in such a healthy economy allowed the working-class teens in the city to grow up flush with optimism and aspirations. A handful of these teens would later go on to form the core of Motown Records. In fact, Diana Ross lived in Smokey's neighborhood. Many others were talented, but never got the opportunity to do the same.

Changes in society continued to take place in 1954 and with the *Brown v. the Board of Education* case. It abolished the segregation of American schools and helped to upgrade the conditions of many inner-city schools. This played a major role in the success of Motown Records because the majority of Berry Gordy's acts came out of the Detroit Public School system, which had one of the nation's top musical programs at the time.

The optimism of Detroit led to the flourishing of music. Gospel, blues, country, pop, jazz, and R&B strains filled the streets of the city, and everyone either loved music or wanted to make it. Smokey and his friends, like many teenagers, chose the latter.

Smokey formed the group, the Five Chimes, with his best friend Ronnie White, and Northern classmates Pete Moore, Clarence Dawson, and James Grice. Two years later, that group was renamed the Matadors and included siblings Bobby and Emerson Rogers in place of Dawson and Grice. When Emerson announced to the band that he was headed into the army, the other members of the band asked his sister Claudette to take his place. At the time, Claudette felt that the band simply wanted to retain the Rogers' basement as their customary rehearsal space.

But Smokey, at 15, had other ideas. He'd been dating Claudette and wanted to keep her close by. With a lady now in the group, the band chose a name that better fit their male/female concept. They called themselves the Miracles.

The Miracles' sound embraced the melodic opulence of doo wop and infused it with the physicality of R&B. Smokey, then listening to archetypal gospel/R&B groups like the Moonglows and Billy Ward and the Dominoes with Clyde McPhatter on lead, absorbed that influence, inspired by McPhatter's high, often feminine-sounding voice. When he saw Ward's band perform in Detroit around that time, he couldn't believe the effect McPhatter's falsetto had on the girls in the audience. From that point on, he never worried about allowing his natural voice—also high and feminine—to shy away from the spotlight.

In the summer of 1957, Miracle Ronnie White had heard that Jackie Wilson's manager was looking for talent to sign. The Miracles woodshedded for their audition. At the time, Wilson was one of Smokey's favorite R&B singers, and he wanted badly to align with his management company. He felt that the combination of Claudette's soprano, Smokey's alto, Bobby's tenor, Ronnie's baritone, and Pete's bass held great potential. They just needed the right material.

But the audition didn't go as well as planned. Wilson's boss saw the Miracles as little more than a rehashing of the Platters and he suggested a few possible configurations they should consider adopting to be more unique. But they weren't about to change what they'd worked hard to establish. So, dejected, they turned to leave. On their way out the door, Berry Gordy stopped Robinson for a chat. Little did each know at that moment that both of their lives were about to change forever.

DISCOVERED

At the time, Berry Gordy, also from Detroit, was a former boxer like Wilson, and a tough, street-savvy personality. Over the years, Gordy had attempted the retail business selling jazz records, gotten married, had three children, and was subsequently divorced. He had been working for Jackie Wilson as a freelance songwriter and had come up with a couple of Wilson's very first hits, including "Reet Petite" and "Lonely Teardrops." He had also produced records by Marv Johnson and Eddie Holland for the United Artists label. Frustrated with royalty checks that were too low and too slow in coming, he decided to go out on his own where he could make real money. Wilson was already signed to Brunswick and Johnson to UA, so he decided he'd set up his own label. Gordy had heard the Miracles audition and wanted to talk about perhaps signing them to his new management venture.

Berry Gordy's Beginnings

Berry Gordy, one of eight kids, began his career in music the way he'd finish it: as an enterprising young man. Gordy loved music, although he had little formal training other than some early piano lessons. One early money-making venture found Berry escorting a friend door-to-door to sing for neighbors. The friend had a beautiful voice and Gordy had the marketing skills to convince neighbors to pay 50 cents to hear a song.

As he matured, he developed an enthusiasm for boxing and he dropped out of high school to concentrate on training to fight professionally. But he abandoned his professional boxing aspirations in 1950 and began writing music. In 1951, Gordy was drafted into the army and sent to Korea. In the army, Gordy earned his General Education Development (GED) certificate, equivalent to a high school diploma.

When he returned to Detroit in 1953, he opened a record shop with a friend. He wanted to sell jazz, but it soon became evident that R&B was the musical favorite of many young African Americans in his Detroit neighborhood. By the time the store closed, he was married and had two children. Pressure to provide for his family forced him into the Ford Motor Company plant in a spot on the assembly line. His salary was $85 a week.

Still, he wrote. One of his first hits was for an artist named Barrett Strong, called "Money (That's What I Want)," a good indication of where Gordy's head was during this time. He then placed a couple of hits with iconic soul idol Jackie Wilson ("Reet Petite" and "Lonely Teardrops"). According to Gordy, Wilson, also known as "Mr. Excitement," could take a so-so song and turn it into a classic.

He began to place other songs with various artists, but soon realized that the royalties he made from those songs were small in amount and slow in coming. Sometimes publishers even refused to pay up. To make sure he received his fair share of royalties, Gordy started his own company, Jobete Publishing, taking the name from the first two letters in his three children's names. Smokey Robinson was the first writer to sign with Jobete. At the urging of Robinson, Gordy set out to form his own record company. To finance it, he approached family members for a loan. Despite his sister Esther's reluctance, Gordy sold his family on the plan and received $800 from them.

He rented an eight-room house on 2648 West Grand Boulevard. This two-story building would serve as both the recording studio and the administrative headquarters for Motown Records. Currently a tourist attraction, they nicknamed the house "Hitsville USA." He employed members of his family to help run the operation.

In 1959, all that groundwork resulted in Motown Records, a label Gordy and Robinson created with the distinct intention of making black music for a biracial audience. He succeeded beyond anyone's expectations; that sound, billed as the Sound of Young America, transformed pop music through the 1960s, thanks to acts as epic and influential as Stevie Wonder, Marvin Gaye, the Supremes, Junior Wells, and Martha and the Vandellas.

The Miracles, with Robinson their unchallenged leader and visionary, were an organized and disciplined group from the very beginning. They rehearsed regularly and took their career in music seriously. Ronnie White spearheaded the band's sober and muted sartorial image. As a jazz fan and "cool cat," he favored the tailored suits and elegant, down-to-earth presentation. Claudette, a business school student, served as the group's accountant and secretary. The boys, like brothers, protected Claudette like a sister. The band functioned as the family Robinson missed while growing up.

As promised, Robinson and Gordy met separately to look over Robinson's songwriting sketchbook. They discussed the pros and cons of Smokey's existing songs; he had amassed hundreds of rough tracks, lyrics, and melodies. They were naive, with subject matter limited to teens—being in love, hating school, and not wanting to go into the army. But Gordy saw through the naiveté to the possibilities beyond. To help Robinson progress past the rather limited purview of his teenage topics, Gordy shared his insight. Smokey put aside his exercise book and started again. He was prepared to embark on a new approach to his work.

In February 1958, coinciding with Smokey's 18th birthday, the Miracles released their first single, "Got a Job," which Gordy had arranged to be issued through the End Records label. The song, an answer to the Silhouettes' hit "Get a Job," resonated with ambition not only literally, but figuratively. The Miracles needed success to continue and the song made enough impact to help them do just that.

The band's second hit, "Bad Girl," another Gordy/Robinson collaboration, made an even bigger impact, hitting the national charts. This one Gordy licensed to the Chicago's Chess label.

But on Gordy's end, the financial arrangement—leasing his acts to other labels—didn't pay off well enough. The shortfall led him, some say at Robinson's urging, to set up his own recording company and label. He did, and called it first Tammie, then Tamla Records. Now he'd be able to sign and nurture his own talent and keep it in house. The Miracles were essentially his first group and they'd serve as the prototype for all other Motown groups to follow.

WEDDING BELLS

In November 1959, Smokey married Claudette, a marriage that would last 27 years, and the band began touring. At first, their show was a mess. A date at the Apollo ended up disastrous, when the band failed to bring the house band music charts. The Miracles' dance steps were frantic and disorganized and their vocal harmonies were shaky. The Apollo's manager half-joked he wanted his money back.

Back in Detroit, Robinson met a musician, Marv Tarplin, an extraordinary guitarist who had been playing with the Primettes, an early incarnation of the Supremes. Tarplin introduced the girls to Smokey, who then brought them to Gordy. Tarplin stayed with Smokey and over time became his most important musical accompanist.

With Tamla now in place, Gordy and Robinson came up with "Shop Around" in 1960. The song had already been cut once and was circulating around Detroit radio stations. But Gordy recut the song, pushing the tempo and simplifying the rhythm tracks. The second version, with Gordy himself on piano and credited to the Miracles (featuring Bill "Smokey" Robinson), hit the national charts, and radio jumped on it. In early 1961, "Shop Around," a bluesier rendition than what the Miracles had recorded previously, topped the R&B chart for eight weeks and sold a million copies. Gordy, intent on making black music for white kids—rock and roll proved white audiences were hungry record buyers—had hit his first jackpot.

Meanwhile at Tamla, Robinson began overseeing the activities of other acts Gordy had signed. Mary Wells and the Marvelettes, two of his charges, began making inroads on the airwaves. The Marvelettes, a five-member girl group from outside of Detroit produced by Brian Holland had a huge hit in 1961 with "Please Mr. Postman," while Detroit's Wells had a hit song at 17 with "Bye Bye Baby," a song she initially offered Jackie Wilson. That song became the company's first Top 50 tune in 1961.

Robinson guided the careers, especially Wells (the Marvelettes had lineup shifts and other personnel problems). He wrote excellent material for her, and the combination of those songs with Wells's natural vocal delivery resulted in some of the label's most creative early work. The pinnacle of their collaborations, though, came a few years later in 1964, when Wells sang "My Guy," a number one pop hit and a worldwide smash. One measure of Robinson's success as a producer is the fact that once Wells left the label, she could not duplicate, or even approximate, the large-scale hit-making she enjoyed with him at Motown.

In addition to overseeing his acts, Robinson became further involved in the rest of the label's lengthy list of responsibilities. He assisted in the business of promotion and he auditioned many of the label's hopefuls who by now were flocking to the successful young company. The Supremes were assigned to Robinson, as were the Temptations, and all of a sudden, he had a full slate of acts to complement his own writing and recording with the Miracles.

Boosted by the success, Gordy and Robinson, by now close friends, set out on the label's first Motortown Revue, although it didn't have that name at the time. It featured the Miracles headlining with other roster acts like Marv Johnson, Mary Wells, and the Marvelettes. This time, when the Miracles returned to the Apollo as headliners, the storyline read quite differently. All of Harlem was blaring the Miracles at the time, so the show was a huge triumph.

Robinson savored the memory. "The evening, at the Theresa Hotel, cars drove by, horns honking, fans waving up at our room, our music blaring from their radios. Seemed like the world was ours" (Ritz, p. 20).

But the tour suffered some setbacks. Smokey came down with America's first certified case of the Asian flu, which took him off the road, leaving the lead singing to Claudette. Smokey remembers it this way.

> I had a complex about my voice, a real thing about it for several years. People would confuse me with Claudette, people would go, "Oh, I thought you were a girl." I remember, one of our first hits, probably "Shop Around," I got sick and couldn't go on stage, so Claudette sang for me. And in the middle of the songs, guys would be yellin' out, "*Sing it*, Smokey!" All of this combined to give me a real complex about my voice. (Dave Marsh, "From the Beginning," *Creem*, 1972)

Meanwhile, Pete was drafted into the army, so the Miracles were reduced to Claudette, Ronnie, Bobby and Marv. To make matters worse, a car accident while on the tour killed the group's driver, Eddie McFarland, and led to Claudette miscarrying her baby. It would be the first in a series of tragic miscarriages the Robinsons suffered.

HITSVILLE!

As a songwriter, Robinson derived plenty of emotional material from his own experience, including the premature birth and death of twins soon after Claudette's first miscarriage. The devastation was palpable, and Smokey turned that tragic experience into a lifetime pledge, "More Love." This would become one of Robinson's hallmarks as a writer. He'd take his own experiences and turn them into empathetic musical numbers. The way he related to his listeners had everything to do with being able to communicate the way he was feeling. His lyrics were simple, casual, and conversational, but his words were precisely chosen, and they could cut deep into a heart.

Clearly, Smokey had a way of looking at things that became uniquely his own. He'd turn clichés upside down or repurpose phrases, twist something familiar into something new, like "My Business, Your Pleasure" and "I Second That Emotion." This allowed virtually all of his lyrics to sound comfortable, relatable, and universal. But it also made his work feel fresh. He could wring his metaphors ("I'm Stuck on You") for every ounce of poetic potential they possessed. He also had a fertile enough imagination to profess love, regret the loss of love, and rue the day love came in myriad ways without sounding too sappy. These were his gifts, and he presented them to every fan of popular music in the 1960s.

In 1963, he succeeded in establishing his voice as a writer, and the work flowed, for the Miracles, the Temptations, the Supremes, and anyone else he'd been assigned to compose for. Because he was faced with writing from morning until night to fill the label's demand for material, he often brought the Miracles into assist, and they ended up with valuable publishing credits. Today, that simple act, brought on out of necessity, feels more like one of kindness. Smokey said much later that he wanted the Miracles to have more publishing income; the Miracles have admitted that Smokey could have easily finished those songs on his own. Such was the generous soul of Smokey Robinson.

The band graduated from the Chitlin' Circuit of the South to the mainstream American touring circuit. The Four Tops, the Temptations, Stevie Wonder, Marvin Gaye, and the Supremes now joined the Motown roster, and the company positioned itself, quite successfully, as the Sound of Young America.

In 1964, Smokey's hits via the Temptations became some of the biggest of his young career, and some of the most enduring tracks in all of the 1960s: "The Way You Do the Things You Do," "My Guy," "Get Ready," "Since I Lost My Baby," and the incredible "It's Growing."

Roughly at the same time, the Miracles' hit parade began marching. "That's What Love Is Made Of," the stunning "Ooo Baby Baby," and, of course, Motown's most memorable cut, the one that Gordy, ever stingy with his compliments, called a "perfect" pop song, "Tracks of My Tears."

In 1965, a few major changes came about. First, Claudette stopped performing with the group, though she continued to record. Second, under Gordy's directive, the Miracles changed their name to Smokey Robinson and the Miracles. He'd also pull the same name change ploy, if somewhat more controversially, for the Supremes with Diana Ross. He assumed that naming a leader of these groups, a front person with a more recognizable identity than the other members, would boost sales. He was right.

Their 1965 *Going to a Go-Go* album, featuring "Tracks of My Tears" and "Ooo Baby Baby," would solidify their standing as something more than a singles act. Though its title track kick-started a brief fad for go-go music—flashy, up-tempo dance music—it's one of the best records the Miracles ever made, and the first six songs rank among the best on any original Motown LP of the 1960s. Even the deeper tracks on the album shine, with "All That's Good," "Choosey Beggar," and "Let Me Have Some," enhance the album as a whole.

Motown's constant pressure to put their acts on national television, appearances secured mainly by Shelly Berger, paid off that year with the Miracles starring on the *Ed Sullivan Show*. It would be the first of many national television appearances, not only for the Miracles, but for many other Motown acts. As an aside, the first time the enigmatic Sullivan introduced the band he referred to them as "Smokey and the Little Smokeys."

And like the Temptations, the Miracles were booking numerous dates on the supper and nightclub circuit, a sure step up from the rather seedy Chitlin' Circuit they traveled in the South. At these upscale clubs they played to more well-heeled, mostly white audiences—Gordy's dream demographic. When they hit television and the Copacabana gigs rolled in, the Miracles had taken a clear step forward as superstars.

During this same period, Smokey had been writing for Marvin Gaye, and the partnership had turned out some excellent singles, including "I'll Be Doggone" and "Ain't That Peculiar." In 1965, the Temptations, largely indebted to Smokey for their early breakthrough hits, released *The Temptations Sing Smokey*, the ultimate tribute. It was then that Bob Dylan praised Robinson as "America's best living poet." As if to justify that praise, Smokey turned out "I Second That Emotion" and "The Love I Saw in You Was Just a Mirage," two complex ballads that proved he wasn't simply content to rest on his laurels.

A confluence of factors halted Robinson and the Miracles' momentum. The music climate began changing once again: the psychedelic, blues-rock, and singer-songwriter movements, with acts like the Beach Boys, Judy Collins, Bob Dylan, and Jimi Hendrix, were swiftly taking hold, stealing the wind momentarily from Motown's soul sound. The hits had been flowing so freely for Smokey's group the lack of progress was surprising. Of course, Smokey himself continued writing hits, for Gaye and the Temptations, especially. But the Miracles' dry spell lasted over a year.

They came out of it in a big way, rather unexpectedly. One song the band had kicking around for a few years was called "Tears of a Clown." Stevie Wonder presented the song, sans lyrics, to Smokey back at a Motown Christmas party.

He liked the tune, iced it with some terrific lyrics, then stowed it away for a rainy day.

In 1970, that rain finally came. Inexplicably, in September of that year it turned into the smash, the likes of which they never expected. Both sides of the Atlantic were crazy about the tune and it became the Miracles' biggest selling single, moving over 3 million units. To enhance the Miracles' rebirth even further, "Tracks of My Tears," a song that had been at the top of the U.S. charts back in the summer of 1965, resurfaced in Britain, where it initially made little impact. This time it hit number one on the U.K. pop charts. "Tracks," incidentally, came from rhythm groove guitarist Marv Tarplin, one of Smokey's go-to instrumental collaborators, came up with after hearing Harry Belafonte's tropical "The Banana Boat Song" at slower than usual RPM.

"Back in those days we had 24-hour access to the Motown studio," Smokey said. "So we went in as soon as we possibly could after writing. This one was a real rascal, because we wanted to make sure the lyrics were real meaningful" (Adam White, *Going to a Go-Go*, liner notes, Motown 1965/2002, p. 4).

"Tracks" became one of the Miracles' most affecting tunes. Miracle Pete Moore often remembered seeing audience members crying while he and the group harmonized. "It had some kind of underlying emotional feel to it, which really tapped into the depths of people's emotions" (White, p. 6).

It helped that the album, *Going to a Go-Go*, featured the raucous title track immediately following "Tracks" on side one. Spearheaded by another Tarplin guitar riff and bolstered by a huge Funk Brothers dance groove, the song would be a concert monster for the group, and one of their best ever dance tracks. Holland-Dozier-Holland had established the Miracles' so-called go-go sound a few years earlier with "Mickey's Monkey," but *Going to a Go-Go* and its follow-up, *Away We Go-Go*, shored up that reputation.

Things began sizzling once again.

Based on that serendipitous re-emergence, the Miracles greeted the 1970s with attractive prospects. But rather than feel hopeful, Smokey felt empty. By this time, he had accomplished so much, been to so many places, enjoyed his career so fully, that he felt like there wasn't anything left to accomplish as a Miracle. In 1970, he sat down with the boys at Ronnie White's house in Detroit and told everyone how he'd been feeling. He told them he loved them, that they were his brothers. But even brothers had to go their separate ways eventually.

"It seemed like we'd done it all," he said. "We'd been around the world and back. I was proud of the success. But man, I was tired of touring. I wanted to stay home with the kids" (Ritz, p. 38).

It would still be a few years, and a handful of reasonably successful, but not smash hit singles, before he left the lineup. But the announcement startled the other Miracles and altered their mindset. They began searching for a replacement.

Business concerns at Motown stretched Smokey considerably at the turn of the decade. His responsibilities as a bandleader and important staff songwriter were time-consuming enough. But as a vice president of Motown, his role as an executive grew just as the company had grown. At this time, Berry Gordy was in the final stages of relocating his entire organization to Los Angeles from its native Detroit. Gradually, Gordy had given up control of sessions in the studio and he began focusing on the business end as well. But the move to Los Angeles, in essence an admission that the Golden Age of the label was over, signified a shift toward a "strictly business" approach.

Gordy had been living in Los Angeles for a while before insisting the company move out there with him. He had his eye on making films as well, so Hollywood made sense as a destination. He spent a lot time trying to convince his fellow Detroiters to move out west to be with him—saying he'd soon be moving the company—but most of the Motown folks chose not to go. In the end, however, the boss had the final say.

In 1971, he brought Motown to Los Angeles, and in 1972, Smokey Robinson, reluctant to leave his home and uproot his family, fulfilled his commitment to Gordy and upheld his promise to the Miracles. He left the group and moved to Los Angeles to join the company. All along, Gordy and Tamla, the label, had really been his first allegiance. Gordy had been his best friend, and Robinson had spent at least half of his time, perhaps more, building the brand, as they say, helping Gordy establish his musical empire. Now, eager to get off the road and be with his family, he proved his loyalty by relocating.

GOING TO A SOLO, 1975–1984

Moving to Los Angeles left the Miracles to their own devices, and also allowed Smokey to embark on a solo career, something he had thought about for a few years.

After struggling mightily to have a child, Smokey and Claudette had two in the early 1960s, Berry and Tamla, both names with obvious origins. Claudette had spent her time with the kids, performing sporadically with the group and having a hand in the band's accounting. With Smokey's solo arrangement, he planned to spend more time with them all at home, his new home, that is, in Los Angeles.

Meanwhile, in an effort to maintain their own career, the Miracles didn't take long to name a replacement for Robinson. A tall, dashing, and talented singer named Billy Griffin, the winner of a long series of national auditions, would take his place. To help smooth the transition, Robinson and the Miracles undertook a farewell tour, with Griffin in tow. They officially announced Griffin as the newest Miracle on July 12, 1972, at the Carter Barron Amphitheater in Washington, D.C.

Without Smokey in the lineup, the Miracles hit the charts two more times, first with "Do It Baby," which reached number 13 in 1974, and then again with the smash "Love Machine (Part 1)," a chart-topping hit in 1976, co-written, incidentally, by Billy Griffin and Miracle Pete Moore. But in 1975, the Miracles left Motown for MCA, and they never had another hit. Not that the group or the group's new label were fully to blame for that. Beginning about this time, the propulsive beats of disco had consumed the country, and, frankly, the world. "Love Machine (Part 1)," a high-energy rhythm track that hinted at jumping on the disco trend, served as evidence that the Miracles knew this was happening. But ultimately, younger and fresher groups were invited into the new dance movement, and the smoother grooves of the Motown Sound sank below the horizon.

After leaving the Miracles, Smokey took a few years to regroup, move his family to Los Angeles, and take care of business and family responsibilities. In 1973 or so, he picked up where he left off as a songwriter, only a little quieter. Oddly, while the country moved toward the tempestuous rhythms of disco, Motown smoothed out the edges of their studio creations, and became considerably mellower. Perhaps this was because the higher-ups at the company, including Gordy and Robinson, were mellowing as they grew older. But their sound by and large reflected a general shift at Motown toward urban contemporary soul.

His first few albums, *Smokey* and *Pure Smokey*, both ballad-driven, polished, and more reflective than his boisterous Miracles sets, were well received but not big hits. In the early 1970s, funk had captivated mainstream urban music listeners, so this kind of product did not have immediate fans, outside of Smokey loyalists.

In 1975, Robinson recorded *Quiet Storm*. It also emerged, well, quietly, at first, creeping into the Top 25 on the album chart but no higher. But soon after, a radio programmer at Howard University, a woman named Cathy Hughes, coined her own romantic ballad radio program *Quiet Storm*, with Robinson's song of the same name as the program's theme. Inadvertently, she and the song triggered a brand-new radio format of the same name. *Quiet Storm* also features the "Wedding Song" which was written for Hazel and Jermaine Jackson's wedding and the "Happy" theme from the movie *Lady Sings the Blues*.

Other Robinson solo hit tunes include "Cruisin'" from 1979, "Being with You" (a U.K. number one hit in 1981), "Tell Me Tomorrow" (1982), and "Ebony Eyes," a duet with labelmate Rick James (1983). "Cruisin'" came from that familiar source, Marv Tarplin. He gave it to Smokey in 1973, and it took him five years to put lyrics to it. He did so after hearing the Rascals' hit "Groovin'" while driving down Sunset Boulevard in Hollywood. It became his biggest hit since "Tears of a Clown."

At the end of the 1970s, Robinson toyed with the idea of playing the disco game; he wrote new songs, or updated old ones, like the Temptations' "Get Ready," that were his version of disco. But as soon as he did, both he and the label realized their miscues and decided to return to more traditional form.

BAD NEWS

Not much has been written about the music Smokey made during the 1980s and it's no surprise. With few exceptions, the 1980s were more about Robinson's personal life than about how effective he remained as a songwriter and a performer.

The troubles started in 1983, when his marriage to Claudette, after nearly 25 years, hit the rocks. The death of "Five," Smokey's father, affected him deeply. He'd turned to his dad over the years for advice and guidance, and without him around Smokey felt lost, even in his 40s. Not even a Miracles reunion, on the occasion of Motown's 25th anniversary, was enough to shake him out of his grief. To make matters worse, Smokey also felt that Claudette had not been present for him emotionally. But, a pretty young woman named Kandi was. While seeing Kandi on the side, she became pregnant with Smokey's child. Smokey insisted the doctors told her she'd be incapable of bearing children. But an illegitimate baby was on the way.

Claudette had known something was wrong. After being married to Smokey for two dozen years, even minor behavioral changes showed up in big ways and she saw clearly that her husband was distracted.

It was also a very sensitive time for the couple. Claudette wanted to celebrate their 25th anniversary with a renewal of their marriage vows. Friends the Robinsons knew were celebrating the same anniversary and suggested they have a double wedding.

Smokey tried to mentally reinvest himself into his marriage, but he couldn't. Claudette felt the distance between them growing. Smokey did too. He'd begun using drugs more frequently. His mind-altering substance of choice had grown from marijuana joints to joints laced with cocaine. He'd hide away at home and get high, then rejoin his family. Everything with Smokey had become clandestine.

Their anniversary came and went without much recognition. When Claudette asked him again, this time more desperately, about renewing their vows, Smokey snapped. "I've had a baby with Kandi," he admitted, after the baby, Trey, was born in 1984.

His admission set the marriage on a downward spiral. "Unlike the past, when she'd always weathered the storms I'd rained on her, now Claudette lost control. She cried; she screamed; she shook with anger; she told me that was it; it was all over" (*Ebony*, May 1989).

Robinson moved out, got an apartment, and began doing harder drugs more often. He sank lower than he thought he ever could. Gordy saw the pain he'd been going through and invited Smokey to his Bel Air mansion in Hollywood to clean up. He spent a few weeks at Gordy's place, in a guesthouse, all the while wondering how he could get high. Gordy, who had a drug-free policy at his home, made Smokey promise him he'd stay clean, and Smokey agreed, knowing full well he'd be getting high as soon as he was free to go.

It didn't matter that Gordy had lined his quarters with literature assailing drug use. He was addicted and he needed drugs.

"Stay as long as you want, Smoke," Gordy urged. "But just promise me you'll stop."

He couldn't. There was too much pain. His father had died. His wife wanted a divorce. His new child didn't know his daddy. His girlfriend was worried that something terrible was happening, and his career was non-existent.

Not surprisingly, Smokey made some of the worst music of his career during this period. *Essar*, his album from 1984, marks the low point of Smokey Robinson's musical career. Co-producer and arranger Sonny Burke, a long-time Robinson recording partner, provides nearly all the tracks, dominating the sound with his synthesized keyboards. In fact, it's hard to recognize it as a Smokey recording at all. This may help to explain why *Essar* was his lowest charting studio album on the Pop LPs list (number 141) ever. It also flopped with R&B fans, peaking at number 35 and becoming his first album not to generate at least one Top 10 R&B hit.

In the late 1980s, Robinson shook free of his drug addictions and began to straighten out his personal life. He wrote his own memoir, *Inside My Life*, and began getting the recognition such monumentally important songwriters deserve. In 1987, Smokey was inducted into the Rock and Roll Hall of Fame—in just the second year the institution made inductions—and the next year he was named a Grammy Living Legend as well as an inductee into the Songwriters Hall of Fame.

In 1991, Smokey left Motown, after a fruitful relationship of over 30 years. He signed with SBK Records, a major start-up that encountered immediate financial problems. Following his Motown departure, Robinson made a single record, without any notable success. Eight years passed in the 1990s—he toured and made special appearances at casinos and other popular hotel venues, but kept a relatively low profile. In 1999, he re-emerged, on Motown of all labels, with *Intimate*. Now a born-again Christian—he had been converted by a faith healer—the singer released his first gospel album, *Food for the Spirit*, in 2004.

The album features nine tracks, all written by Robinson, who sings them with passion and believability. In 2006, he recorded *Timeless Love* for the New Door label, a Universal Music imprint whose sole responsibility is to allow veteran artists to make new records. *Timeless Love* features Robinson singing some very old, as in pre-rock, standards, like Cole Porter's "I've Got You Under My Skin" and "Night and Day."

LEGACY

Save for founder Berry Gordy, no single figure has been more closely allied with the Detroit-based recording empire known as Motown, nor done more to create the sound of that label, than William "Smokey" Robinson.

Today Robinson is one of the elder statesmen of popular music, a writer, producer, and performer who never betrayed his own reputation and, with few exceptions, never sacrificed his legacy with second-rate material, no matter what was happening on the music scene stylistically.

Bob Seger paid tribute to Smokey in *Rolling Stone* magazine's "Immortals" feature:

> Everybody loved his songs, and he had a leg up on all the other singers, with that slightly raspy, very high voice. Smokey was smoky. He could rasp in falsetto, which is hard to do and perfect for sad ballads like "The Tears of a Clown" or "The Tracks of My Tears." Smokey wrote his own stuff, so he had an originality or individualism that maybe the other Motown greats didn't. He was a lyric man as well as a melody man, a musicians' musician. (Bob Seger, "The Immortals," *Rolling Stone*, April 15, 2004)

Over the course of his career, Smokey wrote more than 4,000 songs, including some of the most cherished and beloved of modern times. His list of accolades is almost as long as the list of his songs.

Much of today's soul music launched from the work of Motown and Robinson, from Boyz II Men, India.Arie, Floetry, R. Kelly, New Edition, Kirk Whalum, Gerald Levert, Brian McKnight, Ricky Fante, and John Legend. In fact, not only did he capture much of that archetypal soul sound with the Miracles and as a solo artist, he also helped shape it with the material he provided other Motown artists like the Temptations, the Marvelettes, Stevie Wonder, and Marvin Gaye.

It is virtually impossible to embrace the history of soul without touching significantly on the impact and oeuvre of William "Smokey" Robinson.

SELECTED DISCOGRAPHY

Smokey Robinson

Smokey (Motown, 1973)
Pure Smokey (Motown, 1974)
Quiet Storm (Motown, 1975/1991)

Smokey Robinson and the Miracles

Going to a Go-Go (Motown, 1965/2002)
The 35th Anniversary Collection (Motown, 1994)
Anthology (Motown, 1995)

FURTHER READING

George, Nelson. *Where Did Our Love Go?* New York: St. Martin's, 1983.

Gordy, Berry. *To Be Loved: The Music, the Magic, the Memories of Motown.* New York: Warner Books, 1994.

Ritz, David. *Smokey Robinson and the Miracles: The 35th Anniversary Collection,* liner notes. Motown, 1994.

Robinson, Smokey and David Ritz, *Inside My Life.* New York: McGraw-Hill, 1989.

Courtesy of Photofest.

The Temptations

EMPERORS OF SOUL

The Temptations were the most successful group in black music history. During a career that spanned the early 1960s through nearly four decades, they became the prototype for the modern soul vocal group. When they weren't on the front edge of soul, setting the trends, they were doing what everyone else was doing, only better.

During their prime years, from 1963 to 1974, they defied the odds facing most vocal groups by staying together, enduring hardships, and coping with life in the spotlight. They weathered changing political climates and musical tastes with aplomb. They cut dozens of sublime soul, funk, and R&B sides. In concert, they habitually set the house on fire, and, at the same time, they could take the lights down low and torch their fans with heart-melting, beautifully executed, perfectly harmonized ballads.

The Temptations' songs depended upon the individual members' interaction as a group. Unlike most other R&B groups, each member of the Temptations was a lead singer in some capacity. Although the group always had a main lead singer who dominated most the lead vocals (from Paul Williams to David Ruffin, Dennis Edwards, and later singers such as Louis Price, Ali-Ollie Woodson, and Terry Weeks), that singer was never given more of a promotional push than the other members. Co-lead songs, with two or more singers sharing the lead vocals, are common in the Temptations catalog, particularly among the psychedelic-era recordings of the late 1960s/early 1970s. This gave their best work a bracing feel and a layered richness.

The Tempts worked with Motown's most talented songwriters and producers—Berry Gordy, Smokey Robinson, Norman Whitfield—and struck gold time and again with songs that have become a part of pop lore: "My Girl," "Papa Was a Rolling Stone," "The Way You Do the Things You Do," "Ain't Too Proud to Beg," and the list goes on. Their music veered from glossy pop to supercharged funk.

Their "classic" lineup—Otis Williams, Melvin Franklin, Eddie Kendricks, David Ruffin, and Paul Williams—embodied the concept of classy soul. As a group, they dressed and danced and sang and interacted with elegance and panache. They served as one of Motown's flagship acts and behaved consistent with that highly respected status. One mark of how dignified a band is has to do with how well they handle adversity, and the Temptations handled their fair share of it with more than their fair share of class. The loss of debonair but mercurial frontman David Ruffin in the late 1960s, followed by founding member Paul Williams's departure in the early 1970s began a carousel of lineup changes that tested the band at every turn.

But when all was said and done, their career provided a template for soul acts that is both near perfection, and impossible to match.

THE EARLY YEARS

Detroit in the 1950s blared with music, from pop and jazz to gospel and rock. Most youngsters, white and black, were singing on street corners, mimicking the church revival shows, the harmony groups, and the late-night blues vamps that chimed on radios and through saloon doors. One of those hopeful young voices belonged to Otis Williams, a Detroit teenager relocated from Texarkana, Texas, in 1950. Williams was enthralled by the sweet, soaring sounds of gospel icons like the Dixie Hummingbirds and the Soul Stirrers with Sam Cooke. When those bands visited Detroit, Williams and his friends pushed their way right up to the stage, not only to enjoy the music but to steal some performance secrets. Williams was anxious to compete in the pop music arena.

He had already sung in groups back in Texas, assembling acts as early as junior high school.

He put a band together in 1959 with friends from Northwestern High School, calling it the Elegants. They'd later change their name first to the Questions, and then again to the Distants. Along with him in the Distants were his best friend Elbridge "El" Bryant, Melvin Franklin out of Mobile, Alabama, Franklin's friend Richard Street, the group's lead singer, and James "Pee Wee" Crawford.

The Distants found a local label willing to make a record with them. Their first recording session featured a song called "Come On" in 1959. The tune was picked up for national distribution. In 1960 they recorded "Always" for Northern Records, with Richard Street singing lead.

Meanwhile, two friends, Eddie Kendricks and Paul Williams, had formed a high school group of their own in their native Birmingham, Alabama, called the Cavaliers with Kell Osborne and Wiley Waller. After graduation the Cavaliers moved to Cleveland where they met manager Milton Jenkins, who felt the group would do better based out of Detroit. They all agreed, moved, and changed their name to the Primes.

There was a friendly rivalry between the Distants and the Primes. But, Otis Williams noted, the Primes had a couple of things on the Distants that gave the edge: their harmonies and dance moves. "We were good singers and all, but we knew to do that kind of harmony you had to have great ears, too. The other thing that the Primes had over us were these fantastic dance moves, very smooth and sexy but classy at the same time" (Otis Williams and Patricia Romanowski, *Temptations*, New York: Cooper Square Press, 2002p. 30). Those dance moves came from Paul Williams.

When the recording activity dried up for the Primes, Osborne split for the West Coast. At the same time, as luck would have it, Crawford and Street had just quit the Distants. The workload was heavy and the pay-off, at least to this point, pretty small. They played hops and chicken joints in and around Detroit, but the work outweighed the pay.

Otis heard about the Primes' split and was anxious to replace his own missing pieces. The Primes met the Distants at a house party thrown by a friend of the Distants and the two groups merged into one: Otis Williams, Melvin Franklin, Eddie Kendricks, Paul Williams, and El Bryant.

Together, the new lineup set to work. They rehearsed long and hard, tightening up their voices and fashioning some nifty dance moves. Eddie and Paul brought new dimensions to the Distants' sound. Paul's silky baritone impressed the group and soon he took most of the leads. Eddie handled wardrobe.

Jenkins, still the band's manager, arranged some local live work for the group, which now called itself the Elgins. It was at one of these dates that Berry Gordy Jr. saw them and signed them to his Motown subsidiary Miracle Records in 1961. It was while Otis Williams and Miracles employee Billy Mitchell were standing on the porch of Hitsville, the Motown office, that they came up with the group's new name, the Temptations.

The name embraced all that the band wanted to symbolize: style, elegance, romance, and sex. In their dancing and in their tailoring they were subtle, deliberately more nuanced than many of their overtly sex-obsessed colleagues. They chose to tease and titillate rather than grunt and sweat. The suaveness, when perfected, drove the audiences wild. Paul Williams was the one who made sure they maintained that moderate sense of sexiness. "Even back then [Paul] would remind us, 'We're selling sex'" (Williams and Romanowski, p. 49).

Because of confusion between Gordy's Miracle label and the Motown group of the same name, Berry changed the name of the Miracle imprint to Gordy Records. The new label's first release would be the Temptations' "Dream Come True," Berry's own song. Otis Williams recalls the episode: "We sat around the piano and he said, 'Now you guys got to hit that right on the head because I want it to sound really big. You guys got the harmony to produce this the way I hear it in my head.' It was the first time we were dealing with someone teaching us how to do correct harmonies" (Harry Weinger, *Emperors of Soul* liner notes, Motown, 1994, p. 16). The song charted in 1962, and the Temptations had gotten out of the blocks successfully.

At the time, Gordy had begun assembling the foundation of what would become his Motown empire. While he was rustling up acts to record for him, the Tempts were hustling out follow-up singles. "Check Yourself" and "Paradise," a Four Seasons' rip-off, didn't fare as well as "Dream," but they still helped the group inch toward a sound. "Check Yourself" is remarkable because it was the first Tempts single with the Funk Brothers: bassist James Jamerson, drummer Benny Benjamin, pianist Joe Hunter, and guitarist Eddie Willis.

As an interesting side note, at about the same time, the band recorded a single, "Mind Over Matter" backed with "I'll Love You Till I Die," not as the Temptations but as the Pirates. The notion of wearing Pirates outfits for the rest of their career—had the song become a hit—made them hope for the worst, at least this time. The record sank without a trace, and has since become one of the label's most sought-after collectibles.

By mid-1961 the Motown roster included the Primettes (the Primes' female counterparts that would later become the Supremes), Mary Wells, Marvin Gaye, Eddie Holland (later a songwriter), and Smokey Robinson and the Miracles, among a few others. The stable made for great company. Whenever the bands were off the road, they'd congregate at Hitsville and socialize. Those early days proved to be critically important for the Motown team; they'd become a family. The feuding and tension that cropped up later was still many years away.

The roster of artists interacted and collaborated frequently on each others projects. The Tempts sang backup for Mary Wells, for example, when she played the Apollo in Harlem. In their debut at the historic venue, the Tempts opened with a handful of songs and then backed Wells. It would be the first of many appearances for the boys at the Apollo.

At the end of 1961, Gordy had fulfilled a dream by placing a Motown song at the top of the pop charts with the Marvelettes' "Please Mr. Postman." The accomplishment elevated the competition among the label's acts and also raised the standard of quality. The young label was heating up, and the Temptations were in the right place at the right time.

In 1962, Gordy also enjoyed hits with Marvin Gaye and Mary Wells, along with the Miracles and the Contours. Even though their first handful of singles stiffed, the Temptations were still immensely popular around Detroit. Realizing they had some work to do, the boys put a lot of time into their act, and they accepted assistance from some of the label's respected older guard: Harvey Fuqua, "Beans" Bowles, and Maurice King. They shared ideas about etiquette, fashion, presentation, and performance. It was not, however, the infamous Motown charm school, but something quite like it. The Temptations also spent a lot of their free time going to gospel shows around the city. Paul Williams father, as well as Melvin Franklin's, were Baptist preachers, so the boys were steeped in religion. They were transfixed by the harmonies of the great male gospel quartets.

One Sunday, Gordy came looking for the Tempts at their homes. He had a song and he wanted them to record it right away. Being Sunday, the boys were at a church service, though for some reason nobody thought to look there. In fact, they only attended service when notable gospel groups were playing, and on this day at King Solomon's Church, the Dixie Hummingbirds were singing. When the itchy Gordy couldn't find his singers, he sought out another group, one more readily available. He found the Contours and gave them the song: "Do You Love Me." Gordy's instincts were right. The song rose to number three on the pop charts.

The attention and success stretched Gordy's time. Dedicating himself to his upstart vocal group became problematic. So he turned the reins over to Smokey Robinson, the Motown stable's talented Boy Friday, songwriter, performer, and producer extraordinaire. Robinson and the Miracles had already scored half a dozen sizable hits, and his stock was rising fast. He and Gordy worked together as producers and writers; Robinson credits Gordy with helping him refine his own artistry. Gordy credits Robinson for erecting a financial foundation around Motown with his initial string of hits.

When the Temptations started working with Robinson, the band's luck began to improve. They further refined their vocal style and started performing with confidence, developing moves and bringing a modicum of magic to the stage. Their potential began its realization.

Unfortunately, a stumbling block arose momentarily. Elbridge Bryant, a man of Native American descent, began drinking and his drinking affected the group dynamic. As Bryant's attitude and conduct worsened, the rest of the band had begun searching for his replacement.

One night, when the Tempts were doing a show at a place called Chappy's Lounge in Detroit, David Ruffin jumped out of his seat in the crowd and, nearly possessed, grabbed a microphone. Though few knew him previously, Ruffin had a shtick where he'd throw the mic in the air, jump around the stage, and do full-on splits. The place went wild. They played three encores that night, and the crowd wanted even more. The band, each man but Bryant, had had enough and they strode triumphantly off the stage. There were no more songs to sing or energy to give. But Bryant wanted more. He followed Williams briskly and aggressively. He grabbed a beer bottle and broke it on his colleague's face.

Williams received stitches for his injuries. The rest of the band handed Bryant a pink slip. Enter David Ruffin, that manic "guest singer," the final cog, and the perfect complement to the rest of the band.

RUFFIN'S READY

David Ruffin lived near Otis Williams in Detroit. He had some experience singing, and even a little success on a small, Motown-affiliate label called Anna Records. He and his brother Jimmy Ruffin, also a singer, hung out with the other members of the Primes during their early years until Jimmy went into the service.

David's magnetic stage presence made him the obvious choice to replace Bryant. He had the moves, and his gruff baritone provided the perfect counterpoint to Kendricks's tenor and falsetto. They were concerned, though, if Ruffin, a solo singer to this point, could exist within a strictly democratic entity. Eddie and Paul wondered what it would be like to share lead with Ruffin, a fiery performer who'd no doubt steal much of the spotlight. Their skepticism dissipated when David proved to want a worthwhile career in music as badly as the others; and he worked hard to get there. His entrée into the group in 1963 marked the onset of the Temptations' classic lineup.

It didn't take long for Robinson to write the band its first real hit. In early 1964 he brought "The Way You Do the Things You Do" into the studio. The song, riding an incredible wave of hit singles out of Motown that included the work of Marvin Gaye, Martha Reeve and the Vandellas, Stevie Wonder, and the Miracles, topped out on the pop charts at number 11. The band not only charted high, but crossed over as well. It would be the first in an incredible string of 37 Top 10 hits.

They released their debut album in the spring of 1964. *Meet the Temptations* barely cracked the Top 100 on the album chart, but it served as a source of pride for them. The band had worked hard to make an impression, and the album was proof of that dedication. Gigging increased significantly. The band toured both independently and as part of the Motortown Revues, five or six of the label's acts crammed into the same bus. Undaunted, the young band still enjoyed the camaraderie and social interaction of those early days.

Touring certainly had its fringe benefits for the Tempts. They were all ladies' men, of course; only Otis and Paul were married with children. In those days, the tours provided many thrills, with screaming women throwing themselves at debonair performers.

The parties were frequently epic. One, in Bermuda, even resulted in the band getting thrown off the island. It had started when Eddie and David, roommates at the hotel they were staying, got into a shouting match, and the night debilitated from there. There had been an edge to that relationship since day one, and it periodically came to blows.

They didn't enjoy the badly planned itineraries or the racism they encountered in the South, however. The Tempts often sang to segregated audiences, stayed in segregated hotels, and ate in segregated restaurants. Only certain establishments accepted black customers, especially musicians.

Nineteen sixty-four ended up being a watershed year for Motown. The Supremes ended the year with three consecutive number one pop hits and an appearance on the *Ed Sullivan Show*, the first for any Motown act. At the end of that year, Smokey Robinson brought the band another song, this one called "My Girl."

With excellent basic tracks, Robinson's sweetening, and gorgeous orchestration by Paul Riser, the tune emerged a perfect pop song, and one of the label's best loved tunes. In March 1965, it hit number one on the charts. The continued success empowered the Tempts to work even harder. It also resulted in Motown redirecting its resources from some of its so-called B acts, those bands whose music wasn't exactly hitting it big, to the bigger bands like the Supremes and the Tempts. The emphasis they received caused friction at Hitsville, where lesser artists criticized Gordy's favoritism. (This happened in an egregious way with the Supremes, whom Gordy kept separate from the rest of the Motown roster.) As far as the Tempts were concerned, though, they deserved the resources; Berry's ploys were simply good business. And they were more than happy to be the recipient of Smokey Robinson's top-rate material.

The group released its third album in 1965, a year that saw the band growing bigger than they had ever imagined. They played the *Ed Sullivan Show* that year and sang "My Girl," in what band members refer to as a "dreamlike" state. Appearing on the show, the one program everyone in America seemed to watch, was indeed a dream come true for the Temptations.

THE WHITFIELD YEARS

As the stakes at Motown escalated and decisions had more to do with money than anything, competition between even the biggest acts, as well as the biggest producers within the company, began escalating. Smokey Robinson enjoyed many of the company's biggest hits with his cadre of acts, which included the Temptations. Not to be outdone, Holland-Dozier-Holland, the songwriting/production team responsible for the Supremes and later the Jackson 5, had an unprecedented series of number one hits. Through 1966, H-D-H had eight releases with the Supremes, and six of them hit number one.

Every producer in pop wanted a crack at producing the company's top hitmakers, and one, an understated whippersnapper named Norman Whitfield, was among them. Whitfield had been hanging around Hitsville, dabbling with a number of groups there, attempting to place songs. Gordy's modus operandi held that prospective songs were to be screened by a quality control specialist before being introduced to him and his elite board of executives. This technique proved to be an effective filter in selecting the best songs as singles. Whitfield wrote constantly for the board, directing his rough cuts to the Temptations, but was regularly beaten out when the board opted for Robinson's material.

Whitfield was certain that his string of bad luck was about to change in 1966, when he wrote "Ain't Too Proud to Beg" specifically for David Ruffin. He and Ruffin had labored long and hard to cut the track, and Ruffin, for his part, sang until he could sing no more. The production crackled with a bluesy energy. Whitfield's confidence soared. This would be the Temptations' monster hit, he thought.

But in the song meeting, Gordy chose to release Smokey's newest tune, "Get Ready." Whitfield was devastated and angry. He vowed to not let that humiliation happen again.

"Get Ready," not one of Robinson's top tunes, disappeared quickly from the airwaves. Three months after that original meeting, when "Get Ready" failed to crack the Top 20, the label issued Whitfield's "Ain't Too Proud to Beg" as the next Tempts single. In May 1966, the song hit number 1 on the R&B charts and peaked at number 13 Pop. "Beg," pivoting on Ruffin's strong lead, is buttressed by Whitfield's gritty arrangement and Eddie Holland's lyrics. The song took so much out of Ruffin in the studio that Whitfield actually had to stop and let him catch his breath between takes. The tune kickstarted a remarkable eight-year collaboration between Whitfield and the Tempts, producer and band.

Whitfield's sound would play a massive role in the second half of the decade and through the early 1970s. "Norman could and did write and produce soft, smooth ballads with the best of them but, stylistically speaking, he was headed into another realm" (Williams and Romanowski, p. 100). He introduced a new rawness into their sound, spotlighting David Ruffin as an impassioned lead vocalist, and creating a series of R&B records that rivaled the output of Stax and Atlantic for muscle and grit.

About the same time, 1966, Gordy realized his management was overextended, so he brought in Shelly Berger, a young, Hollywood-based manager hired to oversee a new phase of the Supremes' and the Temptations' careers to take them to the next level. The hiring, made sight unseen, surprised even Gordy, who made the final decision based on a recommendation he trusted. Berger was white.

After the initial shock, Berger set about doing what he was hired to do: get Motown's two marquee acts all the national exposure possible. He said to Gordy, "We are going to get them on television. We are going to produce our own television specials. We are going to produce our own movies" (Weinger, p. 27). He also solicited an album of standards from the group, a real departure aimed at a more sophisticated clientele. It was such a departure that it marked the first time the Tempts cut a record with Motown without the Funk Brothers supporting them. (It was made with an L.A.-based producer.) The record exploded out of the box, and so did the Tempts, whose schedule was busier than ever.

They began showing up, as Berger promised, on many television shows, from the *Tonight Show* to the *Smothers Brothers Comedy Hour*. They rubbed elbows with the Hollywood elite, even sang a duet with Bing Crosby on "My Girl." Elsewhere, the band appeared with Bill Cosby, Muhammad Ali, the Beatles, and all the biggest names. Berger arranged for his two acts to appear together on various shows. On one episode of the *Ed Sullivan Show*, the two swapped material, with the Supremes singing the Temptations and vice versa. The gimmick was a smash and led to an album called *Diana Ross and the Supremes Join the Temptations* in 1968.

MONEY CHANGES EVERYTHING

Along with all this success came revenue; the band members were beginning to see real cash coming in. While it would eventually surface that they weren't receiving nearly their due—what else was new?—they were cashing five-figure checks regularly. But the money flow began to disrupt the band's chemistry. "When your pockets are empty, it's impossible even to imagine that money could ever be a problem. It's what money does to you as a person. When I think about what happened to the five of us, it seems that everything started to unravel about this time. . . . In our own way it seems like we were bent on destroying ourselves" (Williams and Romanowski, p. 109).

For years, the members of the Temptations fought through poverty and financial strife. The fact that money was now coming in affected them in ways they could not foresee. Still young, they had some significant trials in attempting to deal with that issue. All five ended up being lavish spenders. On payday, they'd walk into Hitsville, pick up a check, and go out shopping for themselves: clothes, cars, and other personal belongings.

The man most changed by money seemed to be Paul Williams, the band's creative heart. While Eddie and David earned attention through their frequent leads, Paul also had a large number of serious fans, those who knew the important leadership role he played in the band.

But Paul, who'd married young and already had five children, was conflicted between his traditional home life and the wild life on the road. Money and his access to possessions and women exacerbated that conflict. He started drinking, which was unusual for him. Until this time, he'd been the band's only teetotaler.

For David Ruffin, the money went straight to his head. He began considering himself the group's leading man, an individual, rather than as a member of the group. He traveled in his own car, separate from the others, with a mink-lined floor and his name painted on the side. He had been self-centered to begin with— the other band members, especially Eddie, noticed that early on. He even went so far as to propose, with his lawyers, that the name of the act should change to David Ruffin and the Temptations. The idea was rejected outright, and vociferously, by the band. But the proposal stuck a dagger in the heart of the Tempts. Until then, they'd been a team. Now that team was beginning to fracture.

The Tempts weren't the only band experiencing difficulty. The Supremes were also engaged in a power struggle of their own. Being the label's flagship act brought with it some acute challenges. Diana Ross and Florence Ballard, two of the three Supremes, were locked in a test of wills. The label and Ross wanted her to be billed at the top as lead singer, while Ballard, unstable at the time and drinking, wanted it to remain balanced, as the Temptations were. Both were talented, and both possessed the ability to go solo if they wanted. But in protest, Florence began acting irresponsibly, missing shows, and demonstrating disrespect toward the group. Gordy intervened in June 1967, and a few months later Ballard left the group.

Despite the friction at Motown, the Tempts continued to play and record top-level material. Berger booked them at a prestigious gig at the Copa, and they delved into rehearsals for the songs that would appear on their landmark *With a Lot O' Soul* album.

Considered by many to be their best album of the 1960s, *With a Lot O' Soul* was the Temptations' seventh hit album in a row. Released in July 1967, it shows the band moving in a more progressive direction, thanks to six production credits by Norman Whitfield and some excellent lead vocal turns by Kendricks and Ruffin. Paul Williams also turned in a great lead with "No More Water in the Well," a Smokey Robinson tune. It would be Paul's last lead vocal on a Tempts single. In fact, this album marked the last time the Tempts shared lead duties on their singles. Ruffin would dominate that responsibility until his departure.

The Temptations were at the peak of their popularity in 1968 when they cut *Wish It Would Rain*, and if the album doesn't hold any great surprises in terms of material, production, or performance, it's also a consistently strong set. It also marks the apex of Whitfield's initial phase with the group. His "I Wish It Would Rain," a dramatic ballad, featured the delicate use of sound effects and it became their sixth R&B number one in three years.

MOVING ON

This period also marked many changes in society. Though the Tempts didn't get involved much in politics as performers, not during the 1960s anyway, they were hurt by the assassinations of JFK and Dr. Martin Luther King Jr. They had lived through the riots in Detroit and were relieved when they managed to avoid getting drafted for the war in Vietnam, at a time when many of their brothers were coming back in flag-draped caskets. They did a few benefits that Gordy had arranged.

Just as society was in upheaval, so were the Temptations on the cusp of a number of changes. The problems with Ruffin's ego increased, and the band began looking for a replacement even before he was officially cut loose. One day, they all saw the writing on the wall. Ruffin reported to the band, who were set to play a gig one night, that they'd have go on without him, that he had been caught up with another task. Basically, he bailed on the gig. When he didn't show, they collectively decided it was time to let him go. Otis Williams recalls that the prospect of losing the talented Ruffin still wrenched him.

"Let's face it: Ruffin was a standout. When David stepped out you always knew something great was going to happen. He was a fantastic singer and performer, and no one, from that time until today, does what he did. He was an original" (Williams and Romanowski, p. 133).

Ironically, Ruffin reacted to the news of his ejection with shock and disappointment. In fact, he refused to accept the news at all. Even after getting ejected from the lineup he continued to badger the band, show up for rehearsals, and plead with them to take him back. At a few shows, he'd try to come from the audience and jump on stage to sing his parts. For Ruffin, the change was drastic and uncomfortable. But the Tempts knew they had to move on without him.

David Ruffin

In 1968, after tolerating his drug use, ego trips, and irresponsibility, the Temptations decided they could no longer put up with Ruffin's behavior. One night, after he missed a gig to attend a concert by his new girlfriend, Barbara (Gail) Martin, daughter of Ratpacker Dean Martin, they decided to replace him with Dennis Edwards. Edwards, formerly lead singer of the Motown act the Contours ("Do You Love Me"), was initially apprehensive. He had been looking for a solo career and actually had a friendship with Ruffin. But with the Tempts red-hot, it the offer was too good to refuse and he decided to join the lineup.

Ruffin's ouster left him bitter and upset. He believed he'd been untouchable, and the group owed its success mainly to him. Ruffin began turning up at Temptations concerts. When the group started to perform a Ruffin-era song such as "My Girl" or "Ain't Too Proud to Beg," he'd appear on stage, grab the microphone from Edwards, and start singing, stealing the show and embarrassing the band, but delighting the fans. The Temptations had to hire additional security to prevent Ruffin from attending their shows. Meanwhile, the exiled singer filed suit against Motown, seeking a release from the label and an accounting of his money. Motown countersued to keep the singer from leaving the label and eventually the case was settled. The court ordered Ruffin to remain with Motown and finish his contract. He did, and had solo hits for the first five years of his post-Tempts career. He went on to be the most successful solo Temptation.

After being inducted into the Rock and Roll Hall of Fame in 1989 with the other Temptations, Ruffin, Kendrick, and Dennis Edwards began touring and recording as Ruffin/Kendrick/Edwards: Former Leads of the Temptations. Unfortunately, before that project was fully under way, Ruffin died of an overdose on June 1, 1991, in Philadelphia at the age of 50.

The band members had known Dennis Edwards from around Detroit. He grew up singing in the church, his father was a minister. He attended the Detroit Conservatory of Music and studied voice and piano. At the time the Tempts needed to replace Ruffin, Edwards had just come off a stint with the Motown act called the Contours and he was looking for a solo deal. The Tempts were surprised, frankly, when Edwards accepted their offer. He made his debut with them in July 1968. He had a strident vocal style that fit nicely into the Tempts' new sound, pioneered by Norman Whitfield.

Despite replacing Ruffin, the Tempts continued to splinter. Eddie had begun hanging out with Ruffin when not with the band, and he even proposed the idea of taking him back. At the same time, Paul and Eddie began hanging out together, in a sense taking sides against Melvin and Otis. Paul was now drinking copious amounts of Courvoisier, his beverage of choice. Edwards, in the middle of this unfamiliar maelstrom, tried to his best to remain neutral.

At the same time, things at Motown were topsy-turvy as well. The biggest acts, all of who uniformly believed they were underpaid, had planned a producer-songwriter alliance, a sort of mutiny, which was squashed quickly by Gordy. Gordy felt that all of his acts, as well as his creative talent, were replaceable, dispensable, and conversely, many of his biggest acts considered themselves just the opposite, as indispensable. The team of Holland-Dozier-Holland, one of the most successful songwriting and production teams in the history of pop, left Motown over a financial dispute with Gordy. If they were allowed to leave, virtually anyone else could be shown the door as well. The tug of war that resulted made Motown a very unpleasant place indeed.

PSYCHEDELIC SOUL

Conscious of the psychedelic shift in the rock mainstream, and the inventive soul music being created by Sly and the Family Stone, Whitfield joined forces with lyricist Barrett Strong to pull Motown brutally into the modern world. At first, Whitfield was reluctant to give into the idea of changing with the times. But his charges, namely Otis Williams, had been digging Sly's sound and they felt it was not a passing fancy but a sea change. Sly had fattened the bass lines of soul. Jimi Hendrix demonstrated the power of the electrified guitar. The Beatles, whom the Tempts also enjoyed, were growing their hair out, recording songs about revolution and singing about someone named Sgt. Pepper. Much had happened. Much was still about to happen. Motown needed to come to grips with music's changing landscape.

Whitfield was intent on reflecting that change. "Pop music . . . broadened its ambition, deepened its resonance, and took it upon itself to have something to say, not just about the moon in June and dancing in the streets, but rather about the state of the world" (Leonard Pitts, *The Temptations Psychedelic Soul,* liner notes, Motown, 2003, p. 2).

"Over the next four years, Whitfield and the Temptations pioneered the concept of psychedelic soul, stretching the Motown formula to the limit, introducing a new vein of social and political comment, and utilizing many of rock's experimental production techniques to hammer home the message" (Ben Edmonds, "The Temptations' Final Frontier," *Mojo,* 2001).

The first song Whitfield brought in, and the first song that critics characterized as the Temptations' psychedelic phase was "Cloud Nine." In contrast to so much of what Motown artists had sung about throughout the 1960s—lost love, found love, good love, bad love, young love, old love, and silly love—Whitfield's composition about drug use in the inner city was dark and hostile.

Here was a band that had spent much of the decade pleading for love or pleading for forgiveness, or both—and doing it with incredible success. So hearing this sort of reality check from them, this message song, came as a shock. One can only imagine the song meeting at Motown when Whitfield brought "Cloud Nine" to the company.

Whitfield's choice of instrumentation was also a drastic departure from the customary Funk Brothers sound. Hearing it today, it's clear that the band had been listening to Sly and the Family Stone. The bass became even more prominent than the typical James Jamerson bass lines, and the electric guitar oozed with distortion. Whitfield created the music to match, breaking down the traditional barriers between lead and backing singers—the way the Tempts had worked in the past—and giving each one a recognizable voice within the song. Virtually nowhere in "Cloud Nine" do the voices actually all come together, a risk for a group that made its money on vocal harmonies.

To call it a departure would be a radical understatement. Whitfield essentially destroyed the format of traditional pop. His free-flowing, linear arrangement sounded nothing like the traditional verse-chorus-verse structure so strictly adhered to by the Motown songwriters. But deep down, Whitfield, Strong, and the Motown execs knew that the Tempts could handle just about anything.

"We wrote for the Temptations with the knowledge that they could deliver," says Strong. "It was like writing a script for an actor—you know a certain actor can execute a part the way that you want it, and you gear the words for that person. . . . They were so powerful as people. They had all the ingredients" (Weinger, p. 36).

"Cloud Nine" won Motown its first Grammy, for Best R&B Performance. But more than that, thanks to Dennis Coffey's sublime wah-wah guitar work, it represented the sound of the future. Along with Sly, Curtis Mayfield, George Clinton, and James Brown, the Tempts were responsible for turning soul into funk.

Other songs followed: "Runaway Child, Running Wild" delved into the problem of teen rebellion; "I Can't Get Next to You" sang of the fracturing of personal relationships (and topped the charts with the group's second number one hit); and "Ball of Confusion," a Top Five hit, bemoaned the disintegrating fabric of American society. The Temptations now, oddly, functioned as representatives of the counterculture, a trend that climaxed when they recorded Whitfield's protest against U.S. presence in Vietnam, "Stop the War Now."

The new direction didn't alarm Edwards, who fit nicely into the new sound, but it did unsettle Eddie Kendricks, who felt more comfortable during the collaborations the Tempts did with the Supremes following *Cloud Nine.* That collaboration resulted in the hit "I'm Gonna Make You Love Me" in late 1968.

Hotter than ever, the band celebrated. But that celebration had a bittersweet side; Paul Williams's health was deteriorating—from depression and sickle cell anemia—as the band watched in horror. His skills diminished; they dumbed down their choreography so he could keep up. They eliminated his lead vocals. Oxygen tanks were kept at the side of the stage in case of an emergency. Richard Street, a former member of the Distants, sang Williams's parts from the wings. The heart and soul of the Tempts, and the man responsible more than any for building the group's sexy but elegant image, was on his last legs. He turned to the bottle for solace.

Kendricks, too, began mulling over his departure. But not before he turned in the best lead vocal in the history of the band with "Just My Imagination," an evocative ballad that sounded, thanks to Kendricks's intimate tones, as much like a prayer to love as a pop song.

But the urge to leave took over, and from the time he fist considered exiting, he couldn't shake the notion. At a residency at the Copa in early 1971 in New York City, he walked off the stage after the first set of the night and never came back. The recording landed at number one on the pop chart, the first Tempts song to do so since "My Girl" back in 1964. But Kendricks had left before the song hit the top spot.

They replaced Kendricks with a 19-year-old out of Baltimore named Damon Harris, who ended up staying with the band only four years. The fellas liked him, his personality, and his singing style, so they introduced him in the fall of 1971. About the same time, Williams's health declined precipitously. A doctor told him he had to leave the road. He stayed on the band's payroll and helped them work out new dance steps. But he essentially left the Temptations. That meant three original members departed in three years. Only Otis Williams and Melvin Franklin remained. As promised, Richard Street replaced Paul Williams.

In mid-August 1973, the band members traveled to New York City to attend Harris's wedding when they received bad news. Paul had committed suicide, a gunshot wound to the head. They were devastated, and flew back immediately. 2,500 people attended his wake and funeral. He left a wife and five children.

The psychedelic soul trend continued with "Smiling Faces Sometimes," a rigorous and defiant 12-minute track about duplicity. The song didn't quite make the impact Whitfield had intended commercially, so he allowed a new trio he was producing, the Undisputed Truth, to cut a version of it. That one became the hit Motown expected.

In fact, it happened to be about this time that Whitfield, in demand as a producer now, began to set his sites on other acts. This perturbed the Tempts. They felt their studio leader and chief songwriting talent was betraying them by not staying around to lead them. To make matters worse, he practiced an annoying habit of turning up late, occasionally hours late, for studio dates. This was time the Tempts were being billed for, a fact that irked them. But because Whitfield's stock at Motown had soared through the roof, the Tempts didn't bother to complain to Gordy. That kind of criticism wouldn't be taken too seriously.

"PAPA WAS A ROLLING STONE"

Whitfield recorded the basic instrumental tracks to "Papa Was a Rolling Stone" while the band was on tour. When they returned to the studio and listened to the work, they liked it, but not as a song for the Temptations. "We were just so damned sick of that kind of song," said Otis Williams. "We begged him to go back to ballads" (Williams and Romanowski, p. 158).

But Whitfield foisted the song on them. Worse still, the first few lines of the song, sung by Edwards, identifies the date his father died. Unfortunately, Edwards's father *did* die on that day, and he had trouble singing the song. "It upset me," Edwards admits. "I got so mad that I sang [it] very tightly. . . . But Norman got so good at psyching everybody up that I realized: that was the attitude he wanted" (Weinger, p. 41).

"Papa Was a Rolling Stone," a Whitfield tour de force that is considered by many to be one of Motown's finest achievements. It hit number one, sold 2 million copies, and earned three Grammy Awards. It also helped to solidify the band's legacy by giving them another classic to stow away in its box of treasures.

But the trend of long, elaborately orchestrated tracks, coined "cinematic soul," began to wear on the band. The subsequent album, *1990*, featured only two songs on one of its sides, and the Tempts began hearing it from fans. They felt like Whitfield was hogging too much of the spotlight, as he spent more time on his own drawn-out grooves rather than the band's bread-and-butter: its vocal harmonies. On the back cover of the not-too-humbly titled *Masterpiece*, Norman's photo was bigger than the band's. Critics derisively referred to the Tempts as the Norman Whitfield Choral Singers.

And *1990* was the last album Whitfield produced for Motown.

In 1974, Berry and the entire Motown operations, including the Temptations, moved out to Los Angeles. The band's work was sagging and they needed a change of scenery. They had appealed to Gordy to set up their own publishing company—they had started writing their own songs after Whitfield left—but left that particular meeting with their tail between their legs. Gordy wouldn't budge on that point, and the band began to realize just how important publishing royalties were to the music industry.

The adjustment to living in Los Angeles varied for each member. But it seemed like one thing was clear. Drugs were readily available. New members always started out on a salary, lasting through an 18-month probationary period. So when young Damon Harris, Paul Williams's replacement, made it through that period, and real money came flowing in, his behavior changed. He got lazy, and started taking liberties with the material and his stage banter. Gordy caught wind of his antics and asked that he be removed from the group. He had stepped on too many toes. Money changed his attitude. He was asked to go. They brought in a singer named Dennis Leonard to replace him.

The band recorded one of their best albums, *A Song for You*, one of the pinnacles of their 1970s work. Produced by Gordy and Jeffrey Bowen, a studio guru that had helped the Tempts make the smash *In a Mellow Mood* album, the recording returned the group back to its vocal harmony-oriented roots.

The success of that project left the band in Bowen's hands. But the marriage didn't last long. Bowen, arrogant and demanding, pushed too hard. He wrestled performances out of them, and, as far as the band was concerned, didn't respect them enough. Subsequent albums, *House Party* and *Wings of Love*, were finished and released without the band's consent.

The band was furious. They had just come off recording their best album in *A Song for You* and were now content with cut-rate material and mailed-in performances. *Wings of Love* featured many of Dennis's lead vocals with the backing vocals of the rest of the Tempts pushed way back in the mix. Bowen and Edwards started whispering in the studio. Bowen had put it in Edwards's head that he could cut him into future projects and solo albums, that he didn't need the Temptations, so the seeds of discontent were sewn. Edwards left the fold, and so did Bowen.

MOVING ON, PART II

In 1976, the group's contract with Motown came up for renewal. Up to that time, many of the label's star acts had moved on. The Four Tops went over to

ABC Records, the Miracles left Motown after Smokey went solo, the Jackson 5 jumped ship, choosing Epic Records over Gordy's concern. Other acts disappeared, like the Marvelettes and Martha and the Vandellas.

Renewing their contract presented a good opportunity to review their status at the label, financially and otherwise. An attorney, Abe Somers, working on behalf of the Jackson 5 and the Miracles, uncovered some significant shortfalls in royalties, like $300,000. Hearing this, the Tempts hired Somers, certainly a fly in the ointment when he showed up at Motown's offices.

Dissatisfied with the goings on at Motown, the band decided to look for another label, the first time they had done so in 15 years together. They finished the album they were working on, their last for Motown. It was called *The Temptations Do the Temptations*. The band wrote, produced, and performed the entire album on their own, but because Motown knew the band was about to leave the label, they didn't promote it. The album sold poorly but received excellent reviews.

The Tempts signed with Atlantic in 1976. They began working on their album *Here to Tempt You* for the label with songwriter and producer Ron Tyson. But the heavy dance beats of disco were altering the landscape of pop and soul music at the time. Both their debut, and its follow-up, *Bare Back*, didn't create any impression on the pop charts at all and the band started to get anxious. A third album they recorded for Atlantic was never released.

Amid the crisis, the Tempts heard from Kenny Gamble of the red-hot Philadelphia International label, a company that had helped to shape the sound of 1970s soul with bands like the O'Jays and Harold Melvin and the Bluenotes. Gamble, who had just finished a project with the Jacksons, wanted to produce the Temptations, but on one condition. He wanted it to be a reunion of the group: Dennis, David, Eddie, Otis, and Melvin. When Otis and Melvin told him they couldn't do it, Gamble responded that he felt he could on his end. The prospect of the reunion made the two anxious. But Gamble seemed intent on making it happen.

When they all got together in the room, the mood was tense. Gamble convinced the boys a reunion could work, and the boys had all heard from hundreds of fans that a reunion would really fly. Unfortunately, Gamble's own life had been embroiled in change and his business career was flagging as well. The Tempts reunion, close enough to happening that they had all been in the same room together, fell apart before it could take flight.

A MOTOWN REUNION

While all this was going on, Berry Gordy made it a point to pursue getting the Tempts back on Motown. He'd retained Stevie Wonder, Diana Ross, Smokey, and Marvin, so why not get the Tempts back? While Williams harbored some ill-will toward the company, the rest of the group convinced him to meet with Motown and see what they had to offer.

The meeting with all the company's principals started out jovially, but devolved into a sort of air-clearing, where both Williams and Gordy were allowed to speak their minds and express their grievances. They decided to let the lawyers hammer out a new deal, one that involved a split-arrangement on publishing.

Within three months of their official resigning, the Tempts released *Power*, an album hinging on the strident title cut. But it came out at the time of the Miami riots, and DJs began pulling it off their play lists. The record stalled. Even a summer of 1981 collaboration with Philly soul sound architect Thom Bell, "Aiming at Your Heart," only rose to number 67 on the pop chart. The Tempts were still selling concert tickets, but their album sales flagged.

In 1982, a reunion actually did come about. David and Eddie had come home, as did Dennis. At the time Eddie had enjoyed a string of solo hits, but David struggled to do the same. The subsequent recording session for *Reunion*, hinging on the first single, a Rick James–produced funk track called "Standing on the Top," saw the Tempts regaining some early 1970s form. The tour to support that recording sold out its dates across the country; the demand for the band still existed. Unfortunately, old behaviors returned. David regained his old form, attitude and all.

> I felt I was watching a rerun of a bad movie: the riff-raff, the hangers-on, the leeches seemed to be materializing out of thin air, and, as in the old days, they all gravitated to David. . . . David missed the first three shows in Detroit, and the promoter was on our case. We were letting down our fans and losing money. During all our talks about getting together, this was what I feared. (Williams and Romanowski, p. 205)

On top of that, Eddie's voice couldn't withstand the strenuous nightly performances. In all, the reunion lasted nine months. It ended rather acrimoniously, with Ruffin mired in drugs and Eddie struggling to hold on physically.

The malice between Motown and the band never really dissipated, even when Gordy had reached out to re-sign them. In a meeting with Jay Lasker, Motown's president, David and Eddie acted up. Lasker and the label were in no mood for a fight and they let the band go.

Not long after the meeting, Ruffin was arrested and thrown in jail for tax evasion. Had the reunion gone better, the Tempts still would have been sidelined, given this development.

From here, members came and went. Glenn Leonard left, making room for former songwriter-producer Ron Tyson. Dennis Edwards stayed with the band longer than Eddie and David in the reunited Tempts, but he eventually left as well. His replacement, Ali-Ollie Woodson, had almost replaced Edwards the first time he left. But at the time Woodson sported an orange afro and the Tempts were afraid the style would distort their image.

Beginning in 1985, the Tempts began branching out, doing television spots, playing private parties, and hanging with the kinds of superstar personalities with which they'd earn the right to socialize: Muhammad Ali, Yankees owner George Steinbrenner. The White House had invited them in frequently to play prestigious gigs.

But the emphasis at this time wasn't on recording, or making the kind of outstanding music they'd done through the 1960s and the 1970s. The music industry was a moving target during the 1980s and 1990s so the Tempts had a difficult time hitting the bull's eye. They scored a few R&B hits over the years, but their bread and butter still proved to be touring.

They toured successfully, with ever-shifting membership. Motown re-signed the band a second time, in 1987, a sentimental choice. But the Motown they returned to was a shadow of its former self. It still did decent business. But the idea of it being a great place to hang out, exchange ideas, and watch talented people work had long been gone. The magic had disappeared.

At least they had those glory days to look back on.

The last time they were together was in January 1989 at their induction into the Rock and Roll Hall of Fame. That year the Rolling Stones, Otis Redding, and Bessie Smith were all inducted as well, which gives some idea of the enormous stature they'd attained since forming.

In July 1991, David Ruffin overdosed on crack cocaine and died. He'd been an active drug user, if not an all-out addict, since the late 1960s and had been slipping away for years.

Eddie Kendricks, bitter for most of his post-Temptations years, made peace with the rest of his bandmates before passing away of lung cancer in October 1992.

Melvin Franklin had developed a mild case of rheumatoid arthritis way back in 1968. By 1995 his health had deteriorated badly, to the point where he quite literally couldn't move. Steroids, the treatment for that type of dangerous arthritis, took a vicious toll on Franklin, and his immune system was completely compromised. He lapsed into a coma while recording *For Lovers Only*. Five days later, he passed away.

In 1998, the band released a hit album, *Phoenix Rising*, their 56th recording, and was the subject of a critically acclaimed television special called *The Temptations*. It made a huge impact, and pushed their evergreen anthology of hits all the way up to number four on the album chart.

In the spring of 2000, the band won its first Grammy in 20 years for *Ear-Resistible*. The Temptations were indeed forever.

LEGACY

With their suave look and sparkling choreography, the Temptations set the standard for every male R&B group, in much the same way the Supremes did on the ladies' side. Before the Tempts became popular, most male R&B groups were either gospel or doo-wop derived, or were rough-and-tumble R&B like the Clovers and the Drifters: high energy, but raw of voice as well, unpolished, with mostly improvisational dance steps. Only a performer like Sam Cooke foreshadowed the style the Temptations would come to embrace, one of smooth elegance, simmering sexuality, and lots of class.

Seeing the impact made by performers like Little Richard and Chuck Berry—and how they appealed to both white and black audiences—Berry Gordy insisted that the acts he signed sang and performed the kind of music that would also be accepted by both audiences. His vision was fully accepted by virtually all of his acts, including Stevie Wonder, Marvin Gaye, and the Temptations. Even when they made heavy funk with Norman Whitfield, the music patterned itself after a crossover act like Sly and the Family Stone.

Their choreography, too, created by Paul Williams and later Cholly Atkins, was a sight to behold. It was refined and precise, but dazzling and energetic. The most famous of their moves, the Temptation Walk, was adapted from similar moves by other bands, but they soon morphed into the Temptations' own. Those steps have since been co-opted by many others as has their performance style. More contemporary acts like Boyz II Men, BLACKstreet, Dru Hill, and New Edition all repurposed the Temptations' approach as their own.

Songs the Temptations made famous have been in constant circulation among modern acts as well. Most famously, perhaps, was the Stones' versions of "Ain't Too Proud to Beg" and "Just My Imagination." Duran Duran covered "Ball of Confusion," and Bette Midler sang a version of "Imagination" as well.

In fact, many of the most popular British rock acts, including the Faces, the Stones, and the Beatles, admitted to being enthralled by the Temptations and American R&B. Imitation, of course, is the sincerest form of flattery. And many imitated the Tempts. In 2004, *Rolling Stone* magazine voted the Temptations number 67 on their list of the 100 Greatest Artists of All Time. In 1991, Rod Stewart, who collaborated with the Temptations on the single "The Motown Song," wrote the Temptations entry on that list.

I was on holiday with my parents in the late sixties when I heard "I Wish It Would Rain." I lived in England, where it rains all the time, so it was appropriate. But that's also when I fell in love with David Ruffin's tenor—it jumped out of the speakers and ravished my soul.

Whether it was Ruffin or Dennis Edwards or Eddie Kendricks or Paul Williams singing lead, the Tempts were always an all-star vocal band. Throughout the sixties and seventies, the Tempts had an unprecedented string of hits: "My Girl," "The Way You Do the Things You Do," "Ain't Too Proud to Beg," "Just My Imagination." Later on, they broke ground with the psychedelic soul of "Cloud Nine." I remember listening to the hi-hat rhythms on that record over and over with the guys in the Jeff Beck Group. We'd try to change every one of our songs to try and capture their drumbeats. . . .

My children absolutely love the Temptations, and we try to see them every time they come to town. They always pick me out of the audience with a spotlight, trying to get me up to the stage. But I never do. I'm too frightened. (Rod Stewart, *Rolling Stone*, April 21, 2005, available online at www.rollingstone.com)

SELECTED DISCOGRAPHY

With a Lot O' Soul (Motown, 1967/1998)

Wish It Would Rain (Motown, 1968)

A Song for You (Motown, 1975/2007)

Emperors of Soul (Motown, 1994)

Psychedelic Soul (Motown, 2003)

FURTHER READING

Edmonds, Ben. "The Temptations' Final Frontier." *Mojo*, 2001.
Pitts, Leonard. *The Temptations Psychedelic Soul*, liner notes. Motown, 2003.
Weinger, Harry. *Emperors of Soul*, liner notes. Motown, 1994.
Williams, Otis and Patricia Romanowski, *Temptations*. New York: Cooper Square Press, 2002.

Pictorial Press Ltd./Alamy.

The Supremes

GIRL GROUP ROYALTY

They were, and still are, the most successful female vocal group of all time. They produced some of the greatest soul singles the world has ever heard. Beginning on August 22, 1964, and their first number one hit, "Where Did Our Love Go?," Florence Ballard, Mary Wilson, and Diane Ross redefined the meaning of success for women in the music business. They were the first group ever to score five consecutive number one hits, and were widely regarded as the act the Beatles had to conquer to hold its grip on the American popular music scene.

Mary Wilson, an original Supreme, said, "In 1964, the Supremes showed the world that black was not only beautiful, but black women were gorgeous and talented. We were ambitious. We won. We *were* the American dream" (Brian Chin and David Nathan, *The Supremes,* liner notes, Motown, 2000, p. 33).

Motown president Berry Gordy's original intention was to plug acts into his "machine," to run a sort of assembly line for pop vocal groups, which rings true considering his background as an auto worker himself. He wanted Motown to be the kind of company where someone could enter the back door as raw talent and exit out the front door as a polished star. In between those doors, there'd be the requisite grooming, rehearsing, and indoctrinating.

The Supremes were the first and perhaps most perfect embodiment of Gordy's assembly line process. They came in with all the right tools—the musical, personal, and physical goods—and they left as a masterpiece, a collective thing of beauty, who when they opened their mouths, symphonies emerged.

It also helped if the performers sounded "white," which was definitely the case with eventual Supremes' lead singer Diane (later Diana) Ross. Gordy's intent was to not only find black artists who had the goods, but to find black artists who had a commercial sounding voice that no one could tell was black or white. Ross was not considered to be the most talented voice at Motown; Gladys Knight, Mary Wells, and Martha Reeves all had a leg up on her in that category. In fact, when she arrived at Motown in 1960, she may not have even possessed the best voice in the group. But what she had was a "white-sounding, pop-friendly" voice, one that Gordy coveted and one that he'd be patient for while the group pulled their act together.

Critical revisionism has resulted in the legacy of the Supremes ebbing and flowing, depending on the scholarship and research done, and by whom. But with all the baggage of the Supremes' maddeningly interesting tale stripped away, with only the music laid bare for all the world to hear, the conclusion is plain. In their prime, the Supremes, once known as the Primettes, performed some of the most memorable music the American pop scene ever produced.

Thanks to a cadre of extremely talented, good-natured, and hot writers like Gordy, Smokey Robinson, Harvey Fuqua, and especially Holland-Dozier-Holland, the Supremes reigned throughout much of the 1960s before succumbing to the usual complications brought about by fame and fortune.

And the most fabulous aspect of the Supremes' saga is that it features all the elements glorified by the prototypical American dream: the girls from the projects, eager to turn their dead-end lives around, work hard, determined to change the outcome of their lives. Of course, no one knew just how drastic that change would be.

THE EARLY YEARS

In Detroit in the late 1950s, singing groups were as numerous and ubiquitous as popcorn stands at baseball games. The city, sated with the success of the auto industry, had been kept gainfully employed, and the offspring of autoworkers grew up in relative, if humble comfort. On the streets of Detroit's inner city, this meant living in recently built tenement homes or modest one-family dwellings. There were projects, too, apartment buildings that had sprung up to house the influx of people looking for work inside the auto assembly plants. Cars were rolling quickly off the line and there was a great demand for workers.

Optimism permeated the Motor City. The retail industry boomed, including record stores, which blared everything from gospel and Delta blues to R&B and doo-wop. Good vibrations were everywhere and young people were mainlining music of all sorts. At Northeastern High School in Detroit in 1958, where many of the artists on Motown's eventual roster earned their education, the ambition was palpable.

Paul Williams and Eddie Kendricks of the Temptations—they were then called the Primes—were studying at Northeastern. A group of girls, young high school kids—Diane Ross, Mary Wilson, Florence Ballard, and Betty Travis—came together there as well. Smokey Robinson and Ross grew up across the street from each other in a downtown Detroit project, kicking off a relationship that would come in handy in a couple of years.

Florence Ballard grew up in the Brewster-Douglass housing project with 11 other siblings in a five-room apartment. A step up from seedy tenement living, the project was well kept and relatively safe. Ballard showed a propensity for singing at an early age. She had good range for a young teen, and soon she was singing along with the Primes at local clubs. When she was 15, her father died, and she looked to music for solace.

Ballard originally met Mary Wilson at Brewster-Douglass, where she also lived, and they attended the same local church, where they both sang for the choir. Wilson, born in Greenville, Mississippi, had relocated to Detroit at 11 years old to be with her aunt and uncle, who raised her. Wilson was a perky girl with a permanent smile. She boasted many friends at school because of her upbeat personality.

Betty Travis was another friend they recruited to sing in the original incarnation of the group. At first, they called themselves the Primettes, as a girl spin-off of the Primes. But Travis had trouble singing with the group and getting her homework done, so she left the band to concentrate on academics.

Diane Ross, a thin, young bundle of energy, also came from Brewster-Douglass. Her dad was an autoworker, and her mom a maid in the city's wealthy Gross Pointe neighborhood. Athletic as a girl and ambitious, Ross ran track, swam, and did well in school. But it was her ambition that defined her. Growing up she gave perms to friends, sewed their clothes, and bussed tables.

Diane Ross grew up, like many of girls like her, singing in the church, in her mother's choir. And, like others at the time, she listened to the gospel of the Soul Stirrers as well as the doo-wop of acts like the Moonglows. She'd mime along to Etta James's "Roll with Me Henry" in her bedroom mirror. The reason she didn't attempt to make a name for herself in gospel was because, she admits, she couldn't sing it very well.

"I wasn't the kind of singer that had this range of expression that could go from *booooooooo*," she attempts to demonstrate an Aretha scream. "And all that. I wasn't really like that. My voice was more sensitive, and a lead voice, but the things I did in the choir had more to do with storytelling. So that's part of who I am: my motivation always came from *caring* and *loving* and all that, this expression of *feeling*" (Charles Shaar Murray, "The Gospel According to Miss Ross," *Q*, October 1987).

By the time the girls were 16, they had made up their minds that they wanted to sing for a living. Giddy with excitement, flush with hope, the Primettes sang like songbirds whenever and wherever they could. They were persistent in creating opportunities for themselves. Unlike many other vocal groups at the time, they didn't wait for the music industry to come to them. Rather they seized every invitation and stayed aggressive even at 16 and 17. They were even known to hitchhike around town when rides were unavailable to sing at record hops and talent contests.

In early 1960, they found a record company, Lupine, a tiny local label, to release their first single, "Tears of Sorrow" backed with "Pretty Baby." Diane sang lead on the A side, while Mary sang lead on the flip. At the time, Florence served as the leader of the group. As expected, the record made no impact, but the girls, undaunted, saw the positives of setting out on a career in music. At Lupine, they sang backup for a few of the label's acts, including a young Wilson Pickett and Eddie Floyd. Still, they were searching for a bigger company to handle their music.

Enter Smokey Robinson. Diane Ross knew Robinson from around the city; she was also a friend of his niece. Through Robinson's involvement, the girls had heard about an upstart label run by Berry Gordy. The Miracles, Robinson's group, then called the Matadors, would be taking a shot at a roster spot, and so too were the Primes, a group that would soon change their name to the Temptations. The Primettes scheduled a tryout.

MOTOWN CALLING

The audition didn't go well. The quartet performed in front of Gordy, Robinson, and two other Motown execs. They sang Ray Charles's "The Night Time Is the Right Time," accompanied by Marv Tarplin on guitar. During the audition, Gordy could see quite clearly they had something special. He noticed their talent, but also that they were courageous, unafraid to take a chance. He listened to the Primettes with interest, but ultimately demurred, suggesting they were too young, and that they go back and finish school.

This was not what the Primettes had in mind. (Incidentally, the audition went well for Tarplin, who left the Primettes and became Robinson's musical accompanist and co-writer.) Diane Ross didn't possess the kind of personality that would take "no" for an answer. After school, she'd come and hang around the office. She helped the secretaries with their administrative work, and tried her best to make herself useful; she knew she had to maintain some kind of presence around the office to stay on Gordy's mind.

Which she did, and the more he saw the girls helping out, contributing to the young, growing but burdened organization, the more he appreciated them. He made a conscious decision to keep the girls around the office, where, in addition to that miscellaneous workload, they'd get gigs singing backup on early Marvin Gaye singles, and fill in where necessary.

During the first year or so, Motown was an industrious but sociable place, where the label's young artists not only recorded their music, but served as a support system for each other's inaugural musical adventures. No one quite knew where the ship was headed, just that they wanted to be aboard for the voyage. In the label's nascent days not even Admiral Gordy had a sense of what was to come.

It started with a trickle. In 1961, the Marvelettes had a number one hit with "Please Mr. Postman," a Brian Holland composition. And in 1962 Mary Wells also scored Motown's widescale hit with a handful of Smokey Robinson tunes, "The One Who Really Loves You," "You Beat Me to the Punch," and "Two Lovers." (In 1960, Barrett Strong had a good-sized hit with Berry Gordy's composition, "Money [That's What I Want].") Wells and the Marvelettes succeeded in injecting the young company with hope and energy. The hit slots were there for the taking. They just needed the songs to fill them.

Robinson, Gordy, Clarence Paul, and a handful of other producers, including A&R director Mickey Stevenson, focused their efforts on bringing talent into the label and supplying them with first-rate material. Once the hits started coming, Motown's needs changed. They recruited talent and cut songs as fast as they could put the two elements together. One of the acts they decided to give an opportunity to was the Primettes, now renamed the Supremes by Florence Ballard, who had since dropped out of high school. They were officially signed to a contract in January 1961.

Barbara Martin, a young singer, signed the original Motown contract with Wilson, Ross, and Ballard, but would depart within the year, after the Supremes' first recording session with the label. She chose the relative comfort of marriage over the financial insecurity of a life in music.

The Supremes' first session, in the early winter of 1961, served as a warm-up. No single came of it, and the songs, Robinson's "After All" backed with Gordy's "The Boy That Got Away," are more in the girl group doo-wop mode à la the Chantels, sung by all three women. Another tune, "I Want a Guy," was recorded during that winter session, but saw its release come in March 1961. The spirit in the girls' performance was obvious. But the songs didn't grab much of an audience. Still, they were learning the trade.

> It's not like you're just singing words. You're not a mechanic or a technician, it comes from somewhere, and I usually select songs that have meaning to me.

"There Goes My Baby" was one of the first songs as The Supremes, we were The Primettes, actually, then we won a contest in Canada and that was one of the songs we sang, along with a Ray Charles song called "Night Time Is The Right Time", and I used to sing the high part. (Murray)

Thus began a long string of Supremes singles that didn't make the grade, a phase in the group's career known as the "no-hit Supremes" period. Despite the dry spell, most people around the office—writers, producers, and executives—felt that it was simply a matter of time before the band broke a song nationally. Gordy himself had tremendous confidence in the Supremes, their ability, and their work ethic. So he and the rest of the company devoted a significant portion of their efforts toward making the Supremes happen.

Right up through 1962, the Supremes recorded songs written by Gordy, Robinson, and Clarence Paul but didn't see any of their compositions stick to the charts. Then Brian Holland, Lamont Dozier, and Eddie Holland came to Motown and the Supremes' luck began to change.

HOLLAND-DOZIER-HOLLAND

Each of three songwriters—Lamont Dozier and Brian and Eddie Holland—took their turns trying to make it as a performer, and each one realized in time that they were better suited to writing than recording and performing. Brian had a hand in "Please Mr. Postman," with Robert Bateman, but Bateman had announced he would be leaving. Eddie, a former recording star, threw his hat in the ring as a lyricist. The demand for producers and songwriters had grown intense, and so Motown had issued the order of all hands on deck.

With Gordy and Robinson setting their sites on newer acts, they enlisted H-D-H to begin working with the Supremes. The match worked quickly. H-D-H loved the way the Supremes presented themselves, the way they sounded, the poise and sophistication. The group and their writers went to work.

One of their first compositions together, "When the Lovelight Starts Shining Through His Eyes," landed in the Top 30 on the pop charts, a promising initial salvo. Though the song was standard fare, it wouldn't be long before H-D-H began to understand just what sort of material this group would need to make real impact.

"They all could individually sing," says Brian Holland. "Mary could sing; she was a good lead singer too. Eddie liked the way she sang. There was a uniqueness about their blend. Diane didn't sound like an R&B singer; she had a pleasant voice when she sang, almost as pleasant as Ella Fitzgerald, and that gave a song that element of pop" (Chin and Nathan, p. 20).

When they needed a song to go to next, they pulled an older one out and dusted it off. "Where Did Our Love Go?" had been originally written for the

Marvelettes, but they turned it down. When the Supremes tackled it in April 1964, they didn't like it initially. There were some complicated harmonies that took time for Florence and Mary to work through. None of the girls thought the subject matter mature enough either.

"They were giving us sort of teeny-bopper songs like 'Where Did Our Love Go?' We didn't want to record that at all. They said, 'Trust us. It'll be a hit.' We said, 'Yes, but it sounds like a kid song' " (Nelson George, *Where Did Our Love Go?* London: Omnibus Press, 1985, p. 97).

Worse, they realized the key the song had been written in wasn't comfortable for Diane's lead. But no one bothered adjusting that key, forcing her to stray out of her range. Inadvertently, this lower key brought out a pleading, sultry quality to the song that the folks at Motown had never heard from her before. It gave Diane's voice a sound her listeners could pick out in a crowd. It almost didn't happen this way. Diane, dismayed at the changed key, wanted out of the lead role, while Mary Wilson didn't mind it, and she offered to sing lead. A brief debate ensued, with Lamont, Brian, and Eddie hashing out a decision that would eventually alter the group's path to stardom. Eddie voted on Mary, while the other two urged Diane to sing it. Diane won. The separation of Ross's voice over the others not only made the song a hit, it also drew attention to her singing style, even at this early point in the group's career.

At the time, Mary Wells, the Marvelettes, and Martha Reeves were the dominant female acts at Motown. But in the summer of 1964 that was all about to change after the Supremes worked out their rendition of "Where Did Our Love Go?"

In fact, many female acts in popular music would have a hard time staying in step with the times. By 1964, the Beatles spearheaded the British Invasion and the sound of music on the radio veered sharply from the relative harmonious smoothness of doo-wop and vocal group soul to the rough-around-the-edges jangle of the Liverpool and Merseybeat sounds from England.

In contrast, the acts at Motown sounded polite, even timid. So, to keep up with the changing times, the writers and producers ramped up their own sounds. Unfortunately, Gordy lost Mary Wells from his roster when she turned 21, seeking out greener recording pastures. This abdication—Wells had just recorded "My Guy" and was one of Motown's brightest hopes—may have hurt the label. (Wells, incidentally, recorded sporadically over the next two decades, but never again had another hit.) But Motown's loss proved the Supremes' gain, as the door of opportunity opened even wider.

Despite the obstacles and the events of the time, the Supremes' "Where Did Our Love Go?" went to number one on the pop and R&B charts in July 1964 and because of that, all the resources at Motown were redirected. The producers and songwriters all focused on the girls, who had begun to achieve the stardom everyone at the label knew had been pre-ordained.

Motown also rewrote the Supremes' contract to maximize company profits. They garnered earnings from publishing, personal appearances, and from every other area an artist could possibly earn money. In its way, the new contract simply mirrored the artist-unfriendly arrangements that most black artists encountered from all of the other blues and R&B labels. That is, they maintained the imbalance and unfairness that had begun early on between black artists and music industry executives.

But the meeting in which this new arrangement came about appeared casual, and the girls, without legal representation, simply signed.

Next, the Supremes were sent to Motown's Artist Development department. During the first Motortown Revue, when a busload of musicians and support staff toured the country, some of the Motown execs, including manager/producer Bean Bowles, were startled at the improper and crude behavior of his charges. When they returned, the company decided they'd set aside a certain department for grooming and behavioral issues. The philosophy held that Gordy wanted all Motown artists to cross over, and the best chance of crossing over would always go to those acts that were the most polished and sophisticated.

Harvey Fuqua supervised the schooling, Anna and Gwen Gordy taught decorum and cosmetology. But the task proved considerable so the company hired Maxine Fisher, of the Maxine Powell Modeling School, to do the teaching full-time. She told Gordy that she was grooming his acts—including the Temptations, the Miracles, and the Supremes—to appear in only two places: the White House and Buckingham Palace. This sounded okay to her students, who were used to grabbing most of their meals from cafeterias and were eager to develop taste and class.

On the road, Powell served as chaperone to most of the girl groups, especially the Supremes. She taught them how not to be suggestive while performing; how to sing with their eyes open; how to relate to their audiences; and how to maintain off-stage poise.

Maxine Powell and the Motown Charm School

As one-fourth of the label's artist development department, Maxine Powell partnered with dance instructor Cholly Atkins, musical director Maurice King, and pianist and arranger Johnny Allen to put the finishing touch on recording artists who rolled off the Motown assembly line. The young and rough-around-the-edges musicians that passed through the label's doors and into its recording studios wanted hit records, but Powell and her idol-makers wanted poised and confident stars whose talent would carry them beyond the brief but bright limelight that came with chart success.

Motown president Berry Gordy demanded acts that could transcend class and color lines and reign over upscale audiences in Vegas and New York. In a sense, Powell functioned as Motown's Emily Post, the one person responsible for the demeanor and compartment, not to mention looks and image of the

Motown stars and starlets. Her job was to hone the social skills and stage techniques of the artists. Her system resembled the old Hollywood charm schools set up by movie studios. The Supremes were her students and so was Marvin Gaye, who loved her so much he made her the godmother to one of his sons. Artist development at Motown was considered a four-year educational program and Berry Gordy insisted it be well attended. It goes without saying that many of Motown's young artists were skeptical. But the incredible results and the near universal acceptance of Motown's black soul acts by white audiences, proved their doubts to be groundless.

Powell had a successful finishing school of her own—The Maxine Powell Finishing and Modeling School—before Motown recruited her to work at the label in 1964. She initially worked with Martha Reeves and the Vandellas, the Supremes, and the Temptations, where she was instructed to create the kind of elegant and classy artists that could sing for "kings and queens, lords and ladies." She had connected with Gordy because his three sisters, Gwen, Esther, and Loucye, all attended Powell's school.

"Diana" Ross—she changed her name in the summer of 1964 to sound more elegant—studied at Powell's charm school for nearly a half year. She toned down her perfume, shortened her eyelashes, but Powell couldn't wean her off those bright red three-inch-long fingernails. Together, they spent hours learning how to sit, how to talk demurely about the success they've had, how to stand out in a crowd. Powell understood the potential stardom her client and the Supremes had ahead of them, so extra effort was made to get them through the grooming program as efficiently and completely as possible. Ross absorbed her lessons, and for the next few years, indeed the rest of her career, would put them to good use.

The next cog put in place at Motown was choreographer Cholly Atkins. Harvey Fuqua had worked with Atkins briefly while with the Moonglows and the Fuqua wanted to keep the staff at Motown familiar and comfortable. At the time, Atkins, a former singing waiter, lived in Bermuda, and had to be coaxed to Detroit. But he arrived in 1965 and stayed at the company for six years, working on his patented "vocal choreography" nearly nonstop. Every time a Motown act had a hit single, Atkins needed a routine to incorporate it into their performance. Given the success of the Supremes, Atkins worked steadily with the group from the time he hit the tarmac in Detroit.

He taught them the genteel dance moves that helped turn their stage show into an exhilarating event. While the Temptations were athletic and outrageous and the Miracles were tempered and classy, the Supremes focused on curves and swaying, mild gestures, and elegant posturing. Atkins's choreography for the Supremes set a high standard for girl groups.

BEAUTIES AND THE BEAT

"Where Did Our Love Go?" was the first of an incredible string of chart-topping hits—five in a row—all of which were directed at woman. H-D-H made it a point to target the tracks they wrote for the Supremes directly at a female audience. The girls were buying the records, and it seemed to the songwriters that they were the ones that were doing a lot of falling in love. Teenage girls had crushes, and often those crushes were unrequited. H-D-H pinpointed the feelings of that unrequited love, or the falling *into* love, in their early tracks for the Supremes: "Baby Love," "Come See About Me," "Stop! In the Name of Love," "Back in My Arms Again."

Lamont Dozier explains it:

> There may have been some personal stuff happening; the three of us always had girlfriends, and we had difficulties in our love lives because we spent a lot of time at work, and away from girlfriends or wives, and you have that feeling inside. Basically, our theme was all about love, whether it was a tragic love affair or some happy times, there were moments in there that were about just living and how it affects each individual. (Chin and Nathan, p. 22)

"Stop!" is one of the Supremes' all-time beloved tunes and is one of the team's most exquisite productions. Propelled by James Jamerson's archetypal bass line, and the accompanying vibes, sax, and organ parts, the song's principal element happens to be a tambourine, which adds a gorgeous gospel feel to the entire work. That gospel feel brings out a terrific lead vocal from Diana, who reminds us here that she did indeed come up singing in the church.

At the time, the partnership of H-D-H was writing two or three songs in a single day, piecing together bits of melody, choruses, hooks, bridges, and lyrics like jigsaw puzzles. From 1964 to 1967, their creative momentum carried them through a mind-boggling array of material. At the time, they were trying to keep up with not only the hectic and successful pace they set for themselves, but the music scene in general. The Beatles and the Beach Boys had accelerated their own productivity, so H-D-H and Gordy strived to keep up. The only problem was that Motown had a stable of artists to keep track of. The Beatles and Beach Boys only had to worry about themselves.

Unlike virtually all other black artists, from Ruth Brown and Louis Jordan to Ray Charles and Sam Cooke, the Supremes didn't have to first prove themselves to a black audience. They went to the pop charts straight out of the gate. This happened because Gordy's vision called for it. Powell's sophistication ensured it, and Motown's image-making vehicle nailed it.

By 1965, the Supremes had become a franchise for Motown. Including recordings and personal performances, the Supremes raked in hundreds of thousands of dollars each, despite their inequitable contract. Some of the money Motown made went back into the group, as they raised the standard for the group, with more elegant costumes, an extensive wig collection, and other trappings. They were playing the most prestigious clubs in the country, including New York City's Copacabana, and they could ill-afford to make a false move. Atkins, Powell, Gordy, H-D-H had all hit their stride together, and Motown, thanks to the Supremes—and the Supremes, thanks to Motown—were all moving in lockstep toward fame and fortune.

Because they crossed over to a white audience, they appeared frequently on television. Many performers, like Otis Redding and Aretha Franklin, had to wait for their small screen opportunities, mainly because they were R&B acts that didn't care much about reaching white audiences.

But the Supremes showed up often on the influential program the *Ed Sullivan Show*, where the country would watch them put all that training and polish to the test. They swayed their hips, and sang with perfect enunciation, and just enough soul, to hold the attention of the black audience. If the dance moves and the songs didn't grab the attention of their coveted national audience, surely their designer gowns would. Their first appearance on *Sullivan* came on December 24, 1964, and over the next two years they appeared on national television another 20 times.

Gordy and Motown had designed a plan, a scheme, really, to make sure the Supremes would become the biggest and richest pop group in the world, and for a short time, they succeeded. The girls were buying homes, cars, and clothes like never before. They moved their families into stylish duplexes. When choreographer Cholly Atkins moved to Detroit to work with the label, Mary Wilson was his building's landlady. These were heady times for the Supremes, as they enjoyed their perch at the very top of the heap.

In the summer of 1965, the group encountered its first disappointment. Their sixth single, "Nothing But Heartaches," didn't crack the Top 10, stalling at number 11. They had been on an unprecedented roll and any interruption of momentum felt like a huge letdown. It was at this time that Gordy circulated his now famous mandate: "We will release nothing less than Top 10 product on any artist. And because the Supremes' worldwide acceptance is greater than any of our other artists, on them we will release only No. 1 records."

THE PRESSURE IS ON

Gordy's mandate sent the songwriters back time and again to the drawing board, in an attempt to outdo what they had already done to perfection. The pressure on them mounted, especially H-D-H, who had basically been ordered to write number one hits or don't write at all.

To their credit, they came up with some very ambitious stuff. A few singles immediately following Gordy's order fell short of that high standard. But their next four singles didn't, beginning with "You Can't Hurry Love," then proceeding through "You Keep Me Hangin' On," "Love Is Here and Now You're Gone," and "The Happening."

Originally, most critics dismissed the Supremes. At the time rock was on the rise, and serious music fans focused not on the prefabricated products of Motown, but on the organic and ever-changing rock scene and R&B, where artists like Jimi Hendrix and James Brown were cranking out revolutionary grooves. Still, in hindsight, that criticism may have been misplaced; Motown's "products" have been acquitted over the years, and cited as some of pop music's all-time greatest work. Writer Dave Marsh is one of those proponents:

> "You Can't Hurry Love" is an invigorating groove record which Ross turns into one of the most soulful vocals of her career. Three years into her reign as the Queen of Pop, you can still feel the anxious insecurities that drove Diana into those skinny, spangled dresses. . . . This song's an open, honest reflection of her deep emotions, and that's exactly what soul's supposed to be all about. (Dave Marsh, *The Heart of Rock & Soul*, New York: Da Capo Press, 1999, p. 376)

The Supremes had a total of nine number 1 hits in conjunction with their Holland-Dozier-Holland partnership. The string made superstars out of both parties. H-D-H can lay claim to being at least as important to popular music as any of the artists they composed and produced. Their records had an uncanny coherence, a specific style that transcended the groups that performed them. And while they were in their prime, they managed to keep each record fresh and distinct, without lapsing into formula. They rarely went to the same well twice without at least taking a different path to the water.

Of course, H-D-H did figure out ways to repurpose ideas and spread them between the acts for which they were writing. "They ruthlessly cannibalize olds songs for spare parts; verbal phrases, thematic ideas, musical figures, accompaniments, even sax solos are shuffled together and reworked from disc to disc; every song is a collage" (George, p. 135).

H-D-H did this more or less as a matter of survival. So great were the demands on their time, they had no other option but to return to the wellspring from which the ideas had originally come. Their approach was clinical in its precision, and so, as they honed their process, the musician's personality was gradually phased out. Over time, they delineated specific parts to the house band, leaving less and less up to serendipity and more to precision and calculation. Despite this overt control, the songwriting trio managed to create some of the greatest two-minute pop symphonies of the 1960s, and in all popular music.

But they couldn't do it by themselves. "Love Is Here and Now You're Gone" represents the first time the group recorded a song outside of Motown's studio. To push the Supremes' sense of refinement one step further, they traveled to Los Angeles to record these sessions with an orchestra. The concept of these three girls from the Detroit projects performing lead vocals in front of a talented and very sophisticated symphony orchestra may have been the very embodiment of Berry Gordy's original vision. In November 1967, that song also hit number one. The circle was complete.

THE TROUBLE IN PARADISE

Unbeknownst to Florence and Mary, plans at Motown were being implemented for Diana Ross to begin a solo career. In the summer of 1966, following the smash "You Keep Me Hangin' On," she and Gordy got together—they were also romantically linked at this time—to carefully map out her future as a solo artist. Ballard and Wilson knew nothing of this liaison, or this plan, but they did start seeing some unusual behavior. Ross began demanding her own dressing room at gigs, leaving Florence and Mary to split a second. Diana was assigned virtually all of the group's leads from this point as well, and in interviews, Ross answered nearly all the questions. At events she led the way, sweeping into official functions at the head of the pack, leaving Florence and Mary trailing behind her like bridesmaids.

By April 1967, just as their tune "The Happening" reached the top of the charts, their 10th number one song, Florence and Mary found out that the name of the group had changed. From then on, they'd become known as "Diana Ross and the Supremes." This revelation hurt morale; the girls had both been with the group since inception. It was Ballard who originated the group, coined them the Primettes, and booked their first gigs. And it was Ballard who came up with "the Supremes" when Gordy insisted on a new name. The timing couldn't have been worse for all this injustice; just as the girls were experiencing spectacular success, the two girls felt they were being relegated to the back seat.

If Ross enjoyed the spoils of stardom most, she also, as the vocal leader of the group, bore the brunt of Gordy's criticism. He scrutinized every aspect of the group—from their appearance and image to their dancing and singing—and if they slipped up, it was Diana who heard about it. He'd call her aside after the show, in which he'd often sit in the very front row for a better view, and excoriate her with what he perceived as her mistakes. He frequently reduced her to tears with his flared temper and cruel comments.

Yet just as he criticized her, he'd soothe her. Just as she seemed inconsolable, he'd embrace her and comfort her. He inflated, then deflated, then reinflated her ego with exhausting frequency. Some even referred to Gordy's relationship with Diana as a "modern-day Frankenstein," so firmly was he in charge of her actions.

"When he needed to be, Berry was a master of mind control. Diana wanted 'it'—the love, the acceptance, the stardom—so badly, and he had convinced her that only by living his thoughts, becoming an extension of his dreams, could she live out her own" (George, p. 163).

Florence had actually been coping least well with the group's fast-rising superstardom. Coinciding with the girls' number one hits back in 1964, she started drinking. Before that she'd been a teetotaler, wholesome and well-meaning. But gradually over the next two years, she spiraled into heavy drinking and her work habits slipped. By 1966, she'd put on a considerable amount of weight and had become a changed person. She often called in sick for rehearsals or recording sessions, and on stage her patter became unpredictable and occasionally embarrassing. As her condition deteriorated, she even failed to show up for two concerts, leaving Diana and Mary to perform as a duo.

Berry Gordy saw Florence's decline arise as a result of the power struggle she witnessed between her two colleagues. Mary and Diana had, for the most part, an amicable rivalry as the lead singer of the group. But it always created a source of friction, and Florence dealt with that friction through drink. Florence sang ever fewer leads as the years progressed and she struggled to cope with the rigors of touring and fame. It was a recipe for personal disaster.

At one important rehearsal, with many of Motown's biggest executives in attendance, Flo had stepped to the mic to tackle her lead on "People." Gordy, up front, stopped her after a couple of notes and told her to let Diana sing lead on it. It had been Ballard's song all along, but no more. Flo stepped back and cried. She wouldn't sing a Supremes' lead again.

It all came to a head one night in 1967 in Berry Gordy's living room. He confronted Ballard directly and aggressively about her transgressions, in front of the other girls. Florence expected their support, but received none. Even Wilson could not bring herself to stand up for her friend. During that brief exchange, Ballard saw the writing on the wall. She understood now what the name change meant. She also felt all the time and hard work the group put into their act drift away as if it never existed. As she looked across the room at Berry and Diana, she came to the awful realization that the group didn't exist anymore, at least how she wanted to remember it.

The band that had been emblematic of the rise of Motown, that had perfectly crystallized the so-called Sound of Young America; the very band that had done everything they were told and learned everything they were taught, had begun to fracture.

On April 30, Ballard missed a big show her group was headlining with Buffalo Springfield and the Fifth Dimension. It would be the last show she'd miss with the group. Though she had been truly sick, Diana and Mary were not about to perform such a big show as a duet. Cindy Birdsong had been waiting in the wings to replace Ballard for some time as Ballard's stand-in. Birdsong came from New Jersey and had recently been a founding member of Patti Labelle and the Bluebells out of Philadelphia. Birdsong left that group in 1967, right after the call came from the Supremes.

Motown quietly and unceremoniously replaced Ballard from that day forward; the official announcement was made in July 1967. They offered Ballard $15,000 to leave amicably. A lawyer for the singer, though, entered the scene and Flo left the Supremes with a settlement of $75,000. She signed a contract with ABC Records and attempted a solo career in the early 1970s, which failed miserably. More legal wrangling ensued and Ballard ended up bankrupt. She died in 1976 of heart failure, penniless.

Despite Motown trying to keep the Supremes' schism under wraps, word of the split shocked the music world, and soiled the immaculate reputation of the Supremes. The strife underscored the partitioning that happened within the group. That partitioning, once symbolic, became as real as the sequins on their gowns.

The repercussions of Ballard's departure and Ross's simultaneous rise didn't simply affect the Supremes. It had company-wide ramifications at Motown. All of the label's female stars felt abandoned: Gladys Knight, Kim Weston, the Marvelettes, Martha and the Vandellas. They all felt they stood in the shadows behind an increasingly distant and inaccessible Gordy, and his deification of Ross. Ballard's descent was symptomatic of what was happening throughout Motown.

Not only that, Diana's elevation and the changing of the group's name also piqued the curiosity of the Temptations' David Ruffin, who saw similarities in his own situation. Ruffin had been the main man, and a powerful performer throughout his work with the Tempts. But the act refrained from giving him top billing à la Ross. Still, he began traveling separate from the rest of the group, showing up late for gigs, and allowing his ego to disrupt the band.

The Miracles employed the same name change with bandleader Smokey Robinson. But Robinson's loyal connection with Gordy and the executive branch of Motown kept his situation in check. Still, this splintering heralded a new era within Motown, one that allowed egos to grow unchecked.

THE FALL OF MOTOWN

If the four-year period between 1959 and 1963 proved critical to the young record company, and the years from 1963 to 1967 saw the company reap the rewards from the work it had sewn during that initial four years, then the years between 1967 and 1971 represented Motown's gradual decline.

Gordy spent much of his time grooming Ross for a solo career, at the expense of virtually everything else. Dissension, lawsuits, and pressure from an ever more competitive music industry began taking its toll on what had been essentially a harmonious existence. Gordy moved the Motown offices to a non-descript 10-story building in a more secure part of town; race rioting and crime had soared in light of the powder-keg social climate now gripping the streets of American cities.

Gordy also bought himself a gaudy, marble-floor mansion on the city's flashy Boston Boulevard, quelling rumors that Motown would be relocating to Los Angeles. In fact, Motown did have an office in Los Angeles, and Gordy spent a lot of time doing his business there and phoning in to Detroit executives Barney Ales and Ralph Setzer. That is, when he wasn't playing golf with the Temptations and Harvey Fuqua, or in Vegas hobnobbing with Sammy Davis Jr. and other members of the Rat Pack.

In 1968, Gordy got word that Brian Holland, Lamont Dozier, and Eddie Holland wanted out. Had Gordy been around the office, he would have known that the three were rarely in the Motown building working. They had been producing hits during this time ("Reflections," "In and Out of Love"), but they happened to be pieced together from material they'd written during their most prolific period, 1965–1967.

Fuqua, Gordy's right-hand man Mickey Stevenson, Bean Bowles, and Cholly Atkins all left around the same time, while Gordy clearly had taken his hands off the wheel. Most of these departures concerned proper remuneration and issues of respect. In the case of H-D-H, the trio felt like the time of dues paying was clearly over. They had proven themselves over an extended period and now wanted to participate in a share of the company profits, rather than earn a simple salary. Publishing, of course, was a major revenue stream for Gordy and all of that money was funneled back into Motown and Gordy's pocket.

H-D-H had been trying to pump Motown for a better deal for a while before Gordy even knew of their efforts. So by the time Gordy had heard about their frustration, they were already on their way out.

The lawsuits began. Motown sued first for breach of contract. Then H-D-H countersued Motown for conspiracy, fraud, deceit, and other things. The courtroom process limped all the way into the mid-1970s, eventually settling out of court.

With all this trouble brewing, Gordy and Motown did everything they could to keep Diana hot. They joined the Supremes together with the Temptations, a union that yielded "I'm Gonna Make You Love Me" in late 1968. They crammed all the TV appearances they could for the band into their schedule. For the two years running from January 1968 to December 1969, they appeared on the TV 25 times. Ross became a celebrity thanks to these appearances, and she demonstrated versatility as a personality and actor. In October 1969 the group released another number one hit, "Someday We'll Be Together," co-written by Harvey Fuqua, Johnny Bristol, and Jackey Beavers. Bristol and Beavers performed it back in 1961 for Gwen Gordy's label, Tri-Phi.

In January 1970, at a Las Vegas gig, fully prepped and ready to go off on her own, Ross announced her departure from the Supremes. They were perched at number one on both the pop and R&B charts, which meant Diana was ensuring that she'd go out on top.

GOING WEST

Gordy's move to Los Angeles in 1972 dovetailed nicely with his growing ambition to get involved in the film industry. Though he moved from his strength as a purveyor of pop songs and into relatively uncharted territory for himself, he felt confident that he could make an impact. Motown had done well with its television specials, producing a handful in the early 1970s. Emboldened by that success, Gordy concentrated on seeking film vehicles for Ross.

The problem was, Gordy's disengagement from Motown's music business rendered the company weak and indecisive, all at a time when the industry was undergoing intensive changes. In 1972, Gordy booked Ross as the lead in *Lady Sings the Blues*, a biopic of jazz singer Billie Holiday. While the story suffered from historical distortions, it did showcase an effective and powerful performance for Ross, whose own rise from the projects to stardom paralleled Holiday's. She earned an Oscar nomination for the role, and may have won it outright were it not for Gordy's over-the-top ad campaigning that alienated the Hollywood establishment.

Encouraged by progress, Motown delved into screenplays, putting as many as a dozen into development at once, all vehicles for the cast and characters of the label: Robinson, Gaye, Ross, Wonder, and Michael Jackson. Only five of those came to fruition, including *Mahogany* and *The Wiz*. Given the lackluster performance of these films at the box office, Gordy and Motown never established firm footing in Hollywood. But Diana Ross's career as a solo artist was another story.

It took a while, but she eventually shifted from her impacting turn as Billie Holiday and back into singing pop songs. About this time it was expected that Ross and Gordy would make their relationship public but Diana surprised everybody by marrying Robert Silberstein, a white businessman. She had obviously begun to question Gordy's role as a manager in her career. But not enough to send him away. In fact, Ross, Silberstein, and Gordy spent an unusual amount of time together as a trio throughout Ross's six-year marriage to Silberstein.

Personal relationships aside, Motown had positioned their resources behind Ross's solo efforts at the expense of the Supremes, which were virtually ignored by the label. Ross became a ubiquitous superstar of the 1970s and one of the period's highest paid performers. Recordings like "Ain't No Mountain High Enough," "Love Hangover," and "Touch Me in the Morning" becoming one of the world's highest paid performers.

The Supremes, now with Jean Terrell in place of Ross, continued their successful recording career well into the 1970s thanks to Top 10 hits like "Up the Ladder to the Roof," "Stoned Love," and "Nathan Jones." Wilson, Terrell, and Birdsong continued to draw at concerts and on television. This duality— Ross and her former group competing at Motown for supremacy—proved too complicated for the label. It seemed that as hard as they tried to de-emphasize the work of the Ross-less Supremes, the public embraced them.

Bob Jones began managing the post-Diana Supremes: "We were trying to re-establish the Supremes in the position they had held before. When we introduced Jean [Terrell] to the media, people responded well. However, it became very difficult from a managerial standpoint even though Mary [Wilson] definitely had the ability to keep the group going" (Chin and Nathan, p. 43).

The lack of company support eventually created dissension within the group. By 1973 Jean Terrell quit and was replaced by Scherrie Payne; Cindy Birdsong left the group not once but twice, being replaced in each instance by Lynda Laurence and Susaye Green. Surprisingly, during these confusing times the Supremes recorded excellent material that kept the fans interested, but the group was not destined to be. By the end of 1973, their energy and inspiration flagged. They had a few chart blips in the mid-1970s, up until 1976. But dance music had taken over the soul and pop scenes, and there was no natural place for the Supremes, especially without the support of their label. Motown had quietly pulled the plug on the most successful female trio in the history of the music business.

In tribute, the label made a decision to retire "The Supremes" name.

POSTSCRIPT

In 1979, Mary Wilson released a solo album under her own name. Wilson tried to launch a solo career but record companies backed off, afraid of a problem arising with Motown and their overprotective nature for Ross. Still, Wilson sang around the world based on her past work and likability. In 1986 she issued a candid autobiography titled *Dreamgirl: My Life as a Supreme* that became a best-seller, and actually became the best-selling music autobiography in history. *Dreamgirls*, a warts-and-all tale of the girls' journey, became an award-winning play and motion picture, much to the chagrin of Gordy and the old guard at Motown, all of whom objected to the tell-all depiction. Wilson wrote a sequel to *Dreamgirl*, called *Supreme Faith: Someday We'll Be Together*, which was also well received.

Despite lingering animosities, Ross, Wilson, and Birdsong reunited briefly for a performance at the *Motown 25* special in 1983. However, Ross's grandstanding during the performance—the studio audience witnessed Ross pushing Wilson—rekindled bad feelings and nixed any lasting reunion. Then, in 2000, with her solo career foundering, Ross announced that she would be leading a Supremes "Return to Love" reunion tour. However, mutual distrust and a dispute over the sharing of revenues doomed the reunion from the start, and amazingly Ross chose to stop discussions with Wilson and Birdsong and instead attempted to bring in Lynda Lawrence and Scherrie Payne for the tour. It was a public relations nightmare for Ross and the tour was a monumental failure in every respect; it was canceled after a few low-selling dates.

LEGACY

In Mary Wilson's book, the Supremes were presented as history now views them: part American dream and part American tragedy. The truth is, when they first began their rise, the country, even the world, followed the fulfillment of their dreams. Once they had attained those dreams, however, that same population watched as they slowly began to disintegrate in a maelstrom of egotism, personal demons, botched decisions, and misplaced energy.

As the most popular girl group in the history of modern music, the Supremes were quite nearly perfect. With a gorgeous, cut-glass image and a bevy of nonpareil songs from which to choose, they had it all, and America was willing to get behind everything they did. From 1964 to 1967, the girls had gone beyond all expectations on their way to shaping Motown's Sound of Young America. With their polished sequins and designer dresses, their impeccable etiquette and flawless presentation, they took class about as high as it would go.

But the Supremes were also brittle. In the same way that they could be molded to fit all the right dresses and taught to sing all the right harmonies, they were also human, and incapable of maneuvering through all of the complications, mind games, and corporate traps laid before them. In the end, the relationships that characterized their early rise and incredible successes, the same friendships that brought them together, failed to hold up under the intense strain of the spotlight. It didn't help that folks were constantly trying to pull them apart, with affection, money, favors, and false promises.

All that said, though, they enjoyed a spectacular ride. The template they established for girl groups and all of popular music is easy to see in everything that would follow, from the Beatles' who admittedly adored the Supremes and all of the Motown stable right up through the work of En Vogue, Destiny's Child, and solo acts like Beyoncé Knowles and Gwen Stefani carried the tradition of the girl groups through the 1990s and 2000s, proving how enduring the sound and style really were.

The highly publicized excesses of Diana Ross and Motown have unfortunately gone a long way in obscuring just how good the Supremes were at their peak. Songs like "Where Did Our Love Go?" "Baby Love," "Stop! In the Name of Love," "You Keep Me Hanging On," in addition to a score of album tracks comprise what is one of the most impressive legacies in all of pop.

Their brand of soul was not the kind of soul that James Brown and Otis Redding san in sweaty clubs every night. But it came from the same place. The Supremes' version of soul—penthouse soul—may not have gone over on the Chitlin' Circuit, but it fell on the ears, the hearts, the minds, and *soul* of millions of worshipful fans.

SELECTED DISCOGRAPHY

Where Did Our Love Go? (Motown, 1964/2007)

The Supremes Sing Holland-Dozier-Holland (Motown, 1967/2007)

Diana Ross and the Supremes Join the Temptations (Motown 1968/1991)

The Supremes (Motown, 2000)

FURTHER READING

Chin, Brian and David Nathan. *The Supremes,* liner notes. Motown, 2000.

George, Nelson. *Where Did Our Love Go?* London: Omnibus Press, 1985.

Marsh, Dave. *The Heart of Rock & Soul.* New York: Da Capo Press, 1999.

Murray, Charles Shaar. "The Gospel According to Miss Ross." *Q*, October 1987.

Thompson, David. *Funk: Third Ear Listening Companion Series.* San Francisco: Backbeat Books, 2001.

Wilson, Mary. *Dreamgirl: My Life as a Supreme.* New York: Random House, 1988.

Courtesy of Photofest.

Stevie Wonder

Jesse Jarnow

JOYOUS VISIONARY

The joy pours from Stevie Wonder like a rainbow. Positioned behind his piano in dark sunglasses, Wonder bobs his head from side to side while he performs. His hair, pulled in tight braids and capped with colorful beads, sways along with him. His hands dance across the keyboard, and his smile—whose brightness goes undiminished even when he opens his mouth to sing—stretches across his face.

More than anything, this has been Stevie Wonder's primary contribution to American popular music: happiness. It stretches across every dimension of Wonder's work. Whether as a teenage R&B sensation in the 1960s, a bold funk-jazz experimenter in the 1970s, or a mega-platinum pop singer in the 1980s, Wonder's mission has been one of forward-thinking freedom and redemption, for himself and others.

Prodigiously talented, Wonder taught himself piano, drums, and harmonica at a young age. Originally signed as a novelty act, Wonder worked within the strict confines of a music industry based around regimented, formulaic singles and package tours. Eventually, Wonder levered his talents into an enormous amount of creative and financial control. As a musician, he received nearly infinite leeway.

At his peak in the mid-1970s, Wonder holed up literally for days at a time in the studio, where he played all of the instruments himself, almost always including an array of the latest synthesizers. He often threw away dozens of songs for each one he released. So huge was Wonder's appeal that he was able to negotiate a deal so powerful that he was granted veto power should his label ever be sold (a power he exercised several times).

When Stevie Wonder issued albums—most often with portentous titles like *Songs in the Key of Life* and *Innervisions* that implied a deep wisdom packaged inside—they were treated as major events. As Wonder took more and more time to finish his work, the delivery of the recorded masters to the record company was reported breathlessly in the press, while major advertisements were purchased (including the biggest billboard in history, at one point). Over a dozen of his full-lengths, including a consecutive run of nine beginning in the early 1970s, reached the Top 10. In addition, over 30 of his singles hit the chart's upper reaches, stretching nearly a quarter century, from 1963's "Fingertips (Part II)" to 1985's "Go Home."

It is no exaggeration to say that Wonder's voice has spread joy to all corners of society from calls for social justice ("We Are the World"), to standard songs at weddings ("You Are the Sunshine of My Life," "I Just Called to Say I Love You"), jazz and funk clubs ("Superstition," "Higher Ground"), and in hip-hop beats ("Pastime Paradise"). Wonder has served as a musical ambassador, as well, collaborating with musicians the world over, from Jamaica's Bob Marley to Nigeria's King Sunny Adé. Especially during the years when his musical productivity began to diminish, it was a role Wonder cherished.

"I do believe that Stevie Wonder is the necessary vehicle on which Stevland Morris must be carried on his mission to spread love mentalism," Wonder once said, referring to the dichotomy between his birth name, Stevland Morris, and his professional name, Stevie Wonder. "My mind's heart must be polygamous and my spirit is married to many and my love belongs to all" (Sharon Davis, *Rhythms of Wonder*, London: Robson, 2003, p. 120).

Wonder has followed the same course of action off stage, as well. As a humanitarian, he has addressed the United Nations on human rights in South Africa, and lobbied for a half-decade to designate Dr. Martin Luther King Jr.'s birthday as a national holiday.

That Stevie Wonder rose from poverty to accomplish all of the above without the use of his eyes is not irrelevant to his story, because it *is* his story. But both facets of Wonder's life—his music and his blindness—are merely that: facets. Blind since infancy, Wonder has often said that he never knew what it meant to have the gift of sight and therefore did not miss it. Throughout his life, he has insisted that the people around him have always been more saddened by his blindness than Wonder himself. He has had too much music to play.

THE EARLY YEARS

Stevland Hardaway Judkins was born 100 miles southeast of Detroit in the city of Saginaw, on May 13, 1950. He was a month premature, and immediately placed in an incubator. There, exposed to too much oxygen over the course of the month, Stevie developed retrolental fibroplasia. Membranes grew behind both of his eyes. By the time the doctors removed him from the incubator, one eye was destroyed by a dislocated nerve, and the other by a cataract. He was blind.

His mother, Lula Mae Hardaway, had two sons from a previous relationship. Calvin Judkins, Stevie's father, was never a presence in young Stevie's life, which might have been a blessing. Lula Mae worked as a maid, a job she continued when she brought Stevie and his brothers to Detroit in 1954. They moved in with Paul Hardaway, the father of Stevie's brothers, on the city's west side. Hardaway worked in a bakery, and Lula Mae resumed her domestic jobs. Lula gave birth to three more children: Timothy, Larry, and Renee. When she remarried, Stevie took on her husband's last name, Morris.

Life was not easy in Detroit, either, where the family occasionally had to go without food. Wonder later remembered that "in the winter my mother, brothers and I went to this dry dock where there was coal and steal some to keep warm. To a poor person that's not stealing, that's not a crime. That's a necessity" (Davis, p. 15). Despite the hardships, Lula Mae raised Stevie as best she could. She brought him to numerous doctors, in hopes they could restore her son's sight. None could.

She brought Stevie to Baptist ministers as well, more for her comfort than his, Stevie believed. They told her that what God had taken away from Stevie in sight, it would return to him in other ways. Stevie instinctually believed this, as well. He reasoned that his world was just as beautiful as everybody else's. After all, he never had the gift of sight to begin with, so there was nothing to despair over. In fact, it was perhaps more special, as Stevie discovered, when he began to occupy his own world of sound. He sang in the church choir, but that was only a small part of it.

Around him, Stevie discovered that he could see people without really seeing them. He used his ears to figure out where they were, and listened acutely to discover anything he could. By their movements and the sounds of their voices, Stevie could ascertain their age, their body type, and their moods. "Maybe I can find the truth about them . . . because people who see often tend to choose the book by the cover," Wonder said as an adult. "I have to do it my way. Maybe a person is also beautiful inwardly and that's the side I'll know first" (Davis, p. 16).

The rest of the world was just as fascinating. He experimented with a slingshot and measured distances by the sharp report of pebbles off of his targets. He enjoyed the sound's ricochet. Nor did Stevie let his blindness hold him back from having a childhood. He climbed on barns, flirted with girls, got into fights, and—with his brothers—pulled pranks on his mother. Still, Stevie was not allowed out without someone to guide him. Consequently, he spent much time at home, where his love for music blossomed.

At the age of six, Stevie became a regular listener to WCHB, a Detroit R&B station. Though the station played national singles, they also concentrated on the incredible variety of regional acts, which ranged from early rock singer Del Shannon to fledgling gospel superstars the Staple Singers (from nearby Chicago) to R&B combo Hank Ballard and the Midnighters. Another musician Stevie loved was doomed singer Johnny Ace, who later killed himself in a game of Russian roulette. Stevie memorized Ace's songs and began to sing them on a nearby street corner. When an uncle gave him a four-note harmonica, Stevie's repertoire expanded to include the influence of blues bandleaders like Jimmy Reed and Bobby Bland.

Stevie was a natural musician. His next instrument, the drums, grew from his love for pure sound. Often, Stevie could be found playing rhythms on junk he found on the street, like bottles and tin cans. At a family reunion over Christmas, a relative presented Stevie with a drum kit. He guided his hand along the edges of the snare, kick drums, and cymbals. Within a day, he claimed, he wore down the drum heads. At a neighbor's house, Stevie took up the piano. First, he simply figured out children's songs, like "Three Blind Mice," but progressed to the R&B staples that had taken over his heart. Soon, he could replicate any song he heard. When the neighbor moved, she gave the piano to Stevie.

As much as he could, Stevie continued to have a normal childhood. He attended school, and was an enthusiastic student. Stevie still played on street corners, but brought his talents to parties and dances. Often, he performed with a friend, John Glover, who played guitar. They sang duets, called themselves Stevie and John, and built up a small following around their west side neighborhood. Their performances often incorporated songs by two new local stars, Marvin Gaye and Smokey Robinson, from a brand-new local label, Motown Records.

Founded in 1959 by Berry Gordy Jr., the label was black-owned, and would soon become one of the largest in the world. It had quickly developed a reputation around Detroit. By 1961, securing an audition with Gordy was nearly impossible. But Stevie had an advantage: one of his biggest fans was Gerald

White. Gerald's brother, Ronnie White, was a singer in the Temptations, one of Gordy's biggest acts. At Gerald's encouragement, Ronnie listened to Stevie perform "Lonely Boy," a song Stevie composed himself. Ronnie contacted Gordy, who turned the audition over to Brian Holland, a talent scout who would become one of the label's greatest songwriters.

Lula Mae brought Stevie to Motown's offices at 2648 West Grand Boulevard, where the label's singles were recorded in a basement studio known to musicians as "the snake pit." Stevie showed off his virtuosity as he was led from instrument to instrument. Members of the Supremes, then the youngest act in Motown's stable, watched in amazement. Eventually, A&R director Mickey Stevenson enthusiastically summoned Gordy from his breakfast. Gordy was immediately won over by the young man's personality, and signed him to Motown. Stevie was 11 years old.

On account of Stevie's age, Motown specially prepared the contract. Esther Edwards, a Motown employee, consulted the Michigan Department of Labor so that it would comply with child labor laws. As Stevie's guardian, Lula Mae signed the five-year contract, which she signed again five years later. Motown assumed control of all of Stevie's financial affairs, with all future royalties deposited into a bank account Stevie could access when he turned 21. A private tutor would be employed to teach Stevie as he recorded and toured. Both Stevie and Lula Mae received weekly stipends from Motown, which Lula used to keep her family afloat. Stevie received $2.50 a week.

A MOTOWN TEEN

Stevie Wonder found success at Motown before he found success in the outside world. The musicians and staff took the boy under their arms. One dubbed him "a little Stevie wonder" and the name stuck. Another, drummer Benny Benjamin, became one of Stevie's primary musical educators. Stevie became close friends with Motown secretary (and future Vandellas frontwoman) Martha Reeves, and began a lifelong bond with the Reeves family.

The man who had the most impact on Wonder, however, was Clarence Paul, the producer and songwriter Berry Gordy assigned to his adolescent signee. Paul became a father figure to Stevie as they sang together at Paul's piano. In the meantime, Stevie learned his way around Motown unassisted. An inveterate prankster, Wonder often not-so-innocently wandered into other musicians' sessions, where he would immediately take up a piece of percussion and join the band. With fellow Motown singer Marvin Gaye, the two even spent time crank-calling Gordy.

Stevie also continued his flirting with girls. When he was introduced, he ran his hands over a girl's arms and face to get a sense of what she looked like, before "accidentally" going lower. He would apologize, but shoot a smile in the direction of Gordy or other males in the room.

It was almost a year before Wonder was allowed to record. "I Call it Pretty Music (But the Old People Call it the Blues) (Part I)," a single, was released in August 1962 and failed to sell, as did its autumn follow-up, "Little Water Boy." In the fall, Motown issued two albums credited to Little Stevie Wonder. Though Stevie had begun to write his own songs, his first LP he recorded, while he was still 11, was *Tribute to Uncle Ray*. Released in October 1962, Wonder sang numbers made popular by blind soul and country crooner Ray Charles in a marketing ploy on the part of Motown. In many ways, Motown marketed him as a novelty act. The second album, *The Jazz Soul of Little Stevie*, recorded later, was released a month earlier than *Tribute*. It featured music written for him by Clarence Paul, often with Wonder's direct input. Neither album sold very well.

In late 1962, Wonder joined Gordy's Motown Revue, a 94-date road show to promote the label's catalog and artists. Crammed in a ramshackle bus, Wonder, the Marvelettes, the Contours, Mary Wells, Martha and the Vandellas, the Miracles, Marvin Gaye, the Temptations, Singin' Sammy Ward, and the Supremes played gigs across the Chitlin' Circuit, the unofficial national network of black-owned clubs, bars, and theaters. Because of child labor laws, Wonder was often the first performer on the bill. Though his third single, "Contract on Love," sold better than the first two, Gordy tried a new tactic: a live album.

Recorded at Chicago's Regal Theater, during the Motown Revue, *Recorded Live—The 12 Year Old Genius*, began with what was Wonder's finale: a six-minute rendition of "Fingertips," an instrumental from *The Jazz Soul of Little Stevie*. After the band finished, the crowd cheered for a reprise. Clarence Paul led Stevie back onto the stage, where Wonder pretended to be unaware of where he was. Though it was staged, the crowd went wild when Wonder began to play again. Released as a single on May 21, 1963, the song was split into two parts. Wonder's shtick—known as "Fingertips Part 2"—became his first number one pop hit. Soon, the album followed. He became the first artist to have simultaneous number one albums and singles, as well as the youngest, and the first to top the charts with a live recording.

At the conclusion of the Motown Revue, the Board of Education concluded that Stevie was not receiving a proper education. They demanded that he remain in Detroit's public schools for another six years. "One teacher told me that I had three big disadvantages in life—I was poor, blind and black. Realistically, there was nothing for me, indeed for any uneducated blind guy, but to make rugs for a living" (Davis, p. 34). Wonder and his mother were infuriated, and doubled their efforts to find a solution. At the Michigan School for the Blind, in Lansing, in September 1963, Lula Mae found Ted Hull, a partially sighted man, who was hired as Wonder's tutor.

By agreement with the Board of Education, Stevie attended classes in Lansing for two weeks each month, and was tutored by Hull on the road. Hull explained everything from financial matters to the everyday stuff of life, such as electricity. In Wonder's words, he "connected the blind world with the sighted world" (Davis, p. 35).

Subsequent singles failed to match the success of "Fingertips Part 2," though Wonder remained constantly busy. "Workout Stevie, Workout!" reached number 33 R&B, but many of Wonder's releases from the mid-1960s remain footnotes. One such curiosity is an album of show tunes titled *With a Song in My Heart*. Others include appearances in a pair of Hollywood beach party movies starring Frankie Avalon and Annette Funicello, *Muscle Beach Party* and *Bikini Beach*. In 1964, Wonder dropped the "Little" from his name, a moniker of which he'd grown increasingly intolerant. Stevie continued to tour, and traveled to Europe for the first time to perform in England in March 1965. He loved the attention of the stage, and would pretend that he had to be pulled from his instruments.

Finally, Wonder hit his stride. Recorded in December 1965, his own "Uptight (Everything's Alright)"—about not judging a person over his wealth—reached number one Pop and number one R&B in January 1966. That summer, he issued "Blowin' in the Wind," his interpretation of folk singer Bob Dylan's civil rights anthem, which reached number nine Pop. "A Place in the Sun" followed it to the same chart position. Motown continued to release subpar Stevie Wonder albums, though, such as 1966's *Down to Earth*, which was filled out with covers of acts like Sonny and Cher. Still only 16, Wonder began to feel confined by Berry Gordy's strict release policies, including the practice of following up a single with a sound-alike song, to try to further capitalize on its success.

More and more, Wonder trusted his own muse. Inspired by the voice of a Baptist preacher, Wonder conceived "I Was Made to Love Her," released in July 1967 (number two Pop). After he graduated from the Michigan School for the Blind, with honors, in 1968, Wonder put out "Shoo-Be-Doo-Be-Doo-Day-Day" (number nine Pop, number one R&B). The song was the first by any artist to use a clavinet, an amplified keyboard run through a variation of a guitarist's wah-wah pedal. It became an indispensable part of Wonder's palette, and soon for the rest of the pop world. Not all of Wonder's experiments were as successful, though. When Gordy pressured him to record "Alfie," by Burt Bacharach and Hal David, Wonder returned with an instrumental album titled and credited to *Eivets Rednow* (Wonder's name backward). The album sold poorly, but Stevie continued to follow his instincts though he started to withhold some of his ideas from Motown until he passed his 21st birthday.

Originally released as a B-side, "My Cherie Amour" became a surprise number four Pop hit in 1969. "I wrote it when I was 16 after me and my sweetheart broke up," Wonder said. "It took me 30 minutes to write, but I never did give it to anyone because it was too personal," he continued. "I changed with 'My Cherie Amour.' I suddenly realized it was time I calmed down and started behaving responsibly.". "Yester-Me, Yester-You, Yesterday" (number seven Pop) followed before the end of the year. In early 1970, "Signed,

Sealed, Delivered (I'm Yours)" became the 20-year old Wonder's 10th Top 10 Pop hit. The accompanying album, also titled *Signed, Sealed, Delivered*, featured another important development. On a cover of the Beatles' "We Can Work It Out" (number 13 Pop), for the first time, Wonder played all of the instruments on a track by himself.

In 1970, Stevie Wonder started "behaving responsibly" on several fronts. He recorded "Heaven Help Us All," a song about the horrors of war. In addition, Wonder began working more seriously with other artists on the Motown roster. He had collaborated before, such as on Smokey Robinson and the Miracles' chart-topping "Tears of a Clown" in 1967, but Wonder now began to apply his talents toward specific acts, including the Spinners and a Motown secretary and occasional back-up singer named Syreeta Wright.

Initially recruited to accompany Wonder as he made demo recordings at the Motown office, a romance blossomed between Wonder and Wright. Wonder proposed to her in May. On September 14, 1970, they were married at the Burnette Baptist Church in Detroit. Though it was a joyous celebration whose invitees included nearly all Motown employees, times were changing for the record label. As the business grew, Gordy decided that autumn to relocate Motown to Los Angeles. Many artists soon found homes on other labels. Though Wonder supported the move, he also recognized that it wasn't the same family-run company he once knew.

As the company changed, Stevie took more creative control. With Syreeta co-writing lyrics, he recorded *Where I'm Coming From*, whose songs focused on social issues. It was not only the first album he made without constraints from Motown's offices, but the first full-length he performed and recorded by himself. It sold poorly, but it was no matter to Stevie Wonder. He was about to turn 21.

OUTERVISIONS

On May 13, 1971, Gordy threw Stevie Wonder a massive 21st birthday party in Detroit. On May 14, Wonder flew to New York, where he moved into the Holiday Inn on West 57th Street, and sent his lawyers to the Motown offices. They notified Gordy and Motown president Ewart Abner that, now that Wonder was 21, the contract signed by his mother was null and void. He demanded immediate payment of the trust fund the label established for him in 1961, now worth an estimated $30 million. The label gave him $1 million, and Wonder accepted it as a starting measure. Gordy was stung, but Wonder did not pay attention. He had music to record.

In New York, Wonder met producers Malcolm Cecil and Bob Margouleff. That year, the two had released *Zero Time*, an experimental LP—the first all-electronic album—credited to TONTO's Expanding Head Band. TONTO stood for "The Original New Timbral Orchestra"—the world's first multi-timbral polyphonic analog synthesizer. Stevie took to it enthusiastically. "The whole purpose of me using synthesizers," Wonder said in 2005, "was to make a statement and to express myself musically—to come as close as possible to what those instruments could do, but also to expressing how *I* would allow those things to sound" (Zach Lundy, *Songs in the Key of Life*, New York: Continuum, 2005, p. 53). The palette of sounds available to Stevie increased infinitely.

A History of Synthesizers

Throughout his career, Stevie Wonder has championed the use of new musical technologies capable of creating never-before-heard sounds. Though the golden age of synthesizers didn't begin until the 1960s and 1970s—exactly when Stevie Wonder became a pop star—experiments with electricity and sound are as old as the piano itself.

In 1729, just three decades after the first appearance of the pianoforte in Italy, French Jesuit priest Jean-Baptiste Delaborde, constructed the Clavecine Électrique. Delaborde employed electromagnetics to vibrate tuned metal forks. Over the next 200 years, literally dozens of scientists and musicians all across the world experimented with electronic sound.

The first of any note was American inventor Thaddeus Cahill's telharmonium, begun in 1897 and completed in 1906, which pumped sound from 145 dynamos through, in early versions, primitive horns and, in later adaptations, directly into the early telephone system. At $200,000 apiece, only three were built. In the early twentieth century, the family tree of electronic instruments flowered.

One notable innovation in 1919 was Russian expatriate Léon Theremin's self-named theremin, the first (and only) instrument played without one's hands. In 1928, French cellist Maurice Martenot refined the theremin into the Ondes Martenot, which could be controlled by a makeshift keyboard. Both instruments have been heard on in countless songs and movies, including the Beach Boys' 1967 single, "Good Vibrations."

The true father of the synthesizer, however, was Robert Moog. After selling home theremin kits from his apartment, Moog experimented with his own circuitry. In 1964, he sold his first keyboards, which gained popularity via Walter Carlos's classical-synthesizer adaptation *Hooked-On Bach* (1968). Another early synthesizer was the mellotron, which found an audience through the Beatles' use of it during the introduction to "Strawberry Fields Forever" (1967).

By the 1970s, Stevie Wonder had has choice of literally dozens of synthesizer brands. In addition to the TONTO, the Yamaha GX1, and the Synclavier, which Wonder used, there were models by Korg, Roland, Casio, Oberheim, and others. A true visionary in the field of synthesizers, the electronic keyboards veritably overtook the palette of popular music in the 1980s, especially when they offered musicians the ability to sample and construct new sounds. Even today, inventors are rushing to create instruments to realize the sounds Stevie Wonder has heard in his head for decades.

On Friday, May 28, Wonder, Cecil, and Margouleff entered Electric Ladyland, the studio founded by guitarist Jimi Hendrix. They stayed for three straight days. Wonder jumped from keyboard to keyboard with abandon while Cecil and Margouleff operated the recording gear and attended to the primitive synthesizers. When they emerged on Monday, May 31—Memorial Day—they had 17 new songs.

It set a pattern of working habits for the trio, who—many times over the next two years—worked for days straight, ignoring holidays and weekends. After two weeks, they completed 40 songs. The Memorial Day collaboration began a two-year period of immense productivity and nearly constant recording for the three, both at Electric Ladyland and at the Record Plant in Los Angeles. It is estimated that when their collaboration ended in 1973 they had worked on, if not finished, somewhere between 400 and 1,000 songs.

By the end of 1971, Stevie Wonder and Motown finally came to a five-year agreement whereby Motown would grant him both publishing rights and full creative control over his releases. With a new record deal under his belt, Wonder assembled a new touring ensemble. The eight-piece group, accompanied by four back-up singers, was dubbed Wonderlove and featured former members of Paul Butterfield's Blues Band. For the first time, Wonder brought his Moog and ARP synthesizers with him on the road, for a tour of Europe. Though he had long tackled social issues in his music, such as race and class, Wonder now began to perform benefits and make public appearances in support of his beliefs. On December 10, 1971, he joined former Beatle John Lennon in Ann Arbor, Michigan, at a benefit rally for John Sinclair, the jailed leader of the White Panthers.

Music of My Mind—the first product of his sessions with Cecil and Margouleff—was released on March 3, 1972. Though neither of the album's singles made it into the Top 10 on either the Pop or R&B charts, and the album itself only hit number 21 Pop, number 6 R&B, it was a great critical success. Over the summer, Wonder was invited to open 50 shows on the Rolling Stones' massive tour. Throughout, Wonder clashed in the press with the Stones' leaders, Mick Jagger and Keith Richards, over petty matters. By the end of the tour, they made up to a degree. On July 26, Jagger's 29th birthday, Wonder joined the Stones on stage, where they jammed on Wonder's "Uptight" and the Stones' "(I Can't Get No) Satisfaction," among other songs. Decca, the Rolling Stones' label, planned to release a double-LP recording of the concert, though it was soon scrapped. At the end of the year, Wonder divorced

Syreeta Wright, though the two remained close, with Wonder producing many of her recordings over the subsequent decade.

Between concert dates, Wonder continued his work with Cecil and Margouleff, and released *Talking Book* in October 1972. After Wonder promised to give it to British guitarist Jeff Beck, Motown released "Superstition" as the album's first single. It became Wonder's first number one since "Fingertips Part 2" almost a decade earlier. With its accessible groove and bouncy melody, the song gave Wonder his biggest crossover success yet. "You Are the Sunshine of My Life" followed, and was an even bigger hit. The soft love song sold over a million copies and became a pop standard the world over. *Talking Book* itself reached number three Pop.

Even as *Talking Book* and its singles dominated the charts, though, Stevie was busy. He kept recording and whittling. The result was *Innervisions*. The first single, "Higher Ground" (number four Pop, number one R&B) rushed over the radio in the summer of 1973. Like "Superstition" before it, it was powered with urgency by the clavinet, here dark and driving as Wonder sang of personal and societal redemption. His message was as spiritual as it was political. In April, Ben Fong-Torres interviewed Wonder for *Rolling Stone*. "He sees the earth zigging towards a destructive end," Fong-Torres wrote. "He can see himself dying soon" (Lundy, pp. 108–109). *Innervisions* was released on August 3, 1973.

A NEAR-DEATH EXPERIENCE: THE KEYS OF LIFE

Three days later, Wonder and his cousin, John Harris, left Greenville, South Carolina, headed to the next show, 242 miles away in Durham, North Carolina. While Harris drove, Wonder slept. On Interstate 85, near Salisbury, North Carolina, Harris tried to pass a log truck. Exactly as he did, the truck slammed on its brakes. A log flew from the rear and smashed through Harris and Wonder's windshield. It struck Stevie in the head, breaking his skull, and giving him a brain contusion.

Wonder remained in a coma for a week at North Carolina Baptist Hospital. At Wonder's bedside, road manager Ira Tucker first tried talking to the singer, then shouting, and—finally—singing. For a day, he sang "Higher Ground" and, eventually, Wonder's fingers began to tap along. Gradually, Wonder woke up. Temporarily without his senses of smell or taste, Wonder worried that his musical ability might be depleted, as well.

Tucker brought Wonder's clavinet to the hospital. "You could tell he was afraid to touch it," Tucker remembered. "He didn't know if he'd lost his musical gift. You could actually see the relief and happiness all over his face when he finally started playing it" (Davis, p. 91). Besides several scars, including one over his eye, Wonder suffered no damage in the accident. He returned to the stage on September 25, 1973, joining British pop singer Elton John at Boston Garden in Massachusetts. The 15,000-strong crowd gave Wonder a 15-minute standing ovation, which continued even as Wonder and John jammed on "Superstition" and the Rolling Stones' "Honky Tonk Women."

Wonder returned to work as quickly as he could. *Innervisions* (number four Pop, number one R&B) continued to sell, as did the second single, "Living for the City" (number eight Pop, number one R&B). He recorded and performed sporadically, including a one-off show in Cannes, France, and a jam session in New York with New Orleans pianist Dr. John and blues guitarist Johnny Winter. In early 1974, he hit the road with Wonderlove, who had grown into a tight, jam-happy ensemble. The band now opened their shows with "Contusion," Wonder's only song that directly referenced his accident. Heavy on funk and fusion, it could last as long as 20 minutes, which left some audiences confused.

In 1974, Stevie Wonder was everywhere. In March, he won five Grammys, his first, for Pop Vocal Performance, R&B Vocal Performance, R&B Song, Album of the Year, and Engineering. In June, Motown released *Stevie Wonder Presents Syreeta*, a collaborative concept album about the failure of their marriage. Wonder also penned "Tell Me Something Good" for soul singer Chaka Khan and her band Rufus, who made it a number three Pop hit. Likewise, he wrote "Until You Come Back to Me (That's What I'm Gonna Do)" for Aretha Franklin, who brought it to number three Pop, number one R&B.

In public, Wonder embraced his African heritage. He wore dashikis and spoke in interviews about his wish to retire from music and move to the Republic of Senegal, in western Africa. But retirement wasn't an option for Wonder, who continued to churn out songs with producers Malcolm Cecil and Bob Margouleff. At first, he looked into his already massive archive for material for his next album, but quickly decided to write new songs that reflected the changes in his life.

Though they followed the same pattern of collaboration, with Wonder on keyboards and drums, various musicians joined Wonder on the album. Michael Jackson and the Jackson 5 added vocals to the politically charged "You Haven't Done Nothin'" (number one Pop, number one R&B) released in August 1974, the same month Richard Nixon resigned his presidency. The album, titled *Fulfillingness' First Finale* (number one Pop, number one R&B) was released in July. A second single, "Boogie on Reggae Woman" (number three Pop, number one R&B) came out as Wonderlove undertook a 35-city U.S. tour, before they traveled to Japan. In March 1975, Wonder picked up five more Grammys.

Stevie Wonder and Wonderlove performed for 200,000 people in Washington, D.C., on Human Kindness Day, though most of 1975 was devoted to activities besides music. On April 7, Yolanda Simmons gave birth to Wonder's first child, Aisha Zakiya Morris. All of Wonder's children would take the last name Morris. Wonder became involved in a variety of charities, appearing and answering telephones on Gerald Rivera's One to One telethon, setting up a scholarship at Shaw University in Raleigh, North Carolina, and opening the Stevie Wonder Home for Blind and Retarded Children. Wonder remains involved with many charities, though does not often publicize his affiliations. He also traveled, first to South Africa, where he again considered (and decided against) relocation, then to Jamaica, where he spent time with reggae musicians Bob Marley and the Wailers.

Back in the United States, Wonder started his most ambitious album yet. It was the longest time Wonder had ever taken between albums, but he was prepared to take more. He dismissed the production team of Malcolm Cecil and Bob Margouleff, and hired John Fischbach, an engineer on both *Innervisions* and *Fulfillingness' First Finale*. After meticulously keeping track of Wonder's experiments in their infamous Blue Book, Wonder's prolific work from the previous half-decade was now thrown into disarray. He started fresh.

Meanwhile, as 1976 approached, Wonder's five-year contract with Motown was about to expire. Wonder's lawyer, Johann Vigoda, drove a hard deal with Gordy and Motown. When Vigoda finished the $13 million contract, which included an extremely high 20 percent royalty rate, Wonder had unprecedented control of his future: if Gordy were to ever sell Motown or his Jobate publishing company, Wonder would have full veto. Wonder insisted that, while it was important to provide for his family, the money at stake was not the most important part of the deal. He said:

> [Motown is] the only viable black-owned company in the record industry. . . . Motown represents hope and opportunity for new as well as established black performers and producers. If it wasn't for Motown many of us just wouldn't have had the shot we've had at success and fulfillment. In the record industry we've seen many cases where the big companies eat up the little ones and I don't want this to happen to Motown. I feel young black children should have something to look up to. It's vital that people in our business, particularly the black creative community, make sure that Motown stays economically healthy. (Davis, p. 109)

Wonder signed a new contract with Motown on August 5, 1975.

Even so, Wonder kept Motown waiting. He had a custom shirt made. "We're almost finished!" it read, for anyone who might ask. Motown made a shirt, too: "Stevie's nearly ready." In the studio, Wonder had a new toy: the Yamaha GX1, a prototype synthesizer that weighed 1,000 pounds and cost $60,000. Only a few other musicians, including members of Led Zeppelin and ABBA had them. With three separate keyboards that allowed Wonder to layer different sounds simultaneously, the GX1 was even more complex than Cecil and Margouleff's TONTO. Wonder called the GX1 "the Dream Machine" (Lundy, p. 76).

Songs in the Key of Life was Wonder's magnum opus. Spread over two discs, with a bonus EP, it touched on every element of Wonder's skills and interests. "Ngiculela—Es Uni Historia—I Am Singing" was a song about peace and unity sung in three languages: Zulu, Spanish, and English. "Black Man," meanwhile, was a history of racism. Both a Hare Krishna and West Angeles Church of God choirs appeared on "Pastime Paradise." "I challenged myself to [write] about as many different things as I could to cover as many topics as I could in dealing with the title," Wonder said later (Lundy, p. 9).

The album was given a massive publicity campaign. In New York City, Motown purchased the largest billboard in history, on Times Square, to advertise it. Journalists were flown in a private plane to a farm in Massachusetts, where they were dined and entertained by Wonder himself. Advance orders for the album topped 1.3 million copies. The album went platinum before it was officially on sale.

When *Songs in the Key of Life* was finally released on October 8, 1976, it went straight to number one, where it stayed for 14 weeks. It was only the third album in history to debut in the top spot. Other labels were said to have held back their new releases until Wonder's double-album cooled down. It would be some time, especially with its two number one singles, the funky "I Wish" and "Sir Duke", a tribute to jazz great Duke Ellington, who died in May 1974. Like its predecessors, *Songs in the Key of Life* veritably swept the Grammys, winning five including Album of the Year. Wonder did not collect his award, though was scheduled to perform by satellite from the second World Black Festival of Arts and Culture in Lagos, Nigeria.

WONDERDRIFT

Stevie Wonder's musical activity of the following three years was limited mostly to live performance. Much involved collaborations that expanded his palette. In addition to the performance in Lagos, which included members of Duke Ellington's band and the George Faison Dance Troupe, Wonder appeared with jazz great Ella Fitzgerald, reggae great Bob Marley, and on the stage of the Grand Ole Opry, the home of country music in Nashville, Tennessee. Wonder also reunited with other present and former Motown stars, Diana Ross, Smokey Robinson, and Marvin Gaye to record a poorly selling tribute to Gordy's father, Pops, "Pops, We Love You." Early in 1979, at the invitation of Coretta Scott King, the widow of slain black leader Dr. Martin Luther King Jr., Wonder performed in Atlanta, to mark what would have been Dr. King's 50th birthday, his first of many performances on that date.

Wonder also worked with abnormal slowness on a project that was in an entirely new medium for him: film soundtracking. It was, perhaps, an odd choice of directions, but it was an odd film. Based on a book by Peter Thompson and Christopher Bird, Walon Green's *The Secret Life of Plants* explored the notion that plants might be sentient creatures whose thoughts and feelings were expressed on a different scale than humans and other animals, and sometimes communicated in paranormal ways, such as through magnetism. The documentary employed time-lapse photography, which Wonder set to music.

"Blind people have certain pictures that I believe they are able to draw," Wonder said. "We can perceive the same as another person can visually perceive, but there is no possible way for someone like me, blind from birth, to 'see' in their dreams" (Davis, p. 128). Unfortunately, Paramount deemed the documentary itself unreleasable, and Wonder was left with a soundtrack to a non-existent film. To fill out the instrumental pieces, Wonder recorded several more songs, including "Come Back as a Flower" (with lyrics and vocals by Syreeta Wright, Wonder's ex-wife). Motown experimented with issuing the disc doused in a special perfume, though it was discovered that the odorous chemical corroded the vinyl. Instead, each album cover was marked with a message in Braille. "Inside the embossed square is the outline of a flower with veined leaves," it said, describing the cover.

Wonder performed the work at Manhattan's Metropolitan Opera House on December 2, 1979, a month after the album's release, joined by the National Afro-American Philharmonic Orchestra. Though the album reached number four on the *Billboard* Pop chart, its sales tapered off quickly. Gordy complained that of the 1 million copies Motown pressed in advance, 900,000 of them were too many.

In 1980, Wonder began to work from his new home base, at Wonderland Studios in Los Angeles. He contributed to albums by blues guitarist B.B. King, folk singer James Taylor, and jazz arranger Quincy Jones. Wonder also penned "Let's Get Serious" (number nine Pop, number one R&B) for Jermaine Jackson, a member of the Jackson 5, and received an honorary degree from Fisk University, one of the first black colleges in the United States, founded in 1866. Fueled by the dub and reggae albums Bob Marley sent him from Jamaica, including Lee "Scratch" Perry's *Revolution Dub*, Wonder recorded his new single "Master Blaster (Jammin')", which reached number four Pop. Released on September 29, 1980, *Hotter Than July* reached number three Pop, and went platinum by the next year.

Though the album sold well, Wonder had a more important concern. In October 1980, he held a press conference at Gordy's office in Los Angeles. He "respectfully demanded" that the U.S. government commemorate the birthday of black activist Martin Luther King Jr.—January 15—as a national holiday. The King Day Bill had circulated through Congress since its introduction by Congressman John Coneys (D-MI) in 1968. Despite support from President Jimmy Carter in the 1970s, the bill still did not pass.

"Like no other American, Martin Luther King stood for, fought for and died for American democratic principles," Wonder said. "The holiday would be the first commemorating the enormous contributions of black people in the United States" (Davis, p. 143). In January 1981, Wonder performed at a rally for the cause in Washington, D.C. Between 150,000 and 200,000 people attended, and collected over 2 million signatures for a petition.

In late February 1981, Wonder flew to Montserrat in the West Indies to record "Ebony and Ivory" with ex-Beatles bassist Paul McCartney. McCartney took credit for the song, which reached number one Pop on its March 1982 release. McCartney later admitted that Wonder had come up with much of the song's melody, as well as many of its lyrics, and asked McCartney to take credit for them because he believed the song's calls for racial equality would not be taken seriously if audiences knew a black man wrote it. Wonder's originals continued to bring racial issues to light. He wrote "The Day World Peace Began" in the memory of slain Egyptian president Anwar Sadat, and released "Happy Birthday" about Martin Luther King Jr. The song did not reach the Top 10 in the United States, but it became the centerpiece of Wonder's campaign to make King's birthday a holiday. In 1982, over 50,000 people turned out in subzero temperatures to join Wonder.

As Wonder lobbied for the recognition of Martin Luther King Jr., he became more of a public figure than a musician. Though Wonder returned to the charts periodically and spectacularly during the 1980s, most of the decade was spent on a new course, both commercially and creatively. Especially compared to the prolific years where he virtually recorded around the clock, Wonder spent comparatively very little time in his new Wonderland studio. His interests were wider. In 1981, he vetoed Gordy's sale of Motown's Jobate publishing company, though his own financial state wasn't much better. When he signed again to Motown in 1982, for $3 million, Wonder agreed to release a greatest hits collection, titled *Original Musiquarium I*, with four new songs, including "That Girl" (number four Pop).

Another part of Wonder's new Motown contract was the creation of Wondirection, his own label. Wonder signed bands such as Grease, Boots Rising, and Wonderlove, his own backing band. Though none would release any commercially successful albums, rapper Gary Byrd reached number six on the British charts with his surprise hit, "(You Wear) The Crown." Wonder also appeared on *Saturday Night Live* opposite Eddie Murphy, who had popularized a comedic caricature of the blind singer, moving his head back and forth blissfully while speaking in a spaced-out cadence.

In 1983, Congress voted to recognize Martin Luther King Day. After initial opposition to it, President Ronald Reagan signed the King Day Bill into law on November 3, 1983, and made Martin Luther King Jr.'s birthday a federal holiday, which would be first recognized in 1986. Six states, which included North Carolina and Arizona, at first refused to recognize the holiday. Until they did—Arizona in 1992, New Hampshire as late as 1999—Wonder refused to perform in those places.

Finally, in 1984, Wonder returned to the studio to create his second movie soundtrack. Directed by actor Gene Wilder, *The Woman in Red* was a romantic comedy. The album, released by Motown in August 1984, contained "I Just Called to Say I Love You," which—in October—became Wonder's first number one hit since 1977. It was the fastest selling Motown single of all time, eventually earning Wonder the first ever triple-platinum award. Wonder picked up his first Academy Award for "I Just Called", as well, for Original Song for a movie. The song, a simple ballad, marked Wonder's new pop-oriented direction, which favored directness not heard in the previous decade's more cosmic missives. The follow-up, titled simply "Don't Drive Drunk," underscored this creative shift, and did not chart.

This approach continued the following year with Wonder's participation in "We Are the World," on *In Circle Square*, Wonder's 1985 album, which included "Apartheid (It's Wrong)," protesting the legalized racism supported by the South African government. He spoke out frequently, especially during a speech at the 1985 Oscars, which he dedicated to jailed South African activist Nelson Mandela. "The resettlement camps are wrong," Wonder said. "If they're so great, why don't the whites want to live there?" (Davis, p. 171). Wonder was immediately banned from government-owned South African radio stations. On February 14, 1985, Wonder was arrested in Washington, D.C., during a peaceful protest outside the South African embassy.

In Circle Square (number 4 Pop) was released in September 1985, with "Part-Time Lover" (number 1 Pop), and "Go Home" (number 10 Pop) as its singles. To date, they represent Wonder's last trip to the Top 10 as a solo artist. In 1987, Wonder appeared with Dionne Warwick, Gladys Knight, and Elton John on "That's What Friends Are For," written by Burt Bacharach and Carole Bayer. The song went to number one and won a Grammy for Song of the Year. Like "I Just Called to Say I Love You" and "You Are the Sunshine of My Life," "That's What Friends Are For" became a pop standard, played at social events from weddings to proms to bar mitzvahs.

Characters, Wonder's follow-up to *In Circle Square*, was released in 1987. Though the album, which featured both the anti-crack song "Stop, Don't Pass Go" and a duet with Michael Jackson on "Get It," it was Wonder's first album in over a decade to not make the Top 10 on the album chart. Wonder continued to experiment with electronics, attempting a bicoastal recording session between his Wonderland in Los Angeles and MSA in New York City—a method that would become commonplace with the advent of the Internet a decade later. The album also employed the Synclavier, a new type of computer synthesizer where the composer fed sheet music to the machine, which reproduced it exactly. Live, Wonder appeared more often without a backing band, accompanied only by programmed beats. This became a problem at a 70th birthday celebration for Nelson Mandela at London's Wembley Arena, in June 1988, when the disk with the beats was stolen.

Since the late 1980s, Wonder has recorded little, though continues to be active in other ways. In 1989, for example, he contributed a song, "Parents of the World" to UNICEF. Later that same year, he announced his intentions to run for mayor of Detroit. "I feel that God has an even bigger plan for me, and I would like to move to the plan," Wonder said. "I would like to think of myself as a unity mayor" (Davis, p. 193). Between television specials, tours to former communist nations, the birth of his third child (Mumtaz, born to Melody McCully in 1984), performances with orchestras, and the 1991 soundtrack to Spike Lee's *Jungle Fever*, Wonder never mentioned his political aspirations again.

"While economically it is a great thing to have a record out every year-and-a-half and there are definite drawbacks if you don't," Wonder said of his newer, more relaxed schedule. "The many composers of hundreds of years ago didn't have records out every year-and-a-half. So I don't feel funny about the time it takes me at all" (Davis, p. 211). *Conversation Peace* (number 16 Pop, number 2 R&B), released in 1995, was much delayed. His next album, *A Time to Love* (number five Pop, number two R&B), did not reach stores until a decade later, and featured Prince and En Vogue on the poorly charting lead single "So What the Fuss."

Though Stevie Wonder has not dominated the Pop charts in nearly 20 years, on a given day, his music is likely played more often than most of the currently best-selling artists. Wonder has, of course, been an influence on many of them, including pop songstress (and Motown signee) India.Arie. Like many of his generation of musicians, Wonder's music has been sampled extensively, as well, most notably on "Gangsta's Paradise," Coolio's classic 1995 rap hit, which was based almost entirely on "Pastime Paradise," from 1977's *Songs in the Key of Life*. Wonder's influence has spread even to rock music. In 1995, indie-rock songwriter Liz Phair released *Somebody's Miracle*, conceived as a song-by-song response to *Key of Life*.

Wonder could be heard in his contemporaries as well, like British rock behemoths Led Zeppelin, who employed a funky clavinet on 1975's "Trampled Underfoot" to channel Wonder's "Superstition." And though thousands of jazz-funk bands have borrowed from Wonder's distinct 1970s sound, Wonder's greatest influence is what he conveys: the sheer force of human creativity.

SELECTED DISCOGRAPHY

The 12 Year Old Genius (1963)

I Was Made To Love Her (1967)

Greatest Hits (1968)

Signed, Sealed, Delivered (1970)

Music of My Mind (1972)

Talking Book (1972)

Innervisions (1973)

Fulfillingness' First Finale (1974)

Songs in the Key of Life (1976)

Hotter Than July (1980)

FURTHER READING

Davis, Sharon. *Stevie Wonder: Rhythms of Wonder.* London: Robson Books, 2003.

Hull, Ted and Paula L. Stahel. *The Wonder Years: My Life and Times with Stevie Wonder.* BookLocker.com.

Love, Dennis, and Stacy Brown. *Blind Faith: The Miraculous Journey of Lula Hardaway, Stevie Wonder's Mother.* New York: Simon & Schuster, 2002.

Lundy, Zach. *Songs in the Key of Life.* New York: Continuum, 2005.

Courtesy of Photofest.

Marvin Gaye

THE PRINCE OF MOTOWN

Marvin Gaye could do it all—sing, write, perform, produce—and his massive contribution to soul music reflected all of those considerable gifts. Most of all, though, he possessed the kind of prototypical R&B voice—seared with grit but laced with sweetness—that has lived on through his music long after his 1984 death.

As a musical visionary, he conceived albums as entire works of art rather than simple collections of singles. On the landmark *What's Going On*, arguably his most significant contribution to popular music, he mused deeply on such issues as the Vietnam War, drugs, inequality, the economy, and the environment over a free-flowing musical backdrop that drew on jazz, pop, and classical forms. These meticulously constructed thematic compositions helped to revolutionize pop. In 1994, *Q*, a major British music magazine, noted that *What's Going On* did for soul what *Blonde on Blonde* and *Sgt. Pepper's Lonely Hearts Club Band* had done for rock.

In the early days of Motown, Gaye started out by playing drums and piano on tour and in the studio for the likes of the Miracles and the Marvelettes. He wrote or co-wrote songs for himself and others, including "Dancing in the Street," a 1960s soul classic made famous by Martha and the Vandellas. Gaye recorded in a spectrum of soulful styles, from adult ballads to up-tempo soul to topical message songs.

At the time he was a second-stringer in the Motown scale of priorities, having been produced on a succession of fair-sized American hits by William Stevenson ("Stubborn Kind of Fellow," "Hitch Hike," "Pride and Joy," and duets with Mary Wells, "What's the Matter with You Baby," and Kim Weston, "What Good Am I Without You"); Brian Holland and Lamont Dozier ("Can I Get a Witness," "You're a Wonderful One," "Baby Don't You Do It," "How Sweet It Is"); and his brother-in-law, the boss, Berry Gordy ("Try It Baby").

But his backseat status didn't last long. Beginning with his sublime duets with ill-fated talent Tammi Terrell ("Ain't Nothing Like the Real Thing," "You're All I Need to Get By") and a couple of superb Norman Whitfield creations ("I Heard It Through the Grapevine," "Too Busy Thinking About My Baby"), Gaye burst into the national limelight in the mid-1960s and stayed there for over a decade, propelled by hits and boosted by his mysterious, often inaccessible image. In fact, at every stage in his career, Gaye projected an air of soulful authority driven by a combination of passion, rebelliousness, insecurity, and heartbroken vulnerability.

The product of an emotionally broken family—his father was a deeply conflicted Pentecostal minister that mentally and physically abused his son—was a long-suffering soul who sought relief in music. Throughout his life this mental torment dogged Gaye. It flowed through him constantly, like a river, always rushing through his mind. And it seemed to hit him hardest during the times he was enjoying his greatest successes. He never truly allowed himself the unfettered pleasures of success. Sure, he collected cars, accompanied many women, and had some of the trappings of success. But his psychological instability prevented him from appreciating his success.

His personal relationships also kept him from happiness. His two wives, Anna Gordy and Janis Hunter, were 17 years older and 17 years younger, respectively, than Gaye, and he never fully identified with them. He had children with each, but it never seemed liked he could relate to them as a father, in much the same way his father could never relate to him.

Still, his music provided him relief from a soul that was constantly troubled, from a heart that never felt content. His songs were prayers, meditations on survival, and because they conveyed a sense of importance, because they carried within them a critical emotional, spiritual, and musical weight, they are considered some of the most memorable songs of the modern era.

Gaye's artistry reached its peak in the 1970s, just as his personal life had begun to descend into madness, culminating in his tragic murder at the hands of Marvin Gay Sr. Many who've studied the case feel that his murder was a passive suicide, that Gaye had goaded his father into shooting him. They had despised each other, and by the end of his life, the younger Marvin was a mental and physical mess, a junkie, and psychotically ill.

But history has been kind to Gaye. His image continues to be supported by the sales and airplay of his greatest musical creations. And his voice and legacy are still worshipped by soul music fans young and old, black and white, secular and otherwise.

THE EARLY YEARS

Marvin Pentz Gay Jr. was born in Washington, D.C., in April 1939, the son of a maid and a minister. His father had come from Kentucky and his mother, Alberta, from North Carolina. They met in D.C., where Alberta had moved with her infant son, Michael, Marvin Jr.'s older stepbrother. They married in 1935, at which time Michael was sent, inexplicably, to live with Alberta's sister. The couple eventually had four children of their own: Jeanne, Marvin, Frank, and Zeola. They lived in what Marvin called the "Simple City," also known as the D.C. projects.

Marvin Sr., an opinionated man given to bouts of laziness, spent most of his time at his storefront church, called, improbably, the House of God, the Holy Church of the Living God, the Pillar and Ground of the Truth, the House of Prayer for All People. But his neighbors saw him not only as a preacher, but as a man who found ways to avoid work. He'd bring Kool-Aid to the construction workers on the block, spend hours watering his lawn, or simply ride the bus all day around downtown D.C. In the 1950s, with his son on the brink of becoming a teenager, the reverend started drinking excessively. Because of their differences, Marvin and his father fought constantly.

Those who knew him through the church described him as a charismatic leader. The church itself was intensely fundamentalist, with restrictive laws concerning diet, appearance, behavior, and language. There were no movies, no dancing, no secular music either. They never celebrated traditional Christian holidays such as Christmas and Easter. Church dogma crossed orthodox Judaism with born-again Christianity and enforced the rigidity of both. They did sing during service, loudly and often. It was the one positive element Marvin Jr. took away from his father's church organization.

Marvin Sr. enforced the laws within his congregation and at home, which led to a terrifically tumultuous relationship with his son, and, indeed his other three children as well. But of the four, Marvin was the one who felt compelled to speak his mind. Because of that, Marvin took the brunt of his father's fits of rage, which also came frequently. Frank, Marvin's younger brother, managed to avoid the wrath of his father. But a sibling rivalry cropped up, another element at home that made life in the Gay home difficult. These struggles made his childhood an intensely unhappy one.

Neighbors recall how Marvin Jr. used to avoid his father. He'd get kicked out of the house, and spend the day trying to find something to do. Sometimes he'd stay with neighbors for an extended period, and his mother would be sick with worry. When she found out where he was staying, she'd slip him some money behind her husband's back.

As Marvin Jr. grew older and more mature, the problems increased.

> By the time I was ready to start high school . . . he was still beating me. I wanted to strike back, but where I come from even to raise your hand to your father is an invitation for him to kill you. Father became stricter, demanding that I conform to his ridiculous curfew rules. If I came home late it was like I'd defied the ten commandments. The more demanding my father grew, the more rebellious I became. (David Ritz, *Divided Soul*, New York: Da Capo, 1991, p. 25)

But when he emerged as a young man, at least he had the power of the music inside him. Junior high was when the first serious singing began. At the outset of the 1950s doo-wop was taking hold in a big way across America's urban street corners, and D.C. was no exception. The friends Marvin made were all interested in singing as well and he made an early decision to become a pop singer.

His father insisted that his son's pursuits were fueled by the devil, and that all his friends were good-for-nothing bums. But that didn't deter Marvin. He was hearing the music of Sonny Til and the Orioles from just up the highway in Baltimore. The Coasters and the Drifters both had an enormous impact on him. Music took him over, substituting for God in his life. At about this time, at the violent consternation of his father, he left his House of God and began seeking personal and professional solace in music.

There were a handful of singers that influenced Marvin more than most other performers, two solo acts—Ray Charles and Little Willie John—and two group singers, Clyde McPhatter with Billy Ward and the Dominoes and Rudy West, one of the singers for the Five Keys. As a youngster, Marvin had an impressive voice. He often told his friends that he wanted to be the black Frank Sinatra. He loved Frank's phrasing and style; he also admired Frank's glitzy lifestyle, and he became obsessed with the pursuit of attaining stardom himself.

He also loved listening to Billie Holiday. To Gaye, her voice reflected pain and sadness. He cried along to her album *Lady in Satin*, and memorized every vocal turn and nuance.

Back in the inner city, competition among neighborhood vocal groups heated up. It seemed as if each street corner had a group, and each group brought along with it something unique that presented an obstacle to Marvin's own progress. There were territorial fisticuffs between groups, jealousies, and other disputes.

At the time, the cultural mecca for music in D.C. was the Howard Theater. It was part of the first-run venue circuit that also included the Apollo Theater in Harlem and the Regal in Chicago. It was here that Marvin attended all the shows he could. Watching James Brown and Jackie Wilson and their high performance standards—with their dancing and sexiness—made Marvin feel exhilaration. But he also felt depressed; he knew simply by virtue of his personality that he could not match these magical artists. All he had to impress his audiences was his voice.

He did have one other thing that would eventually serve him as a performer: a deep well of sensitivity. He felt pain and love with equal depth and these feelings permeated his musical delivery. The pain of being unloved by his father stuck with him like the terrible reflections they were, as did the memories of physical pain caused by his beatings.

As students at Cardoza High School, he and friend Reese Palmer had a group, the DC Tones, with a woman named Sondra Lattisaw, the mother of pop singer Stacy. The group distracted Gaye and his schoolwork began to suffer. They skipped school frequently to rehearse. At 15, Gaye's academic struggles grew pronounced. He resented the distorted way his teachers presented history and he began to develop a disdain for the government buildings he could see from his classroom. The life and liberty he knew were not like the values espoused by the history books or the men in those buildings. Life inured him to certain prejudices and biases of being black in the D.C. ghettos, but it also sensitized him.

LEAVING HOME

He and Palmer both considered school a waste of time, and at the same time, Gaye had come to the end of his rope at home. His father created a miserable life for his children and Gaye had had enough. Still 15, he quit school and enlisted in the Air Force.

In recruiting, he'd been promised a slot in the Special Forces division of the Air Force. What he didn't realize was that those Special Forces often served in the kitchen, peeling potatoes and cleaning up. Gaye was sent to bases in Kansas and Wyoming, where he came to the harsh realization that he'd not be learning to pilot a plane any time soon. He began to rebel even more in the military than he had at home.

For eight months his commanders tried every method possible to quell his rebellious spirit, including confinement. Ultimately, he petitioned for release, but he first had to prove that he was unfit to serve. Of course, it wasn't that he was unfit. Rather he simply couldn't handle it any longer. The military dismissed him on the grounds that he couldn't adjust to regimentation and authority.

If nothing else, Marvin's stint in the Air Force lit a fire under him to get his music career rolling. As a man, he felt he still hadn't made anything of himself, so he couldn't face his father after failing in the Air Force. He ended up living with friends and forming a band with Reese Palmer called the Marquees.

Patterned after the Moonglows, one of Marvin's favorite groups, the Marquees sang sweet vocal harmonies. They played sock hops, school assemblies, record shops, and anywhere else they could. But it wasn't until a chance meeting with R&B icon Bo Diddley that they began to feel like they were making progress.

Coming into commercial music amid the easy listening of Mantovani, Diddley's raw and direct post-blues shook the scene out of its malaise and injected it with excitement. When the Marquees met him, they wanted to work with him, but they also felt like they didn't have a whole lot in common with the artist. Bo wanted the Marquees to rock, when in fact they were all natural crooners.

Still, Bo insisted on taking the group from D.C. to New York City so they could cut their first sides: "Wyatt Earp" and "Hey, Little School Girl." Their enthusiasm turned to disappointment when the single didn't fare well. Gaye, who figured his collaboration with Diddley would be his big break, was devastated. They returned to D.C. discouraged.

It took another savior to bail Marvin out of his funk. Harvey Fuqua, leader of the Moonglows and a doo-wop guru, would play a critical role in Gaye's life for the next several years. Marvin first met Harvey when the Moonglows were playing at the Howard Theater and all of the Marquees went to see the group. At the time Fuqua had been successful, but frustrated with the current incarnation of his group, especially lead singer Bobby Lester. Fuqua got rid of the whole group and brought in a fresh crew. In their place, he brought in the Marquees, now the new Moonglows.

Fuqua loved Gaye and his work, and Gaye, in return, treated him like a father. Fuqua taught Gaye and the band to sing, write, and perform. By changing from the Marquees to the Moonglows, the boys had renewed their vision of stardom.

In early 1959, Marvin, just 19, left home for Chicago with Fuqua and the group. Chicago was home to Chess, the Moonglows' record label. In his rearview mirror he rued leaving his mother. But he was also overwhelmed by a sense of relief; he'd never have to deal with his father again.

THAT VOICE

Marvin's voice was never burdened by his turmoil. He never sounded defeated. Even his saddest songs are woven with optimism, partly a function of his tremendous love for singing. But it wasn't easy getting him to sing. He often had to be coaxed or bullied into recording, and he regularly succumbed to deep fits of depression. Those conflicts made Gaye's singing better as he went on, but elusive to capture.

Women, of course, were drawn to his dashing looks and elegant manner. "Throughout his life, Marvin felt sexually obligated to every one of his female fans, a pressure great enough to destroy any man. The irony was that he felt himself playing the role of Dionysus, god of indiscriminate sex, when all the while he only wanted to be Apollo, god of song" (Ritz, p. 51).

Marvin truly enjoyed his first months with the Moonglows. The performances were exhilarating, the women plentiful, and the company affable. He wore tuxedos, sang great songs, and felt himself inching closer to his dream of becoming a star. The group stayed busy, singing backup for other Chess sessions—they were in the studio with Chuck Berry for his "Back in the USA" backed with "Almost Grown" session—when they weren't on the road. One of their major tours featured a young, roly-poly Etta James, an R&B pioneer that had just signed to Chess.

Unfortunately, the happy Moonglows vibe didn't last all that long. Their lead singer, Bobby Lester, appealed to Fuqua and was accepted back into the group, which meant Gaye had to share the lead spot. This created conflict and jealousy within the band. Making matters worse, Gaye tired quickly of the road, and the raunchy clubs and sleazy dance halls the band played every night. The band also encountered racism frequently, especially on the Chitlin' Circuit in the South. Often there weren't segregated accommodations available to the band so they either slept in the car or on the ground outside. The treatment was shabby and humiliating. Gaye suffered the indignity deeply.

To ease the pain, he smoked marijuana. Gaye felt that pot made him more creative. He enjoyed the drug. It put him in a loosened state of mindand helped him compose. Later, Gaye began patterning himself after the young Bob Marley; he knew that Marley and the other Rastafarians used marijuana for spiritual reasons and he felt he needed the same spiritual catalyst. Sex also gave Gaye a temporary high. He worshipped prostitutes for the purity, simplicity, and liberated pleasure they offered.

By the end of the 1950s, Gaye returned home to D.C. for a big date at the Howard Theater with the Moonglows. The gig, attended by his mom, but not his dad, was a triumphant one, and one of his last with the group. Marvin was ready to move on. Fuqua had known for some time that Marvin was poised for a solo career and rather than let him go, Fuqua decided to stay around and work with his young charge. Fuqua had heard about a small record label starting up in Detroit. They quickly packed up and headed there to see what all the fuss was about.

THE MOTOR CITY

In spite of the excitement, Gaye, Fuqua, and the Moonglows felt the ground shifting under popular music. Vocal groups were losing ground to R&B and rock and roll groups. Teenagers in America were going crazy for the rougher, rawer stuff, at the expense of the smooth but dated harmonies of the male singing acts. Doo-wop had certainly seen its better days, and only a few groups were still able to appeal to a record-buying public. When Gaye and Fuqua arrived in Detroit, they were right on time.

Detroit was experiencing a rebirth. The automotive industry had been flourishing. Households, even those in the urban neighborhoods, were flush with cash. Unemployment was low, given the demand for labor. Teens in those homes enjoyed the comfort of at least a modicum of money. Detroit streets were lively and singing. Storefronts boomed the music of the times and kids everywhere had latched onto the possibility of a career in music.

Berry Gordy, a former boxer with an enterprising nature, had already done his time on the automotive assembly line when Fuqua and Gaye arrived together in the city. Gordy had set up his own label, Tammi, and his sister Gwen had a label of her own with Anna Records (named after Gordy's other sister). In turn, Fuqua set up shop with what he called the Harvey label.

Fuqua and Gwen Gordy met through these music dealings and eventually married. Fuqua introduced Marvin to Gwen and Berry's sister Anna, and the two also became romantically linked even though Anna was 17 years older than Gaye. He admits that she was his first girlfriend.

Gordy's label morphed into Motown, while the Harvey and Anna labels merged. The 1950s turned into the 1960s, and Motown, the Motor City Sound, was on the brink of altering the landscape of popular music. Early on things moved quickly. Acts were signed, musicians and songwriters hired. Gaye did all he could to hang on to a fast-moving train. Gaye held on to Anna as a paramour as well as a lifeline to Motown. He admired Fuqua, of course, but saw right away that Gordy possessed a wider worldview, and had bigger dreams, closer to his own.

Gaye's first gig at Motown was as a drummer for Smokey Robinson's young Miracles act. It was the first offer he had after hanging around the studio for a while, so he accepted it. Fuqua actually owned the rights to Gaye, and had since the Moonglows. But Berry bought the contract out and now Marvin belonged to Motown.

Gordy and Robinson composed the label's first hit together for the Miracles, "Shop Around," and it put Motown on the map. Now things were really heating up. And, in 1960, the year the label broke, Gaye was right there in the thick of it.

For the first few months, before he got the nod to enter the recording studio, Marvin had been considered a jack-of-all-trades. He played the drums as well as the piano at various sessions. He also assisted with songwriting. He'd been agreeable for that time, as his relationship with Anna deepened and his willingness to cooperate increased. He confided in Anna, though, that while all the R&B stuff was cool at Motown, he really wanted to do a jazz-pop album. Anna convinced her brother to commit to that type of project and Marvin made a date to enter the studio.

THE MANY MOODS OF MARVIN

Berry Gordy produced Marvin's debut album, *The Soulful Moods of Marvin Gaye*, in 1961. Gordy and the label decided to position Gaye as a crooner, a passionate, jazzy balladeer, and they chose material to adhere to that concept: "My Funny Valentine," "Witchcraft," and "How High the Moon." That in the years after the release of this album Marvin Gaye became one of the greatest and most influential singers in the fields of soul and R&B is hardly up for debate. But this album, which features some tuneful, if unspectacular singing from Gaye, hardly features the sublime talent and innovative vision he'd achieve later.

At the time of its release, Motown had already issued a handful of very successful singles, including "Please Mr. Postman," "Money (That's What I Want)," and the Miracles' aforementioned "Shop Around." Gaye's collection didn't have a standout track, and the album itself didn't sell nearly as well as the products of his label mates.

Marvin, who added the "e" at the end of his surname to coincide with the release of this album, explained why his strategy to do standards simply didn't work. "The plan was to avoid shaking my ass onstage. I'm not a relaxed performer anyway, and I'm self-conscious about dancing. Sitting on a stool and smoking a cigarette while nursing a martini appealed to me. Doing the bump-and-grind did not. My model was Perry Como" (Ritz, p. 25).

Even though the talk at Motown oftened mentioned touchstones like Sam Cooke, Ray Charles, and the Impressions, Marvin continued to believe in his heart that he was a crooner, not a soul singer. Gordy, too, thought that he had a shot at marketing Gaye to an adult audience, despite the fact that the rest of his artists were geared toward the burgeoning teen population. They were both wrong.

Motown's spirit and success were built on a foundation of youthful exuberance and extraordinary young talent. The combination of the two produced most of the label's hits. After *Soulful Moods* flopped, Gaye soon realized that he'd have to play the game like everybody else. He knew he'd have to reach the black audience first, and then, once he communicated with them, he could look beyond it to a wider, more sophisticated crowd.

His first attempt to play that game resulted in the autobiographical "Stubborn Kind of Fellow," a song that roughly follows the trajectory of his relationship with Anna. Gordy always had trouble reading Gaye; his young artist didn't take criticism well, or guidance for that matter. He was, like the song says, "a stubborn kind of fellow."

Gaye's stubbornness and his detached attitude allowed him to call many of his own shots. He refused, for example, to attend the infamous Motown charm school, citing the fact that he already had good breeding. He kept his own hours and often skipped rehearsals. But as his stock rose, so too did the amount of leeway he received from Motown.

> " 'Well,' says Marvin in an offhand tone, dangerously near to becoming touchy, 'the only thing I can say about that is, I'm my own artist and . . . I'll certainly do whatever I like.' My goodness, he sounds almost belligerent for a moment. 'And the *next* album might be the same.' A definite tinge of the defiant 'so theres.' Then he laughs." (Cliff White, "The Marvin Gaye Interview: Earthly Fights and Mystic Flights." *NME*, October 1976.)

In fact, the only thing that matched Gaye's defiance, and, relative to that, his confidence, was his self-doubt. These wide swings made him difficult to understand or get close to. The women worshipped him because he was so beautiful to look at. And they all treated him gingerly. He was the "Prince of Motown," strong, silent, majestic. On stage he milked that sexual allure. In Marvin's mind, there was a close link between singing R&B and having sex. Problem was, this psychological association, no matter how obviously abstract, weighed on him.

Marvin enjoyed three hits in 1963, including "Can I Get a Witness," in which he sings from the point of view of a preacher. Beans Bowles, a musical director at Motown and another father figure for Gaye, noticed that Gaye often spoke quietly about becoming a preacher, like his father. But, of course, the perks of popularity and prestige of a life in pop certainly beckoned. That conflict tore Gaye in two. Those who knew him best, surrogate fathers like Bowles and Fuqua, knew Gaye harbored a tormented soul. Calm on the surface, he never relaxed on the inside.

"Can I Get a Witness" led to other hits, including Holland-Dozier-Holland's "Pride and Joy," and "Hitch Hike." "Pride and Joy" actually crossed over to the pop side of the charts. Now white kids were dancing to his music. "Hitch Hike," a track Gaye himself choreographed a cheeky dance to, complete with thumb out, caught the attention of Dick Clark at *American Bandstand*, and before he knew it, Gaye received significant national television exposure. The impressive string prompted an up-tick in Gaye's stock at the label. But anxiety still ruled in Marvin's world. He couldn't enjoy the success. Rather, he only worried about how to maintain it.

Some of that worry dissipated after his marriage to Anna in 1963. He'd been making some money and his ability to support both Anna and his mom back home built his confidence. He moved his family out of the projects and into a bigger house in a nicer neighborhood in D.C. He didn't visit often, to avoid his father, but he did make sure his mother was taken care of.

DUETS

Before he knew it, Gaye had become Gordy's leading man. He headlined the label's 1964 rendition of the Motortown Revue ahead of the Supremes, Stevie Wonder, and the Temptations. The position of prominence bolstered him and he began performing with strength and fortitude.

In the spring of 1964, Mary Wells had a hit with "My Girl," Motown's third number one pop hit. This turn of events boded well for Gaye; he'd already recorded an album of duets with Wells and the attention she'd been getting made it a prime time to get this release out on record store shelves. The collection, *Together*, based on Wells's own hot image, scored Gaye his first charting album; the duet also notched a number of hit singles, including "Once Upon a Time" and "What's the Matter with You, Baby?"

The ploy worked perfectly and the duets idea garnered Gaye a sex symbol image. Women everywhere wanted to be Mary Wells. They wanted to hear him sing to them the way he sang to her. The country's women fell in love with Marvin. Ironically, it was Anna that got most perturbed by all of this. Unfortunately for her though, the duets would only pick up, with Gaye's astonishing work with Tammi Terrell just around the corner.

In late 1964, the winds were again shifting at Motown. While Gaye and Wells hit the charts hard, the Supremes ("Where Did Our Love Go?") and the Four Tops ("Baby, I Need Your Loving") began to show explosive signs of life. With their fingers on the pulse of popular radio, Motown picked up on that interest and began repositioning their resources to focus on the songs and studio sessions of those groups. This left Marvin momentarily on the back burner. He still had hits, but not the kind the other acts were making. One, for example, the bouncy "How Sweet It Is," a H-D-H composition using a Jackie Gleason phrase, climbed the charts. Despite that tune's juvenile appeal to young love, Gaye still harbored a desire to sing standards, and he followed that single up with the pop-jazz standards album, *When I'm Alone I Cry*.

In something of an exchange program, Britain sent the Beatles to America, and America shipped its Motown acts to Britain. Both sides of that transaction succeeded. For his part, Gaye flew to London for a whirlwind press junket and managed to get the attention of the pop scene even though he hadn't charted a song there yet. At the end of 1964 that would change, as "How Sweet It Is" drifted across the Atlantic and became a hit on the other side as well.

This was a period, 1964 and 1965, that truly distinguished Motown from the rest of the labels trying to break into pop. Through the first years of the 1960s, the label had been doing well. But in 1964, after the Supremes gained traction, the label skyrocketed. The Supremes scored five number one hits in a row, including "Baby Love," "Where Did Our Love Go?," and "Stop! In the Name of Love," all written by Holland-Dozier-Holland. The Supremes were the hottest American act. Only the Beatles were more popular.

As the Supremes surged at Motown, so too did the Temptations, the Miracles, and the Four Tops. Marvin didn't enjoy the same superstardom yet, but his singing, alongside the Tops' Levi Stubbs, the Tempts' David Ruffin, and the Miracles' Smokey Robinson, all comprised the sound, style, and uber-talent of pop music in America.

Amid the musical chaos of 1965, Marvin and Anna had a baby, Marvin III. The baby's arrival came at an inopportune time. Marvin was traveling around the country attempting to take care of business, and when he came home he expected to spend time with Anna. But the baby consumed her and Marvin felt twinges of jealousy.

Gaye's whirlwind schedule went against his calm demeanor. Throughout his life, he preferred taking measured steps, singing quiet songs, and kicking back a little. Not possible at Motown. When things cranked up at Gordy's place, everybody floored the accelerator. Gaye found himself rushing from place to place, and singing songs that felt too fast for his natural ability.

To make matters more stressful, Gordy steamed full speed ahead in his quest to turn every one of his label's acts into a pop sensation. This pursuit extended to image as well, and Gaye reluctantly attended photo shoots playing golf or sailing, things he'd certainly never made a habit of doing in his real life. The facade, the image-making, frustrated Gaye and forced him further into the margins. He was neither destined for nor suited to a pop music lifestyle. He insisted that the Tops and the Supremes were the only pop stars on the label. The rest were natural R&B singers.

Yet the conflict was plain to see. Should he give up his first, best, and perhaps only attempt at real stardom because he felt hypocritical? He certainly had experienced a problem with authority at the label, a pattern of behavior that had begun at home in D.C. He was an upstream swimmer, often based on principle, but occasionally on a whim as well. He baffled his fellow artists, who couldn't understand why he didn't take the path of least resistance. But the answer was simple. He needed to be true to himself.

In the mid- to late 1960s, the political scene caught fire and torched everything in its path. The Watts Riots, the death of Malcolm X, and the recent death of John F. Kennedy prompted Gaye to think more seriously about the kinds of songs he sang. How could he sing silly love songs with all this strife in the world?

In an effort to strike a balance between what he saw and what he had to do, he recorded a couple of standards albums in 1965. Neither did particularly well. They both had heavy doses of big band horns and lavish arrangements, and they feature Gaye in his quest to become the black Sinatra. But it never happened, and it never would. The dissatisfaction mounted.

So did the troubles in Marvin and Anna's marriage. Each experienced problems with the other, and neither made any bones about it in public. They also had some famous fights. At home they'd resort to throwing plates, food, and furniture at each other. Both were unfaithful to the other as well, and both were aware of the other's indiscretions. Things grew more uncomfortable with each passing day.

TAMMI TERRELL

And the hits didn't get any bigger either. While the Tempts were scoring massive chart action, Marvin's were modest in comparison. His romantic, puppy-love duets with Kim Weston made an impression on listeners. An entire album of them, *Take Two*, did excellent business. Marvin's stately vocals pitted against the sexy, but still strong women—created the perfect balance of passion, sex, and muscle.

This formula would reach a peak with Marvin's dazzling duets with Tammi Terrell, a gorgeous, free-spirited singer discovered by James Brown. Not only did she make a good creative and physical match for Marvin, she also matched Marvin's independent will.

Tammi Terrell

"Tammi was the kind of chick who couldn't be controlled by men," said Marvin. "That can drive a man crazy . . . [but] I loved that about her. I knew we could be friends, but never lovers. Independent women hold no romantic interest for me . . . What we chiefly accomplished, though, was to create two characters—two loves that might have been taken from a play—and let them sing to each other" (Ritz, p. 111). James Brown and David Ruffin both had stormy relationships with her, but Marvin kept the relationship strictly professional.

That's all that Marvin Gaye and Tammi Terrell would need. Their duets became the standard against which all other R&B duets would have to measure up. Gaye, with his muscular tenor, played the handsome loverboy, and Terrell, with her sexy soprano, his vulnerable lady love. Together, they embodied a universe of true love and sang about it like they meant it.

With America mired in Vietnam and race riots marring the country's cultural landscape, Marvin and Tammi's exquisite duets blaring from the radio provided a respite from the friction and discontent. They were happy, or at least sounded that way, and the vibe they emitted was infectious. At home, Marvin's vibe with wife Anna had broken down. The baby interfered with their formerly romantic lifestyle, Marvin had lots of temptation on the road, some of which he gave into (as did Anna while he was away), and his business relationship with Tammi, whether platonic or not, added another layer of complexity to his marriage.

Their first hit, "Ain't No Mountain High Enough," in 1967, was written by Nick Ashford and Valerie Simpson. That hit spawned a handful of others: "If I Could Build My Whole World Around You," "Your Precious Love," and the classics "Good Lovin' Ain't Easy to Come By" and "Ain't Nothing Like the Real Thing."

In the summer of 1967, the hit-song joyride came to a crashing conclusion. On the stage Tammi collapsed in Gaye's arms. She was in her early twenties at the time of the occurrence. The incident and her death changed Gaye for the rest of his life.

Their first hit, "Ain't No Mountain High Enough," in 1967, was written by Nick Ashford and Valerie Simpson, a husband and wife team that would go on to become a performing couple themselves. That hit spawned a handful of others: "If I Could Build My Whole World Around You," "Your Precious Love," and the classics "Good Lovin' Ain't Easy to Come By" and "Ain't Nothing Like the Real Thing." Couples everywhere approached them and insisted they were singing their song; their messages were universal. In all, the pair released three albums and watched nine of their songs climb the charts.

His duets with Tammi furthered his image as devoted and somewhat mysterious lover boy, an image he both enjoyed and tried to buck. Equal parts vain and insecure, Gaye didn't know how he wanted to be perceived by his fans. But one thing he did know was that he didn't want anybody to decide for him. If he had an image at all, *he* wanted to be the one to choose it. At one point he began wearing cardigan sweaters and glasses, in an attempt to adopt an Ivy League persona: studious, thoughtful, extraordinary. In a sense, he merely wanted to differentiate himself from the rest of the uniformed Motown artists. Little did he know, Marvin didn't have to worry about being different.

GRIPES, GRUDGES, AND GORDY

In 1967, money came pouring into the Motown offices. By now a millionaire many times over, owner Berry Gordy treated himself to an Italian Renaissance mansion on the outskirts of Detroit. When he did, he gave his former home to Marvin and his sister Anna. That residence, roomy and comfortable with a yard for little Marvin and fancy accouterments, was the nicest "crib" Gaye had ever called his own. But it didn't feel right. Gordy had been the object of considerable resentment at Motown over the last few years, mainly because of money. As the revenues increased, the salaries of his employees, the remuneration for their services, didn't. The staff songwriters and band members especially, those most responsible for the success of the company, felt Gordy didn't show them enough appreciation financially. Many griped. Some, most notably the successful songwriting team of Holland-Dozier-Holland, actually left. Harvey Fuqua, the man who escorted Marvin to Detroit, also departed over royalty squabbles. Mickey Stevenson, another writer and manager, exited along with Clarence Paul and Beans Bowles. Many of the executives who left took their performers with them: Gladys Knight, the Spinners, Kim Weston, and the Four Tops.

Even at this point in his career, Gaye didn't have the financial independence he sought. He felt trapped in Gordy's empire. He fell into another malaise, entwined in a bad marriage, unhappy with his working relationship at Motown, and still insecure about himself and his image.

One of his escapes was the studio, another was cocaine. Motown's demanding schedule put performers under enormous pressure to get records done and stay on the road. Gaye didn't really enjoy performing at all. But he could spend all day in the studio. Clarence Paul, a collaborator and Motown employee, explains Marvin's temperament: "[The studio] was the one place, maybe the only place in the world, where he could really relax . . . And once Marvin got anywhere, he wouldn't want to leave. That was doubly true of the studio. He wasn't a performer. He'd never perform if it hadn't been for the money. In the true sense, Marvin Gaye was a recording artist" (Ritz, p. 114).

Marvin indulged heavily in cocaine. He saw coke as an elitist drug, something rich and slightly out of reach, which perhaps created its allure. But he did it regularly, often rubbing it on his gums or eating it because he had a hard time snorting. This intake heightened Gaye's senses and his energy level, which often flagged, but it also tore him from his spiritual moorings even further. Guilt plagued him after a high. So in order to rid himself of that guilt he indulged in vice further: wine, women, and whatever other luxury the high life afforded him.

In the summer of 1967, the hit-song joyride he'd been on with Tammi Terrell came to a crashing conclusion. On the stage at Virginia's Hampton-Sydney College, Tammi collapsed in Gaye's arms. The illness (a malignant brain tumor) plagued her for three years, during which time she could barely sing.

The strange part about Terrell's illness was that even after she'd been struck by the cancer, the duet's hits continued. This phenomenon, perpetuated by Motown, who refused to release the details of her disease, tormented Gaye. He felt he was an accomplice in what amounted to subterfuge on the label's part. The duet's first album, *United*, came out in 1967, while Tammi was still healthy and singing. Their second, *You're All I Need*, emerged a year later, and featured Tammi's vocals, but was recorded after her illness arose. Their third album "together," ironically called *Easy*, came out in 1969 and featured very little work from the by now very sick Terrell. Gaye later admitted that singer Valerie Simpson, doing her best Tammi impression, laid down most of the vocals. Early on, Simpson had sung many of the demos while teaching Tammi her songs, and so was familiar with her style and the material.

Gaye abetted this deceit because Motown rationalized that the revenue would defray the cost of Tammi's treatment. The double standard irked Gaye. The Detroit riots raged; the death of Martin Luther King Jr. shocked him. One night, badgered by demons and perhaps a bad drug trip, he locked himself in his apartment with a gun and threatened to kill himself. The only one who could save him did. Gordy.

THE REAL THING

As Marvin's star soared, his spirit sank. The only thing that could lift him out of depression was music. Fortunately, the hits kept coming through the period. "Heard It Through the Grapevine," a song Gladys Knight had cut a year earlier, zoomed back up the charts thanks to Marvin's perfect vocals, ultimately selling 4 million copies and becoming Motown's biggest selling single of the 1960s. To this day, it is the one song that Marvin is associated with over all others. What "R-E-S-P-E-C-T" is to Aretha, "Grapevine" is to Marvin.

Of course, there were many other deserving but lesser known songs strewn through Marvin's career. On "Chained" and "You" from 1969, Marvin performs passionately and it oozes from his vocals. His life had informed his art and his feelings were laid bare for the world to hear. Deep down, Gaye felt the hurt and he sang like it. For the longest time, on his way up in show business, Marvin took care of his mother and utterly neglected his father.

Finally in 1970, he tried to make peace. He bought his father a Cadillac. But the gesture served as nothing more than a bandage on a wounded relationship. The divisiveness in his life pushed Gaye close to suicide several more times, even immediately following his huge success with "Grapevine." At 30, Marvin remained a man unable to reap the benefits of all the wonderful work he'd done. "My success didn't seem real. I didn't deserve it. I knew I could have done more. I felt like a puppet—Berry's puppet, Anna's puppet. I had a mind of my own and I wasn't using it" (Ritz, p. 126).

He began working with producer Norman Whitfield, a focused aggressive presence with a rawer vision of R&B than Motown generally held. Marvin looked at Whitfield with skepticism, but Whifield started churning out hits—he wrote "Ain't Too Proud to Beg" with Eddie Holland for the Temptations and would go on to pioneer the concept of psychedelic soul. Even though they possessed polar opposite personalities, Marvin backed off and let the man do his job.

It was Whitfield more than any other Motown executive who realized, in 1968, that soul music was undergoing a radical change. Aretha and Otis sang it, James Brown funked it, Sly Stone screamed it, and Stax and Muscle Shoals set the rules. Motown had been content to stay where it was, comfortable with its proven formula. But not Whitfield. Soon, R&B would be dominated by harder edged acts: Sly, Brown, Mayfield, and Parliament. Thanks to his work with Whitfield, Marvin Gaye gain entry to that elite group as well.

THE 1970s

After nine years of working under other producers, Gaye by now had gained the confidence to produce himself. He'd been through the process enough to know what he wanted and how to get it, so Gordy, who by this time had relocated to Los Angeles and let others run the daily operations in Detroit, consented.

Marvin's confidence also extended to his appearance. He ditched his clean-cut, college-boy image, grew a beard, and started dressing more casually, in sweat suits. He pierced his ear in defiance, and stood up to the Motown execs that dared suggest he go on the road and play in front of audiences. The idea of touring bored him.

He worked on himself as a person. He nurtured his relationship with God; it came as his confidence grew. He focused on his ear as a musician. He bought season tickets to the Detroit Symphony. He also indulged in professional sports, going so far as to seek a tryout with the Detroit Lions of the National Football League. To prepare he plunged into a rigorous fitness regime, running and lifting weights. He worked out with the college football team at Eastern Michigan University. He had never in his life played organized football, but he desperately wanted to prove to himself that he could do something other than sing.

His focus was monomaniacal: "I had every intention of becoming a superstar athlete. I played for keeps. I liked hanging around athletes because I respected their courage. It takes courage, day in and day out, to put your body on the line. I used to laugh when the jocks told me it took more guts to get up and sing" (Ritz, p. 135).

When a few people at the label and the coaches at EMU pulled him aside and told him he wouldn't make it, that he'd get injured and derail his real career, he was devastated.

WHAT'S GOING ON?

At the outset of the 1970s, message songs were selling. Edwin Starr's "War" hit it big, John and Yoko were hot, and so were Simon and Garfunkel. Stone excited the black music community. He saw the hippie movement and was fascinated by its tenets of free love and harmony.

Still, Marvin preferred inaction over action, sulking over socializing. Tammi Terrell's funeral had hit him hard emotionally and he struggled to find a way out of his horrible marriage with Anna. He wanted to withdraw and occasionally did. By chance, he came across a book, *The Teachings of Don Juan*, by Carlos Castaneda. He devoured its metaphysical wisdom, much of which concerned following the desires of the heart. Its abstractions appealed to him and took its life lessons into the studio when he set out to make *What's Going On?*

A conversation with his brother Frankie jump-started the idea. Frankie had just returned from Vietnam and he regaled Marvin with horrifying tales of war. Marvin was appalled by what he heard. It was time to put some of his feelings down on tape. He'd waited long enough, stalled for too long. His creativity restocked, he hit the studio, his head swimming with ideas.

Marvin's relationship with Frankie had been on solid ground. Unlike the one with his father, Marvin's fraternal bond with Frankie was strong and emotionally grounded. Marvin may have even admired Frankie for his courage in going to war. It allowed Frankie to challenge himself the way Marvin always wanted to. Still, Marvin tapped into Frankie's experience for material on the new album.

What's Going On came about at a time when Marvin's life was falling down around him. He found solace in the studio. His new material, addressing all those cultural influences he'd absorbed—hippies, urban funk, message songs, and black politics—reflected that solace sonically.

Set in black urban neighborhoods, the work is complex and thematic, with urgent political and social pleas in the form of words to his mother and father. In fact, the album was dedicated to his parents. It included string-laden pop, smooth soul, and even some jazz.

Gaye had to fight Motown every step of the way to release the recording. They didn't get it. They thought it was too much of a departure for the label and wouldn't sell. But the more resistance they put up, the more entrenched Gaye became in fighting back. He eventually played the "it or me" card. Either Motown releases the album, or they lose Marvin.

What's Going On succeeded beyond anyone's wildest expectations. It hit America's record stores at the perfect time, and its social commentaries, astutely and poetically realized, struck the perfect chord. It also turned Gaye into what he'd always dreamed of being: a serious artist. He no longer had to sing the songs producers served him. He now had to be taken seriously as a composer, producer, and social commentator.

Thanks to songs like "Mercy Mercy Me," "Right On," "Wholly Holy," and "Inner City Blues," the album became Gaye's best-selling Motown effort. At the same time, he widened the parameters of soul music with thought-provoking concepts and insight.

The soul audience was ready for *What's Going On*, but the commercial pop scene wasn't. The NAACP bestowed Marvin with their prestigious Image Award that year and he was recognized by industry publications like *Cash Box* and *Billboard* for his achievement. But the Grammy event, a barometer of artistic popularity, didn't acknowledge him at all. Carole King's *Tapestry* had captured the country's imagination, not Marvin Gaye.

The public clamor for live appearances grew, but Marvin resisted. Then one show, back in D.C., was too big to pass up. It took his mother to ultimately convince him, but on May 1, 1972, Marvin played a gig on Marvin Gaye Day in D.C. Supported by a 10-piece band, and a 20-piece orchestra, Marvin, in front of his family, performed a medley of early hits and the entire *What's Going On*. The show succeeded on a grand scale, and announced Gaye's momentary return to performing.

Next, Gaye undertook the soundtrack to a feature film, *Trouble Man*. The low-budget cop-and-robber flick didn't represent much in terms of film innovation, but Gaye's moody score, mostly instrumental and jazzy, propped it up effectively. Alongside Mayfield's *Superfly* and Isaac Hayes's *Shaft*, *Trouble Man* is one of the principal examples of a blaxploitation soundtrack.

At the end of 1972, Marvin moved out to Los Angeles, finally succumbing to the pressure and doing what everybody else at Motown was doing. Los Angeles had siphoned virtually all of the Motown talent and Detroit had felt to Marvin, one of the last holdouts, like a ghost town. But one concession he made to the move was that he'd bring his family with him, not just his nuclear family, but his extended one. He and Anna purchased a home in the Hollywood Hills. He also kept a small apartment as an outpost. And later in the year he bought a large house for the rest of his family.

In the early 1970s, the climate had shifted in favor of black music and Marvin felt like he'd finally be compensated in the way he should. Money began falling out of the sky. The movie community surrounded him, and opportunities arose. Diana Ross had already made the most of her first chance with *Lady Sings the Blues*, an emotional portrait of Billie Holiday. A Motown executive brought up the idea of Diana and Marvin doing a duets album, something Marvin had said he'd never do again after Tammi's death.

But he reconsidered. Unfortunately, he should have heeded his instinct. The sessions with Ross were difficult and uncomfortable. There was no chemistry. Diana was pregnant with her second child and the two moody, pampered stars could not find any common ground on which to perform; Marvin sulked, Diana was testy. *Diana & Marvin* suffered.

That failure behind him, Marvin set to work on *Let's Get It On* with Ed Townsend. In the studio one night, a friend of Townsend, Barbara Hunter, came into the studio with her daughter Janis to watch Marvin work. Gaye was struck immediately by Janis's beauty. At that moment, Marvin was cutting the title track to the new album, and those in the studio with him swear that Jan's presence pushed Gaye to deliver one of his very best vocal tracks. That song would hit the number one spot on the R&B and pop charts and Marvin was back on top, at least musically. Many say the song suite was a paean to sex. But Marvin insisted the "come to bed" conceit was shallow and inaccurate. He told his friends that he wanted to merge the sacred with the profane, to bring God into a discussion about sex, that sex could be a spiritual experience. There's no good sex without real love.

The record soared, reaching number one. In a year in which many landmark albums were released, including titles by Stevie Wonder and the Rolling Stones, Marvin's album outdid them all. Bolstered by its lead single, the title cut, the album became his most successful so far. It took two laborious years to produce. It actually took all of 13 months just to cut Marvin's vocals. But its tremendous success vindicated that lengthy process.

For as long as he'd been a recording artist, he'd grappled with this issue. Now he finally committed it to wax. His inspiration for the lusty expression? Janis Hunter. Gaye, 33 and still married to Anna, now 50, saw Janis as the girl of his fantasies. The only problem was that she was only 16 years old. Still, she was his dream girl and he felt ecstatic in her presence.

The follow-up, to *Let's Get It On, I Want You*, didn't achieve the same exalted status, but it has come to pass as one of Marvin's most fully realized projects.

DISCO DANCING

Like virtually every other soul artist, Marvin's career took a hit when disco entered the popular music scene. And like many of those artists, he took a half-hearted stab at joining the club, rather than attempting to beat it. Not prone to chase trends, he enjoyed a reluctant and rather eccentric hit with the dance-happy "Got to Give It Up," a song that hit the top of both sides of the chart in 1977.

It proved to be a felicitous moment in another depressing phase for Marvin. Like other moments of overwhelming success, he had difficulty fully appreciating them. At the same time, he and Anna finally consented to a divorce. For years they had remained together in a debilitating relationship that saw both parties finding new and harsh ways of hurting the other. By this time, too, he and Jan Hunter already had two children together.

As part of the divorce settlement, the judge proposed that Marvin give the proceeds of his next album to Anna. Marvin liked the idea. His initial reaction was to record something quick and cheap. But he backtracked. The more he mulled over the project's potential, the more he realized what he could accomplish with this unique kind of motivation.

Gaye made the outstanding *Here, My Dear* and delivered it at the end of 1978. The introduction goes: "I guess I'll have to say, this album is dedicated to you. Although perhaps I may not be happy. This is what you want, so I've conceded. I hope it makes you happy. There's a lot of truth in it, baby" ("Here My Dear").

The record outlines the couple's turbulent relationship. Emotionally powerful songs like "Anger" and "When Did You Stop Loving Me, When Did I Stop Loving You" lay bare the fragility and frustration of their relationship, and they exist alongside tributes like "Anna's Song" and "I Met a Little Girl."

"It was all Marvin, more Marvin than I ever had heard before—Marvin's melodies, Marvin's lyrics, Marvin's harmonies, Marvin's narcissism, spirituality, sarcasm, gratitude, resentments, and, above all, Marvin's inner turmoil" (David Ritz, *Here, My Dear,* liner notes, Motown, 1978/1994, p. 1).

It wasn't until Gaye died that *Here, My Dear* underwent lengthy reconsideration. At the time, pop fans could not have cared less about the album and it died a quick death on the charts.

But he was also beginning to regret his relationship with Hunter. He had been with her four years, long enough for his dream girl to devolve from secret fantasy woman to a very real, very demanding spouse. Her mystique, the powerful allure she held over him for the first while they were together had dissipated and the reality of a troubled relationship set in.

In 1979, now 40, he embarked on a half-hearted tour across the country. If he didn't feel like performing in a particular market, or the bus drove up to the venue at a time when Gaye felt lackluster, he'd just tell his driver to keep going. He bypassed a dozen dates on that tour. To exacerbate the situation, Jan, after keeping Marvin company for six years, left him momentarily for Teddy Pendergrass. He sank into a deep depression and decided he needed to get away. He fled the States for a three-year stint off domestic shores.

GONE AWAY

He initially lived in Hawaii. In that time he hid from public view. Depressed he tried committing suicide with a cocaine overdose and almost killed Jan. Because touring revenue had dried up, he had little disposable income. His mother had to pawn two of his valuable diamonds and send him the cash to cover expenses. Of course, Motown could have sent him some money, but Marvin seemed to prefer destitution. It felt more real.

He hung out on the beach, avoiding contact and doing coke. In Hawaii, though, that proved difficult. Women on the beach recognized him and begged him to go to luaus or more. The drugs distracted him, even, some say, made him impotent. He recorded the rather ironically titled *Love Man*, amid this tangle of personal troubles. The record, fueled by a rather outrageous vision and some quirky experimentation and assembled over the course of a year in a Honolulu studio, was vast and ambitious. But Motown refused to release it. They sent Smokey Robinson, then a vice president at the label, to Hawaii to find out what was going on. Eventually, they cut off his funds, and left Gaye with no financial lifeline.

The recording *In Our Lifetime* heralded the end of his 20-year relationship with Motown. The album, Gaye insists, was released by Motown without his approval. He stepped away from the company, relieved and without regrets.

But the personal slide continued. He moved from Hawaii to London, England, for a few months, seeking anonymity and a fresh start. While there, he deepened his drug habit; he increased his cocaine intake from lines to freebasing. He lay in bed for days, cut himself off from everyone he knew, and stayed stoned out of his mind. He considered suicide again. With nowhere to go, no label, no money, no love and no life, it seemed like as good a time as any to end it. He was only 42, but he felt like he'd had it.

TO THE RESCUE

Strange and serendipitous things happened to Gaye in the two decades he'd been in music, but his meeting with Belgian music executive Freddie Cousaert might have been the strangest. Cousaert, a jazz and R&B lover, had been living in London, doing some small-time promoting when he ran into Marvin. He could see that he was in trouble, and he offered him a line. Why not come to Ostend, Belgium, and spend some time relaxing?

Gaye had been choking on London pollution and he needed fresh air, so Cousaert loaned him money, offered to manage him, and set him up in a seaside apartment in Ostend. Gaye began jogging and biking. He signed a new deal with CBS Records, and just like that, a chance meeting in London with an honest Belgian turned his life around.

In October 1982, Marvin began the first steps of his re-emergence. He released "Sexual Healing." It hit immediately and, according to *Billboard*, became the fastest rising soul hit in half a decade. Harvey Fuqua came around again looking for Marvin, and his former liege signed Fuqua on to produce *Midnight Love*. Fuqua agreed, but on one condition: that Gaye abandon his metaphysical and spiritual dross and make a straight-ahead pop soul album like the old days. Fuqua preferred form over content, and that's what Gaye delivered.

"Sexual Healing" remained at number one on the soul chart for an incredible four months. The song won him his first two Grammys as well, for Best Male Vocal and Best Instrumental Performance, a long awaited validation for him.

It wasn't the success of the album that brought Marvin back to the States. His mother had become ill and required a risky operation. In November, he ended his three-year exile and returned to Los Angeles to be with his family. At the time, Marvin's father had temporarily moved back East to take care of some real estate business. Ironically, the elder Gay didn't even return to look after his wife during the operation and subsequent convalescence. This infuriated his son and drove a fresh wedge between the two. There was no excuse for the neglect his father exercised when his mother needed him most.

In 1983, Marvin descended once again into a sort of oblivion. He had a hit record, but the tour stressed him out. He had new people surrounding him and handling his affairs, but he didn't trust them, and even when he did, he didn't cooperate. He'd become paranoid and erratic in behavior. He began collecting guns and wearing bullet-proof vests.

On tour, the crowds began thinning out. He'd hit the road too late, and the album, *Midnight Love*, had only a limited lifespan. When business hit the skids, Marvin panicked. He started doing crazy things on stage, including dropping his pants at the conclusion to his encore, "Sexual Healing." The ploy was contrived and hokey, unlike Gaye himself.

"How much further could Gaye get from his dream of wearing a tux, sitting on a stool, and coolly crooning like Sinatra?" (Ritz, p. 323).

After the tour, Marvin returned home and sank into a state of comatose exhaustion. In the summer of 1983, Gaye's pathos increased. He began sleeping in his mother's bed, next to her, and he accelerated his drug consumption, doing coke in front of her. He was scared, even more paranoid than before, and losing his grip. To Marvin's mom, he seemed like a monster and a little child at the same time. With Marvin drinking, getting high, and sleeping next to his mother with his father down the hall, the pieces were in place for disaster.

His spirit and energy disappeared. Many of those close to him said it seemed like he *wanted* to die. He threw himself out a car window while it sped down the road in a botched attempt to commit suicide.

Then the inevitable happened. A day before his 45th birthday in April 1984, his father shot Marvin twice, once in the heart, with a revolver that Marvin had given him for his own safety.

Marvin's sister Jeanne, who witnessed the chaos of those final months in the Gaye home, insists that Marvin chose to die and he instigated it purposely. Marvin Gay Sr. pleaded guilty to voluntary manslaughter. A police report cited massive bruises on the father's body, ostensibly given to him by his son.

"I try to pray for my husband," Marvin's mother said. "I want to. I wish I could. But I can't. Now I realize that he didn't love me any more than he loved Marvin. My love for Marvin and Marvin's love for me was so strong. My husband was jealous of that love . . . Jealousy destroys. It destroyed Marvin, it destroyed my husband" (Ritz, p. 340).

LEGACY

Marvin Gaye really had it all: the voice, the soul, the look, everything. He had an intense sex appeal that women were drawn to like bees to honey and his music complemented that sex appeal perfectly. Women saw him perform, heard him sing, and they fell in love, pure and simple.

He wanted to be the black Sinatra. And, while an endless string of extenuating circumstances prevented that from happening, he eventually became one of the most gifted, visionary, and enduring talents ever to call Motown home. He blazed the trail for the continued evolution of popular black music, first with his stunning duets with Tammi Terrell and then with his remarkable song cycles like *What's Going On?* and *I Want You*. He could move from a lithe, potent R&B icon to a sophisticated soul singer, from moody balladeer to angry young man effortlessly. He also helped to further redefine R&B and soul music as agents for social change.

Ultimately, though, his troubles overtook him. Demons had inhabited him from an early age, and, while he freed himself long enough to become a legend, those same demons caught up with him. He struggled endlessly with the sacred and the profane aspects of his life. As a deeply religious boy, he stumbled into a world of indulgence, in women, in drugs, in money. He owned dozens of automobiles and slept with scores of women. But it was these very same accumulations that ate at him. He knew his father, a former preacher would never approve of the indulgences, even though he spent his whole life either trying to gain his approval, or trying to rid himself of the prospect.

He attempted to reconcile the sacred and profane in his philosophical extrapolations as well, much of which he'd lay on unsuspecting journalists. That combination produced the sacredly profane "Sexual Healing" and additional, more vulgar songs he had in the works closer to his death.

But, in retrospect, Marvin produced brilliant music often in spite of himself, in spite of his second-guessing and procrastination. According to Berry Gordy, the chief of Motown and the one man who stood behind him as a surrogate father, Marvin was the one true genius on the entire Motown roster, the one artist who managed in a highly processed star-making facility to think and act for himself.

"Like Frank Sinatra, Elvis Presley, and John Lennon, Marvin is still with us. The entertainment industry continues to celebrate his life and music through television tributes in America and abroad . . . His entire back catalog has been remastered and reissued. Radio plays his records as often today as when they were soaring up the charts" (Frankie Gaye and Fred Basten, *Marvin Gaye, My Brother*, San Francisco: Backbeat Books, 2003, p. 1).

Today, his voice sends repercussions through soul music. He may have wanted desperately to be someone other than himself, but he ended up establishing an incredible musical legacy as the one and only Marvin Gaye.

SELECTED DISCOGRAPHY

Trouble Man (Motown, 1971)

What's Going On? (Motown, 1971)

Let's Get It On (Motown, 1974)

I Want You (Motown, 1976)

Here, My Dear (Motown, 1977)

Midnight Love (CBS, 1981)

The Master: 1961–1984 (Motown, 1995)

FURTHER READING

Dyson, Michael Eric. *Mercy, Mercy Me: The Art, Loves, and Demons of Marvin Gaye*. New York: Basic Civitas, 2005.

Edmonds, Ben. *What's Going On and the Last Days of the Motown Sound*. New York: Canongate, 2003.

Gaye, Frankie and Fred Basten. *Marvin Gaye, My Brother*. San Francisco: Backbeat, 2003.

Ritz, David. *Divided Soul*. New York: Da Capo, 1991.

White, Cliff. "The Marvin Gaye Interview: Earthly Fights and Mystic Flights." *NME*, October 1976.

AP Photo.

Dusty Springfield

THE WHITE QUEEN OF SOUL

Like every icon in popular music, Dusty Springfield was a true original. She had talent, of course, and considerable gifts. As a teen, great singing and great songs intoxicated her and she grew up to possess impeccable taste in style and material. She was also a peerless interpreter. Classic pop songwriter Carole King, who wrote over a dozen songs for Dusty, said she was the best ever singer of her songs. In fact, Dusty ended up performing handfuls of stellar Brill Building material by many of the 1960s' best songwriters.

But Dusty's pop infatuation didn't begin and end there. She was also a student of music, some even referred to her as a musicologist. She recorded music in a handful of different languages, and at her highest point had become a global superstar, an incredible journey for a Scotch-Irish lass who'd attended a single-sex convent school as a child.

She loved soul music, and infused it into all her work. She could sing Motown, one of the first (and only) white pop singers who could claim that, and she wrapped her voice around difficult material, like many Burt Bacharach/Hal David compositions, with ease. She belted out dramatic ballads the likes of which popular music had never heard.

She also participated in the folk boom, with her brother Dion as part of the Springfields. She scored hits amid the British Invasion, one of the only British acts to hit the charts in America after the Beatles arrived. In another important act, she railed against racism on a tour of South Africa, igniting a ripple effect, as other Western artists made their inaugural visits to the country.

Dusty's unique voice set her apart from the more banal singers out of Britain at the time, like Cilla Black, Sandie Shaw, Lulu, etc. She had incredible control of her tone; she could manipulate her voice handily, giving it a hint of desperation or pulling back and sounding vulnerable. She'd open up at the chorus and still sound hurt. She stretched her voice in ways that would infuse every syllable with passion, heartbreak, longing, and loss.

Much of this was instinct, of course. But a significant degree of her vocal dexterity came with study. When she attended concerts of singers she admired, Dusty would observe intently, writing notes to herself about phrasings and vocal styles she liked.

Because she adored Motown, she studied those singers keenly as well, both the men and the women—Martha Reeves, Smokey Robinson, Stevie Wonder. And thanks to her relationship with gospel singer Madeline Bell, she also explored the works of sublime singers like Marian Anderson and Mahalia Jackson. As a result, after observing its nuances with her finely tuned ear, and incorporating them naturally into her own vocal delivery, she'd become one of the few white singers that could sound convincingly black.

Her creative apex came in 1969 when she journeyed to Memphis and recorded at soul music's Ground Zero, with an R&B studio band called the Memphis Cats. The album, *In Memphis*, is one of the true classics of the soul era.

Fans—men, women, blacks, whites, gays, straights—loved Dusty as their own. Yet, despite all the adoration, she was deeply and surprisingly insecure, even to the point of self-loathing. She delved into drugs, consumed inhuman amounts of alcohol, and flirted regularly with tradgedy. A lesbian, she struggled with her Catholic background and the stigma of homosexuality in Britain. Midway through her career, she began to tease prying journalists, dancing around direct questions about her sexuality with coy ambiguity.

At home in the United Kingdom as well as in the United States where she seemed to spend at least half her life, she was a luminous, lovable celebrity who made challenging but accessible music that even the most casual pop fans loved. After a while, her glamorous excesses, heavy makeup, and flirtation with gay audiences turned her into something of a camp icon. But not before she established herself as one of the purest voices in the history of soul music.

EARLY YEARS

Mary Isobel Catherine Bernadette O'Brien, aka Dusty Springfield, was born in the spring of 1939 in an outskirt of London. Her parents, worried about the war and the danger of bringing up children in an urban neighborhood, moved to High Wycombe, a bucolic market town in Buckinghamshire, and then to the more stimulating environment of Ealing, a west London suburb in the early 1950s, long after the "coast was clear" of war.

Gerard O'Brien, Mary's father, known as "OB," had been raised in India during the days of the Raj and worked as a tax accountant. Mary's mom, also known as "Kay," had come from County Kerry in Ireland. They also had a son, Mary's older brother, Dion.

The O'Briens were a religious family and they sent their children to single-sex Catholic schools. On the surface, Mary's childhood appeared peaceful and comfortable. But all was not what it seemed in the family's comfortably middle-class household. The local priest was a fixture at their house for reasons unknown, and family gatherings around the dinner table had a tendency to devolve into heavy drinking and odd food-throwing incidents.

Perhaps it was because Mother Kay yearned for a less mundane existence; she was desperate to spice up her life. Or maybe she enjoyed disrupting her husband's irksome need for neatness and precision. But if someone had a problem with one of her dishes at the dinner table, she'd inexplicably tip it over, throw it across the table, or smash it on the floor. If she was unhappy with the outcome of something she baked, she'd destroy it with a spatula. This happened with bizarre regularity. It's not clear why this happened, but it surely masked underlying family dysfunction. Expectedly, Dusty herself picked up on the eccentric habit and resorted to it throughout her life.

Mary's parents fought often, and the young girl had to blot out the chaos and verbal violence. To cope, she admits to hurting herself as a child, putting her hands on a hot pipe, for example, just to distract her attention from the fighting. In later years, during interviews and in conversation with friends, she'd occasionally refer to her childhood as "wretched," adding that neither of her parents were particularly attentive.

Mary was fond of her brother, but also a tad jealous. Her parents, she says, gave him what little attention they had to spare because he was a motivated child and a good student. Still, the siblings got along. They listened to the radio together and watched TV when the family brought one into the house. Dion would be the first one to admit later on that Mary was the one with the real gift, of a lovely voice.

When Mary was 12 she ventured into a record shop and made her first recording, a version of Irving Berlin's 1912 chestnut, "When the Midnight Choo Choo Leaves for Alabam'," a vaudeville number. Her family, especially Dion, marveled at how well Mary nailed the Afro-American vernacular. The reason for this must have been the musical environment Mary's father provided at home. Though he made a living with numbers, he was a jazz aficionado and actually played some piano. So, while many kids her age were listening to trite British pop music, Mary and Dion were hearing their father's records: Jelly Roll Morton, Ella Fitzgerald, Stan Kenton, and Peggy Lee. She'd hear classical on the radio, some Latin music, and lots of Dixieland.

Similarly, Mary's mother was an avid film fan, and she enjoyed watching them as an escape from her reality. Frequently, Mary would be her accompaniment at these films, and they ended up making a profound impression on her as well. Mary and Kay lost themselves in the glamour of 1940s musicals, the gorgeous gowns, the lavish sets, the dancing, beautiful celebrities.

Through her formative years, Mary's catholic education provided discipline and consistency in her life, even though she wasn't very excited about school and learning. A chubby, bespectacled student with curly brown hair, she was popular among her classmates because of her sense of humor. The same was not true for the nuns, who beat her frequently because of her attitude. Those who knew her, though, appreciated Mary's sense of humor. But she also had an intense mix of other lesser qualities, including anxiety, hyperactivity, and impatience.

MAKING MUSIC

Mary's sweet singing voice was difficult to deny. When she was 17, the O'Brien siblings formed a duet, with Dion on guitar and Mary singing. They booked random gigs at various small cafes and supper clubs in London's West End. The music making whetted Mary's appetite and she was soon scouring papers for other gigs in and around London's music scene.

In 1958, when she was 19, she auditioned for an all-girl vocal trio called the Lana Sisters. About this time in Britain, girl singing groups, often called "sister groups," were popular and the demand great in the late 1950s. The Lana Sisters hired Mary as their third "sister."

The Lana Sisters worked hard to get their act down. The girls also made a conscious decision to be a sort of risqué alternative to some of the more wholesome "sister acts." The strategy paid off. Their reputation grew quickly and soon they were touring the United Kingdom.

While with the Lana Sisters, Mary learned a variety of valuable lessons about the music business: how to take the stage, captivate an audience, and deal with the tedium of life on the road, something she did not handle very well. She made up for that tedium by toying with her identity. She cut her hair, lost the glasses, experimented with makeup, fashion, and even changed her name to "Shan."

They toured incessantly, supporting major performers like Nat King Cole and Cliff Richard, at U.S. airbases across Europe and at smaller clubs closer to home. They even had a hit, a ribald little number called "Seven Little Girls Sitting in the Backseat ('Kissin' and Huggin' with Fred')."

But two years of this rigorous routine was enough. Mary enjoyed the girls and the camaraderie, but hungered for music that satisfied her. When her brother and a friend, Tim Feild, phoned her to ask if she'd be interested in joining their duo, she quickly took advantage of the opportunity and said goodbye to the Lana Sisters.

THE SPRINGFIELDS

Feild and Dion were in a folk group of sorts, latched onto the American folk boom before most in the United Kingdom. They called themselves the Springfields, after, some say, the many towns in America of the same name. They also decided to change their own names. Dion and Mary became Tom and Dusty. Dusty doused herself with hydrogen peroxide and became a blonde.

Their sound embraced different elements of American music, and focused mainly on pop-style vocals, suggesting seminal folk groups like the Weavers. Tom proved himself to be a real student of the American folk idiom and he wrote prodigiously. The Springfields were signed to Philips Records and released their first single, the Civil War–inspired "Dear John," in May 1961. Their debut, *Kinda Folksy*, received warm reviews, and quite a bit of attention in the United Kingdom, thanks to the record's subsequent singles, the infectious "Breakaway" and the follow-up, "Bambino." As writers and arrangers, Tom and Dusty reveled in their influences, offering material as diverse as folk and show tunes. In fact, they were almost too diverse for their own good, coloring their simple pop folk vocal tunes with strings and big climaxes. In performance, as they played to increasing audiences, Tom smiled genially, while Tim shied away from the spotlight. That left Dusty alone in the middle, attractive and alluring. She loved the position and bathed in the limelight. Her hunger for the stage blossomed.

A raucous rave-up of Leadbelly's "Goodnight Irene" failed to attract much attention, but its follow-up "Silver Threads & Golden Needles," broke through dramatically. It made a huge impact in America, hitting the Top 20. It was the first release by a British group to chart that highly in the States, in essence leading the way for the rest of the British Invasion bands. The composition, country in flavor, also opened the doors for highly influential folk-pop acts like Jackie DeShannon and the Byrds.

As hard as they worked, the Springfields were never agsain able to duplicate that success in the States. They had another hit in the United Kingdom, "Island of Dreams," but it didn't make it across the Atlantic. Ultimately, the pressure to break back into the U.S. market wore Tom and Dusty down. In their emphatic and fatiguing attempt to do so, their differences became more pronounced. Tom lived and loved folk music, while Dusty yearned to explore the American R&B she admired as a child. Ironically, it was Feild that left the group first, replaced by Mark Hurst. But Hurst didn't serve as the buffer Feild did and the relationship between the siblings suffered.

In early 1963, the Springfields went to Nashville to record their second album, *Folks Songs from the Hills*. The sessions found Tom and Dusty digging deeper into the folk idiom, covering Leadbelly, Roy Acuff, and other respected American classics. But the record's timing, coming as it did at the end of the folk boom in the States was unfortunate. It collided head on with the oncoming British Invasion.

At that point, the niche for folk-pop almost disappeared at the hands of the Beatles and other Beat groups, and there was literally no place for the Springfields. They tried using electric instrumentation to keep up with the changes, but the sound was forced. They had a couple more minor hits before Dusty responded to the Beat Boom, and its undertones of R&B. The Springfields split before Dusty and her brother could reconcile fully. Their final single was issued in early 1964. It coincided with Dusty's own first single as a solo act, "I Only Want to Be with You." Tom would go on to make a name for himself as a producer and songwriter for the successful pop act the Seekers.

DUSTY, LIKE NO OTHER

Dusty, now 23 and fully composed as an artist, signed a solo contract with the Philips label. Many who regretted the demise of the Springfields preesumed Dusty would be eaten alive in the music business, that she wasn't cut out to go it alone at such a young age and with so little experience. Of course, she'd prove them wrong.

With the Springfields Dusty appeared on the British musical variety television program, *Ready, Steady, Go!* At the time, the show promised that any act starring on the program would be invited back. Well, the Springfields weren't available any longer, so Dusty hit them up for the return favor as a solo act.

RSG complied, infact, Dusty not only performed, but she served as a celebrity host and interviewer. She was hired alongside DJ Keith Fordyce to speak with guest artists, like the Beatles and the Rolling Stones. Viewers and producers alike enjoyed Dusty's natural personality. Perhaps it was the artist's affinity for movies that helped settle her down in front of the camera.

By the time her first single came out, Dusty's name was firmly linked to the program, so it wasn't a surprise that she sang it for that show's audience first. Over the next year, Dusty spent hundreds of hours in the dark hallways of the show's studio, entertaining guests, organizing programs, and performing.

One guest she met, Madeline Bell, a New Jersey gospel singer in London as part of Langston Hughes's show "Black Nativity," had a profound effect on Dusty. The program, which also featured legend Marion Anderson, had been a hit on Broadway and made its way to London, a first for a gospel production.

Bell, a standout in the cast, eventually made a name for herself as a solo act, and Dusty was inspired by her vocal style. For the first time, while studying Bell and gospel in general, Dusty began to hear the emotion and passion underlying a great song. When Bell cut her first single, "I'm Gonna Make You Love Me," Dusty sang back up, and when Dusty's career took off, she invited Bell to sing back-up for her on tour and in the studio.

After establishing herself as a TV personality and pop star, Dusty began putting the pieces of her organization together. This included personal assistant Pat Barnett and manager Vic Billings. Both suited Dusty's modus operandi and both would remain with her for years. Once she hired them, she chose a band.

She hired a full entity called the Echoes: bassist Doug Reece, who'd be a long-term friend and confidante of Dusty's; drummer Bob Wackett, and organist Mickey Garrett. The band had a rough go early on. Dusty demanded perfection; she asked for very specific tone and style from her band and it took a while for the band to achieve it. The bass, for example, had to sound exactly like the soul/R&B records she loved. She also required a lush, full effect even without a horn or string section. With some difficulty, the band figured out how to deliver.

DUSTY'S MOD LOOK

If nothing else, Dusty's look epitomized 1960s Britain. With white boots and velvet coats, Dusty's hip image was a combination of her fascination with Hollywood glamour and the Mod fashion of the times. While her voice proved to be her most distinctive quality, Dusty's look closely complemented it. It helped, too, that *RSG* was quite exclusively a program by and for "Mods," the fashionable London youth movement that caught fire about the same time.

Dusty's eye makeup, featuring dollops of mascara, was heavy and pronounced. She admitted hating the bone structure of her face, saying her face was puffy and round. So she attempted to provide a distraction from that roundness by emphasizing other parts, namely her eyes and her hair, which often covered her ears, making hearing difficult.

After spending time watching herself on television, Dusty also spotted another flaw, this time when she espied herself in a miniskirt with black stockings. She despised her knees. From that point on, around 1963, she refused to wear anything but long dresses on screen. And she cursed her father for giving her what she deemed "knobby" knees.

Dusty's hair, piled into a beehive and artificially blonde, recalled stars of the silver screen like the French goddess Catherine Deneuve and the American icon Marilyn Monroe. She even tied her hair back with a velvety black bow ala Deneuve, a fashion statement that started a fad among English girls. "The eyes blackened with mascara seemingly applied with a paint roller, made her look like both an Italian cinema minx and a West End drag queen." Dusty said, "I used so much hairspray that I feel personally responsible for global warming!" (Rob Hoerburger, liner notes, *The Dusty Springfield Anthology*, 1997).

Dusty's jackets were smart and tight, with many buttons. Her skirts were tight as well, and looked sexy under furs. In a way, her fashion was carefully cultivated and evocative. But it was also a smattering of the things that Dusty loved: glamour, intelligence, fun, America, Mod culture, and television . . .

SEXUALITY

Growing up Catholic and going to a single-sex parochial school, Dusty's life had little, if anything to do with boys or romance. She always rued the fact in interviews and among friends that she passed through her teenage years without really experiencing them. When she was old enough to leave the house alone, she either went to work or had a gig with her brother Dion. At that time, most girls her age were flirting with boys in the back row of movie theaters or hanging out at cafes.

Her life was sheltered for the most part, until her early 20s, when she discovered freedom following her work with the Lana Sisters. To that point her role models were, beyond her confused and unreliable parents, the nuns of her childhood. She never felt truly comfortable around men, especially as she grew older and found herself in the spotlight as a performer.

Until she understood her fondness for women, Dusty would frequently go to confession, a vestige from her Catholic schooling. Oftentimes on the road with the Lana Sisters or the Springfields Dusty would ask to pull over at a church so she could do her penance.

Her lesbian discovery, however, obviated any relationship she had with the church. Her sexual preference was contrary to everything she understood the church to stand for and in 1963, during her first affair with a woman, she thought it best to part ways with Catholicism. The split hurt Dusty deeply and racked her with guilt for the rest of her life.

No one knew who this inaugural affair was with, only that it was with "a famous singer." In fact, throughout her career, Dusty never officially came out. Over time, the clues simply made it progressively more obvious. This repression tortured her and contributed to her many insecurities. "On this whole gay thing, I've been misquoted so on it, that I really—my God . . . I really think, settling back on an old cliché, that it's no one's business, and it really has no bearing on anything." (Len Brown, "Scandal in the Wind," *NME*, February 1989.)

But the remarkable element of all this was that she didn't really symbolize any type of sexuality as a performer. She appealed to both men and women, but not as a sex symbol, a teen idol, or risqué personality like Ann-Margret. She was merely a star, and created hysteria on her own, by virtue of being herself.

"It was amazing, when I first started singing on my own. There were crazy scenes, because it was sort of asexual. They didn't mind that you were a boy or a girl. They would come up sort of on stage. The minute I appeared on stage, girls would scream. Purely because they were so hyped up on the whole atmosphere of a rock and roll show" (Ben Fong-Torres, "Dusty Springfield," *Rolling Stone*, 1973/1999 reprint on *All Music Guide*). In 1970, Dusty conducted an interview with a journalist named Ray Connolly who represented the London paper called *The Evening Standard*. Springfield didn't like doing many interviews, so when she did them she made it worthwhile, both for herself and her fans. She often peppered her quotes with jokey half-truths and silliness, in an attempt to manipulate the session. Her publicist Keith Goodwin quipped that Dusty was "a sort of lovable potty wombat who drove him to distraction with her practical jokes and erratic time-keeping," (Keith Altham, "The Real Dusty Springfield," *Rock's Back Pages,* July 2007.l)

To Connolly she said: "I couldn't stand to be thought to be a big butch lady," she said, "but I know that I'm as perfectly capable of being swayed by a girl as by a boy."

When the piece came out, few took notice. Sexuality was rarely an issue at the time. But when Dusty experienced a career spike in the 1980s and early 1990s, the piece became notorious and was often referred to by subsequent journalists.

Occasionally, even into the 1970s, Dusty felt compelled to fabricate the presence of men in her life. That is, when prodded, she'd conjure up a relationship; the "coupling" was generally short-lived and, ultimately, "didn't work out." This stopgap measure helped clear the air briefly and keep the press off her back.

THE BIG TIME

Dusty's first single, "I Only Want to Be with You," composed by Mike Hawker and Ivor Raymonde, soared up the singles chart on both sides of the Atlantic. The song boasted all the signatures that Dusty favored: the rhythm section and horn charts she loved from R&B, the double-tracked vocals, and the backing singers. The arrangement framed Dusty's sensual lead vocal perfectly. It was also this canny fusion of elements that made the song create an impact on the larger music scene as well.

Up until the early '60s, the American charts had been segregated. R&B records were considered to be for black audiences; white charts were dominated by pop and the odd crooner from the '50s. With the uptown black groups' reliance on white songwriters and, often, producers, the lines were blurred and the teenage market began to cross over. It was a move that was to benefit Dusty, a white singer with a "black" sound. (Penny Valentine and Vicki Wickham, *Dancing with Demons*, New York: Griffin's St. Martin, 2000, p. 54)

Dusty herself, in an unpublished interview done by *Rolling Stone* in 1973, admitted her influences: "When I first started, I copied every black singer. One week I was Baby Washington, next week I was the lead singer of the Shirelles. You know, I had no style at all. I never pretended to be black, and I didn't really sound black. People put that label on me. It was only an influence. There were just certain things in it; an empathy, whatever you like" (Fong-Torres).

Influenced also by the production of Phil Spector, who in 1962 created the Ronettes' "Be My Baby," Dusty's single included a counterpoint string section that elevated the quality of the production and attested to Dusty's musical sagacity even at this early point in her career. Dusty was well aware of Spector's style and effectiveness as a producer and she loved the complex arrangements of Jack Nitzsche. The work of these men on records by the Ronettes and others at the time would stay with Dusty for the next few years.

She performed with her backing band, the Echoes, for the first time in late 1963, the only woman on a package tour with a handful of male performers. Dusty held her own on the stage with popular acts like Freddie and the Dreamers and the Searchers. The audience reaction was as strong for her as it was for the pop idols on the tour. "In those early days I was pretty wild," she admits. "I came in on the wave of Beatlemania, and they somehow associated me with the Beatles. I only had to stick my head out in the street—and [*screams, high-pitched*] AGGGGH!!!" (Fong-Torres,).

THE HIT PARADE

"I Only Want to Be With You" was a perfect way to introduce the artist's style to the world, and the world was happy to accept it. It boasted Phil Spector signatures like lush production and a dramatic wall of sound, and it soared into the British Top 5, while falling just short of the U.S. Top 10. Still, it was the first major hit by a British artist in the States not named the Beatles. But when she released her version of "Wishin and Hopin' " in July 1964, it would be the first of a string of rewarding (and successful) collaborations she tackled with songwriters Burt Bacharach and Hal David. That list would include intricate melodic compositions like "Anyone Who Had a Heart" and "I Just Don't Know What to Do with Myself."

Dusty's first full-length album, *A Girl Called Dusty*, came out in the United Kingdom in the spring of 1964, and received good reviews. By the end of that year, Dusty was the biggest solo act in British pop. She won the first of four consecutive Best Female Vocal awards from U.K. music magazine *NME*.

In 1965, the U.K. hits kept coming: "Losing You," "Your Hurtin' Kinda Love," and "In the Middle of Nowhere." At the time the United States was infatuated with Motown and the Beatles, leaving little room for female solo acts. But the silence in America didn't last long. In 1966, she scored her biggest international hit with the powerful ballad "You Don't Have to Say You Love Me," which topped the U.K. charts and reached the Top Five in the States. The song, with its climbing chord change and intimation of sacrifice, has become the song most closely associated with Dusty's work.

Legend has it that while she was in San Remo, Italy, attending a festival, Dusty heard a song by Pina Donnagio called "Io Che Non Vivo Senza Te," or "I Don't Want to Live Without You." Dusty loved the song and eagerly wanted to remake it, but she didn't know Italian and had no idea where to begin. Vicki Wickham, her manager, and Simon Napier-Bell, another manager in England, volunteered to do a little translating and deliver a new set of lyrics. Perhaps inadvertently, the translators subverted the original intention of Donnagio's song, changing it from a song of lifelong love and devotion to one of nonchalance and aloofness. Dusty had already overseen the backing tracks and arranging, so when Napier-Bell and Wickham emerged with the lyrics 24 hours after receiving the assignment, they entered the studio.

At the time, no one in Dusty's camp held out much hope for the tune. But thanks to the singer's perseverance—the band did 47 takes—and some sweet strings, Dusty's performance was a triumph and the song was a smash. It broadened her appeal and deepened her perception as a mature artist.

By 1966, Dusty had accumulated more hit records than any other female pop artist. She had moved beyond her Mod-based, TV-familiar audience and into the wider world of fame and celebrity. That meant she was recognized everywhere. It also meant that the stories of her eccentric behavior—the anxiety, the obstinacy, her fastidiousness, and her food throwing—all circulated more extensively.

By the summer of the same year, Dusty had her very own television show in Britain. The platform allowed her the privilege of singing anything she wanted and inviting any guest she pleased to join her. The control pleased her, and she took advantage, inviting personalities as diverse as Jimi Hendrix, Woody Allen, and Tom Jones. At the same time, she was also in a worthwhile relationship with a woman named Norma Tanega, a struggling painter with Mexican/Indian roots.

The hits continued through the rest of 1966 and into 1967, with songs like the Goffin-King tune "Goin' Back," "I'll Try Anything," the wrenching ballad "All I See Is You," and "Give Me Time." In the summer of 1967, she reunited with Burt Bacharach for "The Look of Love," a bossa nova–styled song that found a place on the soundtrack to the James Bond spoof *Casino Royale*. The session, a coy and quiet woo of song that sounds like "eavesdropping on pillow talk" (Hoerburger), was overseen by Bacharach. It came at a time when music was growing progressively louder, with acid rock, electric blues, and heavy metal all finding footing, and FM radio gained ground over the once mighty AM band. Still, Dusty had a huge hit in the United States, where DJs preferred it to its original A-side, "Give Me Time."

DUSTY AND THE BRILL BUILDING SCHOOL

Brill Building pop introduced the concept of professional songwriters to traditional pop and early rock and roll. Teams of songwriters worked at the Brill Building—a block of music publishing houses in New York City—and wrote songs for artists as diverse as the Coasters, the Drifters, and Connie Francis. The songs were primarily rock and roll and R&B, but also tipped their hats to Tin Pan Alley, with sophisticated lyrics and indelible melodies. The productions on these early recordings were also more sophisticated than most rock albums, featuring orchestras and big bands. After the British Invasion, Brill Building pop fell out of favor. But its stylings were felt in both British and American popular music for years to come.

In the early 1960s, the Brill Building sound began gripping the imagination of the Mod audiences in London, and, of course, Dusty knew the score. The major writers in the process—Carole King, Neil Diamond, Neil Sedaka, Gerry Goffin, Doc Pomus, Mann and Weil, Ellie Greenwich, Jeff Barry, and the like—created many of the most memorable songs in the history of pop music, including "Splish, Splash," "Save the Last Dance for Me," and "Under the Boardwalk." The Brill Building writers wrote for the best-known acts in the music industry during this time, including the Shirelles, who, in turn, were covered by the Beatles. This gestalt served to introduce the songwriting artistry to British audiences, who devoured it. The Brill Building and Uptown R&B record label opened the doors of pop music, once the sole domain of white singers, to black artists and so altered the evolution of popular music.

Dusty made the pilgrimage to New York in 1964, when Brill Building fever was already under way. She played the Fox Theater in Brooklyn. While there she reveled in the soulful abilities of young artists like Marvin Gaye, Stevie Wonder, and Martha and the Vandellas. She especially loved the insistent yearning of Martha Reeves on tunes like "Heatwave." Watching them perform, she absorbed their gifts and committed them to memory during the day-long concerts at the Fox. She loved the city, the music, the streets, the soul. She felt comfortable.

Back home, Dusty also had the opportunity to host the Motown Revue installment of *Ready, Steady, Go!*, which thrilled her. She was the only white artist on the bill, alongside the Miracles, the Temptations, the Supremes, and Stevie Wonder. She sang her one and only duet for that program with Reeves, their version of Brill Building writer Burt Bacharach's "Wishin' and Hopin'." The program was notable for many reasons, the most salient being Dusty managed to predate the Motown Sound revolution by almost a year. At the time, British radio wouldn't touch the label's work. But a year later, that would all change, and Dusty helped bring about that change. That show is credited with jump-starting Motown's Sound of Young America in Britain.

Springfield would also go on to cut many other Bacharach tunes with incredible success. In fact, "Wishin' and Hopin'" would become one of her biggest hits. Dusty herself admitted to having "to sit down very suddenly" when she first heard Dionne Warwick singing Bacharach and partner Hal David's tune "Don't Make Me Over."

"Nobody can sing Bacharach and David like her. Nobody. It's total gossamer. I knew then that's what I wanted to do. Bacharach and David changed pop music and 'Don't Make Me Over' changed my life" (Valentine and Wickham, p. 72).

The irony of all this is that white singers like Springfield and Cilla Black and their respective versions of Bacharach tunes kept Dionne Warwick's own renditions off the U.K. charts for sometime.

The music climate evolved dramatically at this time. Men and rock groups began to dominate the scene. Hair grew long and unruly. The Summer of Love loomed. Motown hung on by a thread. The Beatles got spiritual in India. As a counterpoint to the heavy rock of this period, a bevy of pop artists, Dusty included, were branded "bubblegum." Perhaps they hadn't seen Dusty's duet with Jimi Hendrix, heard of her work with Napier-Bell, manager of the Yardbirds, or realized that she collaborated with Led Zeppelin's John Paul Jones.

Soon enough she'd stake her place in history with an album that would live on in the annals of R&B and soul as one of the best ever made.

CONFLICTS OF INTEREST

Over the years, Dusty had become known as a problematic personality. She often skipped rehearsals or turned up late to gigs. Those who know her insisted she has been wrongly criticized, that she was simply misunderstood. True, she occasionally had trouble getting motivated for shows, and especially rehearsals for shows. She lived unusual hours, often not going to bed until sunrise and then having difficulty making appointments the next afternoon. She also suffered from anxiety and was prone to suddenly depletion of energy. She loved being on stage, and once she got there she was fine. But, according to her handlers, the effort of getting there was exhausting.

One of the first instances that may have led to this misconception of her being difficult, was a rather noble one. On her first trip to South Africa in 1964, she inserted a clause in her contract stipulating that she and the band would not under any circumstances play to segregated audiences. Although she was not considered to be an activist, she knew well the political problems with South Africa and its apartheid policies. But for someone raised with the respect and appreciation she had for black artists, not allowing people of color into her show made no sense.

Before the first show, Dusty was approached by government officials attempting to dissuade her from holding fast to her clause. Of course, she did, and when the curtain came up to reveal an interracial audience, she was delighted. There were ramifications to her actions, though, and the white minority felt betrayed by Dusty's open-minded demands. She and her crew were escorted to the airport by police to ensure their safety. But not before a line of black airport porters saluted their departure.

The South African government fought back though, with a campaign of disinformation. "Dusty had set this problem up explicitly to create publicity for the American tour that would follow her South African concerts" (Valentine and Wickham, p. 63).

"One of the reasons I'm very insecure is that I have many reputations," Dusty admitted, "and many things that are totally unfounded. Being unreliable. Not turning up for a show. Never finishing an engagement. Doing the craziest things" (Fong-Torres).

At the end of 1965, another situation arose that created something of a controversy for Dusty. She was invited to play the San Remo Festival in Italy, an annual, elegant affair on the country's Adriatic coast. Dusty prepared extensively to perform "Face to Face with Love." But something wasn't right. At rehearsals, her voice kept breaking down and Dusty panicked. She'd pushed herself to fight through it, but her condition worsened. With a worn and weak voice, she pulled out of the festival. This wouldn't be the first time, or the last, that she did this. The pattern recurred. Her voice, often taken to the limit, grew weak frequently. Dusty's anxiety exacerbated the problem.

Another incident occurred in 1966 at the height of her popularity in the United States. Dusty had been enjoying a run of hits and her first two albums had sold well in America. She was booked to headline a three-week stint at a New York City venue called Basin Street East. Buddy Rich, the disputatious jazz drummer, and his 17-piece big band orchestra were selected to support her.

Rich took his opening slot with disdain. That he had to support a "third-rate pop singer" irked him and he let the audience know his feelings. "Opening night was a disaster. Rich managed to sabotage Dusty's moment of glory" (Valentine and Wickham, p. 71). That first night, he played an hour over his allotted time, and effectively served as "a star killer." On subsequent nights, despite the protestations of Dusty and her management, little changed. Rich berated the headliner, shortchanged her of rehearsal time, and did whatever he could do to obstruct her success.

The engagement wore on Dusty. One night, after Rich denied her more rehearsal time to work on new tunes, she entered his dressing room and slapped him across the face. On the last night of the stand, as she finished her final set at Basin Street, Buddy Rich's sax player entered the stage, grabbed the mike, and made a presentation to her: it was a pair of bright red boxing gloves.

Deserved or not, Dusty's new reputation as a combative performer dogged her for the rest of her career.

DUSTY GOES TO MEMPHIS

In 1967, Dusty was hot, especially in the States, where she spent almost half of her time. Her third album, aptly titled *Where Am I Going?* chalked up another hit for the artist and songs like Clive Westlake's "I Close My Eyes and Count to Ten," rivaled her best material.

That year, Dusty's contract with Philips in the United States was up and she didn't want to renew. So when Ahmet Ertegun and Jerry Wexler of Atlantic Records approached her with sincere interest, she was thrilled. Atlantic had been the home of some of her very favorite soul artists: the Drifters, Aretha Franklin, Otis Redding, and many others.

Wexler and Ertegun knew Dusty's capabilities well. But she was still surprised when they asked her to fly to Memphis, where so many soul musicians were based, to record her first album for the label. In fact, her Atlantic contract included in it a "key man" clause; Dusty was required to make her first album for the label with Jerry Wexler.

Wexler remembers prepping for those initial Memphis sessions with Dusty at his home on Long Island. "We must have had 75 songs there, of which she liked exactly 0," (Hoerburger). Wexler exaggerated. That first batch of songs did include two songs that Dusty eventually cut: "Son of a Preacher Man" and "Just a Little Lovin'." "Poor Jerry Wexler," said Dusty. "I drove him mad, because originally I only picked two . . . And then we plowed ankle deep through the demos. We disagreed on a couple that I let him win on, 'The Windmills of Your Mind,' for one, and he was right . . . He knew something I didn't" (Jim Feldman, *Dusty in Memphis*, liner notes, 1993).

Delays in choosing material and pre-production required a postponement of studio time. A second batch of cuts proved to be better targeted. Two songs from Randy Newman, four tracks from the tried and true pairing of Goffin/King, a track from Bacharach/David, and one from Mann/Weil, among others, were selected. It is perhaps the most illustrious batch of pop songs ever chosen, and none were written specifically for Dusty.

Dusty flew down to Memphis with arranger Arif Mardin and engineer Tom Dowd late in the summer of 1968. At first being in Memphis intimidated Dusty, what with all the city's musical history. She had to overcome jitters in the vocal booth as well. "They'd take me to the studio and tell me, 'This is where Wilson Pickett stood!'" she fretted. "They didn't have a clue that it absolutely froze me" (Feldman).

Could she measure up to her heroes? Her voice, breathy and delicate, wasn't a cinch for the task, and neither was the figure she cut—slight, British, and blonde—a familiar one in an urban studio. But she settled down and laid down her basic vocals in about week. The studio band, known as the Memphis Cats, did their work in about the same time. She had the support of the city's best musicians, including the Memphis Horns, and backing vocalists the Sweet Inspirations. The accompaniment was spare and tasteful, allowing the full brightness of the songs to shine on Dusty's voice.

Dusty also had a strange way of recording her voice in the studio. On *In Memphis*, she generally recorded her vocal tracks very late at night, in the dark, with the backing track turned up so loudly that she had a hard time hearing her own voice. Still, she had miraculous pitch and nailed it, to the delight of all present.

Wexler and Dowd insisted that her voice would carry the album and the musicians would provide her with a subtle cushion. This didn't make Dusty happy. For much of her career, she abided by the Spector-esque approach of burying her voice in a lush wall of orchestration. "She used to say that most of all she wanted her voice to be another instrument in the overall sound of the production" (Wickham and Valentine, p. 113). But that wasn't the way it would happen. She returned to New York City to cut final vocals. Dusty, along with the Atlantic posse, produced and mixed the album.

"Her head tones, and the way she put a falsetto on, and her phrasing," were impressive, says Tom Dowd (Feldman). "She's one of the important singers. Her voice contains the essence of soul."

Upon its American release in March 1969, the album received excellent reviews, but did not meet with commensurate sales. The record-buying public was perhaps unready to accept Dusty as a serious artist. "The Windmills of Your Mind" received a song for Best Oscar from the film *The Thomas Crown Affair*, giving the record a boost.

In the United Kingdom, the album sat around for months before shipping to stores. In London, her previously album, *Dusty Definitely,* still had legs, and her management wondered what a British audience would want with a bunch of southern soul tracks from their West Hampstead diva? When it was finally released there, critics adored it, but the record received little commercial attention. It peaked at number 99 on the album chart. 1969 was, of course, more about Woodstock than a British pop singer's journey to Memphis.

Dusty herself couldn't listen to it for a year after it was complete, and she had trouble singing "Preacher Man" when he career resurged in the late 1980s.

With all the accolades, *In Memphis* was destined to live on as an underground classic, the kind of album that would grow in legend rather than in sales. With each passing year it's name-checked more and more as new soul converts continue referring to it as a touchstone.

In the fall of 1969, Dusty went to America again to record, this time to Philadelphia to work with Kenny Gamble and Leon Huff. The two music men would later single-handedly account for that would come to be the Philly soul sound or "the Sound of Philadelphia." Gamble and Huff had worked with Wilson Pickett and Jerry Butler among others, but they had yet to refine their sound. Dusty was familiar with Gamble and Huff and their collaboration was casual, comfortable, and low-key. The album *A Brand New Me*, aka *From Dusty . . . With Love* in the United Kingdom, was well received, but it fell to the same commercial ennui that plagued *In Memphis*. The tepid sales depressed Dusty and she contemplated her next move.

1970 AND BEYOND

Following her work in the late 1960s, Dusty became a major artist and a superstar. She had tremendous visibility. She sold out clubs regularly and earned huge fees for her appearances. She appealed to pop fans of both sexes, all ages, white and black. No one was immune from Dusty's popular spell.

Ironically, at about the same time, Dusty was wearing down physically and emotionally. She'd been reaching for the top since going solo in the early 1960s and her super-controlling, high-energy approach sapped her endurance. She also wanted to put more time into her relationship with Norma Tanega, who had moved back to California at the behest of Dusty's manager after their relationship had grown stressful. So Dusty made a commitment to spend more time in America.

Over the next couple of years, she'd jet back and forth from L.A. to London, working sporadically.

She'd tour the English provinces up north. The club circuit had always appreciated her special brand of soul. But by the end of 1972, she felt like she'd done all she needed to do in this phase of her life. She said goodbye to her band, packed up her dresses and wigs, and headed once and for all to America. She'd hired an American crew; her personal assistant and manager were both based in London and declined to make the move with Dusty.

She enjoyed solid popularity in America, and had confidence that her management would know how to plot her future course. She respected American music and American audiences, and took heart in the fact that the country's scene embraced all different kinds of music. The first thing she did was tour "the circuit." In contrast to the British circuit, where she'd play glorified pubs, the American venues were generally posh rooms, often connected to hotels. Dusty loved a good hotel and she reveled in the luxury of the places she stayed during this time.

But as a solo performer, it was also lonely. Rather than traveling with her band, she'd play with the house bands at each stop, so that required extensive rehearsals and sound checks. After the show each night, Dusty was so tired all she could do was eat and sleep. Not the glamour she was accustomed to, but the money was good and so were the audiences.

In 1972, at the tail end of the tour, Dusty met Faye Harris, a photojournalist, based in Los Angeles. They bonded and ended up spending the next six years together, off and on. Harris was taken with Dusty's intelligence and passion. When Harris suggested they move from their small apartment, Dusty went out and bought a large home with a pool for the two of them in Laurel Canyon.

By the mid-1970s, the hotel circuit was wearing thin. The rise of corporate rock loomed over the pop charts. Bands like Aerosmith and the Doobie Brothers were now dominating radio, turning acts like Dusty into quaint artifacts of a bygone age. Hotels were also no longer trendy venues. Soon, stadiums would hold all the very biggest and boldest musical experiences. Dusty had weathered the folk boom, the British Invasion, the Sound of Young America (Motown), the British Blues Boom of the mid-1960s, and the rise of hippie and acid rock of the late 1960s. She made it through with bold and honest music. Now, though, it was looking more and more like she'd be squashed by this latest musical juggernaut, with its decibels, drugs, money, and hedonism. In fact, she didn't have much of a chance at all.

DRINKING AND DRUGS

One night, amid a bender involving lots of drinking and drugs, Elton John, a longtime friend of Dusty's and a huge fan from her days on *Ready, Steady, Go!*, asked her to sing on a session of his. Dusty had already worked with him on his *Tumbleweed Connection* recording, albeit in better days, and Elton really wanted to see Dusty get back to her old self, maybe even make a new record.

Initially, Dusty resisted his requests. But when she heard she'd be singing with some old friends, including Cissy Houston, who sang on her *In Memphis* sessions, she couldn't resist. She showed up to do some supporting vocal tracks.

The track in question, "The Bitch Is Back," would show up on his album, *Caribou*, but Dusty's voice wouldn't be on it. Not that she didn't try. It became immediately apparent that her voice was quite nearly gone. She struggled to hit the high notes. Her vices were catching up with her. The girl with the once mighty voice was losing what she'd had for her entire professional life. The Elton session was humiliating and plunged her deeper into drinking.

Sometime later, Anne Murray managed to convince Dusty to sing at some sessions. Occasionally, her voice bounced back, and she took advantage. She sang demos in Los Angeles, a substantial step down from her former superstar pedestal.

By the summer of 1975, Dusty's life was in a tailspin. She had had four commercial failures in a row and drinking and popping pills consumed her. She began attending AA meetings—at small town churches to minimize the risk of being found out—signing in as Mary O'Brien. Her public image had always been so important to her, and she guarded it closely.

But she felt such low self-esteem that she had also taken to the violent, self-effacing act of physically cutting herself. A few years back, when her voice let her down right before the eve of a residential booking for the London-based Talk of the Town series, Dusty cut herself repeatedly—acting out her frustration and violent depression—and now she was reprising that deviant behavior. From this point on, she had to wear long sleeves to hide her wounds.

Royalty checks had decreased in size. Her relationship with Faye was strained. She was constantly on drugs. The record company, seeing she was in no state to reenter the studio, occupied themselves by releasing compilations. While this was a boon to Dusty financially, it also made her feel that her only future was to mine the past. If she had no real future, then, what did that mean for her as an artist?

Dusty was eventually diagnosed as manic depressive. But she refused to look back. She hated ruminating on her unhappy childhood. Beyond living in the shadow of her brother Tom, Dusty had little affection from either parent. Call it emotional neglect. She lived for her music, and managed to survive without affection the way a cactus requires little water.

For the next several years, Dusty would be in and out of detox or psychiatric wards. Each time she lapsed she'd be rescued by one or another of her courtiers. She had a handful of lovers and friends who kept a watchful eye on her, including Harris, Helene Sellery, Suzanne Lacefield, and Peggy Allbrecht. She spent lots of time with professional tennis players as well, including Billie Jean King and Rosie Casals. They often came to her aid.

It was now 1976 and four years had passed since Dusty attempted to sing in front of an audience. Nona Hendryx, an old friend, was red hot as a member of LaBelle. The soul trio implored Dusty to sing with them on stage in front of a sold-out Oakland audience. Dusty agreed, and the crowd went wild. It would be one of Dusty's best nights in years. Sadly, it would be her last successful performance for a long while.

In the winter of that same year, Dusty was working on her new album, *It Begins Again*, with Roy Thomas Baker, a producer who catapulted to fame thanks to his successful work with the rock band Queen. Despite her efforts in AA, Dusty managed to stay sober for only a week or two before relapsing into drugs and alcohol. Her relationship with Faye Harris was again on the skids and the recording wasn't going as well as she'd hoped.

One night, her friend Helene, who received phone calls religiously from Dusty nightly for years, hadn't heard from her. Suzanne Lacefield, her sponsor at AA, didn't hear from Dusty either and both began to panic. Suzanne rushed to Dusty's place and found her unconscious on the floor. The evidence of an overdose was everywhere: pill bottles, vodka, and dirt, where she had fallen into a potted plant.

LOVE, AGAIN

Dusty most often found love from the stage, from her fans and friends. This could explain why she made such a super-human effort to stay in the public eye. When she discovered how much "love" she felt from her audiences, she seized it and did her best to hold onto it. For a decade she lived on the love of her fans. And when she started to lose that love, she began dying, if not literally, certainly in the eyes of those who knew her best.

Dusty recaptured that love in the late 1970s when her act turned toward campy cabaret. In London, especially, where she found her dearest fans, Dusty came into her own as a person who could at last be honest with herself. At the age of 40, she was finally comfortable with being herself.

She granted an interview to *Gay News*. It was ostensibly to promote *It Begins Again*. Her handlers identified a potentially huge audience that had already silently begun to gather at her feet: gays and lesbians.

"The gay community has been extremely loyal to me as a singer," she'd said in an interview. "I value that fiercely."

"For them, Dusty had always been the supreme diva. It was her very 'single-ness' that so appealed . . . They loved her for being cosmopolitan and exotic, for recording singles in Italian and French over the years, for knowing about Brazilian music before it was fashionable, and for being well-traveled, as much as for her 'over-the-top' looks." (Len Brown, "Scandal in the Wind," *NME,* February 1989.)

In 1979, four years before AIDS became a health issue, homosexuals were beginning to enjoy a visibility of their own. They'd respond enthusiastically when Dusty acknowledged them, and they began to love her, her campy shows, her roller skates, and audacious clothes, all over again.

The shows, both in London and in America, went well, but Dusty was hanging on by a thread. Her voice needed cortisone shots to get through, followed by heavy doses of Gran Marnier to recover. She'd begun a new addiction as well, to barbiturates. She said she loved the euphoria it gave her.

That euphoria only temporarily masked her unstable behavior. She continued cutting herself and resorting to even more violent acts. One night in a fit of rage she detached a restroom sink from the wall and smashed it on the floor, bloodying herself in the process.

In 1983, at an AA meeting, Dusty fell for an exotic, wild-haired woman named Tedda. She had just come off a stint in prison for violent behavior, but Dusty was taken by her beauty. After a brief courtship, they engaged in a civil union, a legally binding same-sex arrangement. They were married, surrounded by family and friends at what Dusty insisted would be a dry wedding. But no sooner had the wedding wrapped up that the newlyweds were fighting. Their relationship was turbulent from the start and deteriorated rapidly. For the first time in her life, Dusty had teamed up with someone as unstable as she. One day, that instability surfaced violently.

Tedda, enraged about something Dusty had done, clobbered her partner with a frying pan. Dusty was hospitalized and her face never truly recovered. Tedda was sent to prison, a repeat offense. Helene extended Dusty money for plastic surgery on her mouth, but rumor had it she opted for the cheapest cosmetic procedure possible so she could spend the rest on drugs.

Helene also took Dusty out to visit Tedda in prison. This forgiving gesture had a dual purpose. Dusty needed her "spouse's" signature for food stamps. Rock bottom, the clichéd destination for junkies and ne'er-do-wells, was close at hand. She lived in fleabag motels in the seediest neighborhoods of Hollywood. One night, 11 months into sobriety, she celebrated by appearing at a charity event. Sadly, Dusty wasn't ready to sing.

"A few phrases into her first song, she collapsed under the weight of her drug intake. She left the stage, to return a few moments later with a Hoover [vacuum cleaner]. To the astonishment of the audience, Dusty proceeded to hum to herself as she cleaned the stage" (Valentine and Wickham, p. 221).

The incident is considered the most bizarre of Dusty's career.

MORE BATTLES, OCCASIONAL VICTORIES

One day, in 1987, after several recording misadventures, including *White Heat* and the single "Sometimes Like Butterflies," Dusty received a phone call. It was from a songwriter named Allee Willis, a woman who had just written a song with Neil Tennant and Chris Lowe of the Pet Shop Boys. During the process, the dance-pop duo, popular at the time in the United Kingdom and the United States, had mentioned to Willis how much they adored Dusty, and how they'd love to have her sing on the track. "What could they possibly want from me?" Dusty was said to have asked herself.

On the verge of retirement, the prospect lured her back into the studio. The track, "What Have I Done to Deserve This," featured the monotone Tennant trading lead with Dusty. The juxtaposition was magical and the song became a hit on both sides of the Atlantic. Incredibly, it became the second biggest hit of her entire career.

The Pet Shop Boys would go on to produce half of the songs on Dusty's next album, the U.K.-only *Reputation*. The set yielded a handful of hits and Dusty was back on the charts again, on the dance floors, and impersonated on the drag bar circuit.

The first hints of serious illness for Dusty appeared in 1994, when she was in Nashville recording with Mary Chapin Carpenter and K.T. Oslin. Her manager, Barry Krost, envisioned Dusty's next project to be a country music set, called *In Nashville*. But bad weather sidelined the project. Just days after the stint in Nashville, she felt a lump in her breast and called her friend Vicki Wickham. With no doctor of her own, Dusty went to Wickham's doctor. The tumor was malignant. For the first time in her life, the worst was actually happening to Dusty.

"Because she'd beaten so many other things in her life, Dusty always believed she could beat breast cancer" (Valentine and Wickham, p. 257).

The cancer went into remission for a few years, and Dusty celebrated by releasing *A Very Fine Love* in 1996. When the cancer returned, it had spread into her bones. She called her friend Faye Harris to ask her some advice: "I'm going to die and I don't know how to do it—I've never done it before" (Valentine and Wickham, p. 286).

In January 1999, she received word that she'd be inducted into the Rock and Roll Hall of Fame's class of that year. The actual induction ceremony, in which her friend Elton John served as inductor, came four days after Dusty died. She died on March 2, a few weeks before her 60th birthday.

SELECTED DISCOGRAPHY

In Memphis (Atlantic/Rhino, 1969/1999)

The Dusty Springfield Anthology (Mercury/Chronicles, 1997)

In London (Atlantic/Rhino, 1999)

With the Springfields

Anthology: Over the Hills and Far Away (Phillips, 1997)

FURTHER READING

Feldman, Jim. *Dusty In Memphis,* liner notes. Atlantic/Rhino, 1999.

Gaar, Gillian. *She's a Rebel: The History of Women in Rock and Roll.* New York: Seal Press, 2002.

O'Brien, Lucy. *Dusty: The Queen Bee of Pop.* London: Pan, 2000.

Valentine, Penny and Vicki Wickham. *Dancing with Demons:Dusty Springfield.* New York: St. Martin's Griffin, 2000.

Pictorial Press Ltd./Alamy.

Aretha Franklin

THE QUEEN OF SOUL

"I'd like for you to receive the First Lady of Music, Miss Aretha Franklin!" Reverend James Cleveland introduces Aretha Franklin on her brilliant 1972 gospel album *Amazing Grace*. Cleveland used "First Lady of Music," rather than the more accepted "Queen of Soul," her acknowledged nickname. For close to a 10-year span, Aretha Franklin was indeed the premier woman in music, and one of a very small number of true soul music giants. At the point in her career in which she recorded this album, "Queen of Soul" seemed too restrictive, so great were her accomplishments.

In the late 1960s, Franklin became one of the biggest international recording stars in all of popular music thanks to an incredible string of gospel-infused performances like "Chain of Fools," "Respect," "Natural Woman," and "Baby I Love You." This run earned her the "Queen" crown, and she has worn it proudly ever since.

During the course of just a few years in the mid- to late 1960s, Aretha reigned over the charts with her Atlantic label releases. She amassed chart-topping hit after hit in both the R&B and pop music categories; her choice of material—ranging from soul and gospel tracks to pop covers—enabled her to cross over and appeal to all fans of music. This phenomenon, accomplished by only Sam Cooke and Ray Charles until that time, allowed her to reach a vast audience and her music, firmly rooted in gospel and R&B, became universally accepted.

Based on the power of her music within the African American community, many also viewed Aretha as a symbol of black America. Her strength and confidence embodied the mission of her brothers and sisters during a critical time in American history. Even though she refrained from much politicking in her public life, the power of her performance and her potent presence helped to advance the cause of the civil rights movement.

If Aretha became a symbol of black pride and womanhood in the black community, she *personified* soul to white audiences. Black women, less threatening than black men to white audiences, have always been the first to introduce new black musical styles.

Part of Aretha's greatness was that she could be both uptown and downtown at the same time. She was a country girl at heart, who in the wink of an eye could transform into a glamorous celebrity. She loved a home-cooked meal, but she was also dazzled by the style of Hollywood's glitziest celebrities. She loved being at home with her family, but she also enjoyed dressing up, buying clothes, doing hair, and looking fabulous.

Other 1960s soul queens—Diana Ross, Dusty Springfield, Dionne Warwick, for example—conveyed a smooth, high-fashion elegance. In contrast, Etta James and Mavis Staples were gritty gospel singers, more comfortable belting it out than finding their way through complicated Bacharach songs, or nuanced Motown pop hits. Aretha's dazzling versatility and breathtaking virtuosity became her signatures, not whether she was urban or rural, earthy or elegant. She was both. Aretha was Aretha, and boy, could she sing it.

Aretha's voice soared, singing out as if she wanted to lose herself deep within a song. Her timing, compression of phrases, emphasis and dynamics were natural and astonishing. In the 1960s, after refining her vocal chops with John Hammond at Columbia Records, Aretha found a musical place that allowed her instincts to take over. The music—largely the soul of the South, with horns, rock-solid rhythms, and Aretha's own piano—combined an unstoppable sense of energy and range without losing the full power of a great interpretation.

Not surprisingly, the Aretha of the 1980s, 1990s, and beyond, of guest cameos, award winning, and superstar duets, saw her power diminish somewhat. Her voice, airier, huskier than the feisty days of the brilliant "I Never Loved a Man (The Way I Love You)," one of the great soul performances in all of popular music, somewhat tired. The dizzying, five-octave range of her youth was gone. But even her middling performances contained immense soulfulness. And her skill of interpretation, of understanding the heart of a song and nailing it for the world to hear, is a vastly underappreciated gift.

Lena Horne once said, "Inside every woman there's an Aretha Franklin screaming to get out." The same could be said about Aretha herself. She began her career quietly, unassumingly, in her father's church choir, and soon after, playing small clubs as the opening act for comedians. Inside, there was an Aretha Franklin, an outsized soul talent, just waiting to emerge. Soon enough, she did and everybody heard about it. Each song she sang—oozing with subtle eroticism, funky sounds, and shimmering harmonies—was a full-throated and ragingly spirited message to the world. Woman, hear her roar.

THE EARLY YEARS

Aretha Louise Franklin was born in Buffalo, in 1942, to the Reverend Clarence LaVaughn Franklin and Barbara V. Siggers. One of five children, she was named after her father's two sisters, Aretha and Louise, and was the second youngest. Aretha's grandparents both worked in the cotton fields of Mississippi. But her father dreamed of a better life. He walked miles to school in order to achieve that, but he still toiled in the fields to help support the family.

He met his wife Barbara in Mississippi. Taking advantage of his education and ambition, he became a preacher and together the Franklins moved to Memphis. While there, he attended a college, LeMoyne, and began to widen his view of the fundamentalist upbringing he'd had. Religion still played a critical role in his life, but at this point he was becoming more liberal. He took his open-minded views to the couple's next destination, Buffalo, New York, where his wife's family lived. There he presided over the congregation of the Friendship Baptist Church. Aretha was born while the Franklins were in Buffalo.

When Aretha was two, the family eyed the economic landscape in America and decided that Detroit would be where they'd make their next home. The city had been exploding thanks to the thriving automotive industry, and the Reverend Franklin saw an opportunity to get established. He asserted himself as the pastor of the New Bethel Baptist Church, with a congregation of over 1,000, and the family at last began to establish roots.

Aretha's Mom, a nurse's aide by day, had a beautiful voice. She treated her daughters with fairness and generosity. But she didn't want to be in Detroit and the Franklins had trouble making their marriage work. So Aretha's mom moved back to Buffalo with her parents, along with her oldest son Vaughn.

At the time, Aretha was six. Rumors hold that she had left her family, but Aretha, in her autobiography, emphatically stated that this was not the case: "Despite the fact that it has been written innumerable times, it is an absolute lie that my mother abandoned us. In no way, shape, form, or fashion did our mother desert us" (Aretha Franklin and David Ritz, *Aretha: From These Roots*, New York: Villard, 1999, p. 5).

Aretha's father was a stately man, tall at over six feet. He was affable and kind-hearted, able to speak with his intellect as well as his heart. His singing voice was booming. Many say he could have been a gospel star had he chosen to. The most celebrated pastor in Detroit, he took great pride in his appearance, often dressing in finely tailored suits. He was the first black minister on the radio in the Detroit area and one of the first to tour the country thanks to his syndicated sermons, which he sold as recordings through the Chess label.

All those who saw him in action recall how great a storyteller he was, and how he always managed to whip his congregation up to fever pitch. There were actually nurses in attendance with smelling salts ready to revive fainting churchgoers, so potent was his message. As a friend of Dr. Martin Luther King Jr., he became a national figure during the civil rights movement. He capitalized on his notoriety by going on the road to preach and in so doing earned the nickname of "The High Priest of Soul Preaching." On a darker note, the Reverend had a penchant for partying; he was arrested for possession of marijuana. And while he never remarried, he did have an appetite for women.

At the time, Aretha (also known as "Ree") and her siblings had no idea why their mother left, and the subject was never discussed. Both of her parents spoke with respect about the other, and both households remained positive. Aretha and her siblings would spend enjoyable summers with her mother in Buffalo.

In Detroit, the Franklins grew up in the church parish home, a six-bedroom residence in an upscale neighborhood on the north side of Detroit. Music filled the house. There were two pianos and all the children played them, especially Erma who Aretha says had the skill of a virtuoso. Reverend Franklin had many musician friends, including jazz piano genius Art Tatum, and they'd often come to visit.

Erma Franklin

Erma Franklin, Aretha's older sister, also had her heart set on a recording career. As a teenager, she formed a singing group called the Cleo-Patretts. They recorded locally in Detroit, but disbanded quickly. Erma went on to win local talent shows and early on developed a reputation as a fine singer and songwriter. In the late 1950s, eventual Motown president Berry Gordy and his songwriting partner, Billy Davis, decided Erma would be groomed as their label's first recording artist.

Her father, Reverend C.L. Franklin, had different ideas, though, and convinced Erma that continuing her education was more important than singing. She attended college in Atlanta. While she was gone, three songs originally intended for her had passed her by, recorded by other artists: Marv Johnson, "You Got What It Takes;" "All I Could Do Was Cry" by Etta James, and "Sweetest Feeling" by Jackie Wilson. After college, her father brought Erma and Aretha to Columbia Records for auditions. Erma signed with Epic (a Columbia subsidiary), and moved to New York. Aretha signed with Columbia. When Erma's contract ended, she became the featured vocalist with the Lloyd Price Orchestra for five years. Erma then signed with Shout Records, where she recorded her hit song "Piece of My Heart" in 1967, later covered definitively by Janis Joplin. The song, which made the Top 10 on the national R&B charts, helped garner her a Grammy nomination for Best New Artist in 1968. Right after "Piece of My Heart" hit it big and she was ready to record her next album, Bert Berns, the writer and co-owner of Shout, died suddenly of a heart attack. Chaos led to disappointment and she obtained a job with a computer programming firm. Her career was hampered by misfortune and by contracts with recording companies who could not find appropriate material for her. In the 1970s she left the music business entirely, apart from engagements with her sister Aretha. She died in 2002 after a long battle with throat cancer.

THE GOSPEL SINGER

Without question, church played a central role in the Franklin family, and the children, especially Aretha, looked forward to the pomp and tradition of Sunday service. The day often began late morning and the service would run for hours. By that time, the worshippers were tired and hungry and the family would retire to the house for a pan full of fried chicken.

As a young girl, she was exposed to the gospel talents of singers like Clara Ward and the Reverend James Cleveland, two of gospel's most revered icons. Reverend Franklin had befriended Clara Ward and her gospel group and so Aretha found herself in an important circle of talented people at a very young age. Marion Williams, who became an international star thanks to her role in *Black Nativity*, also served as an influence. Cleveland, one of the first modernizers of the gospel tradition, served as Minister of Music at the Franklin church, and, as Choir Director, he spent much of his time working to develop Aretha's natural vocal talent.

At the same time, R&B served as a supplement to Aretha's musical diet. After coming home from school, when her father wasn't around, she'd turn the radio on and listen to Ruth Brown and LaVern Baker, two of the first female R&B stars and Aretha's direct musical ancestors. As a teenager, she roller-skated to songs like Baker's "Jim Dandy," Dinah Washington's "Let's

Go Around Together," and Frankie Lymon's "Why Do Fools Fall in Love?" She loved the Falcons, led by Wilson Pickett, as well as Little Willie John. In Detroit at large, the optimism of a booming economy led to the city's jubilant saturation of music. R&B and doo-wop were on virtually every street corner, as were gospel and jazz. Segregation within the city hadn't become a devisive factor, so the strains of pop music—Sinatra, Bing Crosby, Perry Como—could also be heard and Detroit, along with few other integrated cities across the country, would become America's musical crucibles, the places where it all happened.

Aretha sang her first solo in her father's church when she was 10. As the daughter of a famous singing preacher and a mother with a gorgeous voice, Aretha was on the fast track to stardom, following in the footsteps of gospel greats like Ward and Mahalia Jackson. Up to that time, she'd been singing with the Junior Choir and Aretha recalls how much fun it was rockin' the church with them. But she also felt ready to take the big step out front. At the time, in the early 1950s, the Soul Stirrers, who'd counted Sam Cooke in its lineup beginning in 1952, was the most popular group on the gospel circuit, and Aretha's first solo happened to be "Jesus Be a Fence Around Me," a Soul Stirrers hymn.

Chicago's Cooke was the biggest heartthrob of Aretha's teenage years, and a man she could not stop talking about. He was instrumental in gospel; he represented a departure for traditional lead singers of gospel groups. Aretha took notice. She knew who the gospel stars were: the Swan Silvertones had Claude Jeter, the Dixie Hummingbirds had Ira Tucker, and Julius Cheeks had the Sensational Nightingales. She observed how the girl groups in gospel looked so beautiful with their flowing robes and pretty hairstyles. She also knew of the handsome young singer named Cooke who was in the process of turning the genre on its ear with his looks, his voice, and his sensual approach. Cooke, like many high-level artists, often paid the Reverend a visit. Sam's visits were exciting for Aretha, as they would be for any young girl who had set her eyes on him.

"Sam was certainly an inspiration to me. I was so influenced by him that my Daddy told me to stop emulating Sam and instead express my own heart and soul" (Franklin and Ritz 1999, p. 52).

In 1952, Barbara Franklin died. She had suffered a heart attack. The family journeyed to Buffalo to grieve and attend the funeral. Aretha, always close to her mother was devastated.

In the mid-1950s Aretha and the Franklin sisters, all aspiring musicians, met a Detroit songwriter named Berry Gordy. Gordy, of course, would go on to establish the Motown empire. But as an upstart, he was an aggressive presence on the scene, playing and writing music for anyone who'd have him. Erma Franklin, Aretha's big sister, actually chose not to work with Gordy. But she did record a version of his song, "All I Could Do Was Cry." Unfortunately, Etta James's version reached radio first and Erma's version failed to chart.

Aretha first toured as a teenager as the opening act on her father's gospel show, along with Lucy Branch and Sammy Bryant. Those early tours, though brief, opened Aretha's eyes up to the wider world. She may have been singing gospel, but she was traveling on the secular side of life. She'd always have gospel in her blood, in her voice, and her heart and soul. But the secular world and its many vices began to beckon.

The R&B material at the time made a deep impression on her, as evidenced by the numerous tunes from this period that she'd go on to cover. Songs by Ray Charles, Sam Cooke, and Johnny Ace all became a part of her repertoire, and it became easy to understand that R&B, as well as gospel, had cast a spell on her as a young girl.

Unlike many other prodigies, especially children of clergy, whose parents urged them further and further into religious involvement, Aretha's father urged her out of it. Ironically, C.L. Franklin was responsible for introducing his daughter to pop and jazz music. He actually encouraged her to sing secular material. Perhaps this happened because father Franklin himself was a liberal man. Perhaps because he was smart enough to observe that the riches in pop music were much greater than they were in gospel. Whatever the case, he had a broader vision of his daughter's future. He opened the door and showed her the way out of gospel.

ALL GROWN UP

Admittedly, Aretha loved boys. Visions, she said, of handsome faces and physiques danced in her head. She had high standards, but when those standards were met, she didn't hesitate. She had her first serious boyfriend at 12, and enjoyed an endless string of paramours. Her social life was active; she attended ballroom dances, parties, and other functions for young people. When she reached her teens, she got pregnant for the first time. The childhood that she adored was now in danger of passing her by.

Six months into the pregnancy, she dropped out of school. After she became pregnant and had the baby, she was comforted and accepted unequivocally by her family. They didn't judge her, and they helped her any way they could. Having an accepting father helped with that attitude. The baby, Clarence, arrived just after Aretha had turned 14. By 17, Aretha had fallen in love with a Casanova she had met at the roller rink; months later she gave birth to her second child, Eddie.

All of the Franklin daughters were strong, independent women, a reflection of the masculine upbringing they had. In the early 1960s Erma toured with R&B star Lloyd Price, while Aretha and Carolyn were also trying to break into secular music. In 1956, the folks at Chess, the label involved in the Reverend's sermons and other recordings, asked Reverend Franklin if they could record Aretha. He consented. The recording, *The Gospel Soul of Aretha Franklin,* is comprised of sacred songs recorded live, some at the New Bethel Church and some at the Oakland Arena in Detroit.

Touring enabled Aretha to see both New York and Los Angeles. In L.A. Aretha spent some time with Sam Cooke, who by the late 1950s had left the Soul Stirrers and embarked on his career in pop music. For Cooke, the transition from sacred to secular drew ire from gospel fans, and it became one of the most controversial moves in the then-young world of pop music. Whether swayed by Sam's rocky voyage or not, the 18-year-old Aretha would embark on the same trip.

Being from Detroit, Aretha's logical first move into pop music would have been to start with the young Motown label. Many of the talented teens from urban Detroit, including the Marvelettes, the Miracles, the Primettes (later the Supremes) all opted into this up and coming music company. Indeed, agents from the label, eager to sign her on, approached Aretha with a contract. But for some reason, she was reluctant to sign it. Even though the label, in her own backyard, would have made for a convenient arrangement, she refrained from joining the Motown roster. "Both Daddy and I had our sights set on something bigger. At that time, Motown was a fledgling local label. Little did we know that they would be one of the greatest record labels of all time. Instead we concentrated on national and international labels" (Franklin and Ritz, p. 80).

THE COLUMBIA YEARS

In 1960, Aretha moved to New York City and signed with Columbia based on a demo she had cut of jazzy standards. John Hammond, a producer at Columbia at the time, heard the demo and contacted Jo King, Aretha's manager, immediately. Hammond was a storied executive at that point, having signed Bessie Smith, Billie Holiday, and Count Basie. Hammond told Aretha she had the best voice he'd heard since Billie, which, of course, thrilled her.

Across town, RCA had entered into the sweepstakes for Aretha. Sam Cooke, who himself had signed with the label just a year earlier, dearly wanted her on the roster. But up till Sam Cooke, RCA had been a country and rock and roll label, so their soul pedigree suffered. Still, the romantic Aretha's soft spot for the dashing Cooke might have made her do some ill-advised things.

But Columbia led the way in terms of mainstream music throughout the 1950s, thanks to hit performers like Johnny Mathis, Mitch Miller, and Leslie Uggams. That's exactly where Aretha wanted to be: swimming with the big fish in pop music's mainstream. Her signing to Columbia was overseen by her father.

Her first album for the label, released in 1961, was *The Great Aretha Franklin: The First 12 Sides*. These were Hammond-produced songs, foreshadowing her later work with Atlantic. They were pop songs that drew on the spirit of gospel and the blues, and they would become known as the best material she'd record for the Columbia label.

To work as frequently as possible, she made a home for herself around New York City. She lived at the YWCA for a while, and then down in the arty burg of Greenwich Village. Her children, back home with their grandmother, were safe and content. Aretha began to find her own way in the world.

Jo King, a feisty NYC woman, booked Aretha's first gigs in the city. She insisted her client take some finishing classes as well, to work on her presentation. Aretha worked on choreography and had a vocal coach as well.

In her earliest years, hits were elusive. But at least she was laying the groundwork. She played reputable venues and began to attract a considerable fan base. Hammond saw Aretha as a blues and jazz artist, not a pop hit maker. At Columbia, they focused their efforts on that side of her talent. In retrospect, this nearsighted approach to her ability doomed her tenure on the label. She did polish her vocal technique and she began to develop a style uniquely her own. But commercial hits were still a few years away.

Rather than singing in the gritty Ruth Brown vein, she opted to sound more like Nina Simone or Betty Carter, powerful singers fronting small, jazzy combos. Her jazzy period overlapped a time when the genre seemed to be going through a soul phase. So the confluence put her in the company of some of the greatest jazz musicians of the age. She played dates with John Coltrane, Charles Mingus, Blue Mitchell, Freddie Hubbard, and Art Blakey and the Jazz Messengers. The Village Vanguard, one of the jazz world's most respected and influential clubs, booked Aretha for months at a stretch, allowing her to work out improvisations, alternate arrangements, and learn how to entertain an audience.

At the same time, Aretha had the chance to jump on a couple of R&B bills, one being with Sam Cooke. In fact, she experienced a variety of tours, bouncing from jazz clubs to R&B venues on the Chitlin' Circuit to high school hops. But this exposure created some confusion for Franklin. She wondered what kind of material she was meant to sing. She shifted between singing for adults and singing for teens, singing improvised jazz and singing more scripted R&B. She had the ability to do both, but had difficulty deciding which audience would be best for her career.

In 1963, Aretha earned a slot on the *Ed Sullivan Show*. Thrilled, she gathered some dresses and went to the studio. Not long before she was slated to go on, however, a producer told her she'd been bumped from the night's program due to an overbooking. Better luck soon followed, though, with appearances on *American Bandstand* and *Shindig*. Was she cut out for the urbane Mr. Sullivan, or the raucous Dick Clark?

While Aretha's career experienced upheaval during the early 1960s, so too did America suffer from similar turbulence and conflict. Urban renewal had gotten under way in Detroit and elsewhere around the country. The events precipitating the civil rights movement were unsettling, culminating in the

1963 assassination of President Kennedy. Devastated by this blow to the African American community, Aretha plunged into her work.

She still visited Detroit regularly. On one of her trips home, she met a man named Ted White. White's management company included mostly small name acts and little known songwriters. One of them, Ronnie Shannon, would go on to play an important role in Aretha's career.

Back home, White was a man-about-town. He knew all the in-places and he escorted Aretha around. They explored the after-hours club scene and became friendly. Well-connected, White helped Aretha get acquainted with the talented and party-inclined groups from Motown, including the Four Tops and the Temptations. White's wherewithal impressed Aretha and after a few months of hanging around together, she asked him to be her manager. Not long after that, they began dating.

They were joined together in matrimony by a justice of the peace after a show in Ohio. The union was spontaneous; Aretha, after the fact, regretted not having a big wedding at her father's church. The Reverend felt disappointment as well. Both White and Franklin knew that their relationship was not built on solid ground. Still, Aretha gave birth to her third child, Teddy, in 1964, while in her early 20s.

Aretha's relationship with White was unsteady. He failed to remain faithful, and he drank to excess, resulting in destructive behavior. Aretha tried to stay calm with her kids and she focused on her career. She continued recording and performing, while White did some behind the scenes work as her manager. The relationship didn't last long, but White was present when Aretha experienced her first truly big break.

THE ATLANTIC YEARS

Atlantic Records served as the home of many of Aretha's favorite R&B acts, from Ruth Brown and Ray Charles to the Drifters and the Clovers. After searching futilely for an artistic identity with Columbia, the writing was on the wall that she needed a clean break and a fresh start. When her Columbia contract expired, she signed with Atlantic in 1966. She was all of 25 years old.

Jerry Wexler, Atlantic's visionary producer, welcomed Aretha with open arms. He made her feel comfortable. "She fit into the matrix of music I had always worked with—songs expressing adult emotions," wrote Wexler. "Aretha didn't come to us to be made over or refashioned; she was searching for herself, not for external gimmicks . . . I urged Aretha to be Aretha" (Jerry Wexler, *Aretha Franklin: Queen of Soul*, liner notes, p. 13).

To Wexler, letting Aretha be Aretha meant sitting her down at the piano and allowing her to sing. It helped illuminate her natural ability; what she chose to sing and what her organic tendencies were, both in song choices and in performance techniques. Wexler observed her, made some notes, and considered two options for his new client.

He first called Jim Stewart at Stax in Memphis to get his thoughts. He told him he could have a percentage of Aretha's recordings if he paid her the $25,000 advance she was owed. Oddly, Stewart passed on the opportunity, and the chance to work with one of the greatest singers in the history of popular music. Wexler dodged a bullet as well. No one would want to go down as the person who passed on Aretha.

So, with his first plan nixed, Wexler opted to take Aretha south to Alabama, to record at Rick Hall's Fame studio in Muscle Shoals. There, he knew from experience, they would find the type of Southern soul musicians that would best complement Aretha's natural style.

At Muscle Shoals, Aretha encountered a brilliant band: Jimmy Johnson, Spooner Oldham, Dan Penn, Roger Hawkins, David Hood, Tommy Cogbill, and others worked full-time laying down tracks at the studio. She and Jerry had pinned down some material, including a Ronnie Shannon song called "I Never Loved a Man (The Way I Love You)." The camaraderie in the studio, free and easy, lent itself to a great session. Aretha loved the looseness, the chemistry, and the sound of the band. Compared to her more rigidly defined work with Columbia, this was real and raw and had Aretha written all over it.

But trouble had been brewing. Apparently, Ted White, who accompanied Aretha to Alabama, had a run-in with one of the musicians. The fact that the band was all-white had been a source of consternation for White, and Aretha recalls that friction arose the first day in the studio. "I vaguely recall loud noises and voices shouting and doors slamming. I never learned the details" (Franklin and Ritz, p. 109).

Aretha felt uncomfortable enough though that she decided to leave Muscle Shoals the next morning, after only one day of recording. She met White—who also made his own decision to leave Alabama—at the airport. They flew separately, and didn't discuss the incident. But the recording experience, while it provided a magic moment or two, had ultimately failed. Setting out, they planned a slate of 11 songs and only finished 1, along with a fraction of a second.

When Wexler heard the song they did cut, he pressed a dozen acetates and shipped them to disc jockeys. For the moment, the one song ended up being all he needed. Radio went crazy for it. The fact that there was no B-side, not yet, didn't affect the single's success. Shannon's song, "I Never Loved a Man (The Way I Love You)," became Aretha's first hit.

To finish the second song the band had begun at Muscle Shoals, Dan Penn and Chips Moman's "Do Right Woman, Do Right Man," Wexler tried a different strategy. Instead of sending Aretha back down South, he brought the musicians to New York City. The ploy worked and Aretha had a complete, two-sided hit.

"RESPECT"

Aretha began to build the songs that would become her Atlantic debut. They came from different places—her own tune, "Dr. Feelgood," a Ray Charles cover ("Drown in My Own Tears"), two King Curtis tunes ("Soul Serenade" and "Save Me"), a song she wrote with her sister Carolyn ("Baby, Baby, Baby"). One tune in particular came about rather serendipitously.

At the tail end of 1965, Otis Redding had seen his roaring tune called "Respect," climb into the Top 10 on the R&B charts. Carolyn and Aretha, between takes of other tunes, began toying with it on the piano, singing and playing together. Playfully, they coined the phrase, "Sock it to me," and used it after the chorus. Everyone in the studio heard what they were doing and they chose to cut the record. Aretha turned Otis's version inside out. With her forceful performance, the song became a concert staple. She made it resonate with boldness and courage. It became an anthem, a command, a statement of ferocious intent. It also, inadvertently, became a battle hymn for the civil rights movement, and has lived on as one of the best-known and most-loved tunes of the 1960s soul era.

It also served as, her breakthrough, and the tune that sent her following the same sky-high trajectory as her heroes: Ray Charles and Sam Cooke. At Columbia, she struggled with material that felt like a compromise. With her first efforts on Atlantic, in a place where she had actually been given the freedom and guidance to create and do what came naturally, Aretha had crossed over without even trying.

> Look over the selections on this first album, and you see that soul was the key. There was no compromising, no deliberate decision to go pop. As it turned out, these records crossed over and sold on the charts. But we weren't trying to manipulate or execute any marketing plan. We were simply trying to compose real music from my heart. (Franklin and Ritz, p. 111)

The success awakened Aretha's creativity. From her first Atlantic album she gained focus; after nearly a decade of singing professionally she began to understand what her true mission was.

The first four Aretha albums, released two a year those first two years, combined to yield 10 Top 10 pop hits and six chart-topping R&B tracks. The material surged to the leading edge of soul music. After Sam Cooke and Otis Redding had both passed away, Aretha became the standard bearer for the style.

As the country stood on the brink of war—abroad in Vietnam, and at home with Woodstock and civil rights—Aretha's voice echoed from East to West. She devoted much of her time and energy at this time to the work of Martin Luther King, not as a strident spokesperson, but as a woman who knew the difference between right and wrong and simply wanted to represent, and do what was best. She acted purely, out of the simplest expressions of her faith.

"It was neither my intention nor my plan, but some were saying that in my voice they heard the sound of confidence and self-assurance; they heard the proud history of a people who had been struggling for centuries. I took these compliments to heart and felt deeply humbled and honored by them" (Franklin and Ritz, p. 113).

The widespread acceptance twisted her life in many different ways. As the demands on her time increased, her relationship with Ted White continued to spiral downward, ultimately ending in divorce. She had a new and exciting career, but no real support system. The stimulation, and wholesale changes in her life weighed heavily on her and she responded by retreating. She became sulky and unpredictable. She'd often not report to the studio until hours after her expected arrival. Some days she'd disappear completely.

Wexler recalls Aretha this way: "I call Aretha 'Our Lady of Mysterious Sorrows.' Her eyes were incredible luminous eyes covering inexplicable pain. Her depressions could be as deep as the dark sea. I don't pretend to know the sources of her anguish, but anguish surrounds Aretha as surely as the aura of her musical genius" (Wexler, p. 17).

Wexler and Franklin made 14 albums in eight years, and during that time, he said, she never hit a sour note, and never showed a second of self-doubt. Wexler provided the framework within which Aretha did her very best work.

Her third album, *Lady Soul*, released in 1968, became her true masterpiece. Strengthened by a powerful song list that included "Chain of Fools," "(You Make Me Feel Like a) Natural Woman," Aretha's own "Since You've Been Gone (Sweet Sweet Baby)," sister Carolyn's "Ain't No Way," and covers from Curtis Mayfield, Ray Charles, and James Brown, the recording became as an instant classic. It didn't hurt that in addition to the Muscle Shoals rhythm section, Wexler recruited the services of soul singer Bobby Womack and guitarist Eric Clapton. In June 1968, based on her accomplishments at Atlantic, *Time* magazine chose her as a cover subject, a rarity for a musical artist. Her presence on the cover announced the mainstreaming of R&B, the second musical art form (along with the blues) to receive such status.

In 1969, Aretha and Wexler decided to change things up. They put her in front of a jazzy big band, featuring Fathead Newman, Ray Charles's former sax man. Along with the support of the Muscle Shoals band, Aretha enjoyed the accompaniment of jazz greats like Kenny Burrell and Ron Carter. The album was a quiet smash, that is, one without commercial radio hits, and is now considered one of Aretha's artistic apexes.

She also married a man named Ken Cunningham, a tall, handsome executive she met in Miami. At the time, Cunningham was representing a group of young, black entrepreneurs and wanted Aretha to invest in his company. They met and clicked. She nicknamed him "Wolf." Together, they accepted each other's children, and were true to the relationship, at least for a while. Aretha's sexual appetite interfered periodically, mainly in trysts with Dennis Edwards, a member of the Temptations, and another liaison she indulged in with some regularity, a high-profile celebrity she refers to only as Mr. Mystique. Despite the occasional transgression on her part, Wolf and Aretha grew steadily stronger. Aretha continued to develop as an artist, and she began to appreciate the closeness that Wolf provided.

That stability helped Aretha remain on strong footing while she evolved musically. At the end of the soul era in the late 1960s, her music gained a harder, funkier, more danceable edge. Sly Stone, Curtis Mayfield, and James Brown all grew in stature, making funk the new breed of soul. Fortunately, Aretha wasn't far behind. She'd always been able to sing with toughness, just as the best of the R&B singers, Wilson Pickett, Otis Redding, could.

Soon, singles began ebbing in importance, and the concept of the full-length album rose. At Motown, that meant acts like the Supremes and Smokey Robinson would give way to Marvin Gaye and work like *What's Going On?* Sly and the Family Stone made *There's a Riot Goin' On* and Curtis Mayfield issued *Curtis*. These album-length statements, musical experiences made to be heard in their entirety, stood in stark contrast to the two- and three-minute pop songs. Aretha could play that game as well.

In 1971 she released *Live at Fillmore West*, one of her best-loved recordings and a fine example of a classic Aretha performance. At first, she hesitated to play the venue. It was located in San Francisco, in the middle of a white-dominant hippie enclave. But a few years earlier, Otis Redding played the same place and received an outstanding reception from the audience. Aretha took her best shot.

"It was a night to remember. Whatever the capacity of the hall, three times that number were there. They stood toe to toe, wall to wall. The place was so packed it might have been scary were it not for the warm and accepting vibe. The flower children embraced me with gusto" (Franklin and Ritz, p. 138). It helped to have none other than Ray Charles join Aretha on stage for a version of "Spirit in the Dark."

At this point, Aretha had grown comfortable not only with herself but with her team, her studio comrades, and supporting musicians. Arif Mardin, her arranger/producer, Tom Dowd, her engineer, and musicians like Cornell Dupree, Donny Hathaway, Bernard Purdie, and Chuck Rainey formed the nucleus of her stellar musical organization.

In 1972, Aretha switched gears by going back to the church and making a gospel record. But not just any gospel record . . . *Amazing Grace* would become Aretha's most acclaimed gospel work and is considered *the* gospel record of the 1970s. Buoyed by confidence, powered by her incredible commercial success and the knowledge that she had the assurance of her fans, the album includes some of Aretha's best vocal work. Intense and spontaneous, it soars with the majesty that great gospel deserves. "With all due reverence to the Almighty, I don't think it would be an overstatement to claim that if God were a female soul singer, She'd possess a voice not unlike that of Aretha Franklin" (Reggie Collins, *Amazing Grace*, liner notes, Rhino/Atlantic, 1999, p. 2).

From here, there was a gradual tapering of Aretha's output. In 1973, the questionable *Hey Now Hey* featured one of Carolyn's very best ballads, "Angel," a high-water mark for her as a songwriter. But much of the rest of the album, produced by Quincy Jones, seemed intent on changing with the times and those times were inching toward disco and dance. In 1974, she released the hot and cold *With Everything I Feel in Me*, a set featuring her classic "Without Love," also written by her sister Carolyn along with Ivy Joe Hunter.

DISCO FEVER

During the disco craze, veteran R&B acts like Aretha suffered. Radio programmers, eager to appeal to a younger audience, went with all the new music coming out at the time, and left the rest, even the legends, behind. Aretha herself could have sung disco had she been inclined. But she avoided trend-hopping and remained as true to herself as she could without sounding dated. In the short term, her obstinacy in the face of changing times prompted her sales to slump. But they'd rebound soon enough.

In the late 1970s, after a down period, Aretha made two albums that jump-started her commercial and creative comeback, both with producer Curtis Mayfield. Mayfield, originally with the Impressions and then as a highly regarded solo act, had experienced one of the most impressive careers in R&B and soul. He had occupied himself through the 1970s serving as the chief musical architect of the blaxploitation sound on film scores like *Superfly*. Aretha dug his "sweet funk" sound and considered their collaborations one of the highlights of her career.

The late 1970s posed commercial as well as personal problems for Aretha. She moved to Los Angeles and separated permanently from Wolf, who remained in New York City. Her husband had encountered difficulties with Aretha's brother Cecil, who was also working in Aretha's business arena. They squabbled over business decisions, a conflict that trapped Aretha in the middle of two family members.

The freedom also allowed her some time to herself, which she appreciated, for the short time it lasted. It came as a surprise to meet a man, Glynn Turman, a film actor she admired. They began a courtship and ultimately pooled their families, seven children in all. They were married in April 1978, in the New Bethel Baptist Church.

THE FINAL CHAPTERS

After 10 years at Atlantic, Aretha felt it was time for a change. Sales had tapered, falling consistently short of gold, and the singer thought that perhaps the label wasn't being as innovative as they could have been in marketing her image and keeping her current. This discord forced Aretha to make the difficult decision to switch over to Arista Records, led by Clive Davis, one of the most successful record executives in the history of the business and the man behind many of pop music's biggest stars, including Barry Manilow, Janis Joplin, and Earth, Wind and Fire.

The change was one of many traumatic moments Aretha confronted at the end of the 1970s and throughout the 1980s. In June 1979, Aretha's father, the Reverend Franklin, was shot and killed in a robbery at his home. He lapsed into a light coma—one not involving life support—for five years, during which time they were never again able to communicate with him. His struggle and eventual death devastated the Franklins, and the entire spiritual, musical, and political communities.

But the show for Aretha went on. She entered the studio for her first Arista album, *Aretha*, in 1980, producer/arranger Arif Mardin, her longtime Atlantic collaborator at her side. She also recruited Cornell Dupree and Fathead Newman. Their presence calmed her and brought her back to the glory days of her prime soul era. The album came out to a warm reception.

After a tour of England, in which she sang for British Royalty, she hurried home to build on the momentum established by her first Arista release. Co-produced by Mardin and Aretha, *Love All the Hurt Away* hinged on a beautiful duet with George Benson.

Through the rest of the decade, Aretha managed to stay afloat. She did some charity work by sponsoring a formal ball and inviting her elite celebrity friends. She was honored with a star on the Hollywood Walk of Fame, and made a hit record, "Jump to It," with Luther Vandross.

At home, Aretha and Glynn's marriage grew rocky. He traveled almost as often as she did, so they were rarely together. They agreed to separate, and eventually divorce. They had signed a prenuptial agreement, so the split came quickly and easily. Glynn moved outside of Los Angeles, where he set up a ranch for underprivileged children. Aretha moved back to Detroit, the city of her childhood, and the only place she'd ever truly called home. Besides, her father, still convalescing at the house, needed her care.

In 1984 at 69, the Reverend died, his family and friends watching over him, as they had been for five years. That same year, Aretha's close friends, unparalleled soul singer Jackie Wilson and close friend and Detroit native Marvin Gaye also died. They had both played important roles in Aretha's life and she took the news of their deaths particularly hard.

After taking some time off, Aretha enlisted Narada Michael Walden, a talent she discovered via her enjoyment of soul recording artist Stacy Lattisaw, to make her next record. Titled *Who's Zoomin' Who?* the record featured star turns by the Eurythmics and E Street Band saxman Clarence Clemons, on "Freeway of Love." The tune became a smash in both R&B and pop; Aretha even made her first video for it.

A follow-up to that album, also titled *Aretha*, boasted a portrait of the singer done by Andy Warhol, not to mention a hit duet with George Michael and a few collaborations with Mick Jagger and Keith Richards of the Rolling Stones. In 1987, 15 years after recording her gospel comeback *Amazing Grace* Aretha returned to the idiom with *One Lord, One Faith, One Baptism*. That same year, Aretha was bestowed with the honor of being the first woman inducted into the Rock and Roll Hall of Fame.

She followed the gospel album with another secular work, this one saturated with stars. The highlight, a duet with James Brown, got most of the attention. But Aretha also partenered with Elton John, Whitney Houston, and the Four Tops' Levi Stubbs.

Family matters again played a critical role in her life at this point. Both her brother Cecil, now a reverend like his father, and younger sister Carolyn contracted cancer and in both cases the disease proved fatal. Carolyn died of breast cancer in 1988, and Cecil, diagnosed with lung cancer, died the next year. To make matters worse, still hurting from the death of her siblings, her grandmother, affectionately known as Big Mama, the woman who took such good care of Aretha's boys while she was on the road throughout her career, passed away as well in 1990.

Throughout the mid- to late 1990s, Aretha began to receive the honors a career artist of her caliber deserved. She sang in the Clinton White House. She was the youngest artist to receive the prestigious Kennedy Center Award. In 1994, she released her *Greatest Hits* set representing her Arista years, which had begun in 1980. The album included a couple of bonus tracks of note, one with Kenneth "Babyface" Edmonds and another with the C+C Music Factory.

During the spring of that year, the Grammys honored Aretha with a Lifetime Achievement Award. Lauryn Hill of the Fugees wrote "A Rose Is Still a Rose" for Aretha. She liked the song, a message of empowerment for all women, so much that she and Clive chose to use the name as the title of her 1998 album. The next year, Aretha became the ultimate diva, thanks to VH-1's presentation *Divas Live*. Aretha closed the show with a gospel number, "I've Got a Testimony," after a handful of other divas, Gloria Estefan, Mariah Carey, Celine Dion, and Shania Twain all sang. Months later, she even stood in at the last minute—that is, she had only 15 minutes to prepare—for an ailing Luciano Pavarotti to sing his signature aria, "Nessun Dorma," from Puccini's *Turandot*. The world was watching, as the performance was televised, and she aced it. Only Aretha could pull that off.

LEGACY

When the subject is woman singers in pop music, the first and last word is "Aretha." It is the one word, the one woman, who sums up the joy, pain, majesty, redemption, and triumph of soul music. Of course, there have been other women who've mattered in popular music in ways that Aretha has not. But in many respects, nearly all in fact, it is impossible to hear the sound of the female voice in pop without at least considering the work of Aretha Franklin.

As Aretha once learned from Mahalia Jackson and Clara Ward, so new generations learn from Aretha. She has established the eternal template for all talent—all the aspiring girls and women looking for a life in music—to follow. When they sing, they, inadvertently or not, pay homage to her life's work. We hear her voice in the prideful hip-hop of artists like Mary J. Blige. We catch glimpses of her 1970s presence in Erykah Badu's head wrap, and in the soulful vocal style of singers like Alicia Keys and Christina Aguilera.

Also, skilled as a pianist and songwriter, Aretha made an impact on popular music many ways. She cut the music that now loops continuously in the soundtrack of our lives. That is as big an honor as a recording artist can ever ask. Not that her career is over—she admits to having huge dreams still, including attending Juilliard and doing further charitable work. There are still people she'd love to work with, awards she'd love to win, and songs she'd love to sing.

Aretha's voice is the sound a woman's voice learns to make. It is the sound of growing up, the sound of your first heartache. It's the sound of a slamming door as one walks out on an unfaithful lover, or closing quietly as one enters the room to slip into something more comfortable. Her voice resonates with the joy of life, with the pain of death, with the promise of renewal. It is a template that will never be replaced.

SELECTED DISCOGRAPHY

I Never Loved a Man (The Way I Love You) (Atlantic/Rhino, 1967/1999)

Lady Soul (Atlantic/Rhino 1968/1999)

Aretha: Live at Fillmore West (Atlantic/Rhino 1971/2006)

Amazing Grace: The Complete Recordings (Atlantic/Rhino 1972/2006)

Queen of Soul: The Atlantic Recordings (Atlantic/Rhino, 1992)

FURTHER READINGS

Bego, Mark. *Aretha Franklin: The Queen of Soul*. New York: Da Capo, 2001.

Dobkin, Matt. *I Never Loved a Man the Way I Love You: Aretha Franklin, Respect, and the Making of a Soul Music Masterpiece*. New York: St. Martin's Griffin, 2006.

Franklin, Aretha and David Ritz. *Aretha: From These Roots*. New York: Villard, 1999.

Courtesy of Photofest.

Otis Redding

CROWN PRINCE OF SOUL

Even when Otis Redding was singing low-rent gigs in the deep wooded towns of Alabama, way back with the Pinetoppers, he'd say, "I'm gonna be a star. Just you wait." (Scott Freeman, *Otis!*, St. Martin's Griffin, 2001).

He was right, of course. But the irony surrounding his life and early death was that he'd just started coming into his own when he left this world. As an upstart, Otis knew nothing about the art of singing other than the raw sounds that came out of his throat. Then came that hunger to be famous.

This desire, this fire inside Otis, propelled him to the very front of the class of '1960s soul singers, which included some of the best voices in the history of popular music. His coarse and unrehearsed singing style featured power over finesse, passion over polish. What you heard was what you got, whether in concert, in the studio, or on record. What he lacked in technique, he made up for with immediacy. He'd win listeners over by sheer force. Rather than touch them with subtlety, he'd wallop them with a single line, over and over until those words took hold and a spell was cast.

Stax VP Al Bell called Otis "the true soul messenger." And because his artistry was built on emotion and pure instinct, he didn't labor in the studio. In fact, he was known to cut an entire album in just a couple of days, so as not to lose that immediacy and spontaneity.

"When I go into a studio to record a song," Otis told a U.K. journalist for *Melody Maker* in an undated interview, "I only have a title and maybe a first verse. The rest I make up as we're recording. We'll cut three or four times and I'll sing it different every time. We cut everything together, horns, rhythm and vocal, six songs in five hours." The spontaneity had a huge impact on popular music. After listening to Otis's impromptu approach Aretha Franklin and Wilson Pickett took advantage of the Stax recording style to capture the same sound, as did white rock bands like the Allman Brothers and the Rolling Stones. Everybody was looking to achieve that Southern soul vibe.

One of Otis's grand ambitions was to fill the void created by the death of Sam Cooke in 1964. Stylistically, he was a long way from the suave tones of Cooke, but at least it prompted Otis to temper his growl occasionally and color his singing with subtler hues. He could be gentle, and he did share a sensitivity with Cooke that many urban soul singers never bothered to attempt.

Otis began his singing career infatuated with Little Richard, an artist he had the good fortune of watching as a child. Little Richard also hailed from Macon, and was the talk of the town when Otis was growing up. Otis idolized him, and began singing and performing in a fashion that was almost identical to him. Once he shed his desire to be someone else, though, he came into his own.

That started when he began writing his own songs. His first song that made regional impact was "Shout Bamalama" in 1960, a pretty good Little Richard imitation. But his first composition out from under Little Richard's shadow, "These Arms of Mine," demonstrated how powerful Otis could be when he sank his teeth into something uniquely his own. It took two years, but the song finally grew into a hit and eventually sold 800,000 copies. It was not only the beginning of an incredible career for Otis, but it also marked the onset of the Memphis-based soul sound from the Stax studio. With its mix of gospel, punchy R&B instrumental acts like Booker T and the MG's and the Mar-Keys, it opened the door for a flood of classic soul acts including Sam and Dave, Carla Thomas, Arthur Conley, and others.

More than any other soul singer of his generation, Otis was all about the voice. While he didn't start with gospel, he still communicated the passionate spirituality of the genre and translated it into an emotion that reached vast audiences. Because he projected an Everyman kind of vibe, and a rare vulnerability, Otis was a born entertainer, with an easy demeanor and the ability to communicate with crowds easily. White and black audiences alike responded to his act in ways that more rigidly defined singers like Wilson Pickett and James Brown did not.

Unfortunately, tragedy prevented Otis from seeing through his evolution as a talent and from fully embracing his potential. Nor did he see his first number one recording, "Dock of the Bay," reach the top of the charts. Released in 1966, the song captured the essence of his artistry better than any other. Written with Steve Cropper, a member of the Stax studio band, the song's mellow vibe and country flavor sounded like the first page in Otis's next chapter. Sadly, he would not see that chapter written. Today, we are only left to guess what size and shape his mainstream success would have taken. He died in December 1967, leaving a wife and four children behind, as well as an enormous, unfulfilled legacy.

The life of Otis Redding embraced all the paradoxes of his time in history. A black man from the South, his closest friends were white. He was a charismatic performer at the peak of his sex appeal, yet he took great care of and paid much attention to his wife and kids. Struggling to reach a significant level of success himself, he often took time out of his schedule to help other musicians in more desperate struggles than his own. As Steve Cropper told *Hit Parader* (August 1968): "My original feeling for Otis wound up to be my final feeling, he was a pure man. His love for people showed in his songs. He was always trying to get back to his baby—or he missed her, she was the greatest thing in the world. His approach was always positive."

THE EARLY YEARS

One of six children, Otis grew up in a traditional, working-class household in Macon, Georgia. He was born in Dawson, Georgia, but moved to Macon in 1942, when he was three. He bounced around a couple of housing projects, including one called Belleview, also known as "Hellview" to its residents.

His father, a part-time preacher and gospel singer, began his working life as a sharecropper, then moved on to more conventional work at Robins Air Force Base, one of the area's main employers. But Otis Sr.'s health was precarious; he was sick with tuberculosis for much of Otis's childhood. The rest of the family—a younger brother and four older sisters—coped the best they could. His mother Fannie worked as a housekeeper.

As a family, the Redding girls were mild, well mannered, and respectful. Otis, though, was on the wild side. He was fidgety and adventurous, and gave his parents, simple, old-fashioned folks, a lot to worry about. He was also athletic—over six feet tall and 215 pounds—with a lean frame and a great deal of agility. He and the kids in the project would have daily games of tackle football, an exercise in toughness that helped Otis later deal with the grueling routine of nightly performances and endless touring.

When he wasn't hustling around the ball fields, Otis loved to sing. He loved the sound of his voice, and he used it all the time. He was never quiet. When he wasn't talking, he'd be singing. But he also loved rhythm. At 10, he had picked up the habit of banging on things with his hands, pounding out rhythms to whatever music happened to be playing. He eventually began to play the drums as well as sing behind his church's gospel choir. In seventh grade, he entered a talent show to both sing and play a drum solo.

In 10th grade, the 15-year old Otis had grown tired of watching his family struggle financially. His father was in the hospital more than at home and making ends meet became more and more difficult. He felt it was his responsibility to get his family through its financial crisis, so he quit school and got a job. Initially, he found work drilling wells in the area. From there, he bounced from job to job, delivering groceries and working construction. Often, he quit these jobs as quickly as he obtained them, sometimes within a single day. He never liked working. Having to be accountable to others made him irritable.

Throughout his laborious trials, he never stopped singing. He loved his music; it was his lifeline. At night, after a long day of work, he'd sneak out his window and head to the Hillview Springs Social Club to hear live music. Music played a big role in daily life, especially in downtown Macon along Broadway, which was lined with thriving live music clubs. Otis's favorite musician at the time was another Macon act, by the name of Little Richard. When Otis was 12, Little Richard's career was in full swing; the Macon community considered his shows "can't-miss" events. At the same time, James Brown, still another artist who called Macon home, was on a similar trajectory.

Otis's first brush with fame came very early. Someone from the Upsetters, Little Richard's band, heard him sing at one of the talent shows he competed in, and extended an invitation to Otis to accompany them on the road. The boy jumped at the chance.

Unfortunately, it was too much too soon; it didn't take long to see that Otis was in over his head. He had no idea what life was like on the road and the experience overwhelmed him. He failed to captivate his audiences, and he suffered from a poor vocal technique and an awkward sense of rhythm. He returned home after a few months and went back to roofing.

At the time, a local club was hosting a weekly talent show called "The Teenage Party," and winning became Otis's obsession. He worked at his singing technique, and after studying enough performances, recruited some of his roofing buddies to form a band. Eventually, Otis felt confident enough to enter the club's contests.

His debut appearance failed, for the same reasons his work with the Upsetters fell short. His timing was poor, he sang out of key, and his notes were out of place. A guitarist named Johnny Jenkins, saw him perform that night and approached him later. Jenkins had played with some of the bigger acts around

Macon and he had a stellar reputation of being a showman destined for stardom. Jenkins witnessed Redding's struggles and offered to help. They agreed that Otis should attend one of Johnny's next gigs, which he did. He even got up to sing a Little Richard tune that night. A relationship developed and the two began playing together.

Jenkins saw that Otis had potential; he just needed proper accompaniment. "You can take a man that can't sing and if you put the right kind of music behind him," said Johnny, "he'll sound good" (Freeman, 2001, p. 29). Jenkins enhanced Redding's stage presentation. He was a handsome, flamboyant performer who played guitar with great skill. Many credit Jenkins's wild antics— playing fast, behind his head, behind his back, with his teeth—for inspiring Jimi Hendrix. At the time, Hendrix was frequently around Macon playing guitar in James Brown's band, the Famous Flames, and it's not a stretch to assume that Hendrix would have seen Jenkins play on numerous occasions.

With Jenkins's able support, Otis began picking up the rudiments of singing: tempo, key, phrasing, and performance. With persistence, and a few more tries at it, Otis ended up winning the talent contest, not once, but a staggering 15 weeks in a row. His streak ended when the club barred him from entering it again.

During that streak Otis was winning with the Little Richard tune "Heebie Jeebies." It was his bread and butter song. Otis's act became synonymous with Little Richard, or at least an imitation of him. He didn't yet have an identity of his own.

But, Otis didn't see his stylistic limitation as an impediment. After his incredible run of talent show victories, he'd become something of a celebrity in Macon. Only 17, he had girls hanging on him and enough friends so that he'd be with someone wherever and whenever he went. Friends, girls, a little cash, a big reputation . . . to Otis, these were the fringe benefits of stardom, and what little success he'd seen only made him hungry for more. He moved from talent show venues to more legitimate clubs. Otis would tell anyone who'd listen how famous he'd become.

In a short time, he received an invitation to replace Little Willie Jones as the frontman in Pat Teacake's Band, an act that also featured Johnny Jenkins. "When he'd get to singing, he'd put his whole heart into it," said Jenkins. "He didn't just sing to be singing a song. With Otis it was real. You could hear it in every word" (Freeman, p. 51).

Otis explained his style to an uncredited journalist in 1967.

I watch people when I sing. If they're stompin' their foot or snappin' their fingers, then I know I got something. But if they don't move, then you don't have anything. Five years from now, I know the kids are going to be tired of my singing. If I can keep a good mind with the help of the good Lord, I'm gonna keep producing records. You can't have anything else on your mind but the music business. When I go into the studio, I'm strictly for business. I can go in there any time of the day and cut six songs if I want to. I don't like any fooling around in the studio. (*Hit Parader*, August 1967)

Still, his father's worst nightmares were coming true as he began to lose control of his first-born son to the worldly temptations of downtown Macon.

EARLY CAREER

Fronting Pat Teacake's band, Otis began touring again, mainly the Chitlin' Circuit of the South. Of course, the Chitlin' Circuit wasn't a circuit at all, but rather a ramshackle network of juke joints in each town's ghetto that featured lots of fast women and alcohol. Again, the routine was grueling and not exactly lucrative. Johnny Jenkins would be the first to leave Pat Teacake to form his own band, the Pinetoppers, and he brought Otis right along with him. Then came a big break.

His name was Phil Walden.

Jenkins met Walden on the Macon club circuit. Phil, a white college kid, born in Greenville, South Carolina, and relocated to Macon, dared attend black shows around Macon, often the only white face in a sea of African Americans. Unlike many Southern whites, Walden didn't patronize blacks. At the time, around 1960, segregation was in full sway, especially around Macon. But Walden didn't buy into it.

At the time, African Americans were beginning to galvanize, making Walden's journey into the world of race music somewhat risky. Rosa Parks had made an impact in Montgomery, and a young Baptist preacher named Martin Luther King Jr. was beginning to get word out as well. Episodes of the population demanding civil rights grew more vocal and vociferous. Both sides of the frisson were on edge. But Walden and Redding would eventually meet to bridge this great divide with grace and class.

One night Walden stepped into a Little Richard show; he was the opening act for the more reknowned Amos Milburn, a popular pianist at the time. Walden would come away lukewarm regarding Milburn, but Little Richard had set the place on fire. He had just written "Tutti Frutti," and his performance of it had driven Walden crazy.

With his ear to the ground around Macon, Walden had witnessed the rise of "race music," and rhythm and blues. Not only did he enjoy it, he thought of ways to take advantage. One way to cash in was to open a booking agency.

Phil Walden and Associates, his first company, was Phil Walden on his own. He'd answer the phone in a falsetto voice, and pretend to transfer it to another extension, which he'd pick up and use his normal speaking voice. He also accumulated standard publicity photos, and taped "Phil Walden and Associates" stickers on them, to give the impression to people that he was working with many clients. The illusion held that Walden was a young and successful businessman, and anybody coming into his office would see it firsthand.

He had been booking Pat Teacake and a few others, when Johnny Jenkins was with them. So when Jenkins moved to form his own band, the Pinetoppers with Otis Redding, Walden got that booking business as well. At the time, everyone thought Jenkins was the real star of the band. His guitar antics were entertaining and his look dashing. Little did Walden know that he'd be starting a lifelong friendship and business relationship with Redding as well. When the Pinetoppers debuted in 1959, Redding dazzled Walden. Backstage after the show, they shook hands and struck up a friendship.

Another friendship that would help advance Otis's career occurred when he met Bobby Smith, a young, white upstart businessman with a small office in downtown Macon. Ostensibly, Smith ran a record label, Confederate Records, and was interested in the music Otis played. Otis ran through a version of "Shout Bamalama," his first real composition and a spot-on imitation of Little Richard. Despite its obvious derivation, Smith showed some excitement, and a willingness to print up the song. He only had a single artist on his label, a white kid named Wayne Cochran who was a popular rock and roll singer in the outlying areas of Macon.

Eventually, Cochran would take on bass duties for the Pinetoppers; Smith changed the name of his label when he took on Otis's song. "Confederate" wouldn't wash in the Macon clubs—and together they began going places.

With his modicum of clout, Cochran helped the Pinetoppers get into clubs normally closed to R&B acts. Together they visited rural radio stations, pushing "Shout Bamalama," the Pinetoppers, and Cochran's band the Rockin' Capris. They'd fill places with both white and black audiences, and succeeded in blurring the racist lines in Macon's music community.

"THESE ARMS OF MINE"

At 19, Otis fell in love with Zelma Atwood, a girl he had met originally at one of the Teenage Party shows in Macon. She was a canny woman and a fast learner, and when she denied Redding's initial advances, it made him that much more curious. Within weeks of his conquest, she was pregnant and Otis made a commitment to marriage. They had their first child, a son named Dexter, in the summer of 1960. They were married one year later, in August 1961, just two weeks before Otis turned 21.

Once he made the decision to begin sounding like someone other than Little Richard, Otis was always writing music. Following the near-success of "Shout Bamalama," he presented Bobby Smith with another of his songs, "These Arms of Mine."

About the same time, Phil Walden, still unprepared to act on the talent of Otis Redding, was peddling Johnny Jenkins to record companies. Joe Galkin, the southeastern representative of Atlantic Records, heard about Jenkins and proposed an idea: send Johnny Jenkins to Memphis's Stax studio to record. The label had recently signed a deal with Atlantic and they had an up-and-coming instrumental R&B act Booker T and the MGs that came highly recommended. Jenkins and Otis packed up and headed to Memphis.

Jenkins's song, "Love Twist," would be the focus track. Jerry Wexler heard Galkin's proposal and liked the idea as well as the song. Galkin wanted $2,000 from Atlantic for the rights to Jenkins, even though Jenkins wasn't Galkin's to sell. Bobby Smith had the rights to Jenkins, and so began a lengthy controversy.

Yet beyond the friction created by Galkin, the real story occurred before the conflict, when Jenkins hit Memphis. Otis had driven Jenkins to the gig, with the intention of simply standing by and watching, helping when he could. He carried Johnny's equipment into Stax and sat around while Jenkins and Booker T worked out the arrangement to "Love Twist."

Here's where the legend grows a little fuzzy. The original story goes that Jenkins finished early and the band had a little time for Otis, who had waited patiently for Jenkins all day. Otis took advantage. He first sang an up-tempo thing called "Hey Hey Baby," but it didn't create much excitement. Then, at the urging of Galkin, he sang his new ballad, "These Arms of Mine." Jenkins played guitar, while studio guitarist Steve Cropper played piano; Booker T had punched out for the day.

"Everybody was fixin' to go home," said studio chief Jim Stewart. "But Joe Galkin insisted we give Otis a listen. There was something different about [the ballad]. He really poured his soul into it" (Freeman, p. 77).

"The original idea was for Otis and Johnny to go out as a duo," writes Peter Guralnick, "with Otis providing the singing and Johnny the spectacular effects." (Peter Guralnick, *Sweet Soul Music: Rhythm and Blues and the Southern Dream of Freedom*, New York: Harper Collins, 1986, p. 147). The problem was, it was widely known that Johnny wouldn't travel. He had a fear of flying, and so wrote his own ticket to forever remaining a local act. (Of course, there is the irony of Otis's impending death which confirmed Jenkins's worst fear.)

This, of course, led to bitterness. Especially after Jenkins witnessed Otis's incredible rise in the soul music pantheon, the guitarist receded into the shadows of paranoia. One of his stories involved Galkin bringing Jenkins into the studio for hours simply to provide a guitar template for Stax upstart guitar player Steve Cropper. They recorded Jenkins for hours, Jenkins growled, and then they went back and analyzed his style in detail, to imitate it.

Many say that the talented guitar player's career essentially stopped on that day in the studio in 1962. He'd continue on the Southern frat circuit for many years, and worked steadily with Phil Walden, but he never took his career to the next level. He made a record, *Ton Ton Macoute*, during his prime in 1970. Twenty-five years later, he produced a "follow-up," *Blessed Blues*.

Jim Stewart was unsure about Otis at first, but credits Galkin for pushing the envelope. "Joe promoted Otis day and night. Otis Redding was his life. He certainly saw more than I did initially in Otis" (Jim Stewart, *Otis!* liner notes, p. 8). Stewart admits he began warming up to Otis after his third single, "I've Been Loving You Too Long." But it was Galkin who deserves the credit for Redding's stardom. "He would walk into a station and tell the guy that if he wasn't playing the Otis record, then he'd go back to the DJ booth and take out every Atlantic record [and say], 'If you're not playing Otis Redding, then give me all my records!]" (Stewart, p. 9).

But because Stewart and Stax were unsure about Otis from the outset, Galkin and Atlantic sweetened the deal for the label, promising Stax 50 percent of the publishing royalties on Otis's first single, "Hey, Hey Baby" backed with "These Arms of Mine." The deal-making worked. Galkin's push vaulted Redding over Jenkins and obviated any chance for Jenkins's Pinetoppers work to earn attention. Stax would now focus on Otis Redding, their up-and-coming star. In return, Redding would help to define the Stax sound as well. As an arranger, producer, and artist, Otis brought the label a different feel than they'd had in the past, especially when he was backed by the explosive MGs.

Stax Records: "Soulsville, U.S.A."

No one can say for certain just when "rhythm and blues" became "soul." By about 1960, the word "soul" was frequently used in the lexicon of African American music: in 1958, for example, Ray Charles and jazz vibraphonist Milt Jackson released an album titled *Soul Brothers*. Nor is it easy to describe the musical elements that differentiate soul music from earlier styles of R&B. James Brown's hard-hitting, syncopated rhythms marked one evolutionary change; so did Jerry Butler's deep, gospel-infused lead vocal with the Impressions on their 1958 ballad hit, "For Your Precious Love."

Once soul music took hold, small and large record companies in urban centers across the nation began pumping out countless records in the new style. In 1959, Jim Stewart and his older sister Estelle Axton created Stax Records (initially as Satellite Records) in Memphis, Tennessee.

Unusually for its time and place, Stax Records was an integrated operation. Its white partners built their offices and recording studio in a converted movie theater in the heart of Memphis's black community. The artist roster was virtually all black, but Booker T and the MGs—the house rhythm section that played on most of the label's greatest hits—were comprised of two black musicians (drummer Al Jackson Jr., keyboards player Booker T. Jones) and two white ones (guitarist Steve Cropper, bassist Donald "Duck" Dunn). Black producer/songwriters like Isaac Hayes and David Porter worked alongside the white recording engineer Ron Capone.

In 1959, Rufus and Carla Thomas provided the fledgling company with its first national hit, "'Cause I Love You." For Rufus Thomas, this was his second career on a pioneering Memphis label: his song "Bear Cat" (1953) had been the first significant hit on Sun Records. In 1970–1971, "Do the Funky Chicken" and "The Breakdown" were Top Five R&B hits for the man known as "The World's Oldest Teenager." Rufus's daughter Carla became the label's most popular female artist with such songs as "B-A-B-Y" and "I Like What You're Doing to Me." In 1967, she recorded a humorous, funky duet called "Tramp" with a singer from Macon whose music epitomized the Stax sound: Otis Redding.

Redding was a classic "down home" soul singer whose gritty voice sounded older than his years, especially on pleading ballads like "I've Been Loving You Too Long." He sang with a pronounced Southern accent, punctuating the lyrics with trademark phrases like "GOT-ta, GOT-ta" and "my-my-my." Otis wrote or co-wrote many of his best-known songs, including "Respect" (later a career-making hit for Aretha Franklin) and "Pain in My Heart" (which was covered by the Rolling Stones). His galvanizing performance at the Monterey Pop Festival in June 1967 was captured in the documentary film *Monterey Pop*.

Otis Redding died at age 26 in a plane crash in Madison, Wisconsin on December 10, 1967, soon after recording an unusual new song. With its prominent acoustic guitar and surf sound effects, "(Sittin' on) the Dock of the Bay" was a striking but wholly natural departure from Redding's usual hard-charging style. Released posthumously, it became his first and only number one hit (on both the Pop and R&B charts) and won two Grammy Awards.

After Otis Redding's death, soul-blues man Johnnie Taylor brought Stax back to the top of the charts in 1968 with "Who's Making Love" (number one R&B/number five Pop). The Staples Singers' blend of social consciousness and gospel fervor on "I'll Take You There" and "Respect Yourself" made them one of the most popular R&B groups of the early 1970s.

"I've Been Loving You Too Long," written with Jerry Butler, hit the Top 10 and its success instilled everyone with confidence. Phil Walden, Joe Galkin, the executives and other bands at Stax, all now had financial stability on the horizon, and a focal point for their efforts. Otis's soul was beginning to take shape and his world began to expand in a vast way.

He began touring extensively, and found himself in the company of many of the men who originally influenced his vocal style. He met and worked with artists like Solomon Burke, Jerry Butler, Joe Tex—all revolutionary singers in the soul idiom, and all artists who had an effect on Otis's own voice.

In 1963, Stax decided to release Otis's first album, *Pain in My Heart*. Though singles were by far the biggest money makers—thanks to the popularity of jukeboxes and AM radio—Jim Stewart felt like Otis had enough material to fill an LP. He did, but barely. The singles released to this point were on the record, as was a cover of Little Richard's "Lucille." But the song that made the most impact would become his next big hit.

"Security," credited to Otis, represented a departure for the singer. To this point, he had become best known for his ballads, yet this song was a burner. But it wasn't in the Little Richard rave-up style. Rather Otis began developing his own rockin' attitude, characterized by a mesmerizing power. When he kicked into this gear, Otis became a force of nature.

The follow-up songs to "Security" were more of the same pleading ballads, which made the ladies happy. It got to the point where the women, intoxicated by Otis's well-cut figure and romantic voice, would swoon. One night in North Carolina, a jealous boyfriend, angered at the fawning reaction his date had to Otis's singing, charged the stage and sucker punched Otis while he had his eyes closed finishing a tune. Otis put the microphone down, and calmly walked off the stage. He found the perpetrator and beat him senseless. He did, after all, grow up in a fightin' neighborhood where that kind of unprovoked action was punished severely.

Because of all the lovesick ballads he sang, radio DJs began referring to him as "Mr. Pitiful." The unsolicited nickname became a blessing for Otis when Steve Cropper came up with an idea for a song. It would have the same name, "Mr. Pitiful," but it would be a barnstormer, full of energy and sarcasm. Cropper and Redding wrote the song in one 10-minute drive to the studio, and from this point on these kinds of soulful tour de forces would displace his balladry as his signature. Unlike "Security," or any other single he'd recorded so far, the song stuck immediately to both the R&B and the pop charts. The single's B-side, "That's How Strong My Love Is," became a hit as well. Otis and Stax had finally enjoyed the breakthrough they'd been anticipating.

The next big impact Otis made came in early 1965 when he had a chance encounter with Jerry Butler, a classy and talented Chicago soul singer with close ties to Curtis Mayfield and the Impressions. The two stars met in a first-class lounge at the Atlanta airport and, after getting caught up on things, set to writing. Jerry had the seeds of a song, and the two threw some ideas on to it. Otis, convinced of its potential and encouraged by Butler, took it home and worked it up in his own way. "I've Been Loving You Too Long" was the result, and it would become Otis's biggest crossover hit and one of the greatest ballads of the soul era.

His success on the soul scene had a positive financial impact on Otis. He bought a home on the outskirts of Macon and a car for Zelma to go along with the Cadillac he drove himself. After a few of his hits, he managed to make enough money to move his parents out of the projects—a gesture that made his father eat his words about Otis being a thorn in his side. His press releases would boast of his expanded wardrobe and shoe collection. When his success grew, he and Zelma moved to a 270-acre ranch in the Georgia countryside. He called it the "Big O Ranch."

To take advantage of the airplay and chart success, Otis toured constantly. He toured every venue he could, from frat houses to theaters. Thanks to Phil Walden, who'd been to the army and back, he secured a handful of "cattle call" tours, where a half-dozen or so performers would travel together from place to place, play a few songs to a packed house, and then rush to the next stop.

In those days, traveling was perilous, especially for a young black performer in the South. Martin Luther King Jr. had just begun captivating the imagination of Americans, and a racist backlash had overcome the Southern states. These gifted artists saturated the region with nice cars, fashionable clothes, and pretty girls on their arms. That image didn't wash with the racist-minded folks in Georgia and Alabama.

Otis's situation was exacerbated by the fact that he played with the MGs, which included two white men—Cropper, and bassist Duck Dunn. Hornman Wayne Jackson was also white. Every few miles, in Mississippi for example, the band would get pulled over and searched. Otis would have to order his meal at a different window than Cropper and Dunn. Ironically, the racism worked in reverse too. When Otis played black clubs in the area, his white bandmates were accepted only begrudgingly, and Otis had to work twice as hard to win over his audience.

While his non-stop touring proved profitable, Otis and his label folks had a hard time setting studio time aside for a new album. Finally, in the summer of 1965, they pinched three days off the schedule and hit the studio for a marathon recording session. Otis had only two new songs to record, but, as was the practice at the time, that's all he needed. Most albums were just glorified singles, with a couple of focus tunes and a bunch of filler. Not so with the new album. *Otis Blue: Otis Redding Sings Soul* would come to be known as one of the great recordings of the soul era.

Cut in a single day, *Otis Blue* captures the essence of Redding better than any of his work before or after. Released in September 1965, the album included Sam Cooke's "A Change Is Gonna Come," the Rolling Stones' "Satisfaction" (a record picked up by Cropper earlier that day that Otis had never heard), and a few other covers along with Otis's own "Respect" and "Ole Man Trouble." Split into an afternoon session and a very late night/early morning session (due to many of the musicians having 8 P.M. club gigs, much of the success came after midnight, when the creative juices were really flowing (and as their time together was running out).

Perhaps it was because he now had the confidence of a true superstar. Perhaps it was because his entire band, including the MGs and his horn section, known as the Mar-Keys, were also hitting their stride and defining their own legacy as well. Or perhaps it was because the material was largely loose and improvised, leaving the creativity to the very fertile minds present in the studio. Or maybe it was because the band had only one day to get their ideas down and recorded, resulting in a sense of desperation. Whatever the case, *Otis Blue* is majestic work.

The recording zoomed to the top of the R&B album chart, and remained on the pop charts for nearly nine months. In the first weeks of its release, it sold only about 50,000 copies, despite its long-standing chart presence.

But the album's statistics don't do justice to the tremendous impression it left on the landscape of popular music.

Atlantic Records hovered around the Stax studio waiting for the levee to break, waiting for a profitable act to turn up, and it at last began to happen with *Otis Blue*. Jerry Wexler of the label became aware of what was fast becoming "the Memphis Sound," and, at the same time, was growing tired of his New York City studio product controlled by Mike Leiber and Jerry Stoller. Yes, they too had enjoyed many great hits, largely with Northern pop and soul groups, but they had grown rote in style. Memphis was fresh, and Wexler was inclined to shift his focus southward.

His idea? Make the Stax studio more than just a label. He envisioned it as the Southern outpost of the Atlantic's R&B sound.

He brought Atlantic R&B artists to Stax to record, and began in earnest to develop the careers of icons like Wilson Pickett and Sam and Dave. There was reluctance at first. DJs were put off by the crude and raw nature of Southern soul. Unlike the super sophisticated Motown sound, it wasn't polite, polished, or euphemistic. The Stax grooves roared with sex and sexuality.

But Wexler encountered problems with Jim Stewart at Stax. It seemed that the Stax owner was averse to converting his studio recording equipment to a stereo version. At the time, stereo had begun replacing mono as the current vehicle, and Wexler's engineer, the soon-to-be legendary Tom Dowd, had become quite adept at capturing the new stereo sound. Still, Stewart was afraid that the transition to stereo would spoil the sound Stax had spent a great deal of effort establishing.

In the end, Stewart and Wexler compromised. Dowd would record in stereo, but use a technique that would allow Stewart to mix any record down in either mono or stereo. The compromise was equitable and for the next five years the two labels would set about altering and subsequently dominating the R&B landscape.

Stax's association with Atlantic helped the label gain exposure north of the Mason-Dixon line. Until that time, Southern R&B, and bands on the Chitlin' Circuit, were known as a kind of "country" music. DJs in the North refrained from playing Otis for a time. But Atlantic's cash infusion helped Stax reach further with their artists than they ever had before, and Otis Redding was their biggest priority.

That cash from Atlantic also proved to be dangerous. When Otis's first contract with Stax neared its close, rumors arose that Atlantic had offered Otis an additional $50,000 to sign with the label. That amount, substantially more than Stax could shake loose, seemed too attractive to pass up. But Otis, as honest in business as he was in life, promised Stewart and the label early on that he'd stay with them, and he honored that promise. He passed over the rumored advance and signed on with Stax for another five years.

From this point, the momentum only grew. The hits came more consistently, the money flowed, and with it Phil Walden began signing more hit acts, like Percy Sledge and Johnnie Taylor, Clarence Carter and Eddie Floyd. Stax did incredibly well. Together, Redding and Walden had designs on a company, something they drew up as Redwal Music. They sought to do business in music publishing, record production, and management. In fact, much like Stax was doing in Memphis, only in Macon.

One last hurdle remained. Otis had never truly crossed over to a white audience. Yes, some of his music appealed to whites and made it onto pop radio outlets in the North. But the saturation was spotty. Otis and Phil began an ambitious plan to reach the audience that had so far resisted Otis's musical entreaties.

It helped that the Beatles, in 1966, had sought out Otis, and professed to loving the music coming out of the Stax studio. This validated the bands, and emboldened Otis. Based partly on the Beatles' vote of confidence, Walden booked a three-night stand in Hollywood at the Whiskey A Go-Go. If they wanted to reach a more rock audience, Los Angeles was the obvious destination, and these Whiskey gigs were considered the most critical in Otis's career so far.

At the time, authentic, Southern R&B had not reached Los Angeles. Otis Redding would be one of the first. When the lights went up at the Whiskey and Otis kicked into gear with his 10-piece band, all the doubt and apprehension about whether R&B would go over out West were erased. The dates were packed and the performances memorable, even historic. They led to more mainstream exposure than he had ever received before. *The Los Angeles Times* fawned over his performances. Bob Dylan, in attendance at the Whiskey, sought Otis out after the show and handed him a copy of his new song, "Just Like a Woman."

"TRY A LITTLE TENDERNESS"

In the fall of 1966, Otis entered Stax again to make a record. Though in typical fashion he appeared with just a handful of scraps and a few complete songs, he set about doing what he did best: record on deadline, in a sort of quiet desperation. At the time, Otis needed a jolt to stay on top. Now that he had arrived, he had to work to keep his vaunted pole position. One song, a tune Sam Cooke famously covered called "Try a Little Tenderness," would provide Otis with just what he'd need to do so.

"Tenderness" was originally written in the 1930s, a ballad, and enjoyed interpretations by some of music's most important singers: Ella, Frank, and Bing to name a few. But thanks to a nifty arrangement by the MGs, Otis turned his version into one of his greatest vocal performances. It took three takes to nail it.

Everyone involved with the song knew it would be a hit. Phil Walden had the notion that he'd be able to get Otis on national television outlets to sing it.

And while that didn't happen, it would become the song that his fans most closely associate with the singer.

"If there's one song, one performance that really sort of sums up Otis and what he's about, it's 'Try a Little Tenderness,'" said Jim Stewart. That one performance is so special and so unique that it expresses who he is . . . If you want to wrap it up, just listen to [it]" (Stewart, p. 8).

Complete and Unbelievable: The Otis Redding Dictionary of Soul was the album that included the song, and though the tune was a hit, the album was not. Walden and his crew decided it was time to head overseas to London, in an attempt to seek out an audience that had already been receptive to the Beatles' own attempts at the Stax sound ("Drive My Car"). The Rolling Stones also championed American R&B, so many music fans in the United Kingdom were prepared to be impressed. A short, 10-day stint on the continent went over well for Otis, and he headed back for more work in the Western United States knowing he'd have an eager audience in Europe.

In December 1966, Billy Graham, a successful booking agent in the Bay Area, contacted Otis to play a three-night stand at the legendary Fillmore. The spectacular gigs astounded even a scene veteran like Graham. "By far Otis Redding was the single most extraordinary talent I had ever seen. There was no comparison. Then or now . . . That was the best gig I ever put on in my entire life" (Bill Graham, *Bill Graham Presents*).

After recording a duets album with Carla Thomas, another Stax artist, in the winter of 1967, Otis went back to Europe to headline the Stax/Volt revue, a cavalcade of the label's stars all backed by the MGs. The European press was excited and hyperbolic. The reception was incredible, the reviews adulatory. Bandmate Wayne Jackson felt like he was backing Elvis Presley. "We had guards along the stage who actually had to keep people off the stage. I mean, drag crying women away . . . They were crazed, their eyes were glassed over, and they were wanting to be involved with Otis so bad. Of course, he egged them on" (Freeman, p. 171).

The experience for the entire Stax/Volt revue was triumphant. For five weeks they were at the top of their game and the ecstatic reception matched their performances.

Out of that crazy maelstrom of acceptance came *Otis Redding: Live in Europe*. Bolstered by the publicity buzz and Otis's superstar status, the recording shot up to the Top 40 in the pop album category. Yet with the accolades came petty jealousies. In addition to the positive notices Otis received and the plethora of interview requests he got, animosity reared up in the Stax camp. The tour provided a good look at the contrast between the way Stax treated Otis Redding, the superstar, and the way the label treated the rest of its artists. Otis was the man, and the others on the tour simply his underlings.

Actually, that wasn't quite true. Steve Cropper, the Stax A&R man and, Otis's guitar player/arranger/songwriter, also received some of the spotlight, with interview requests and other attention. That would earn him some animosity as well, particularly from Al Bell, a Stax employee and musician who, at a late-night meeting while overseas, successfully removed Cropper from his post at the company.

LIVE AT MONTEREY

Even though the Stax/Volt Revue's U.K. odyssey had enjoyed more success than anyone anticipated, the pop crossover wasn't quite complete. "Try a Little Tenderness" and the wildly successful U.K. tour were important elements involved in Otis's ultimate ascent, but they didn't push him over the top. He was still in the shadows of Motown's incredible pop-soul domination and the rock scene, led by the Beatles and the Stones, left little room for Otis. Then came a booking at the Monterey Pop Festival and all that would change.

At the time, music festivals were just beginning to take hold. Newport and producer George Wien had revolutionized live music in both the jazz and folk idioms by featuring those styles exclusively in an outdoor, weekend-long setting. But Wien had purposely stayed away from pop music for fear of it getting out of control.

To fill the void, West Coast rock promoter Ben Shapiro took a stab at it. At the time, the San Francisco scene had exploded, seeped as it was in the hippie culture of the city's Haight-Ashbury district. At first the hippies were skeptical. They saw the festival as a capitalist enterprise and vowed not to accept it should it be staged. But after a little cajoling, and after handing over the production to one of their own, John Phillips of the Mamas and the Papas, along with his manager Lou Adler, the festival became more appealing. Bill Graham from the Fillmore pitched in $10,000. The Grateful Dead, who had been one of the voices of resistance, said they'd buy in if Paul McCartney and Mick Jagger could oversee the festival profits being directed toward charity. Bands like Jefferson Airplane, the Byrds, and Janis Joplin all committed, as did the Dead. With those bands on board, the Monterey Pop Festival, the pop scene's very first rock festival, became a reality.

Phil Walden had heard they were booking the festival and was entertaining the idea for his client. He had also heard that virtually every other soul performer who was offered a slot on the bill turned it down, uncertain of the effect and perception it would have on their careers. Certainly, the downside was real. Flopping in front of thousands, and the publicity that failure would generate, could be a death blow to many performers. The stage was large in many ways.

But Walden was more courageous and hopeful about the experience. After all, Otis had owned the Fillmore and its white audience, and the idea of winning over thousands of "Flower Power" fans and their psychedelic perspectives, was intriguing. When Walden received encouragement from Atlantic and Jerry Wexler, he bought in.

Estimates put the crowd at Monterey, held at the Monterey Fairgrounds from June 16–18 in 1967, at anywhere between 50,000 and 100,000. Orchids were flown in from Hawaii and handed out at the door. LSD was widely dispersed. A police presence had been called in for security, but many were sent home on the second day; the crowd was tame and unthreatening.

Otis played on the festival's second night, following acts like the red-hot Jefferson Airplane and the fiery Janis Joplin. But, the prospect of following these rising stars didn't intimidate Otis. He had been following Sam and Dave on stage for months, and few acts put on a better show than that dynamic duo.

Ten minutes before his set, Otis still hadn't put together a song list. With a panicky Walden by his side, they decided that the MGs would go on and play "Green Onions," then Otis would come out and open with "Shake," as rousing an opener as he could think of. The idea worked. From the opening shouts of his first track, the crowd was fully absorbed by the big soul man. He kicked into "Respect," after catching his breath, and the audience was his, just as it was on all the other dates of the European tour. There was something about his energy, passion, enthusiasm, and soul that left no spectator untouched.

The upshot was miraculous. Despite quality sets from the Who and Hendrix, Otis stole the show. Rock journalist John Landau, a man who'd go on to manage Bruce Springsteen, wrote in a local newspaper that Otis Redding's performance constituted the highest level of expression rock and roll had yet attained. "Otis Redding is rock and roll!" (Michael Lydon, "Monterey Pops!," *Newsweek*, June 1967).

SITTIN' AROUND

After the overwhelming victory at Monterey, Otis had one more punch, the knock-out blow, to deliver. It came in the form of a song. As usual, he only had a few lines of it, a few scraps, a lyric or two. The interesting thing about it was how different it sounded. It felt more like folk music than R&B.

At the time, relations with Stax, and even with his very close friend Phil Walden, began to falter. Stax resisted the talents of Otis's protégé Arthur Conley, a man Otis truly believed in. So Otis ended up having him record in Macon instead of Memphis. The song Conley recorded, "Sweet Soul Music," became a hit and legendary in the soul genre. Conley drove another wedge between Otis, Stewart, and the Stax operation.

Then there was the issue about the polyps on his larynx. For a number of years, Otis tried to soothe his ravaged throat with tea and lemon or honey. But the pain became too great. In the summer and early fall of 1967, he could barely reach the notes that he'd normally hit with ease. A doctor in New York City advised surgery. Otis immediately saw his career flash in front of him. At 26 years old, and set to become the new king of pop, Otis, his family, and his associates worried that he'd never be able to sing again.

The doctors assured him that worry was unnecessary. The surgery happened in early September, and Otis was laid up for a few weeks, incapable of speaking. The fact that he couldn't get out and run around town, that he was confined to his home for a while was both a blessing and a curse. The up side was that he spent more time at home with his family. By this time he and Zelma had three children. Dexter was now five, Karla was four, and Otis III was three.

It was also a time for reflection. He took another look at his life, where he was headed, and made a few decisions. He decided he wanted to leave his wife Zelma. He had also planned to leave Phil Walden, citing money issues. And finally, Otis wanted to split from Stax. He yearned for a fresh start, a clean slate, to erect something completely new. He envisioned a studio scene in Macon that would rival the work done at both Stax in Memphis and Muscle Shoals in Alabama. The latter had become a location that the Atlantic label and Wexler had established as an alternative to Memphis.

But before he enacted these changes, Otis still had commitments in the pipeline. His career still sizzled, and there were dates—both on the road and in the studio—he had to fulfill. Once he was sure he could sing, he plunged back in with both feet. In the winter of 1967 he returned to Stax. He was fired up, aggressive, and the material he cut mirrored those feelings. "Hard to Handle," for example, sounded as much like rock and roll as R&B, not surprising considering the rise of rock on the scene in acts like Clapton and Hendrix, and Otis's subsequent exposure to it.

The sessions lasted two weeks. At the tail end, he sat down with Steve Cropper to finish writing the song he had first begun conceiving months prior. Redding and Cropper, facing each other on the studio floor, each one with a guitar, worked out some melodic details and some chords. Slowly, the MGs straggled in to contribute, as they'd done so many times with all of the Stax artists. And when they finally came together on "Sittin' on the Dock of the Bay," the band hit its groove on the very first try.

The song was unlike anything ever recorded at Stax, closer to pop than R&B, closer to the Stones than Sam and Dave. A few of the people in the studio that day knew in their bones that it would be a hit, and not just any hit, a smash hit. Cropper, for one, loved the feel of the song and stood behind it steadfastly, as did Booker Jones on keys.

But for some reason Jim Stewart had a problem with it. So did Otis's wife Zelma, who was afraid her husband was changing his spots as an artist. Stewart thought it was too far outside the Stax style to release as a single. He had great taste in R&B, but his tastes ran conservatively and, like a protective parent, he remained in the stylistic box he had built around the Stax sound. He didn't like the song's lack of energy. He felt it didn't embody the classic Otis style his fans had come to expect.

The whistling that faded out the song didn't help. He had decided to work with it more, perhaps make it more soulful, bring in some guests, take out the whistling. He really wanted to add seagulls and the sounds of the ocean . . . another idea that didn't go over too well.

But, like always, Otis had to rush off to another commitment. He boarded his plane, piloted by Dick Fraser, an experienced, 26-year-old pilot. There were also members of his touring band the Bar-Kays with him. They flew to Nashville, then to Cleveland. He called home from Cleveland, and according to Zelma, he was tired. He spoke briefly with Otis III, but Fraser knocked on his door and told him it was time to leave. Otis told his wife to be good, something he never did, seeing as how she was as faithful to him as he could ask, and hung up the phone.

Sunday night's Madison, Wisconsin, gig was the last commitment of this early December weekend. They were slated to play two shows at a venue called the Factory, a white rock club. At the Cleveland airport, Fraser accompanied a mechanic to check out Otis's plane to ensure it was ready for flight. Six passengers boarded; all that could fit. This meant one member of the band, always rotating, would have to fly commercially. This time it was bassist James Alexander's turn to take another flight.

Otis sat in the co-pilot's seat for the three-hour flight to Madison. The entire flight was uneventful and the band members, all in their teens, slept. About four miles from the airport, Fraser radioed in for permission to land. The visibility was poor and landing would be tricky due to heavy rain.

Ben Cauley was on the plane. He heard a jolt, then an awful sensation of falling. The plane had tipped to the left he said, and everybody was eerily quiet as Fraser struggled to right the plane and bring it down safely. It was not to be. They crashed in Lake Monona, just outside Madison, in freezing cold waters. Cauley heard screams for help from familiar voices, but they disappeared after a couple of minutes. Cauley himself held on to a seat cushion until he lost consciousness. Just then he felt an arm pulling him out of the water. The others had all died.

The aftermath of the crash affected everyone in the industry. Otis had many friends and business partners, family members, and best buddies. He had made so many people in his life feel important and good about themselves. Now they had lost one of their own.

Cropper coped with the news by going into the studio and working. He found a tape of sound effects featuring eagles and crashing waves. Pulled up the rough mix of "Sittin' on the Dock of the Bay" and added the seagulls Otis wanted. He'd later go on to say that finishing that song during those next few days would be the most difficult thing he would ever do.

LEGACY

The life of Otis Redding embraced all the paradoxes of his time in history. A black man before desegregation, his best friends were white. As a man in the peak of his sexual prime, his primary considerations were his wife and kids. As someone who was in the position to make thousands of dollars with Atlantic Records, he chose to remain with Stax, an independent, family-run operation with whom he promised he'd stay.

"He had a strong inner life," said Jerry Wexler. "He was emotionally centered . . . He had a positive sense of racial identity. He was one of those rare souls beyond color. He dealt with you as a human being, not as a white or a black or a Christian or a Jew" (Freeman, p. 134).

Jim Stewart, a famously curmudgeonly music critic, appreciated the fact that Otis was a constant source of hope at Stax. "Otis Redding was like a magic potion," he said. "When he walked into the studio, the studio lit up and all the worries and problems just sort of vanished. You knew something good was going to happen" (Freeman, p. 137). One critic's comparison of Otis to Elvis was prescient. At his peak, U.K. publication *Melody Maker* named Redding the Top Vocalist of 1967, an honor previously reserved for Elvis.

That Otis Redding influenced today's musicians comes off as a gross understatement. He was a singer of such commanding stature that to this day he embodies the essence of pure soul music. His name is synonymous with the genre; he is a distillate of that form of music that arose out of the black experience in America, wound its way through the transmutation of gospel and rhythm and blues into a form of funky, secular testifying.

From his first sessions for Stax/Volt Records in 1963 until his death in 1967, four short years, Redding left behind a deep legacy of recordings, from which virtually every soul performer draws, from his colleagues Aretha Franklin and Arthur Conley to Marvin Gaye, Al Green, Janis Joplin, and every critical performer who ever claimed to sing real soul music. "He didn't have an obsessive drive. He wasn't out to conquer the world. He didn't have that attitude, yet he spent more time writing songs and coming up with new things than any artist I know. Even when he was on the road for ten days straight, he'd be in a hotel or on the bus with a guitar in his hands working on ideas" (uncredited writer, "Steve Cropper: The Otis Redding I Knew," *Hit Parader*, February 1968).

SELECTED DISCOGRAPHY

Complete & Unbelievable: The Otis Redding Dictionary of Soul (Atco, 1966)

Otis Blue: Otis Sings Soul Music (Atco, 1966)

In Person at the Whiskey A Go-Go (Atco, 1968)

Otis Redding and Carla Thomas: King & Queen (Stax, 1967)

Otis! The Definitive Otis Redding (Atlantic/Rhino, 1993)

FURTHER READING

Freeman, Scott. *Otis!* New York: St. Martin's Griffin, 2001.

Guralnick, Peter. *Sweet Soul Music: Rhythm and Blues and the Southern Dream of Freedom.* New York: Harper Collins, 1986.

Stewart, Jim. *The Definitive Otis Redding,* liner notes. Rhino/Atco 1993.

Miller, Jim, ed. *The Rolling Stone Illustrated History of Rock & Roll.* New York: Rolling Stone Press, 1976.

Courtesy of Photofest.

Sly and the Family Stone

THE FREAKY FATHER OF FUNK

When Sly and the Family Stone came together in 1967, there had been nothing on the pop scene even remotely like it. But in the bubbling cauldron of the late 1960s known as the rock and roll subculture, audiences were eager to try anything, and the more unusual the better. Different strokes for different folks. Sly and the Family Stone were more than happy to bestow that open-minded audience something fresh and new. Without blinking, they managed to amass all the disparate social trends—civil rights, feminism, integration, and free-spiritedness—and roll it into an explosive juggernaut of sound. Between 1967 and 1970, their peak years, Sly and the Family Stone, an interracial, mixed gender combo that took even the tolerant hippie generation by surprise, skillfully fused soul, funk, jazz, R&B, and psychedelia and redefined the boundaries of popular music.

It is said that Sly influenced the very extremities of contemporary black music. By incorporating polyrhythms and jazz tempos, he touched the work of Miles Davis and Herbie Hancock. By subverting soul's pop side, he added substance and meaning to the sound of Motown. In doing so, he took the first wave of R&B, music from the likes of Ray Charles and James Brown, merged it with white musicians, and brought it to the entire spectrum of pop fans, black and white, young and old, male and female.

Led by their namesake Sly Stone (née Sylvester Stewart), the band started out with pure intentions and joyful noise, espousing high ideals and earthly harmony. Albums like *A Whole New Thing* (1967) and *Dance to the Music* (1968) were celebrations, a vibrant mélange of group vocals, infectious rhythms, and simple, soaring melodies. These recordings offered the thrill of discovery, the excitement of the unexpected. Sly's lyrics appealed to the head and the heart while the band's ebullient rhythms moved the hips and the feet.

The music, indeed the entire presentation, was monumental. And the effects of what Sly and his band accomplished live on, first in the work of epic acts like the Temptations, Parliament, the Isley Brothers, and Prince, and later still in the artistry of Michael Jackson, the Beastie Boys, and the Red Hot Chili Peppers.

And if the band itself was monumental, Sly Stone the man was the image imposed upon it. He was, personally speaking, at least as large as the band itself, a hero who had as many faults as attributes. As he ascended to the throne of rock star—he was the first black rock star of the era in both good and bad ways—those faults came to bear and his attributes receded.

On the one hand, he took tremendous advantage of his popular acceptance to indulge in an incredible amount of debaucherous and indulgent behavior. On the other, his popularity took him out of his comfort zone, and he often seemed like he was pretending to be someone he wasn't. The duality tore him apart, and his disintegration occurred quickly and with devastating effect.

There's a Riot Goin' On, the album at the fulcrum of his musical canon, reflected that duality. One of his stunning achievements, the recording is Sly's deeply personal artistic statement. Unlike his previous dance-oriented work, *Riot* is introverted and disturbing, not easily understood. In retrospect, we know now that it also offers a glimpse into Stone's troubled soul.

Sly also functioned as the poster child for the Woodstock era. After playing what many deemed to be Woodstock's most memorable set, he became the symbol of the festival's spirit. His anthems, "I Want to Take You Higher," "Dance to the Music," and "Everyday People" were soundtracks of the times, and as effective as any in the Flower Power movement in sketching out the agenda of a generation.

But nearly as fast as his star rose, it came crashing down. Indeed, Sly Stone's fall from the top was as precipitous and ignominious as any in the history of popular music. It was hard to pinpoint a pivotal moment that may have triggered Sly's fall. Many say it was a confluence of things, from his ill-advised move to Los Angeles, his fascination with mind-altering drugs, including PCP, his extravagant $12,000 a month Bel Air mansion, or the hiring of his "pit bull" bodyguard, the street-smart Hamp "Bubba" Banks, whom he leaned on. All of these factors are stories in themselves, and make Sly Stone's arc through the music business Shakespearean in scope and tragedy.

To many with a passing interest in his music, Sly simply disappeared, squashed by a changing music scene and capricious tastes. But to those in the know, Sly's descent had more to do with harsher concepts like the ego, vice, and indulgence associated with the rock star lifestyle. Sly's drug habits were notorious and they dimmed his ability not only to front his own band, but to perform at all. He was habitually late to gigs, sometimes showing up hours after his appointed set time. He'd too often betray his fans by not showing up at all. A megalomaniac from early on, Sly always had control issues. But his ability to control himself, no less his band, became a liability and in time he lost everyone and everything that had made him what he was, including the Family members in his band.

Still, it was one remarkable day in the sun.

THE EARLY YEARS

Born Sylvester Stewart to Alpha and K.C. Stewart in 1944, Stone and his family moved from his home state of Texas to Vallejo, California, about 40 miles north of San Francisco, in the 1950s. He was singing by the age of five with a family gospel group that called themselves the Stewart Four. Sly tinkered on piano at about the same time and picked up the guitar by the time he was nine. The family lived modestly and spent much of their free time together with the family at church.

He began singing gospel with his siblings, Loretta, Freddie, Vaetta, and Rose, at the Church of God in Christ. They were good enough to record, and they cut a handful of 78 rpms. This experience gave young Sly his first taste of making music, and many of these same siblings would be at his side during Sly and the Family Stone's rise and fall as well.

Influenced by blues and the R&B of Ray Charles, Sly began putting more secular groups together. The Cherrybusters and the Royal Aces were gimmicky groups with creative costumes that Sly assembled during high school. The Aces wore white suits with aces on their sleeve. In 1961, when Sly was 17, he formed the Viscaynes, another gimmick group. It was an integrated band, featuring different races and both boys and girls. With this mix, the Viscaynes foreshadowed Sly's future lineup.

Smooth talking and handsome, Sly had trouble staying in school. He was more preoccupied with music and girls than his studies. Many say he had a singular mind about music. While his other classes suffered, Sly would stay late in his music classes, working hard and earning straight A's. His voice matured, and he developed tremendous range. His compositional skills also blossomed as a result of his dedication. Instrumentally, he was playing guitar, drums, and bass in addition to keyboards.

"He was always singing, always humming, messing around with drumsticks. There was always a certain kind of young hipness to him," says Autumn Record executive Carl Scott. "He was constantly The Musician. He was a rock and roll guy. He was certainly not what we consider to be R&B. He had a pop sensibility to him and that was always obvious" (Joel Selvin, *Sly and the Family Stone: An Oral History*, New York City, Avon, 1998).

He released a single, "Yellow Moon," in 1962. It went nowhere commercially, but it did earn him the attention of some record executives at the Autumn label, Tom Donahue and Bob Mitchell. Impressed with his talent, they hired Sly when he was just 19. Soon after jumping aboard he penned his first hit for the label, "The Swim." Pop artist Bobby Freeman cut the record, which subsequently went gold. Sly played organ, guitar, and bass for the sessions as well. With the royalties he received from the song, he put a down payment on a house.

ROCK AND ROLL STAR

Suddenly legitimate, Stewart attracted more and more work as a producer. His highest profile job came quickly, when Donahue and Mitchell convinced hot Bay Area band the Beau Brummels to sign on to their label and use Sly as a producer. The Brummels made their entire first album with him and ended up with a handful of hits, including popular tunes like "Laugh, Laugh," "Just a Little," and "Still in Love with You Baby." Based on their work off that first album, the Beau Brummels signed to Warner Bros. and Donahue's organization enjoyed a nice payday.

Stone was fastidious in the studio. He used overdubs and multiple takes extensively. He was so demanding that he often played instruments for the band, rather than the band's own musicians. He had very specific ideas about sound and he did virtually anything to achieve it.

Sly also used his clout and musical know-how to snag a DJ job at KSOL, a race music station in San Francisco. When he was hired, the station was suffering in the ratings. Most black stations in the area were playing sedate, establishment music, and the more pop-oriented sounds of the times, like Motown and Girl Groups. When Sly began spinning at KSOL, he had big ideas. He and his crew wrote and sang jingles, invented "dedications," held contests and other skit-type performances. Sly captured the essence of a good vibe at the station, with a vibrant personality and command of the medium. He also helped ignite the free-form FM-radio revolution by playing outside-the-box artists like Dylan, James Brown, and Jimi Hendrix back to back.

It didn't take long for his innovations to turn the station around, and soon KSOL, much less powerful than its competition decibel-wise, overtook the bigger commercial stations in the city in the ratings. Sly's night shift was number one in the area and his success earned him celebrity status.

After his shift, which ended at 11 P.M., Sly prowled the clubs of North Beach. He'd hang out with friends like musician Billy Preston, at the time a member of the Rolling Stones. He'd also have a hand in booking entertainment at these clubs, another aspect of his musical career that afforded him clout.

It was about this time that Sly connected with the street-smart Hampton "Bubba" Banks. He liked Banks's toughness and kept him close by. He felt secure on the city's mean streets with Bubba by his side. Banks would come to play a much more prominent role in Sly's life a little later, when his fame became a larger issue.

Sly sat in with bands frequently at neighborhood clubs. The patrons and musicians knew him, and were excited to have his seal of approval. It was widely understood that where Sly was, the party soon followed. He'd pull up in his green Jaguar XKE, a lady on each arm, and take a place over.

THE PLAYERS

One afternoon in 1967, Sly convened a meeting of hand-selected musicians in the basement of his home to jam. They were both white and black, men and women—the mosaic was unsurprising, given Sly's diverse background. The group included his younger brother Freddy, a guitarist, bassist Larry Graham, drummer Gregg Errico, reed player Jerry Martini, and trumpeter Cynthia Robinson, a holdover from Stone's previous group, the R&B-flavored Sly and the Stoners, as well as a blues veteran of Lowell Fulsom and Jimmy McCracklin.

"He was so far ahead of his time," says Martini. "He intentionally had me in his band. He intentionally wanted a white drummer. He knew exactly what he was doing. Boys, girls, black, white" (Selvin, p. 37).

At the time, Martini was a decorated musician, having recorded and toured extensively with various bands. He had a family to support, but was so convinced of Sly's promise that he passed up a good-paying gig in Las Vegas and moved out of his apartment to give the band a try.

Bassist Larry Graham was playing with his mother Dell Graham's band. She'd toured the world as a jazz/blues pianist/vocalist in the mold of Dinah Washington, and Graham was playing guitar for her. One night, as the story goes, the band's organ broke down, and was irreparable. They needed a bottom end to their sound, and so Graham rented a bass to play. To provide that bottom—the band didn't have a drummer—he began playing the bass in a unique way, thumping the strings to mimic a bass drum beat, and plucking the higher strings to imitate the sound of the snare drum.

Graham didn't realize that he was developing a new way of playing bass.

> It was just out of necessity. Just trying to do the gig right, make it sound good and feel good. After a while of doing this, that's just the way I played. I never thought about playing the overhand style, the way bass players were playing then, because I wasn't going to be a bass player . . . At the same time, I'm not listening to bass players to be influenced by them, because I'm not a bass player. I'm a guitar player. In my brain, this was just a temporary gig. (Selvin, p. 29)

Whether Graham had it in his mind to play bass didn't matter to Sly Stone. He loved how Graham pushed the sound of his instrument and the funky rhythms emanating from it. Though Graham had designs on being front and center of his own band after leaving his mother's act, he'd eventually become a background player for Sly, albeit a famous one. His bass sound would be a signature ingredient in Sly's stew—he never went back to guitar—and it ignited an instrumental evolution in funk.

Not only did Sly's band sound different, they looked different as well. Even while the free expression era of the hippie and the Flower Power revolution were under way, Sly and the gang had managed to cultivate their own very unique look.

Sly himself coordinated their outfits. At first that meant combing second-hand shops for duds. Sly chose the stores; the members could pick their own outfits. Stripes, polka dots, period outfits, leather, pajamas . . . He'd have nothing to do with the clichéd, Temptations-style uniforms that were popular at the time. He also designed the band's hairstyles. He told Martini for example to spray his hair black, grow a beard, and dye it black as well. When all else failed, band members often donned wigs. It was all part of the eclectic presentation Sly was going for.

The band also refrained from doing much choreography. "We don't rehearse any dance steps," said Sly, in an unattributed interview in the liner notes to *A Whole New Thing*. "What happens when we're dancing is spontaneous. We just have to get up and do something if we feel like doing it."

Together, they began playing Top 40, only in a very different way. Sly arranged the songs, like Ray Charles's "I Don't Need No Doctor," the first song they ever played together, in such a way as to emphasize punch. While he was regarded first as a rock and roll musician because of his affiliation with Autumn Records and the Beau Brummels, he enjoyed putting together a set list of R&B covers. His horn charts were powerful, the bass prominent; even the players were surprised by the muscle of Sly's spiced-up arrangements. "It shocked me because I had never played in a group that was that together," said trumpeter Robinson (Selvin, p. 33).

Freddy Stewart felt that he had just witnessed a miracle. "I was just excited because I knew we were going to do something great," said Stewart (Selvin, p. 34). He was right. After just a few months of rehearsals, the band was packing a northern California club called Winchester Cathedral in Redwood City. At first their material included covers, then they began introducing originals into their sets, and they'd receive the same enthusiastic response. Musically, they'd come on stage one at a time, beginning with Errico who'd lay down a beat. One by one they'd come and add their own parts, and by the time Sly came on the stage, the groove was entrancing. And it never stopped. Errico wasted little time between tunes, revved up the next before Sly had even introduced it. They'd play into the wee hours and bring the house down, flooring audiences with non-stop dynamite. In no time Sly and the Family Stone exploded.

ENTER DAVID KAPRALIK

Tipped off by a promotions rep in San Francisco, David Kapralik flew from New York City to check out this new band. At the time, Kapralik had climbed his way up the corporate ladder at Columbia Records before splitting off to start his own management company. "I walk in, the place was jammed," he says. "This group came on and I was electrified . . . I knew right there that I wanted to sign them" (Selvin, p. 43).

Kapralik understood immediately that Sly was a true original. His task was to convince the artist that a middle-class Jew from the East Coast was the right man to manage a street-savvy artiste from San Fran. Kapralik said to him: "I can help you accomplish your dreams and you will be a star. At that point, you are going to have power, and at that point, I won't be able to help you. Only you can decide what you are going to do with that power" (Selvin, p. 34).

Based on Kapralik's management successes, Clive Davis, president of CBS Records, rehired him as head of Epic, a CBS affiliate. In turn, Kapralik signed Sly's band to his label.

His first move after the contract was to book the band on a three-month, six-nights-a-week gig at the Pussycat a Go Go in Las Vegas. It was there that the band tightened its sound. They weaned themselves off their covers— though they were encouraged to play as many as they could to keep audiences entertained—and they began crafting originals.

The crowds in Vegas were plentiful and star-studded. Anyone who played the Strip knew of Sly's gigs and their shows were attended by the cognoscenti. The presence of people like Ike Turner and James Brown, some of their musical heroes, encouraged the band and made for great press.

During their stint in Vegas, Kapralik had the band start recording their debut album. They had Mondays off from performing so they flew out to Los

Angeles, to the CBS Recording Studio and spent the day making music. This went on for a month until they had enough material together for an LP. For those sessions, they imported a couple more of Sly's family members, Rose and Vet from the all-girl gospel singing group Little Sister, to help them in the studio. Their spiritual voices bolstered the vocal sound of the material and they became an integral part of the Family Stone for some time.

The Vegas gig ended inauspiciously though. The club owner, an ex-cop and apparent racist, espied Sly with a white girl on his arm. He asked her to leave, that she shouldn't be with a black man, but she refused and Sly came to her defense. There was a verbal confrontation, but no immediate resolution. That night on stage Sly recounted the story of what had happened to a packed house.

When he left the stage that night, he found a gun pointed at his head. The owner, angry at the affront and intolerant of Sly's attempt to humiliate him, sent the band packing. With a police escort, they made their way out of Vegas and back east.

In New York City, Kapralik and the intense East Coast record industry could keep close tabs on Sly and the Family Stone's progress. They booked a gig at a Greenwich Village venue called Electric Circus, owned by Jerry Brandt, formerly of the William Morris Agency. As they did on their torrid run at the Winchester Cathedral, the band destroyed audiences. Perhaps it was staying at a lousy residential hotel, their lack of cash, or the crowded, dangerous conditions in the city, but when the band hit the stage each night, they let loose with dazzling energy. They signed to the William Morris Agency for booking and hit the road.

As many black and interracial bands discovered, the conditions on the road were daunting. The band, loaded into a two-car caravan, including one rickety van that Sly drove, encountered problems, mainly racism, in many areas. In Detroit, for example, they were cornered by the National Guard. In each tour stop they played sleazy, undesirable rooms. Morale sank. Then they were informed that their debut album, *A Whole New Thing*, recently released, wasn't generating much interest either.

A WHOLE NEW THING

"The myriad innovations dreamed up by Sly and his talented cohorts— including the hot-potato trading off of lead vocals, the staccato horn riffs, the archetypal popping attack of Larry Graham's bass lines, the celebratory lyrics, which espoused community and diversity, the acid-rock flourishes and the racing rhythms—were introduced on *A Whole New Thing*" (Bud Scoppa, *A Whole New Thing*, liner notes, Epic/Legacy, 2007).

Indeed, the album was full of early band trademarks on songs like "Underdog," the first single, and the playfully diverse "Run, Run, Run." There was a fresh dynamic at work. The band was onto something that would happen soon enough.

Unfortunately, the album came out, as they say in the industry, "dead on arrival." It may have been fresh, but it wasn't in the pop idiom. It sounded innovative, but too unfamiliar. Much of it was on the fringes of pop, but not far enough out to appeal to a progressive audience. It didn't fit into any genre; didn't appeal to any specific demographic. Of course, this was an offshoot, a result of the band's own stunningly unique approach. Still, it received no airplay, which meant that a very small audience heard it. The band, once hopeful and optimistic, was devastated. Sly wanted out of his contract. It was their first real setback.

Kapralik talked the band out of its mindset. He told him they needed to streamline their style. Musicians and writers dug the band's sound, but it was too sophisticated for a mainstream audience in 1967. Sly headed back out to San Francisco, insisting he'd focus on giving music fans something they could not only figure out, but never forget.

DANCE TO THE MUSIC

In contrast to the iconoclastic work of the band's early days, *Dance to the Music* was a creative compromise for the band. Because *A Whole New Thing* flopped, Sly and company were forced to rethink their formula, or rather develop a formula in the first place. At first, it felt like a cop-out to Stone and his collective; they were proud of their edgy funk, jazz jams, and improvisational R&B workouts. But the general public didn't warm to them and so they revisited the drawing board.

Released at the beginning of 1968, "Dance to the Music," the song, embraced a simpler sound. Gregg Errico's drumming and Larry Graham's bass were basic, as were the song's hooks, including the "boom-boom" background singing, each member's concise solo, and the party theme. The song entered the Top 10 the week of its release and the band began to impact the commercial scene.

They would have never arrived at this point had *A Whole New Thing* not fallen flat. But their debut provided a crucial starting point for the material on the *Dance* album, and served as a critical transition. Instead of jamming out complicated patterns and unexpected hooks and rhythms, *Dance* hit hard with its immediacy. It also managed, in its simplicity, to include his requisite social and political commentary.

"The trick is that it continues to sound poised to pivot and reposition the world of music on its agile axis," says Greg Tate in the liner notes to the reissue of *Dance to the Music* (Epic/Legacy, 2007). "Even Sly's throwaways and tangents possess that kind of life-altering juju. The most remarkable thing about Sly's talent, like that of Ray Charles and Prince, is that he could pick and choose from an abundance of options and select those that fit his vision of life."

Dance to the Music's success thrust Sly and the band squarely into the limelight. They began playing bigger venues. They fit perfectly into both the Black Power and Black Is Beautiful movements. They also attracted white audiences as their music began crossing over boundaries and back.

Everybody from Frank Zappa and Jimi Hendrix to Steely Dan and George Clinton took notice. Herbie Hancock named a song "Sly" on his multimillion-selling disc, *Headhunter*. Sly Stone had begun to put his stamp on popular music, just as he had planned.

STUMBLING BLOCKS

With *Dance to the Music* a smash, Sly and the Family Stone enjoyed the weeks and months that followed. They played to bigger and more enthusiastic crowds, got a massive amount of press and publicity, and in the summer of 1968, they began receiving festival slots.

They went overseas on a tour of Great Britain, but ran into a few obstacles. Their first London gig, a sold-out show, was marred from the start. The promoter, a man named Don Arden, didn't come up with the proper organ for Sly to play. In fact, the organ he supplied was dilapidated and missing keys. Sly, fastidious about his stage set up, refused to play the show without it. Arden, a dodgy businessman, stood up to him and dared Sly to cancel. Sly did, telling the audience the situation, and then doing two a cappella numbers before bolting. It would be a harbinger of unpredictable behavior to come.

Another incident that cut the tour short was Larry Graham's bust for possession of marijuana. Not that it was Graham's pot; Jerry Martini had originally planned to throw it away before landing in the United Kingdom, but Graham told him not to, that he'd hold it. The bust put an abrupt and premature end to the tour. It also foreshadowed much more significant narcotic trouble.

Following the botched U.K. tour, the band returned to the States to make another record and play more dates. They'd so far shared the stage with an eclectic roster of acts, including Jimi Hendrix, the Stooges, the MC5, and anyone who dared compete with the band's energy and virtuosity.

At the end of 1968 they released *Life*, their third album. Issued during their surge of popularity, expectations were high. But instead of benefiting from that popularity, the band's fan base chose to stick with tracks from *Dance to the Music*, an album that still had chart presence. *Life* tanked, barely charting, and only remained in the Top 200 for five weeks.

Not that it wasn't worthy. While there were no obvious hits on the album of the magnitude of "Dance to the Music," it possessed a richness and innovation that characterized Stone's best work. It also boasted a certain confidence, a swagger that marked this period of the group's career. At this time no one was better known or more highly regarded, and *Life* reflected that attitude. Sly and the Family Stone had succeeded in expanding the ideals and consciousness of soul music. They injected it with folk, jazz, rock, and psychedelia, and infused it with something much larger than themselves. *Life* was, perhaps, the perfect crystallization of that kaleidoscopic approach. Yet nobody heard it.

HIGH TIMES

Though *Life* disappointed the band, they still maintained huge popularity. And with that popularity came money, which they used much of to throw parties with and purchase drugs. Sly had well-documented contacts in the medical and pharmaceutical community, including doctors and dentists. All of them, for the price of an office visit, were willing to supply Stone and any of his band members prescriptions to whatever drugs they desired. This did not account for the bags and bags of cocaine that began showing up.

With all the partying, behavior became increasingly erratic. Egos and dark, drug-laced moods grew pronounced and more frequent. At this point, though, the band hadn't allowed drugs to affect its performance. In fact, 1969 was a banner year. They played the *Ed Sullivan Show* in early 1969 and nailed their song. The act featured Sly spontaneously walking into the audience with his microphone, the first time that had ever been done on the show, and perhaps in all of television history.

STAND!

In February of that year Sly and the Family Stone recorded *Stand!*, kicking off a watershed of productivity. Creatively, it was their most fertile and harmonious time and the album is considered by many to be their crowning achievement. By consensus it remains a pop music masterpiece with its messages of social harmony and exuberant egalitarian ethos.

Recording at Pacific High Studios in San Francisco, just a few blocks from the Fillmore theater, Stone pushed his band harder than he ever had. The work paid off. The set's lead single "Stand!," a euphoric social anthem which has since become a pop culture artifact, hit the top of the singles chart in March and stayed for a month. The album itself never rose to higher than number 13, but it eventually sold more than 2 million copies. It also sparked an impressive string of hits for the band, including the aforementioned "Stand!" and "Hot Fun in the Summertime," and also counting "I Want to Take You Higher," "Everyday People," "Everybody Is a Star," and "Thank You (Falletinme Be Mice Elf Agin)." No act at this time in the late 1960s could rival the success of Sly and the Family Stone.

"The irony is that while *Stand!* virtually invented the 'progressive' funk of the Seventies and Eighties, jettisoning the trappings of Sixties soul and paving the way for P-Funk, Prince, et al, Sly and the Family Stone themselves fell apart in a mire of drugs and almost solipsistic introspection" (Barney Hoskyns, *Stand!*, liner notes, Epic/Legacy 2006).

In the summer of 1969, the festival circuit was hungry for the band, and vice versa. In July, the Newport Jazz Festival had booked them on their prestigious bill. Sly worked his magic on the fans there, stirring the audience up in an astonishing display of reverse crowd control. "Sly had this Napoleonic or Hitler-type control when he was on," said horn man Jerry Martini. "He could make them riot. He could make them sit down . . . We were the reason that the Newport Jazz Festival was closed down" (Selvin, p. 73).

A newspaper story covering the event described what happened in Newport:

> The Newport Jazz Festival was invaded last night by several hundred young people who broke down a section of the ten-foot fence surrounding Festival Field and engaged in rock-throwing battle with security guards. When the main gates were opened to prevent further assaults on the fence, they swarmed down through the 21,000 spectators, leaping chairs and railings. As they rushed toward the stage where Sly and the Family Stone, a rock group, was playing, they drove paying customers from their seats, occupied the boxes at the front of the field, and filled a pit in front of the bandstand intended for photographers. (*New York Times,* July 7, 1969)

Stone and the band generated enormous hysteria.

That same summer they were booked at Woodstock. The band had a 10 P.M. time slot on the second night of the festival. But due to delays and technical snags, they didn't end up going on until the dead of night: 3:30 A.M., a time that saw much of the massive audience tucked into their sleeping bags. It had been raining. There was mud and dirt everywhere. The band itself had grown tired from anticipating their set, coming down off that excitement, revving up, coming down.

"We started out doing the best we could," recalls drummer Errico. "You could feel it drag and then, all of a sudden, the third song, I think, you started seeing heads bop up . . . You could feel everybody start to listen to the music, wake up, get up, start dancing. Halfway through the show, the place was rocking" (Selvin, p. 79).

Rolling Stone magazine reported that the band had "won the battle, carrying to their own majestically freaked-out stratosphere."

Larry Graham recalled the experience: "To play anything after [Woodstock], you know you have capabilities beyond. So that took our concerts up a whole 'nother giant notch, to where the concerts became an experience for the audience and for us" (Selvin, pp. 77–78).

In January 1970, Sly followed up his August 1969 smash, "Hot Fun in the Summertime," with "Thank You (Falletinme Be Mice Elf Agin)." The single soared to number one, the second chart-topper for the band. It may have been a simple, one-chord romp, but it sizzled, and audiences responded.

THE CITY OF ANGELS

The bigger the audience the more intense the experience. Along with Sly's fame came challenges of getting along, personally, musically, and professionally. After Woodstock, Sly decided to relocate his business from New York City to Los Angeles to establish his new company, Stone Flower Productions. Many feel that this move West was the beginning of the end for Stone, including Jerry Martini. "There's a cloud flying over Sly from the time he moved to Los Angeles . . . It was havoc. It was very gangsterish, dangerous. The vibes were very dark at that point" (Selvin, p. 81).

Following his move, Sly was still a vital creative force. He was constantly making music, jamming, writing, recording, and spending long days in the studio. He began opening up his perspective musically as well, embracing country and jazz in addition to his traditional pop, R&B, funk, and soul.

Toward the end of 1969, he moved into Coldwater Canyon, a mansion in the Hollywood Hills owned by John and Michelle Phillips of the Mamas and the Papas. Sly was renting the two-acre estate for $12,000 a month. It was at this point that Sly began to change. Stone and the band's life had been altered immeasurably since Woodstock. He was a smash that night, and was on a high from that point forward. He had hits. He found a vast audience that included everyone from soul daddies to young white rockers. He captured the musical imagination of an embattled nation with style and verve. Pithy slogans ("Different strokes for different folks"), a profound social agenda, and an optimistic portrayal of racial harmony all merged in creating what was essentially a phenomenon.

These accomplishments changed Sly's mental state dramatically. Life at the Bel Air home became dark and dirty. Drugs and drug suppliers were everywhere. So were guns, big, dangerous, loaded guns. And dogs. Sly had grown fond of dogs, and bought many of them. Unfortunately, he chose not to take care of those dogs, so they had run of the house.

"There was no real separation between life and drugs," said Stephani Owens, Sly's personal assistant and part-time love interest. "Life was drugs, and it was music. They would spend so many hours collectively in the studio wearing out the engineers. But they were doing drugs, too" (Selvin, *Mojo*, August 2001).

The drugs essentially destroyed the bonhomie the band had enjoyed since those early days at Winchester Cathedral. The narcotics heightened Sly's need to control. He began dictating where his band members lived and when or if they should report to work. He petitioned them less and less for suggestions and advice. Sly had become a one-man show who seemingly would have done it alone on stage if he could. This isolationism was difficult for his bandmates to comprehend.

Because he ignored those around him, he heard few voices that made sense—in business, morally, ethically, musically. He began missing gigs and showing less responsibility. In 1970, Stone failed to show up for 26 of the 80 live dates booked for the band. In the first half of 1971 he bowed out of 12 of the group's 40 shows, including 6 in a row on a swing through the South. Those he did make he appeared late. Yet far from feeling remorse for this behavior, he glorified in the power this arrogant unpredictability provided.

Bubba Banks, normally a tough guy, didn't like what he saw: "It all fell apart at Coldwater. That is when Sly did the PCP and was just out of it . . . It was over . . . He was through . . . He and Freddy walked around the house all day like zombies. I started sleeping with a pistol" (Selvin, p. 95).

> Showing up late to concerts just started to sneak up on the group. At first, Sly liked to heighten the dramatic tension by keeping an audience waiting. Then it became a power trip he needed to pull—they would have him on his time, not the other way around—but soon he began to not show up at all. Yes, there were drugs involved, but nothing was quite that simple in Sly Stone's increasingly twisted world. Soon he would be philosophizing about the irrelevant nature of time ("I make time," he would tell his people), and it would become a psychological battle between the audience and Sly. Getting Sly to every single concert soon became a huge struggle, a convoluted, malevolent little game that he insisted on playing over and over again. (Selvin, *Mojo*)

One extraordinary moment happened on national television when Sly and the band were scheduled to appear on the *Dick Cavett Show* on the ABC network in 1971. At the time Cavett was a smash on the daytime talk show circuit and the appearance of Sly and the Family Stone was critically important for the band. Yet Sly nearly missed his moment.

The night before, he had been out with Muhammad Ali in New Jersey, and on the spur of the moment, he announced he intended to fly back to Los Angeles. Fortunately, his keepers, Banks and singer Bobby Womack talked him out of it.

When his manager Kapralik found out Sly was flaking, he had him helicoptered into the Manhattan TV studio. It was nearly too late. Stone missed his original show time. Cavett introduced the band, but Sly wasn't on hand yet, so the host cut to a commercial. He chatted with a few other guests, essentially buying Stone time. Nearly 30 minutes later, he introduced them again, and the entire band, including Sly, hit the stage for a blistering extended version of "Thank You." Musically speaking, the band acquitted itself.

The same couldn't be said for Sly's interview with Cavett following the performance. He looked stoned, with a runny, coke-plagued nose. He slurred his words, stammered, and supplied bizarre and oblique responses to simple questions. "I look in the mirror when I write," Sly drawled when Cavett asked him about his songwriting. "The reason why I do that is because I can somehow be a great critique for myself, and I can react spontaneously before I realize that I'm going along with what I'm doing, and dislike it or like it before I realize that I'm doing it" (*Dick Cavett Show: Rock Icons* DVD, Shout Factory, 2005). Cavett smiled wryly and wondered what to ask next.

As the story goes, Sly did anything he could to miss that Cavett performance, even going so far as demanding the pilot turn his helicopter around, that he'd forgotten something. When he got to the studio, he made seven or eight trips to the bathroom in an attempt to miss his time slot. It was the ultimate drug-induced meltdown, and it was becoming more the rule than the exception.

On tour the band was still drawing well; ticket sales were brisk. The problems came down to whether Sly would grace fans with his presence. "We were late and it would create a tension," said Gregg Errico. "The promoter would be nervous. The audience would be nervous. Everybody was trying to get the band there . . . After all was said and done and we played, it was cool" (Selvin, p. 101).

"It was pretty nightmarish," Martini agreed. "What you don't know is that the band went. We were there. We showed up to a lot of gigs in 1970 that we didn't play" (Selvin, p. 103).

In July 1970, Sly bailed on a headlining gig at a free concert in Chicago's Grant Park, inciting a riot. It began shortly after 4 P.M. and by 10 P.M., 150 people had been arrested, and 25 were injured, including 10 police officers. The press and the politicians blamed the band, mainly because they had established a pattern of behavior and that night the behavior had tragic consequences. But band members insisted that the Chicago riot had started even before they were set to go on. "We were used as a scapegoat because of our reputation," Martini explained. "We were there and we were totally ready to play, Sly was ready. We got blamed for that on Page One. That just ruined us, ruined our careers" (Selvin, p. 107).

In January 1971, Kapralik, powerless over his difficult star client, filed suit against Stone to collect $250,000 in back commissions and unpaid loans. Kapralik had been feeding Sly money for years and there weren't enough funds to go around. With the prospect of having his box office proceeds attached, Sly's response to the suit was not to play more, but to skip the next six concerts. About the same time, Sly, desperate for cash, also resented his initial publishing deal with Kapralik. When Kapralik first signed Sly, they formed a 50/50 partnership to publish Sly's music. Now strapped, Sly wanted Kapralik's 50 percent as well. The success of "Thank You" and a subsequent *Greatest Hits* effort enabled Kapralik to renegotiate Sly's original contract with CBS and secure some money for his client. Of course, that money disappeared quickly, too.

THERE'S A RIOT GOIN' ON

Just as the band was beginning to achieve its full musical potential, in some cases true genius, they were self-destructing. They had completed *Stand!*, a work on the short list of influential 1960s pop albums, and they had subsequently come up with an equally inspired series of singles. In between tours and even on the road, Sly had been writing and recording. He spent days on end in the studio. And when he wasn't in his own home studio he moved down the road to the Record Plant; he'd park his RV outside the studio and spend days editing tracks and partying with his friends.

Very little of this work actually included his band, with the exception of session cameos by Errico and Martini that often went nowhere, and his brother Freddy, who had been completely consumed by the same narcotic subculture. Trumpeter Robinson found a small place in the pool house along with Martini. But bassist Graham, so integral to the sound, remained in Oakland, away from the lunacy, and he overdubbed his parts when he came down to L.A. Rumor had it that some of Graham's bass tracks were actually erased and replaced with Sly's own bass parts. Overall, there was very little of the communal interplay that characterized the early ethos of Sly and the Family Stone, and more recently, that made *Stand!* so brilliant.

No one really knew what was going on with Sly, though, not his manager, not Clive Davis, his record company president, not even his band. His music, on tapes scattered everywhere, often disappeared. His engineering staff was all on drugs. All the people who had been around Sly when he first moved to Los Angeles that avoided falling into the narcotic trap, had moved away. Stephani Owens, for example, observed that Sly preferred to surround himself with madness. That way madness appeared normal.

At the time, Sly and Freddy were both doing PCP, angel dust, a severely crippling drug that transported users to another place, often incapacitating its victims and leading to total breakdowns. "PCP really had a big influence on everything that was going on," said Owens (Selvin, p. 97). Sly was also spending indiscriminately, oblivious to the exorbitant financial ramifications of endless studio time, not to mention the cost of living like royalty. He phoned Clive Davis, president of his label, to ask him for money. By this time, Sly's reputation had almost completely soured, and Davis, a seasoned pro in the business, would have none of it. Stone's abysmal attendance record at shows had made him a pariah with booking agents, so his revenue stream as a live act was drying up. The only question Davis had for Sly when they spoke was when he was going to deliver a new album. Epic had not heard any new music from him for more than a year, a long time to wait for the follow-up to a number one record.

So Davis waited impatiently for new music. David Kapralik had become subservient to Sly, and was no longer able to obtain answers from him, no less ask him to work harder or faster. Frequently Sly and Freddy were too stoned to even stand up. Asking them to play would have been like forcing them to re-enter reality, which neither of them cared to do. Occasionally, artist friends like Joe Hicks or Bobby Womack would hang out at the Bel Air mansion and make some music with Sly, but the resulting material was a far cry from the ebullient sound that made *Stand!* so unique.

Slowly, somehow, an album began to take shape.

Sly grafted lyrics on top of his simmering, supple grooves, bursts of half-finished thoughts that fused with the percolating instrumental tracks. The feel was very dry, the vocals sounded as if Sly was singing over your shoulder, straight into your ear. The tracks chugged along invisible grooves that guided the careful chattering of guitars and electric keyboards. No more punchy horn builds. No big dramatic panoramas. No more sloganeering. This was stripped-down funk, raw as an exposed nerve, shadowy, mumbled, electronic voodoo. (Selvin, *Mojo*, p. 76)

Released in the winter of 1971, *There's a Riot Goin' On* is the antithesis of *Stand!* In the nearly two years that had passed between albums, Sly's rainbow-coalition glee had faded, and his optimism soured. Whether these were conscious turns he had taken or whether they were simply byproducts of a drugged-out imagination, his writing had grown dark, restless, and murky. Disgusted with the sagging civil rights movement and in a vise grip of addiction, his band's former joy turned to cynicism, Flower Power turned to free love turned to sleazy porn, and his energy receded into weary resignation. Even the sound of the album, the actual production, was fuzzy low fidelity.

"He'd get women he wanted to sleep with and ask if they wanted to be on his album," said Martini. "They'd lay down some terrible vocal, Sly would get the goods and then erase it. That's why *Riot* is a lo-fi record. The tape was worn out" (Selvin, *Mojo*).

It's a long way from the celebratory family jam "Thank You" to the spare "Family Affair on Riot," the latter nothing more than a drum machine, Billy Preston on keyboards, and Sly and his sister Rose singing through cupped hands. On the album there were no co-writes, no producer credits, just Sly Stone/Stewart/Stone Flower Production ringing out starkly on the label. The album's title? It could have been literal, perhaps a reference to the debacle in Chicago, or even reaching back to Newport. More likely though the "riot" was in his own mind, and this "Riot" served as the effective end of his career as a popular recording artist. He still had one more significant album to make, but it was after this pivotal point that he lost his momentum and most of his fan base.

After the record was done and before it was released, David Kapralik managed to convince a promoter to present Sly and the Family Stone for three nights at Madison Square Garden. It was a considerable gamble, but the shows all sold out, breaking box office records in the process, and Sly pulled himself together long enough to be present for each one. (According to writer

Joel Selvin, he still missed six flights out of Los Angeles before he finally caught the plane to New York.) "Family Affair" was released about the same time and ended up being Sly's third chart-topping hit.

RECORDINGS, PHASE II

Sly Stone's recording career entered its second phase following *There's a Riot Goin' On*. In 1972, after *Riot*, the band was in irrevocable disarray. Sly, no longer the "happy black hippie who'd made 'Everyday People'" (Touré, *Fresh*, liner notes, Epic/Legacy 2007), had seen founding drummer Gregg Errico leave the band. He had engaged in a bitter feud with bassist Larry Graham, a vital member of the band who'd always avoided Sly's troublesome traps. Graham exploded and was asked to leave the band. Guns were involved. Rumor had it that Sly had asked one of his henchman to actually murder his former bass player.

Outside of music, there were conflicts like Vietnam, the enervated civil rights movement, Bloody Sunday, the Munich Olympics massacre. Turmoil within, turmoil without. It's amazing that Sly and the band were able to get their heads around a new album at all.

Many critics think that *Fresh*, from 1973, is one of the most important funk and soul albums of all time. It's livelier and more vibrant than *Riot*. But *Fresh* is also an album of resignation. Sly saw the writing on the wall for his band, and a handful of tracks on this album sound like he's stepping away from the industry, albeit reluctantly. "If You Want Me to Stay" and a cover of Evans/Livingston's "Que Sera, Sera" are weary goodbyes, marked by melancholy and blue moods. The album sold well, reaching the Top 10 on the strength of the single "If You Want Me to Stay," another tune with "goodbye" overtones.

Small Talk followed in 1974. It reflected a calmer, gentler artist, perhaps as a result of changing musical times, or perhaps because he'd married and had a child. Sly wed Kathleen Silva, still a teenager, in 1974 in a huge ceremony/concert held at Madison Square Garden. Nine months later they had a baby, Sylvester Bubb Ali Stewart Jr. Five months after the baby's arrival they were in divorce court. At least Silva and the baby were able to live on, infamously, on the *Small Talk* album cover. "He said he loved me. He always said he loved me," said Silva. "I think he really did want that kind of world that was a special world" (Selvin, p. 169).

One of the reasons for their divorce emerged when Silva bumped into trumpeter Cynthia Robinson on the plane. Robinson dropped a bombshell on Silva. Despite strong advice to remain quiet, she explained to the new bride that she'd already had Sly's child, a girl, a few years before. Silva was crushed. "It was one of the first spikes in my heart," she admitted.

The album reached number 15 on the charts and attained gold status, selling over 500,000 copies. But that was largely based on Sly's loyal, lingering fan base rather than creative merit of the recording. *High on You* released in late 1975, was the first record he made that dropped "The Family Stone" tag. It served as the end of an era, but the album had no lasting impact.

By this time, disco had overtaken funk as the R&B idiom of choice, and soon Sly found himself antiquated, or at least out-dated. His drug problems hung on, and he had some run-ins with the law. Epic honored one more album from Sly before letting his contract expire. That album, *Ten Years Too Soon*, was a compilation of previously released material that replaced his funky rhythm tracks with disco beats.

Warner Bros. picked up Sly, and Sly went back in time to reunite with members of the family Stone for *Back on the Right Track*. But no one cared and when the album bombed, Stone retreated from the limelight and returned to drugs.

Stephen Paley served as the band photographer for a while as an employee of Epic Records and he stood in as Sly's best man at his wedding (a slight to both Banks and his brother Freddy). "The main problem was that Sly lost his perspective. He didn't know what was good and what wasn't good anymore. He erased wonderful things and re-recording things over them that weren't so good . . . He kept thinking that he'd make it better, but sometimes he would make it worse" (Selvin, p. 166).

In 1981 Sly partnered with 1970s funk icon (and Stone acolyte) George Clinton on Funkadelic's 1981 album *The Electric Spanking of War Babies*. He toured with Clinton's P-Funk Allstars and did a stint with old friend Bobby Womack. To take advantage of his new visibility, he tried issuing a comeback album in 1983 called *Ain't But One Way*. When that album received no notice, he hit the cocaine hard, got arrested, and finally entered rehab.

After emerging from rehab, the potholes continued. He was arrested and imprisoned again for possession in 1987 and never truly able to recover from this final arrest.

Sly and the Family Stone were inducted into the Rock and Roll Hall of Fame in 1993. To the surprise of everyone presenting attendance, Sly actually appeared for the induction and joined the band. Two years later, a hopeful label, Avenue Records, crossed their fingers and granted Sly a record deal. But they never released anything, not a single song.

In February 2006, a Sly and the Family Stone tribute took place at the Grammy Awards, at which Sly and the band (minus Larry Graham) gave his first live musical performance since 1987. Sporting an enormous blonde mohawk, thick sunglasses, a "Sly" belt buckle, and a silver lamé suit, he joined in on "I Want to Take You Higher." Producers admitted that Sly refused to leave his hotel room until he was given a police escort to the show and then waited in his car until the performance began before coming to the stage.

"It's sad to say," says Freddy. "He knows what he didn't do. He knows what we wish he had done. I know he wishes he could have done better. By me and by a lot of people. I think he thinks about it all the time" (Selvin, p. 191).

Sly Stone: Where Is He Now?

Inducted into the Rock and Roll Hall of Fame in 1993, Sly kept both band and audience waiting as the Family Stone ran through a version of "Thank You." "As usual, it's just us," Rose Stone sighed on stage. Finally materializing in an electric-blue leather jumpsuit, the reclusive Stone gave the most perfunctory of speeches, muttered, "See ya soon," and disappeared into the night. It was the first time the six original members of Family Stone (drummer Errico, bassist Graham, saxophonist Martini, trumpet player Cynthia Robinson, and the siblings Freddie and Rose Stone) walked onto the stage together, and Sly didn't even stick around for photos.

Since then Stone sightings have been few and far between. No one is entirely sure where he even resides. Funk legend and friend George Clinton believes he's in Malibu, California. His manager Jerry Goldstein admitted the singer, now in his mid-60s, is in frail condition. When Stone attended his father's funeral in 2002, his back appeared hunched, likely the result of poor nutrition and chronic drug use. "Sly went down the aisle of his brother's church with his mother on his arm, and nobody recognized him, because he has a hunchback," journalist Joel Selvin commented (DuLac, *Washington Post*, January 27, 2006).

"He's been in seclusion for so long, he's like J.D. Salinger," said Greg Zola, who is producing and directing *On the Sly: In Search of the Family Stone*, a documentary about the elusive musician and his bandmates. "He was so famous for a period of time, but he's just not around anymore. A lot of people who you'd think are in-the-know actually believe Sly Stone is dead" (DuLac, *Washington Post*, January 27, 2006).

Stone's younger sister, Vaetta, acknowledges as much on her Web site, where she's selling T-shirts proclaiming "Sly Lives." "I don't think Sly has been hurting from his underground status—I think he likes the mystique," said Rickey Vincent, author of *Funk: The Music, the People, and the Rhythm of the One* and host of a funk radio show in the San Francisco Bay area.

There are also unconfirmed reports that Sly has done recording sessions in seclusion and then erased all the tapes, not surprising, considering that was his practice in the mid-1970s as well.

"He's got hundreds of songs that he's sleeping on," former drummer Errico said. "He's been writing the whole time. Where are all those songs? I haven't heard one in 20 years. He's written and destroyed who knows how many great songs over the years with all the insanity he's been through" (Du Lac, *Washington Post*, January 27, 2006).

SELECTED DISCOGRAPHY

Dance to the Music (Epic/Legacy, 1968/2006)

Life (Epic/Legacy, 1968/2006)

Stand! (Epic/Legacy, 1969/2006)

There's a Riot Going On (Epic/Legacy, 1971/2006)

Fresh (Epic/Legacy, 1973/2006)

The Essential Sly and the Family Stone (Epic/Legacy, 2002)

FURTHER READING

Du Lac, J. Freedom. "Sly Stone's Surprise." *Washington Post*, January 27, 2006.

Hoskyns, Barney. "Looking at the Devil." *Observer Music Monthly*, March 19, 2006.

Lewis, Miles Marshall. *Sly and the Family Stone's There's a Riot Goin' On*. New York: 33 1/3, 2006.

Selvin, Joel. *Sly and the Family Stone: An Oral History*. New York: Avon, 1998.

Thompson, David. *Funk: Third Ear Listening Companion Series*. San Francisco: Backbeat Books, 2001.

Courtesy of Photofest.

George Clinton

"SUPERGROOVALISTICPROSIFUNKSTICATION"

Popular music had seen nothing quite like it, and will likely not see it again. The Parliament-Funkadelics, a musical collective roughly 50 members strong, changed the landscape of R&B forever, and elevated funk, its musical religion of choice, to a wildly entertaining art form, one that has exerted more influence on black music than virtually any other artist since its emergence in 1978.

The story of P-Funk is vast and colorful. At the outset of the 1970s, a man named George Clinton, the band's guru and an apostate from his own 1960s soul vocal groups, was eager for something new. He was bored by the black vocal groups of the early 1960s, the mild harmonies, the velvet tuxedos, the predictable dance steps. He yearned for something exciting that would rouse the music industry from its sleepy contentment.

Attracted by the hippie movement, Clinton wondered what would happen if he merged Flower Power with Black Power. He wanted to take the soulfulness of R&B and mingle it with the outrageous, anything-goes philosophy of the Haight-Ashbury hippies. He put a call out for willing souls, and has since hosted a continuous flow of hippie and post-hippie musicians looking for an alternative to the super-polished sounds of Motown in Detroit and Gamble/ Huff in Philadelphia. Clinton set his mind to creating the sounds of tomorrow, and in doing so expanded his loose-groove empire to ridiculous proportions.

Undertaking this project, Clinton, perhaps unwittingly, shaped and redefined the future of soul music in the same way Gordy did at Motown a dozen years earlier. In the process, he became a superstar, spawning numerous unorthodox spin-offs from his Parliament-Funkadelic empire, all of which had a look, sound, and feel of its own. Like a puppeteer pulling the strings of a bizarre kids' marionette show, Clinton controlled a magalopolis of funky music, and did so with imagination, whimsy, a strong work ethic, and a surprising sense of discipline.

Parliament-Funkadelic's principal offshoots—Parliament, Funkadelic, Bootsy's Rubber Band, and George Clinton—released over 30 studio albums, many of which were critical, to the evolution of 1970s funk. Despite its outlandish presentation—which featured wedding gowns, platform shoes, blonde wigs, astronaut costumes, and feathery headdresses—the P-Funk ensembles became a tremendous commercial force, verging on the mainstream even though it appeared to many as marginal and cockamamic. Indeed, it touched many mainstream acts in R&B, funk, and dance music at the time, as well as some rockers like the Red Hot Chili Peppers and the Beastie Boys.

All the labels for which P-Funk recorded made money, including Warner Bros., who netted something close to $30 million from the work of Clinton, Funkadelic, Bootsy, and the Brides of Funkenstein. The money started pouring in with the band's 1975 album, *Chocolate City*. But it really kicked in later that year with Parliament's epic *Mothership Connection* album and accompanying tour, which was a colorific take on R&B as seen through the eyes of Isaac Asimov. That is, an off-the-wall traveling road show, a kaleidoscope of sight and sound. By the end of the decade, Clinton parlayed that peculiar presentation into his own label, Uncle Jam Records, distributed by CBS.

As far as Parliament was going, we wanted to be saying something to black people, so we just took them and put them in a situation people had never seen them in and one they could be proud of. First, we put them in the White House.

> It made sense because [we] call DC "Chocolate City." Then, since *Chocolate City* worked, we had to find another place which ain't used to seeing blacks and somebody said, "Outer space." So we got us a Mothership and started doing what we'd be doing if we were in outer space. (Lloyd Bradley, "The Brother from Another Planet," *Mojo*, September 1996)

Clinton's desire to give his fans something to be proud of worked, thanks to the way he pushed the envelope theatrically and musically. Together, the collective worked on the presentation, and with the help of some mind-altering substances, developed characters, storylines, and running jokes to keep it as whimsical and funky as possible. Clinton admitted that during his songwriting stint at Motown he learned that if something was working it's best not to figure out why. Just feel the ingredients and run with it. Once the momentum kicked in, no explanations were necessary.

Between 1974 and 1981, Parliament-Funkadelic leveled an assault on the pop-rock-dance-funk scene, with music and musicians saturating every corner and sub-genre within reach. Music spewed not only from the conglomerate's principal bands, but from guitarist Eddie Hazel, keys genius Bernie Worrell, the Horny Horns, Parlet, and many others. And when Clinton set up his own label, he issued albums by an additional bevy of R&B personalities, including the Sweatband and former Motowner (and Spinner) Philippé Wynne. Sales totals of these acts hit eight figures and Clinton was seen as both a visionary and a successful businessman. There was something for everybody in what he offered, from go go and mainstream funk, to Philly rap, West Coast electro, Detroit house, and white funk. The fun never stopped. That is, it didn't stop until the lawyers and the corporate executives put a stop to it for him.

"We made it cool to be funky again, like James Brown had done," said Clinton.

> Once, you'd have to hide your James Brown records just like you had to hide Funkadelic records, 'cos they was nasty as hell. Even though when you went to a party where you'd look for the James Brown records and you'd party your ass off, you wouldn't admit to that because you wanted to be cool like Smokey or The Temptations. Funkadelic was the same way—anybody trying to be cool didn't want to admit to being down with that nasty, funky shit, not until well into the '70s. (Bradley)

THE EARLY YEARS

George Edward Clinton was born in 1941 in the small town of Kannapolis, North Carolina. He and his family relocated first to Washington, D.C., then to Virginia, and finally alighting in Newark, New Jersey, where he sparked his involvement with music.

At 14 he formed a vocal group called the Parliaments and they played local dances, hops, street corners, and small clubs for a couple of years, cutting their teeth. He and his singing partners all worked in a barber shop that Clinton eventually owned by the time he turned 18, in the neighboring ghetto town of Plainfield, New Jersey. The storefront was a gathering place for music fans and musicians, both young and old. Clinton took the shop over after the original owner died, and ran a reputable business there. During this time, in the urban neighborhoods of the 1950s, hair-cutting parlors provided a good living. Plus, Clinton and his gang needed a hassle-free place to hang and rehearse.

Clinton remembers those days with a chuckle:

> The way a barber usually advertised himself was to have the slickest hair imaginable, the sleekest process with nothing nappy showing through. Most of the time I was working so hard I never had time to get mine done so my slogan was always, "Come get your do done or you could end up looking like me!" It must have worked though, because we were going to school in Cadillacs and sharp suits! (Bradley)

Several of the regulars at the shop would often bring instruments for after-hours jam sessions. These included keyboard wiz Bernie Worrell, a graduate of the Boston Conservatory of Music, and guitarist Eddie Hazell, both of which would later form the nucleus of the band Funkadelic.

In the late 1950s, the Parliaments—a close harmony, doo-wop style singing group—recorded a couple of singles, the first, "Poor Willy," for ABC Records, and the second "Lonely Island," for a label called New Records. Both went nowhere, but the group didn't despair.

Shortly thereafter, in 1960, the Parliaments signed a contract with the New York City bureau of Detroit's Motown Records. But due to instability between the Detroit and New York branches, the Parliaments were lost in the shuffle. They never released any music on the imprint. Clinton would often joke that the band couldn't match their outfits well enough to suit the label.

George moved to New York City in 1962 to work for Jobete, Motown's publishing company. During this time he managed to collaborate briefly with the legendary songwriting team of Holland-Dozier-Holland on a few songs, including "Baby That's a Groove," which is credited to Clinton-Dozier-Holland. A few Parliament tracks the group never cut were eventually recorded by the Jackson 5 and the Supremes.

In an effort to shore up the tenuous arrangement they had with Motown, the Parliaments—Clinton, Ray Davis, Calvin Simon, Clarence "Fuzzy" Haskins, and Grady Thomas—uprooted from the barber shop and New Jersey and moved to Detroit. With their contract about to expire, they were torn. At the time, Clinton was leading a difficult double life. He worked in the music industry between Monday and Thursday, and flew back to Plainfield on Friday to take advantage of the lucrative weekend at the barber shop.

Clinton and the Parliaments wanted desperately to sign with Gordy's hot label. But they also had problems with the working climate at Motown, a place where Gordy treated his artists as if they were in military school. Certainly, the discipline didn't suit a renegade like George Clinton, and when their contract ran out, they opted to sign with another label.

Golden World would give the band their first taste of chart success with the minor hit "My Girl." But shortly after, Golden World was acquired by Motown, and the band was again out of a home. LeBarron Taylor, a top executive at Golden World, left to form a new Detroit label, Revilot, and when that label's first recording ("Our Love Is in the Pocket" by Darrell Banks, with Clinton co-writing) became a hit, Taylor made the Parliaments his next signing. "(I Just Wanna) Testify," the group's first song on Revilot in 1967 hit the charts hard. It reached Top 20 on the pop chart and Top 5 on R&B. Taylor loaned the band his red Cadillac to promote the album and by the time they did enough dates to push the record over the top, Taylor told them to keep the Cadillac.

But Revilot never had proper financing and they soon went out of business. They sold their Parliament masters to the Atco label in an attempt to recoup some of their losses, but Atco didn't reissue it or any new material soon enough to suit the band. Clinton and the boys moved back to New Jersey and pondered their next move.

> I was disillusioned. The whole pop success thing had wooed black music to the point where lyrical and melodic sophistication was everything, and the rhythms had become so predictable because they wasn't supposed to get in the way of the melody. The blues influences had been lost. This happened at Motown, and although it was cool to a point, it had got to where everybody wanted to do it that way. Except for James Brown and some of the stuff coming through from Memphis. (Bradley)

Atco eventually released a collection of Parliament singles and released the band. They realized Parliament was still under contract to Golden World/Motown for another year. Motown had indirectly tied the Parliaments up in one form or another for five full years, and the band had nothing to show for it.

THE SPLIT

Then, in 1969, George Clinton devised his first brilliant, nonconformist idea. Rather than remain inactive for that year, bound by a useless contract, he thought that he'd free up the musicians behind the Parliaments, the ones who created and played their instrumental tracks. Those artists weren't under contract and so were able to work under a different name. The band "Funkadelic" was born.

Prior to that arrangement, in 1966, the socio-cultural landscape began to change and Clinton had gotten caught up in the excitement. Music was transforming, becoming more rock-oriented, and increasing the volume, growing more unkempt, a perfect transformation for an eccentric like Clinton. Drugs entered the picture more prominently, another plus for the artist, who'd been smoking marijuana since his earliest days in the barber shop.

One of the reasons Clinton didn't push hard to get through the Motown door was because of the pressure they put on their artists to conform—in look, sound, and behavior. With the Parliaments, Clinton was never comfortable in their mohair suits, and so he wrestled with the idea of "playing the game," or attempting to do their own thing. In the back of his mind, he'd been toying with a strange twist on soul music, something really innovative, to suit his personality. Perhaps he didn't know what that meant exactly, only that he'd know it when he heard it.

Funkadelic financed its own first single, "Music for My Mother," and sold it to another new Detroit label called Westbound. Once the Parliaments' contract at Revilot was up, they were snatched up by Invictus, a company helmed by Holland-Dozier-Holland, the star songwriting team behind many of Motown's biggest hits. The writing trio had also rebelled against Motown and Berry Gordy and splintered off to start their own label. This meant that the 10 people in the Parliaments, including the band, which was now called the Funkadelics, were recording for two separate labels. This unorthodox arrangement ended up being the first of many bizarre contractual entanglements the Parliament-Funkadelic talent would encounter throughout their career.

"Sure, neither company liked it much," George explained at the time,

> but we had been caught before in the business, so we felt it safer if we had an escape clause. Funkadelic stays with Westbound and Parliament stays with Invictus and, though they don't really like it, it keeps both companies working hard trying to do better than the other. (Simon Witter, "Taking Funk over the Hump," *I-D,* May 1988)

Having temporarily lost the rights to the Parliaments name and concept for a year because of the binding contract, Funkadelic became Clinton's focus. His whole crew, the band and his fellow Parliaments worked on the new project, becoming active in the business again. They recorded an album and naturally, only the heretofore unknown musicians, the Parliaments' backing band not under contract already, were given songwriting credit.

Meanwhile, in 1970, ownership of its name reverted back to the band. Only this time, the singers decided to call themselves simply "Parliament." The Parliament-Funkadelic empire, also known humorously as Uncle Jam's Army, now had its first two principals, and they were on the lookout for more.

JOINING THE ARMY

"Where I figure that I might have done at least one thing that had a little intelligence in it was the fact that we tied all the groups together," said Clinton. "One could support the other when necessary; it made us less vulnerable. Also I knew how the system likes to play one artist off against another, so we were able to get around that" (Cliff White, "The Noble Art of Rhythm'n'Biz," *New Music Express*, November 18, 1978).

The circus assembled by George Clinton and the Parliament bunch began to expand soon after the band received its name back. In the first decade of its recruiting, that funky force numbered as high as 55 members, all serving in one capacity or another in George Clinton's burgeoning army.

As the numbers grew, the contractual complications also multiplied. Individuals on the bandwagon were signed to Clinton's own company Thang Incorporated, not to a record company. Then Clinton would negotiate individual deals with those labels under group names that do not stipulate any particular personnel. That way specific individuals avoided any sort of record company politics and other legal entanglements; it also allowed the artists freedom to move from group to group when the spirit felt so inclined, or when their specific services were required. This also meant that songs themselves could shift between bands, depending on the vibe or instrumental direction. If a song was half finished but the groove wasn't right, one band could always pitch the composition over to another more appropriate outlet. That way no notes went to waste.

It also meant that P-Funk could pursue as many musical projects as they could concoct names for, release as many albums as they could record, and no player would be contractually bound if something went wrong. The only drawback was that the labels involved were competing against each other to sell basically the same interchangeable act.

The magic of P-Funk lay beneath all the outrageous get-ups and crazy theatricality: the musicianship. George Clinton was once asked by the host of a German music TV program how he could arrange a song for up to 27 musicians and still have it sound okay. Clinton answered, "The secret is to get cats who can really play. Then you just have to offer them the possibility of chaos and order on the same plate, and they'll go for it every time" (source unknown).

Of course it helped that in addition to having the best musicians he could find, Clinton also made sure ego never came into play. In fact, all personalities with the exception of Clinton's took a backseat to the group's wild stage antics and madcap concepts.

THE MAIN CHARACTERS

The main strands of P-Funk were Parliament and Funkadelic. Parliament featured relatively traditional funk performances with sizzling horns and gospel harmonizing amid colorful storylines. Funkadelic incorporated more rock and roll. They were also politically minded, and more outlandish in terms of songs and song structures. The surprising aspect of this dichotomy was that oftentimes the same musicians would form the core of both. At last count, there were a total of 17 horn players who had passed through the P-Funk gauntlet, 11 guitarists, 6 bass players, 10 drummers/percussionists, 10 lead vocalists, and over 25 background singers.

Bernie Worrell and Junie Morrison were genius keyboard players. Worrell, a classically trained pianist, mastered a vast cache of effects and instruments, and nearly single-handedly formed the nucleus of Parliament's sound. Then there was guitarist Eddie Hazel, often considered to be one of rock music's top 100 electric guitarists. Hazel received assistance from guitarists Mike Hampton and DeWayne "Blackbyrd" McKnight, both talented players in their own right. Hazel did his best work in Funkadelic, especially on iconoclastic funk-rock LPs like *Maggot Brain*.

Fred Wesley, Maceo Parker, and Rick Gardner comprised the horn section. Wesley, a trombonist, was the longtime musical director of James Brown's band and helped to orchestrate the precise, note-perfect solos Brown favored. Parker, a household name for funk fans for his 1960s work, also with James Brown, earned his reputation for memorable, stinging saxophone solos. Parker, legend has it, is the only musician James Brown ever had the humility to ask back into his band.

P-Funk had almost as much talent in the singing department. Ray Davis sang bass, Glen Goins and Gary Shider the tenors, and cartoonish voices of P-Nut and Mudbone, who sang later for Bootsy Collins's band, provided the voice over entertainment for some of the act's more outrageous characters. In addition, there was a group of women, called the Brides of Funkenstein, within the P-Funk ranks, and a platoon of part-time dancers, actors, and background singers.

FUNKADELIC

Initially, Funkadelic was a tough sell. The original band, Hazel and drummer Tiki Fulwood, guitarist Tawl Ross, bassist/bandleader Billy Nelson, and Mickey Atkins on organ, were not as well-polished as the Parliament crew, not as schooled in the aspects of performing, and they had little formal music training. They were essentially a rock band. Their sound, fuzzed out and distorted with lots of effects, had more in common with early punk rock bands like the Stooges and MC5 than the soul of Philly or Detroit.

Funk's Lineage

Funk originated as something of a successor to soul music. It combines a wide array of different elements pilfered from various musical types that had come before: soul, R&B, blues, rock, psychedelia, be-bop, and the polyrhythms of

African percussion. "Funk music is a direct offspring of the blues in terms of its intimacy, intensity, and meaning for 'common' black folks in the decade of integration" (Vincent, p. 19).

In sound, funk began with a specific set of elements: a steady, insistent groove, a heavy bass presence punctuated by aggressive horns, and a certain amount of sexiness, or intimacy. It was also designed to get people up and dance. But not any dance would do. Funk was designed to entrance listeners, to the point where one forgets she's dancing at all and instead fills that feeling of sultry, uninhibited bliss. James Brown mastered the art early, and his legion of spawn skillfully picked it up and brought it to new heights.

In the 1970s, a funk scene had already existed thanks to Brown, Sly Stone, and Curtis Mayfield, the triumivirate largely responsible for funk's original evolution. Brown, nicknamed "The Godfather of Soul," derived the formula, while Stone and Mayfield took their cues from him and expanded the genre's sound. In the early 1970s, a myriad of bands arose in the wake of this activity, including Otis Redding's former backing band the Bar-Kays, who billed themselves a Black Rock Funk as early as 1972. About the same time, George Clinton's P-Funk empire began its quest to spread funk throughout the nation. With its many tentacles, including Parliament, Funkadelic, Clinton, and Bootsy Collins, it succeeded in dominating the funk scene through the 1970s. Their musical output would, beyond all the others at the time, prove to be the most influential. Their music reached all types of fans, too, from soul to rock, and their memorable grooves would provide the young rap/hip-hop scene with a bounty of samples from which to build their own grooves.

Also in the 1970s, bands such as Kool and the Gang, the Ohio Players, Earth, Wind and Fire, the Commodores, and War, each of whom would deserve a unique chapter had these volumes been elongated, were early funk proponents that added unique elements to the James Brown sound. They were key players in the 1970s funk revival. There were also heavier pure funk bands like Slave, Lakeside, and Cameo, among many others that sold records in significant numbers during funk's peak era.

In the 1980s, the P-Funk repercussions continued. Performers like Rick James, Prince, the Time, the Gap Band, and Roger Troutman's Zapp all issued quality material. But in the middle of the decade, the funk/soul scene petered out. These performers had run dry. Radio had abandoned the sound, leaving a gap in black music quickly filled by the innovative urban rhythms of early hip-hop. Afrika Bambaataa began to concoct his heady grooves, and the revolution of rap music in the wake of funk's death, began in earnest.

They were also different in that they were less willing to play the P-Funk masquerade game. They wanted to rock, without all the pageantry. And they backed up those intentions on record. *Funkadelic*, released in 1970, communicated the concept of black blues-rock with clarity; and many yielded important moments, including the intro beat, which has since become a classic hip-hop sample.

In 1971, Funkadelic released *Maggot Brain*, their masterpiece. At the time, Ross had grown addicted to narcotics, and the band decided to leave him behind. That left the guitar spotlight on Hazel, who excelled as a presence on the record, especially on the Clinton-penned title track, in which his eight-minute solo has become funk's most lauded guitar workout, and one of the most memorable in rock and roll history. Jimi Hendrix himself would have been proud of Hazel's work. In fact, Hendrix died as the band was making the album, so it was a fitting tribute.

The Funkadelic gang, emboldened by the widespread acceptance and appreciation of *Maggot Brain*, reached for more. They'd record through 1976 on the Westbound label, laying down a formidable foundation of rock, funk, R&B, and eccentricity. They also earned a reputation for torrid performances and became a band difficult to follow on stage. *The Rolling Stone Record Guide* said of them: "The music of Funkadelic is an urban soundscape—not always pretty or appealing but perhaps the truest representation of urban life offered in black music."

BOOTSY COLLINS

In 1972 a bass player named William "Bootsy" Collins out of Cincinnati joined up with the caravan. Collins had formed his first band, called the Pacesetters, back in 1968 with his brother Phelps, Frankie Waddy, and Philippé Wynne. At first, they were a sort of house band for the King Records label, assigned to supply backing for popular King roster artists like Arthur Prysock and Hank Ballard. When King signed superstar James Brown in 1969, Collins and company were assigned to him, and they spent the next three years backing him as Brown's JBs.

The road became quite rigorous, as the JBs soon found out, and their leader was notoriously dictatorial. Brown would often dock the pay of a musician who hit a wrong note, or screwed up a dance step. So the routine grew wearisome, and after three years, the band decided to ditch the Godfather of Funk and go it alone. Bootsy was only 19 by the time he left Brown, so there was plenty of music left to play.

Returning to Cincinnati, they formed the House Guests, a band of outrageously dressed, dubiously behaved musicians out looking for a good time. Clearly, they had left the stern discipline of the JBs behind. One band, the Spinners out of Detroit, had approached them to be their backing band, but only one of the members, Wynne, accepted the offer. The Collins boys had a feeling they were onto a good thing, and stayed the course.

Eventually, the paths of both Parliament-Funkadelic and the House Guests crossed. George Clinton checked out the House Guests in 1972, and invited

Bootsy in as a collaborator. Many feel that Parliament truly kicked into gear when Collins joined the fray.

> Both artists had fantastic imaginations, single-parent upbringings (raised by their mothers), and years of drug-induced psychedelic soul music behind them. Clinton and Bootsy quickly became an interlinked creative songwriting duo, a partnership that flourished with the social insight of Lennon and McCartney, the folksy warmth of Simon and Garfunkel, and the strength of Chuck D and Flavor Flav. (Rickey Vincent, *Funk: The Music the People and the Rhythm of the One*, New York: St. Martin's Griffin, 1996 p. 239)

Together, they pushed the Parliament-Funkadelic concept to new heights.

Bootsy Collins, under the moniker Bootsy's Rubber Band, would later become one of the most bankable artists to come out of the P-Funk conglomerate. Among bass players, he was legendary, a prototype of funk bass much in the way Larry Graham from Sly and the Family Stone was. As a musical unit, they were the most liberated of all the P-Funk tribes, stretching out their jams (hence, their name) into elongated spasms of rhythm. Their first album, *Stretchin' Out*, released in 1976, resonated with bass-heavy craziness and fit the P-Funk raison d'etre perfectly. They recorded another handful of successful albums through the end of the 1970s, including *This Boot Is Made for Funkin'* on Warner Bros. The outfit received so much attention that the band's vocal chorus split into another outfit, called Parlet, for a few releases.

Other noteworthy acts popped out of Clinton's posse. Fred Wesley and the Horny Horns made two records. Female vocalists Lynn Mabry and Dawn Silva formed the Brides of Funkenstein. Hazel made the acclaimed solo album, *Games, Dames, and Guitar Thangs*, proving his immense value to the P-Funk gathering. Bernie Worrell made a couple of albums of his own, as did Maceo Parker under the name Maceo and the King's Men. Obviously, production hit overdrive when these talents began feeding off of and inspiring each other.

THE PURE FUNK SOUND

One of the major benefits of having so many talented musicians around him was the Technicolor sound that came out of them. Clinton enjoyed the services of many creative people, and he simply let them do what they did best: play. That meant the collective style would be altogether indefinable, indescribably and completely wacky, spanning every black musical style from traditional gospel all the way to Jimi Hendrix's electric-blues psychedelia. The doors had come open and the winds of creative freedom blew freely.

Often, a song started with a riff or chant, occasionally both at the same time, both designed to move feet. Then came an invasion of musical variations, genres, and oddball ideas. The combination, rhythmic and steadily building, entranced audiences. Through it all, lyrical lines from Clinton's demented brain addressed one of his comic-book characterizations in some nonsensical story or tale.

With Parker and Wesley handling the horns, Clinton could arrange the tunes however he wanted. Throw some rock and roll on top, and finish it off with close-harmony doo-wop vocals and you've got what Clinton often referred to as his big sandwich, "the kind Scooby Doo used to eat." As far as he was concerned, despite the number of layers already crammed into a tune, there was always room to "throw something stupid on top."

At the time, P-Funk was getting away with just about everything sonically. Because they were in the process of writing, or re-writing, the rulebook, no one acknowledged any limitations. No one cared to define them. Making this kind of wacked-out music was too much fun, too good to be true. This attitude enabled them to transcend white and black. Like Sly Stone was doing about the same time, or perhaps a year or two earlier, P-Funk liberated black musicians from simply playing to a black audience and they eliminated any notions of selling out to a white audience by maintaining a solid grip on their African American heritage.

Since the late 1960s, the social climate was changing in their favor as well. The hippie movement, which led to Hendrix and garage/heavy/psychedelic rock had quieted down after Monterey, Woodstock, and Vietnam. The Motown Sound had phased out of pop and into what the Temptations were doing with producer Norman Whitfield during their "Ball of Confusion" psychedelic-funk phase. Marvin Gaye, Stevie Wonder, and Sly and the Family Stone had surged to the vanguard of black music with its hard message albums like *What's Goin' On?* and *There's a Riot Goin' On.* Curtis Mayfield helped give black cinematic music, or blaxploitation, some credibility with his landmark soundtrack to *Superfly.* In fact, black music had at the time become eminently commercial. Black cinema had begun making money as well. Black was in. "Even white people wanted to be black," said Clinton.

> We had to change up and we couldn't just leave the following we'd gained over the last few years, we still had to offer [blacks] a little bit more. We wanted to be able to put the intellectual shit on top of the rhythm, because by then the rhythm was becoming so hip that it could support intellectualism, or just plain foolishness, and still sound cool. (Bradley)
>
> James Brown was the hottest shit around on the black side, white people was trying to be black and that was what was taking over the radio again. Motown had had the radio for ten years but now it had wore itself out. We started checking out Lee Dorsey, stuff like that, and figured, "Aaaah, they ain't got this shit, that real nasty shit that makes you shake your ass," and we went that way, but we got to wah wahs and fuzz tones and it sounded really nasty. Then I started talking about, "Lick my soul and I will suck your funky emotion." Knowing that black was popular with black folks and white folks alike we just did the *blackest* of the black shit. (Witter)

PARLIAMENT'S MOTHERSHIP

In 1973, Clinton signed his operation to a contract with Neil Bogart's Casablanca Records imprint. The eccentric Bogart had an eye for a gimmick—he'd soon sign KISS as well—and Clinton and Bogart made a good match. Clinton appreciated Bogart's support, especially financially, and Bogart knew he'd be paid in kind. It was Bogart's money in those early years that allowed Clinton to expand his empire, and when the singles like "Up for the Down Stroke" in the summer of 1974 started to make headway, Bogart's wallet opened even further.

When Bootsy convinced the Maceo Parker and Fred Wesley, two fellow JBs, to join the mob, thereby adding an adroit brass section, Clinton had Parliament right where he wanted them.

1975 was the year it all came together, the Year of the Mothership. Everything to this point had been a dress rehearsal for this critical phase in the collective's development. As Clinton relays the story, he was driving with Bootsy and they saw this light bouncing from one side of the street to the other. Clinton thought, "the Mothership is angry with us for giving up the funk without permission." Then the light hit the car and all the other area lights went out. The weirdness freaked Collins and Clinton, but also sparked the idea: Clinton's "Mothership Connection."

"The *Mothership Connection* LP was a motherlode of concepts and rhythm on a level never witnessed before" (Vincent, p. 241). Lyrics were vividly rendered scenarios, part fantasy, part science fiction, part madness. Clinton called it "supergroovalistic-prosifunkstication." Charged with energy to go along with that imagination, the album featured wall-to-wall funk, with no ballads in between for pacing. It served as Parliament-Funkadelic's mission statement, its defining moment, a towering monument to R&B. It's the one album they will, despite the mob's myriad side projects, be best remembered by.

Since its release, hip-hoppers have had a field day with the *Mothership Connection* album, grabbing samples off it like kids fighting for the last lollipop. Dr. Dre's dazzling classic *The Chronic* made ample use of *Mothership* as have many other old school rappers like Snoop Dogg and Public Enemy's Chuck D.

In June 1976, a track off the album, "Give Up the Funk (Tear the Roof Off the Sucker)," a complex, hard-hitting dance track, broke into the pop charts and became the country's number one R&B single. Within that year, P-Funk had completely seized the imagination of the record-buying public; they had released five albums under four different names for three separate labels.

While millions of fans took notice of Parliament's work, apart from "Tear the Roof Off the Sucker" Clinton and company were ignored by radio.

"It took me a while to realize that I wasn't getting played on no white stations because I was black and I didn't get played on black stations because to them it sounded like I was white. So then I had to go back and meet 'em halfway with the Parliament situation, the horns and things, and then hand-walk 'em up to where Funkadelic is at. (Bradley)

Other funk and R&B acts—the Ohio Players and Earth, Wind and Fire— were more widely accepted. Where War's "Low Rider," the Commodores' "Brick House," and the Ohio Players' "Skin Tight," for example, were being played on a wide swath of FM stations, Parliament couldn't *buy* airplay. They were marginalized, considered too extreme.

They took the "Mothership Connection" show on the road to support the album. The tour was an outright spectacle, a sweaty mish-mash of sci-fi, funk, rock, and gospel revival. Produced with an unprecedented $275,000 budget, it featured the band alighting on stage in an actual spaceship. There were outrageous, animated props, musicians flying through the air, choreographed tribal dancing, church vocals, and an array of mind-blowing visuals. The band hit the road for four months on this maniacal journey, and dazzled audiences nightly. The production involved exhaustive planning and excessive attention to detail, all of which Clinton oversaw. The odyssey culminated with a best-selling live album, *Parliament Live: The P-Funk Earth Tour*. People by the thousands would remember the tour as one of the most memorable, and out-rageous, of the decade.

The band finished out the 1970s with a modicum of radio success. Songs like "Flash Light" and "Aqua Boogie" caught the ear of pop radio as well as R&B stations, and soon black and white music fans alike had caught onto these funky madmen. In fact, P-Funk became so popular that Mattel, the popular toy company, entered into negotiations to create a series of dolls based upon Clinton's diverse and colorful P-Funk characterizations.

In the end, those negotiations broke down after licensing and royalty dis-agreements arose, so the plan was scrapped. It wouldn't be the last time the P-Funk troupe would see the inside of a courtroom.

TOILS AND TROUBLES

All good things had to come to an end, though, and so it was with Parliament-Funkadelic. The empire had expanded to an out-of-control point by the time it had subsumed Bootsy's Rubber Band, and was now numbering upwards of 70 total characters and artists. For a long time, Clinton's scheme of keeping them all under his aegis worked beautifully. He engineered licensing deals for each separate operation as they formulated, and so he was able to keep track of where everybody was headed and what everyone was doing. This also proved effective in cross-pollinating the acts, allowing each musician the opportunity to share his gifts with not just one but any number of collective members.

Eventually though, there were so many people involved in so many different things, cracks started to form in its cumbersome foundation. In metaphorical terms, George Clinton had elevated funk to a lifestyle. He created it as something to strive for, like sainthood, or a job promotion. But the lifestyle he created was a vast illusion, not a reality. It was an illusion he succeeded in projecting to his audience from the stage.

The reality of P-Funk, the day-to-day mechanisms behind the workings of the band, was something quite different. In the beginning, that ideal was reasonably close to P-Funk's reality; as the musicians and the different bands were reveling in the creative adrenaline spawned by such inspired work. But as the band began to succeed, gaining notoriety, money became a more serious issue.

Like any successful operation, P-Funk gained legions of hangers-on, people looking to ride the coattails of success in hopes of picking up some of the financial scraps. But as many of these hangers-on latched onto to the band's wagon, it groaned with all the excess weight.

These people also brought with them alluring goodies: stronger drugs and other temptations that many in the band had already dabbled with and enjoyed. There were other distractions—parties, girls, side projects, vanity deals—that also served to add temptation to every day.

To make matters worse, the music industry climate had begun to change. Throughout most of the 1970s, until about 1977, funk had a firm footing and good representation within popular music. But it also dug its own grave. Hard funk bands proved they couldn't get much mainstream airplay, so, in an attempt to circumvent that problem, lighter funk bands came into being. Radio loved *them*, so much so that they wanted more and more, and the lighter the better. This explains in part the birth of disco music.

Like funk in the early 1970s, late 1970s disco became a whirling dervish, leveling everything in its way. Dance floors everywhere exploded with its super-lightweight sounds. Funk virtually disappeared, a relic from an immense movement of music and mayhem.

For Parliament-Funkadelic, tensions were high and morale was low at the turn of the decade. In fact, Clinton retired, at least temporarily, from music right before his band was slated to play a week-long stint at the Apollo Theater in Harlem. The band soldiered on that week, and Clinton appeared in a few cameo roles. He eventually returned full time.

Somehow, Clinton and P-Funk held on through the disco onslaught. Not only did they compete with the genre's mercurial rise of disco, they had to contend with a slew of lawsuits and other legal complications, most of which stemmed from Clinton's bizarre jumble of arrangements he had made with members of his crew.

As early as 1978, he experienced desertions of crew members. One of them, Jerome Brailly, was especially outspoken of his time with the Mothership in the work he did with his own band, Mutiny. The title of the band's first album, *Mutiny on the Mamaship*, explains it all.

To compound problems for P-Funk, Clinton's most faithful ally, Neil Bogart of Casablanca, died of cancer in 1982. Warner Bros., who represented many of the acts, demanded the band cut their upcoming two-disc set *The Electric Spanking of War Babies*, down to a single disc. They also censored artist Pedro Bell's phallic album art. The band didn't expect these affronts, for they had just come off two million-selling albums, and despite the surge of disco, still expected substantial commercial success.

For the *War Babies* album, Clinton had recruited funk pioneers James Brown and Sly Stone. But star quality wasn't enough for their label. Warner Bros., convinced that Parliament-Funkadelic was more trouble than it was worth—perhaps they looked at their complicated contracts?—decided to let them go. This meant that Clinton had lost Funkadelic, and now Parliament. Discouraged, he signed with CBS Records as George Clinton and the P-Funk Allstars. That deal experienced a similar fate as the one with Warner Bros., only quicker.

Roger Troutman, a newish member of the Clinton posse, had secured a deal with Warner Bros. through his childhood friend Bootsy Collins. After entering the P-Funk fold, Clinton helped Troutman put together the monster single, "More Bounce to the Ounce," one of the most sampled songs in the history of pop. It went to number one on the R&B charts. To this day, the tune qualifies as one of the P-Funk oeuvre's most enduring. But after seeing the writing on the wall, Troutman left the Clinton gang to record on his own; he managed to escape with his band Zapp and did so with style and substance.

Troutman's abrupt departure represented another straw that helped break P-Funk's back. Clinton's loss was Troutman's gain and Zapp went on to make memorable, successful music throughout the 1980s.

In 1983, a country band called the Rubber Band sued Bootsy for using the band name unlawfully and, after a protracted legal fight, won. Bootsy could no longer call his act the Rubber Band, and he lost nearly $300,000 in future royalties to pay for court costs. It would be five years before Bootsy could pay off his debut and get free of his contract. By 1988, he was faced with starting over.

Clinton's relationship with Sly Stone, a notorious drug consumer, also ended up being detrimental. They were busted in California in 1982 for possession of cocaine. It's hard not to take note of the symbolism: two out of three of funk's grandest icons tossed in the slammer.

SUCCESS, ETC.

Through the rest of the 1980s, Clinton survived, but largely underground. He worked with a variety of performers, including Stone, James Brown, Thomas Dolby, Prince—all artists whose careers had also taken a nosedive at the time.

Clinton had been virtually banned from radio as well. But that didn't mean his audience had left him. He toured continuously through the late 1980s and early 1990s on the strength of one of his biggest hits, "Atomic Dog." The song, off his album *Computer Games*, remains an oft-sampled classic, and one reason George Clinton's name is still on the lips of R&B/funk fans to this day.

But his label at the time, Capitol, refused to service the record to many radio outlets. Clinton's reputation preceded him, and few wanted to get involved in more complicated entanglements. Clinton, though, had adopted new business policies; he had already headed toward new and hopeful territory, free of complications.

When radio finally got a hold of "Atomic Dog," it shot up the R&B charts to number one, passing Michael Jackson's "Billie Jean" along the way. Oddly, the record didn't even crack the Top 100 on the pop side. Generally, number one R&B hits were a cinch to hit the same spot on the pop charts. But Clinton, ever the iconoclast, failed to make even the slightest impression on the pop side. Never was there a more clear distinction between black music and white music.

Label difficulties again dogged Clinton at Capitol and he eventually ended up at Paisley Park, the soul music star Prince's imprint. Together, they issued a few lofty jams. Clinton stumbled on a production job: working the console for the second album by Los Angeles white funk rockers the Red Hot Chili Peppers. He, his group, and the Peppers all teamed up for a gigantic jam session on NBC TV's *Saturday Night Live* program, one that eventually led to Parliament snaring a slot on the main stage for the 1994 Lollapalooza summer rock tour. White rockers began taking notice and Clinton put himself back on the map.

At about the same time, so was hard-core rap, which was beginning to make itself heard with groups like Public Enemy. The first Public Enemy single, "Bring the Noise," off their first album, *It Takes a Nation of Millions to Hold Us Back*, made good use of Funkadelic's "Get Off Your Ass and Jam." As militant rap expanded and rappers were seeking to expand their sampling beyond old school James Brown, Parliament vinyl was the next place to look.

Virtually all of the early 1990s rap outfits—EPMD, De La Soul, and Schooly D—sprinkled P-Funk samples liberally throughout their jams. Digital Underground, a rap act from Oakland, professed deep fealty to Parliament by naming their third album *Sons of the P*. Clinton cameoed on the recording.

Since then, Clinton has reaffirmed his place alongside many of these hip-hop and rock acts, not as a washed-up sideshow, or as some kind of dated mascot of the funk genre, but as a viable performer who still exudes hipness and great ideas.

LEGACY

Taking his cues from the hipster lingo of the beboppers, early black radio deejays, and the apocalyptic anti-slavemassa edicts of black nationalist sects lik the

Nation of Islam, Clinton reconceived funk as the antithesis of everything that was sterile, one-dimensional, monochromatic, arrhythmic and otherwise against freedom of bodily expression in the known universe. (Greg Tate, *Parliament: Tear the Roof Off, 1974–1980*, liner notes, Casablanca/Chronicles, 1993)

Throughout his career, Clinton blurred the lines between funk and life. "He placed the African American sensibility at the center of the universe" (Vincent, p. 254). For fun, or perhaps in all seriousness, Clinton postulated that it was the Africans that built the pyramids, essentially throwing down the philosophy that blacks were responsible for all of civilization.

Clinton would later tackle the idea, this one became more of a joke, that the P-Funk tribe was responsible for the Big Bang itself. "That fuss wuz us!" they sang. Because they wallowed a sort of good-time preposterousness, it didn't matter what they claimed or how they claimed. They edified the African American culture, reassured them through funk that their lives had purpose. The turned the negative stereotypes of blacks inside out. By delivering this message to the right crowd, with the right tenor, and via the perfect medium in their music, Bootsy, Parliament, and Funkadelic managed to sell over 10 million records in just six years.

The ascendancy of George Clinton's P-Funk establishment marked a new phase in the post–civil rights movement for black America. Where Martin Luther King Jr. spoke to the hearts of his congregations using religious and passionate, precise language, George Clinton appealed to their booties and spoke in an oblique, bizarre, and often totally inscrutable language. Funk was his religion. Oddly enough, they accomplished some of the same things. King spoke from the dais, or the rooftops; Clinton delivered his sermons from the doors of the Mothership.

But they both empowered black America to be proud of their heritage, proud of themselves, and proud of their community. "Since P-Funk is the direct link between hiphop culture and the legacy of black music and political struggle that preceded that Bronxborn revolution, Clinton's fakeout of the powers that be—hiding astute social commentary in "interplanetary funksmanship'—worked like a charm" (Tate).

The fact remains that in addition to providing black youth with a musical focal point for nearly a decade, Clinton provided the cornerstone—in both sound and content—for virtually all black music to follow right through the present day. With P-Funk, there would be no Afrika Bambaataa, no Grandmaster Flash and the Furious Five, the progenitors of rap and hip-hop often credited with inventing the genre. With the work of Parliament and Funkadelic, we would almost certainly have no black rock and roll. Bands in that rubric, like Fishbone, 24-7 Spyz, and Living Colour all took their cues directly from the grooves emanating from this wide circle of talented music makers.

P-Funk's current circle of influence stretches way beyond even these amazingly inspired performers. They also touched Philly rap, West Coast electro,

Detroit house, and white acts like Was (Not Was) and the Red Hot Chili Peppers. P-Funk was such a commercial force in the 1970s, it reached anyone who was into dance music at the time.

The vision of Parliament, Funkadelic, Bootsy, and George Clinton was consistently positive. Collectively, they viewed the African American population as strong and creative, important and full of potential. All that population needed was a little guidance, some direction, a handful of great grooves and a few catchphrases, perhaps. To that end, they came up with one of funk's most memorable statements. The melding of P-Funk with MLK still sounds extraordinary today.

SELECTED DISCOGRAPHY

Parliament-Funkadelic

> *The Mothership Connection* (Casablanca, 1976)
> *The Clones of Dr. Funkenstein* (Casablanca, 1976)
> *Funkentelechy Vs. The Placebo Syndrome* (Casablanca, 1977)

Funkadelic

> *Free Your Mind . . . And Your Ass Will Follow* (Westbound, 1970)
> *Funkadelic* (Westbound, 1970)
> *Maggot Brain* (Westbound, 1971)
> *One Nation Under a Groove* (Priority, 1978)
> *The Electric Spanking of War Babies* (Priority, 1981)

FURTHER READING

George, Nelson. *Hip Hop America*. New York: Penguin, 2005.

Larkin, Colin, ed. *The Virgin Encyclopedia of R&B and Soul*. London: Virgin Books, 1998.

Vincent, Rickey. *Funk: The Music the People and the Rhythm of the One*. New York: St. Martin's Griffin, 1996.

Michael Ochs Archives/Getty Images.

Kenny Gamble, Leon Huff, and Thom Bell

"THE SOUND OF PHILADELPHIA"

It's been said before on quite a few occasions, but it bears repeating. "The Sound of Philadelphia," developed by Kenny Gamble, Leon Huff, and Thom Bell, was to the 1970s what Berry Gordy's Tamla/Motown sound was to the 1960s. With a proven songwriting approach and a long roster of hit makers, the Philly music svengalis forged a style and identity as powerful as any in the history of pop.

The trio collectively produced 28 gold or platinum records, and 31 million-selling gold- or platinum-certified singles. These mainly hail from a pool of more than a thousand songs they'd written over the years for their vast stable of artists. Many of Gamble and Huff's artists went on to become superstars, including Teddy Pendergrass of Harold Melvin and the Blue Notes, the O'Jays, the Spinners, and the Stylistics. To soul and pop fans in the 1970s, *these* were the sounds of commercial radio. These, and many other Philly soul acts, ruled the airwaves with hit after gorgeous hit.

More than any gimmick, it was the *sound* of these hits that set them apart. Gamble, Huff, and Bell took the rhythmic push of Motown and Stax, smoothed it out, added strings, punchy horns, crisp melodies, chill vocal harmonies, and amazing hooks. Many critics and other music experts say, not half-joking, that the soul music out of Philadelphia at this time featured the most memorable melodies in the history of pop.

Certainly, songs like "Me and Mrs. Jones," "Rubberband Man," "Love Train," "You Make Me Feel Brand New," and "When Will I See You Again," make for a solid case. They are indelible in every sense, archetypal works of soul, featuring layer after brilliantly arranged layer of instrumentation and orchestration.

The label they represented, Philadelphia International Records, was the last of the great independent music empires, and Gamble, Bell, and Huff (hereafter referred to as GB&H) ruled that empire. They wrote, arranged, and often helped perform the songs that erected such a glorious edifice. They nurtured the artistry that became critical to its look and feel and sound. Time after time, they nailed the emotions of the human heart circa 1973 and had their finger on the pulse of musical, societal, and cultural trends.

"They represented the creative process at its most evolved. They brought American music to another level. They followed their instincts and it showed, in the range and breadth of their music" (Boz Scaggs, *The Philly Sound*, liner notes, Epic/Legacy, 1997, p. 48).

When it exploded, Philly Soul had been laying in wait for a few years. At the time, the Temptations, Sly Stone, and Curtis Mayfield were dominating the charts and minds of black music fans the world over. Motown still had significant pull, as did funk geniuses like James Brown and George Clinton. Sly and the funk sound, though, had come out of the hippie era, almost directly from the Flower Power aesthetic of Haight-Ashbury, a long way from the mean streets of Philadelphia. The urban street corners had already seen doo-wop and *American Bandstand* pass through the city. The music scene in Philly had throughout the 1960s produced much in the way of soul, and its best musicians had spent the latter part of the decade refining their chops. So when GB&H made the calls, this talent was raring to go.

Knowing they had a good thing, and following the template Gordy at Motown had set forth, GB&H developed a soul system that allowed them to control every aspect of their artists' output. The formula was simple: amass the most talented musicians on the scene, write effective songs that appealed to the righteous black music fan and the casual pop fan alike (black and white), and find the artists that could sing them as well as they were written.

At their peak, the label had a 40-plus piece orchestra hashing out their songs, a large and dexterous band that did their best work live in the studio. They could swing with the skill and verve of a big band, funk it up with the nastiest groove masters, and take it down to create the perfect "quiet storm."

Unlike the classic Motown period, in which each track contained the same formulaic elements and ran habitually two and a half minutes in length, GB&H often wrote loose arrangements, within which groups could experiment, stretch out, or improvise. Harold Melvin and the Blue Notes often stretched their jams into six- or seven-minute workouts.

Legend has it that the principals of the Philadelphia international empire were laughed at when they sought employment with the major record labels at the time. They were treated with prejudice, and that unfair treatment propelled them on a mission. For a brief, shining moment they overcame that prejudice and set the world on fire with a great business model and even greater music that captured the imagination of audiences worldwide.

Eventually, as it so often did, the music industry caught up with GB&H. As the decade wore on, their influence changed as the times themselves changed. But the world will always hear the influence of the Sound of Philadelphia on dance floors everywhere, and even on your radio, over 40 years later.

THE EARLY YEARS

Against a backdrop of intense racism beginning in the 1930s, Philadelphia, like many cities in America, coped with its troubles through music. Beginning with gospel sounds of bluesy spirituals, the city began to develop a musical identity as a center of Northern black gospel. Gospel and blues had dominated the black cultures of the South, jazz had come of age in New Orleans and New York, and gospel and the blues were prominent in cities like Chicago.

Two of the most famous gospel performers in the history of the genre had roots in Philadelphia, the Clara Ward Singers and the Dixie Hummingbirds. Both had migrated north to escape the poverty and prejudice of the South and by the early 1940s they were nationally renowned. In their journey, they took gospel out of the churches and began performing it in nightclubs.

At the same time, vocal groups began popping up in both Philadelphia and New York City that resembled the gospel singing acts in dress and style. But their lyrics were secular rather than sacred in nature. Groups like the Ink Spots and the Mills Brothers sang songs of love and devotion not to God, but to women, and the landscape of popular music began to shift.

The Ink Spots, in particular, led by debonair lead singer Sonny Til, were the first of these secular singing groups to appeal to a nationwide audience. Til, with a sweet falsetto, was sexy and alluring. Many feel that the Ink Spots, and Til's gorgeous tenor, functioned as the blueprint of the music of Philadelphia.

Because of the large black population in the city, groups, nightclubs, and radio programs featuring this kind of music flourished and the city developed a reputation for smooth vocal music. Further, they seemed to have innovated their own specific and peculiar style of singing, characterized by a falsetto lead with two tenors, also singing a kind of lead. The backdrop was high, without much in the way of bass or heavy drumming. The arrangements were light, making sure to illuminate the lead vocals and group harmonies.

Groups like the Castelles, the Buccaneers, and the Dreamers grew in prominence; they sang in clubs and at high school dances, and their music saturated the city's neighborhoods. Each precinct of the city had its favorite group, occasionally called "corner boy" groups; the competition was friendly and exhilarating. Music ruled Philly's urban culture and it became an acceptable way to cope with the city's tense and friction-filled social climate.

It was in this climate that a young Kenny Gamble, growing up in south Philly, came of age. His own experience, influenced by a singing group called the Turbans, reflected his musical surroundings. The Turbans weren't classic Philly, but they did feature some of the city's sound signatures. For a brief time in the mid-1950s, they managed to break out nationally, and they caused quite a stir at home. The excitement infected Gamble, who himself wanted to be a singing star in a popular vocal group. He dedicated himself to learning all he could about the music industry, and as a young teen he sang all the time.

Thom Bell moved to Philadelphia from Kingston, Jamaica, as a toddler, one of 10 children and the son of talented parents. Dad worked hard at a local fish market while studying accounting and turned his son onto classical music at an early age.

Soon after he moved to Philly, excited by the music he heard around him, he began playing drums. Vocal groups like the Platters and the Flamingos, groups that went beyond the typical three-chord song structures, appealed to him most. In high school, his musical appetite grew and he picked up the piano, playing ballet recitals and other events for cash. The earnings potential whetted Bell's appetite and he stepped up his involvement.

In the summer of 1957, the fuse that had been lit by the great Philly vocal groups earlier in the decade detonated the bomb. ABC Television came prowling the city looking for a show to air afternoons after school. The time slot was difficult to fill. Most kids were busy after school, while their parents were working. The nine to five employment culture had gripped America firmly during the 1950s and because of that, most families were forced to be industrious. Still, ABC was searching for a reason for people to stay in and watch their televisions, and they found it in Philly.

The program was called *American Bandstand*. The year was 1952.

Hosted by a dashing young white man named Dick Clark, the program, originally just *Bandstand*, featured the latest popular music numbers while a happy group of teenagers, mainly white, Italian American kids from south Philly, danced to the recordings. The show was an immediate smash. It soon became critical for aspiring music groups and their labels to secure a spot on the show, thereby reaching millions of eager record buyers. And it all went down in Philly; *American Bandstand* turned the city into a metropolitan focal point for pop music.

But there was a big problem, one that most black music fans in the area witnessed immediately. The show invited only white acts and white audience members. Unlike Philadelphia itself, *American Bandstand* did not serve as an accurate microcosm of an interracial city. Kenny Gamble and Thom Bell lived only blocks from the studio, and they watched the program each day, observing how they featured mostly a homogenous white audience, acts, and dancers. Even when a black fan made it into the set to attend a taping, the cameras tended to avoid him.

That racism affected Gamble and his circle. They were musicians and fans with an intense desire to break into the industry. But when an opportunity presented itself in their own backyard, they couldn't take advantage. By 1957, *American Bandstand* had become the biggest pop phenomenon since Elvis Presley. It towered above the teen music world and dictated what kids every-where would listen to. Surely, it hadn't been the first time these young Philly men experienced racism, but, still, the bitterness mounted.

Nearing the end of high school, with his interest in music escalating along with his abilities to perform and write, Gamble met an attractive classmate named Barbara Bell. When Gamble visited Barbara at her home, he was happily surprised to see she had a brother, Thom, who was practicing the piano. The two embarked on a musical friendship.

At the outset of the 1960s, Bell and Gamble were ready for work as musi-cians. Bell had taken piano lessons and aspired to be a musical director of some kind. He traveled north to New York City to take a conductor's test, but, though he passed, he was told that Broadway wouldn't hire colored people. They sent him to Harlem, to the Apollo Theater, where he became the house pianist for a while. Disillusioned, he figured he could play piano closer to home, so he moved back to Philly and took a job doing the same thing at the Uptown Theater. Not long after that he met a man named Luther Dixon, a musical talent affiliated with the Shirelles. He apprenticed with Dixon in New York City for a couple of years, playing, writing, and learning the ropes.

With that experience, he returned to Philly in 1962. He had heard that a new local label called Cameo-Parkway was hiring musicians. But when he went to the audition, they stopped Bell at the door. No colored people were being hired for the band.

He sought out Gamble, his friend, who had just graduated from high school. They knocked unsuccessfully on a few doors before encountering a man named Jerry Ross, an upstart music mogul who had good connections with the *Bandstand* production, as well as the larger music industry. Gamble hit Ross up for an audition, with Bell at his side. The audition went well, and resulted in the duo's first record together, "I'll Get By," a straight soul ballad.

The song failed, but the relationship between Ross and Gamble had just begun. Ross discovered that Gamble could write as well as sing, so he signed him to a songwriting contract. Bell, newly married, began to see that if he was going to make waves in music it would have to be without Gamble. Gamble, not Bell, had the relationship with Ross, and Bell thought that deep down, something about Ross wasn't quite right. He was too shrewd of an operator for the down-to-earth Bell. So from that point, Bell made his own way.

With Bell temporarily out of the picture, Ross and Gamble were without a real musical presence. Enter Leon Huff.

Leon Huff, a pianist from across the bridge in New Jersey and the son of a local barber, gained his musical education on the gritty street corners of Camden and nearby Philadelphia. Having heard his father's blues guitar, he picked up the drums as a child and became a premier musician in high school. By the time he graduated in 1960, he was playing sessions. He couldn't find the work to stay busy in the area, so he ventured to New York City and knocked on doors at the Brill Building, a songwriting factory where musicians were needed for countless recording sessions.

For a time, Huff shuttled back and forth between the Brill Building and Schubert Building, the Schubert being the Philly songwriting equivalent of the Brill, a songwriting assembly line. It was at the Schubert Building that Huff encountered Jerry Ross, and through Ross, Gamble.

In one particular session Huff fronted a group called the Lavenders for a Ross recording, and he played some impressive piano. Gamble appreciated his talent, and so Huff showed up on Gamble's radar.

THE 1960s

As the 1960s began the phenomenon of the Teen Idol began to dominate the charts, and because *American Bandstand* was located in Philadelphia, the city became a mecca for idol worship.

While this didn't bother Huff and Bell, it irked Gamble. He was the only aspiring performer of the three, so while Huff and Bell simply focused on what tune to write next, what lyric to turn or melody to hum, Gamble was busy jockeying for stardom.

Beginning around 1959, when Ray Charles released the controversial "What'd I Say," R&B music had become a force and everyone in the genre wanted to piece of the action. Acts like the Impressions (featuring Curtis

Mayfield), Wilson Pickett, Otis Redding, and Garnett Mims with the Sweet Inspirations were at the fore of the original soul movement, as was a Philly boy, Solomon Burke, the son of a local preacher.

In the late 1950s Berry Gordy, a former boxer, started up his own record label at the urging of Smokey Robinson. In 1961, Robinson and the Miracles had their first hit, "Shop Around." It would be the first of a handful of hits they'd have that year, and a harbinger of things to come.

In Memphis, Stax beavered away at its own version of R&B, and the same thing was happening down in Muscle Shoals, Alabama. Satellite points all over the country were picking up on the trend, and working tirelessly to win over the new, young, record-buying public.

Gamble, now 20, began rounding out his musical experience. He'd been teaching bands to harmonize in the studio and he started familiarizing himself with the publishing side of the business.

In 1963, the assassination of President Kennedy, the great white hope for integration and the civil rights movement, hit the black communities of Philadelphia especially hard. They had embraced Kennedy as the man who would once and for all end the segregation and the turmoil of race. When he died, their hopes died, at least momentarily.

But the integration that Kennedy had precipitated before his death took hold on the music charts. Thanks to crossover artists like Ray Charles and Sam Cooke, black musicians began to assert themselves in the pop realm. The arrival of the British Invasion in 1963 and 1964 ensured that the pop charts were in a constant state of upheaval.

In 1964, with Motown really humming along, the folks in Philadelphia wondered what it all meant. The Cameo-Parkway label reps saw the Motown empire growing before their eyes and decided to open their doors up to any and all talent. Jerry Ross joined, as did Bell, even though he had been rejected on his first attempt to enlist.

Mimicking Motown, Cameo-Parkway formed a black house band of its own over which their vocalists could sing. Bell controlled the formation of the band, recruiting two brothers, Roland and Karl Chambers on drums and guitar. He found Louisiana transplant Win Wilford for the bass. They called themselves the Romeos.

When Gamble caught wind of the Cameo-Parkway house band, he immediately envisioned it as his own backing band. They didn't have a singer of their own, and so they were looking for one or more as a frontman. With Gamble in the fold, the band rehearsed frequently. They played sessions for label artists during the day and gigged at night.

The arrangement worked, by and large, but it soon became apparent that Gamble had limitations as an entertainer. The band began to record with other frontmen as well. In the meantime, Jerry Ross entered into an agreement with Columbia, a major label, to develop talent. One of the three artists he brought with him was Kenny Gamble.

Columbia wasn't all that interested in Gamble's work, though Ross pushed his debut album into the marketplace. At the time, major labels left the real R&B to independent labels. The majors were more focused on the "black" music of Johnny Mathis or Brook Benton, easy listening stuff that their predominately white-run radio stations and white record buyers could handle. Even though Gamble had a real pop side to his material, the album flopped.

Meanwhile, the Cameo-Parkway label's fortunes had taken a turn for the worse as well. In an effort to stem their cash losses—with lots of overhead and few hits—they asked Ross and Gamble to write for them at the Schubert Building. While their song, "The 81," didn't do much to make the label money, it brought Ross and Gamble back to Philadelphia, where Gamble met Leon Huff.

In an elevator one day at the Schubert offices, the outgoing Gamble struck up a conversation with Huff, and asked him if he wrote songs. When Huff told him he did, they made a date to get together, to see if they could work on something, just the two of them. In their brief conversation, they commiserated, coming to the conclusion that producers, mostly white folks, didn't "get" the music as well as they needed to, and so didn't know how to work with the song, or promote it. The two started skipping out of work at their day jobs, pooling their experience and hope, and sketching out their own material.

THE FIRST HITS

In the mid-1960s, civil strife raged through Philly and America, quelled temporarily by Lyndon Johnson's Voting Rights Act in 1965 and a few other political concessions. The rise of Black Power and Malcolm X strengthened and solidified their movement, though their ascendance caused a backlash with white America.

It was also about this time, around 1965, that popular music began to split down the middle. Rock and roll became known as "white music," while R&B and soul music was for black audiences. This racial fissure was dramatic, especially considering that young rock and roll had come directly from the R&B and blues of the early 1950s, both black musical idioms. The split deepened from the start, and has existed ever since.

It is amid this backdrop that Gamble and Huff began to write together. They were not, personality-wise, completely compatible. Gamble, outgoing and direct, enjoyed interaction and communication, and he had strong business acumen. Huff, on the other hand, was tough, taciturn, and completely focused on music. Together, they scraped together some cash and started their own company.

Their first signing was an already established Philly band called the Intruders. They had been together since the early 1950s, when they sang on street corners. The fact that they had experience gave Gamble and Huff's young company, called Gamble Records, a leg up.

Despite a good first signing, Gamble and Huff struggled in those early years. They had patterned their sound after what was coming out of Detroit, and avoided too much politically motivated subject matter. Still, they scoured the streets for acts, and had to work second jobs to stay afloat. Gamble had a small record shop and Huff did as much session work as he could muster.

Their first big break came when they encountered a group called the Soul Survivors, an all-white act from New York and Philadelphia that had designs on cashing in on the so-called blue-eyed soul phenomenon made popular by the Righteous Brothers and Dusty Springfield. Gamble and Huff, along with engineer Joe Tarsia, produced the song "Expressway to Your Heart," an epic soul tune with overtones of pop and rock. The record shot out of the gates and up the charts. Gamble and Huff were officially in business.

At the same time, Thom Bell, still at Cameo-Parkway, saw his company going in the opposite direction. He had one promising band, the Delfonics, but he didn't know what to do with them. He took them into the studio one last time under the auspices of his suffering label and recorded "La-La Means I Love You." Bell's partner, Stan Watson, formed his own label to release the record, and it became a massive hit, rising high on both the R&B and pop charts.

An Intruders' novelty song called "Cowboys and Girls," a Gamble and Huff track, marked something of an early turning point for the organization. The recording served as the debut of producer/arranger Bobby Martin, a talented but unheralded studio presence with lots of experience.

Martin became instrumental in helping to create the Philly Sound of Gamble and Huff. In many cases, he'd piece together exactly what the bosses had ordered, but in others he'd fill gaps with strings and horns. He fit seamlessly into the modus operandi of Gamble and Huff and his abilities enabled the studio to develop a more fully realized sound.

The last piece of the Philly Sound came about when the Romeos, the band that had played many of the studio sessions up to this point, broke up, and its members headed in different directions. In its place Gamble and Huff assembled a new studio band patterned after Motown's Funk Brothers. They'd become the company's house band: white guitarist Bobby Eli, Norm Harris on guitar, bassist Ronnie Baker, guitarist Roland Chambers, drummer Earl Young, and percussionist Vince Montana. They called themselves MFSB—mothers, fathers, sisters, brothers.

They worked together closely and comfortably.

If someone was in a bad mood or wasn't feeling well, Kenny would cancel the date because he knew that there wasn't going to be a record if the rhythm section wasn't comfortable. Kenny didn't play any instruments, but he had the best ears. Sometimes we'd sit around for a couple of hours, talking, joking, eating and relaxing before we ever talked music. The outsiders, they didn't get that. They'd come to town, hand out the charts and expect us to make them a hit. (Earl Young, *Philly Soul*, liner notes, p. 52)

The next project for the company was to revive the career of Jerry Butler. A former member of the Impressions with Curtis Mayfield, Butler left that band early on to embark on a solo career. The hits lasted from the late 1950s to the mid-1960s and began to taper.

The first song they had Butler do, "Never Give You Up," became the biggest single he'd had in six years, and it would be the first of many eloquent soul ballads Butler would place on the charts.

As business picked up, GB&H picked up an act named Archie Bell and the Drells. Bell, no relation to Thom (he had changed the spelling of his name), was an energetic young R&B singer from Texas that Atlantic had signed through Stax. When Gamble and Huff approached Bell, he was still under contract, and, in fact, was enjoying his first huge hit, "Tighten Up." But Atlantic gave GB&H the go-ahead to record Bell at their New York studio. The resulting session produced "I Can't Stop Dancing," a Top 10 hit in the summer of 1968.

While Gamble and Huff were rolling, so too was Thom Bell with his work in the Delfonics. "La-La Means I Love You" had become a huge hit, and Bell resorted to using the same backing band for his sessions that Gamble and Huff were using for theirs. The entire operation moved into a two-story building on North 12th Street in Center City. Joe Tarsia, of the ailing Cameo-Parkway label, saw the writing on the wall of his previous company and jumped ship. He bought a studio in the same building, which was idle at the time, and named it Sigma Sound.

Nationally, Martin Luther King Jr.'s assassination roiled the population again, even as the rise of Sly and the Family Stone—with its sexual and racial integration—hinted at the harmony a peaceful America could achieve. But the Philly musicians decided to back off the politics and focus on their strengths.

It was Jerry Butler who nailed the first real prototype for the Philly Sound. More polished than any song they'd done so far, "Only the Strong Survive," recorded in a single take, best embodied what GB&H were after. With its strings, strong rhythm track, passionate tenor lead, the song had all the elements of the perfect soul single. Audiences thought so as well. It hit the top of the R&B charts and Top 5 on the *Billboard* Hot 100. The song, producers Gamble and Huff, and the subsequent album were all nominated for Grammy Awards.

Aware of impending changes in the soul marketplace, GB&H wanted to balance out their sweet, Intruders/Butler sound with a tougher soul approach. To distinguish between the two approaches, they formed another label, this one called Neptune. Their first signing to Neptune was an Akron, Ohio–based band called the O'Jays.

Their first session for Neptune came in 1969. "One Night Affair" showcased the rugged vocals of the O'Jays' Eddie Levert and his foil, the fluid tenor Walter Williams. R&B radio accepted it warmly, but AM radio banned it because of its free-love subject matter: the song was sung from the perspective of a recently available man who wanted nothing more than one night with a woman. The embargo hurt GB&H who felt certain the song would be its a smash.

They followed that up with the O'Jays' more conservative love song, "There Is Someone Waiting at Home." The first message song from Gamble, he wrote it from the point of view of a soldier in Vietnam. Admittedly, the subject matter was strange for Gamble. But he did have a younger brother serving in Vietnam, and he did come to realize that black America was overrepresented in Southeast Asia, something he felt he could broadcast without much risk to his listening demographic.

In keeping with their desire to work with proven artists rather than develop new talent, they also signed on experienced talents Bunny Sigler and Dusty Springfield. The Springfield arrangement seemed strange. One year earlier, Dusty, a white, blonde British soul singer, had just come off a hit with her brilliant *In Memphis* album recorded at Muscle Shoals in Alabama. The album yielded four singles, but a follow-up platter held none and her label, Atlantic, discovered they needed a new sound for the artist.

Jerry Wexler understood the power and aptitude of the Philly outfit and he wanted to give them a shot. Gamble and Huff had written or co-written each of the 10 songs on the resulting album, and the title track made some waves on the pop chart. But the album, *A Brand New Me*, ultimately met with a tepid reception.

As the 1960s came to a close, soul music as GB&H knew it appeared to be on shaky ground. But where was it headed?

THE 1970s

In the same way they recruited GB&H for Dusty Springfield, Atlantic Records also loaned them another R&B icon, Wilson Pickett. Just prior to getting the call from Atlantic, they lost out in negotiations with their big star Jerry Butler. Butler, looking for greater control of his own material and career, begged out of his deal with GB&H to go it alone. Begrudgingly, they consented.

So when Wilson Pickett showed up on their doorstep, ready to record, their relief was palpable. By this time, Sigma had a beautiful new recording console, 24-tracks, which meant a lot, considering the fact that they lavish envisioned arrangements for their artists, the kind that would certainly keep the board as busy as possible.

Initially, Pickett expressed concerns about all the expensive technology. The earthy soul singer had never put much money into his recordings and the sight of the new board really set him on edge. His concerns were valid. The recording ended up costing him $60,000, $40,000 more than his customary cost.

Many feel that the album, *Wilson Pickett in Philadelphia*, justified the expense. It was the artist's biggest selling record in years and it yielded two substantial hit songs, "Engine Number 9" and the exhilarating "Don't Let the Green Grass Fool You."

Having now produced sessions for Atlantic, Stax, and Chess, the Philadelphia crew was ready for a major label affiliation. They had proven themselves with established stars, and had begun marking the trail for real success. But they wanted more and they could only get it with the financial clout of a major corporate machine. Five major record companies controlled more than half of all the music sales market. The rest was divided between hundreds of other smaller companies that would fight over that share like hungry sharks.

Socially, in the early 1970s, the country was opening up to blackness. Black pride had taken root. Black music had crossed over completely and now appealed to every audience. Black executives were on the payroll at major record labels. *Soul Train* became a black counterpart to *American Bandstand*. Artists like Curtis Mayfield proved that they could run their own labels, as he did with Curtom, successfully.

At Columbia Records, a man named Logan Westbrooks ran the "Special Markets" department, a shrouded term for black music. Westbrooks was enlisted with the responsibility of creating a black marketing staff to penetrate the black market.

Columbia wasn't as evolved and urbane as the Atlantic label, who'd been mining rhythm and blues artists since 1950 and Ruth Brown. In fact, Columbia commissioned a report called "A Study of the Soul Music Environment Prepared for the Columbia Records Group."

Gamble and Huff also understood that there was money to be made in a radio market where newly expanded progressive FM stations were more interested in supporting album-oriented artists than commercial hit singles. Columbia Records was the first to be sold on the idea, and the company most desperate for an R&B presence. Together, eagerly, they formed Philadelphia International Records in February 1971, with a $75,000 advance for 15 singles and a smaller number of albums financed at $25,000 each. It didn't take long for the Columbia investment to pay off for both parties.

Elsewhere, things weren't quite so rosy with Thom Bell and the Delfonics. Poogie Hart, the group's talented lead singer and lyricist, began demanding greater control and label owner Stan Watson took more money and more credit for the band than he could rightfully claim. Frustration reigned, the band broke up, and Bell moved on to concentrate on arranging songs for Gamble and Huff. The Delfonics' loss was Gamble and Huff's gain.

The Columbia arrangement started slowly. They released 16 songs over the next few months, by a banal group of no-name artists, few of which had hit their mark. The beautiful Philly Soul classic "You're the Reason Why," by the Ebonys, a band Huff had discovered in Camden, was a notable exception. At the time, Gamble and Huff had taken their eye off Columbia by choosing to get their own Gamble Records label back on track. At the time, Gamble Records had been a vehicle only for the Intruders. But the distraction hurt their efforts at Columbia.

It took another seasoned R&B star, Joe Simon, to revitalize the Columbia relationship. Simon, a former gospel singer, had recorded over a dozen hit singles in five years, but his streak had cooled and he was eager to get his mojo back. He felt at home at Sigma Sound. "Drowning in the Sea of Love," recorded in late summer of 1971, became a million-seller and it set the stage for his next megahit, "The Power of Love," released in early 1972.

Columbia exercised its right to assign acts to PIR with two of its artists: Laura Nyro and the Chambers Brothers. The latter, four Mississippi-born hippie gospel folk artists, had a hit with its monstrous, 11-minute psychedelic epic "Time Has Come Today," years earlier, but the act had since grown stale. They were unpredictable and difficult to work with. But the collaboration was ill-fated from the start. The band had come in with its own material and its own vision, a situation that GB&H had never encountered before, and the project collapsed.

In the aftermath, the band accused Gamble and Huff of stealing its material and giving it to the O'Jays, something the folks at PIR flatly denied. Meanwhile, Bell had been looking for a band to work with since the Delfonics' bitter split. A call one day granted him his wish. Hugo Peretti and Luigi Creatore, an Italian writing and arranging duo who'd helped Sam Cooke become a superstar, implored Bell to hear out a band they had hit a wall with called the Stylistics. While Bell didn't see much potential in the group, he liked the high falsetto singing of Russell Thompkins Jr. in that it reminded him of the Delfonics' Hart. He took the gig and set out to write songs for the group with a new partner, Linda Creed, a 22-year old French Jew who specialized in writing lyrics. In the fall of 1971, they had their second hit, "Betcha By Golly Wow," a million-seller, and their debut album set the new standard for sweet soul. Bell had hit it big for a second time.

Gamble and Huff, however, had not. They were busy meeting with Columbia President Clive Davis in an effort to beg out of the distribution deal they had with the label. Columbia proved to be inept at promotions and the Philly businessmen felt they couldn't possibly sell records successfully with the current arrangement. Davis was staggered. No one had ever asked to be let go from Columbia. He promised to change the way things were done. He granted Philadelphia International the right to use its own promotional department. The two men in charge of that department, Harry Coombs and his colleague Ed "Lord Gas" Richardson, would see to it that matters were set right. In a short time, they were. PIR began producing hits. Within nine months, they had sold 10 million singles.

In March 1972, Gamble pieced together a single by a group called Harold Melvin and the Blue Notes. He had wanted to sign the Dells out of Chicago, but couldn't get them to leave their Chess label home. Melvin and the Blue Notes were an established lounge act that had long ago given up hope of becoming recording stars. They were content to tour the lounge circuit, and made plenty of money doing it.

But Gamble and Huff were looking for a vehicle for their songs, and this band fit the bill. Right before recording, they brought their drummer Teddy Pendergrass out front to sing lead. Twenty at the time, Pendergrass was a powerful presence with vibrant sex appeal. His shift to frontman was integral to the Blue Notes' success.

Their first single, "I Miss You," fell a little short of expectations. But their second hit, "If You Don't Know Me by Now," hit the Top Five on the pop charts and earned the group a Grammy nomination for Best R&B Act. The event strengthened Columbia's feelings about their deal with Philadelphia International.

The O'Jays were next. Though they had returned home to Ohio during their hiatus, they had kept in touch with GB&H, and were pleased with the news that they had signed on with Columbia. After a little cajoling, and a few guarantees, they returned as a group inked with Philadelphia International. The first track Gamble wanted them to record came from songwriters Gene McFadden and Joe Whitehead, two artists who had made a name for themselves singing back-up for Otis Redding. When Redding died suddenly in 1967, they were out of a job.

McFadden and Whitehead traveled to Philly with a bunch of song ideas in a desperate attempt to get work. The two literally hung out by the company soda machine waiting for Gamble to show up. When he did, the ploy worked. The first track they played him was a song called "Back Stabbers," an up-tempo tune that had a slightly negative connotation. But, the O'Jays weren't crazy about it. It was too dark, not uplifting enough. Still, Gamble talked them into giving it a shot.

Arranged by Thom Bell, the song is a masterpiece of orchestration, with violins, horns, and Leon Huff's beautiful piano. It was acknowledged as one of the best songs to emerge from the Philadelphia music empire of the 1970s, and it made the O'Jays, like the Blue Notes, superstars. The song topped the R&B charts, and, like the Blue Notes big hit before it, cracked the Top Five on the pop charts. It enabled the O'Jays to cross over, and it made everyone involved with the company, especially Columbia, ecstatic.

Not long after the O'Jays' success, another PIR artist, Billy Paul, sent his first single on his second album, "Me and Mrs. Jones," a song about infidelity, soaring to the top of the charts across the board. Written by Gamble, Huff, and Huff's friend from Camden "Hippie" Gilbert, the tune earned Paul a

Grammy and became Gamble and Huff's top-selling single to date. At this point, the PIR machine found its groove literally and figuratively. The hits started rolling. The house band hit its stride, and the mood was high.

When it came time to record a follow up to Paul's single, all signs pointed to another massive tune. White audiences ate up "Mrs. Jones," and were anxiously awaiting another killer track. But in a rare error in judgment, Gamble opted to release the confrontational, "Am I Black Enough for You?" It was an antagonistic song that went against the grain of white acceptance. Bell and Paul pleaded with Gamble not to issue it as Paul's next single, but ultimately it was Gamble's call and he released it with Columbia's approval.

Those who knew Gamble around this time weren't totally surprised by his behavior. He had been absorbed in more political and spiritual pursuits and the song fit his mindset at the time. Unfortunately, there were many who saw this decision as a poor one. Paul's career never truly recovered. As memorable as his first single was, so its follow-up was equally forgettable.

From here, Gamble actually did succeed in writing more and better message songs, just not for Billy Paul. While the Blue Notes were into more romantic-based, gospel-derived material thanks to the presence of Pendergrass, the O'Jays made the perfect message-oriented vehicle for Gamble. "Put Your Hands Together" and "For the Love of Money" were the next huge hits for them, their third million-seller and the label's seventh. The album it was on, *Ship Ahoy*, also ended up selling in vast numbers, and it anchored on the *Billboard* album chart for nearly a full year.

Gamble and Huff finally convinced Bell to enter into a more formal agreement with them in 1973, though it wouldn't be in a musical fashion, ironically. Bell had resisted Gamble's overtures for a partnership more than once. He had insisted that he wanted to remain independent, producing records and making his own decisions. He had done well so far with the Delfonics and the Stylistics, and various other projects.

The venture that he joined in with his friends was a publishing and real estate agreement. They bought the old building that once housed the Cameo-Parkway label, the same company that had turned them all away at one time or another, when they were young kids looking for jobs in music. Poetic justice prevailed once again.

"LOVE TRAIN"

As 1973 came to a close, the Philly soul titans took their traveling caravan of talent to Europe in search of a newer and larger audience. For his part, Bell found a band to work with from Detroit called the Spinners. Like the O'Jays and the Blue Notes, the Spinners had been around the block. They'd been mistreated at Motown and were bitter from the experience. When they signed on with Atlantic, at the recommendation of Aretha Franklin in 1971, they recorded four songs, wasted a lot of money on some unfulfilling sessions, and developed a reputation as an underachieving band.

But Bell wanted to give them a shot. Atlantic was right. They were difficult. But he managed to record with them in a way they could both feel good about. Their first session yielded a masterpiece: "I'll Be Around," the B-side to what had intended to be the first single, "How Could I Let You Get Away." The Spinners' eponymous debut album stayed on the charts for seven months.

The Spinners' success pulled him away from the Stylistics, who were still hot as well. In 1974, their triumph "You Make Me Feel Brand New," sold in big numbers and topped the charts. But Bell didn't feel right about working both bands. His success had prompted him to be called "the maestro of symphonic soul," but something had to give. The Spinners would get the majority of his time.

In the spring of 1974, he conceived the idea of putting Dionne Warwick, who had been hot in the late 1960s with Burt Bacharach material, with the Spinners on the song "Then Came You." The Spinners had been the opening act on Warwick's tour the previous summer. It was another stroke of genius, with an instrumental arrangement to match.

As early as 1974, things at the Philadelphia label began to transform musically. A year or so earlier, the nascent strains of disco began to emanate from the clubs to radio. Gamble, with his ear always to the ground, picked up on it and appreciated the dance style's energy. One day at work, he mentioned it to his studio band. Drummer Earl Young recalled playing disco tempos—fast, strong steady beats—before disco was even existed as a term on tunes like the Blue Notes' "The Love I Lost" and "Bad Luck."

Gamble and Huff's next project was a trio of black women billed as the Three Degrees, Linda Turner, Shirley Porter, and Fayette Pinkney. Formed in the 1960s in Philadelphia, the group recorded for a couple of labels, including Swan and Roulette, but hadn't had anything resembling a hit. They had moved to Boston and enjoyed some notoriety on the supper club circuit in the Northeast, but success eluded them.

Gamble and Huff changed all that. Though their first attempt at a hit, "Dirty Old Man," was as misguided as Billy Paul's "Black Enough," the idea came up to lay the girls vocals over an instrumental track laid down by MFSB, the studio band. That track, "TSOP," was already well known as the opening theme to the television program *Soul Train*, and dance fans had already been digging it. Gamble and Huff's remix of the song with the Three Degrees hit the top of both the pop and R&B charts and the ladies were in business.

Gamble and Huff now had five million-selling acts on their roster. The Sound of Philadelphia dominated the country's music scene. But all this success was taking its toll behind the scenes.

Gamble and Huff's current situation was a far cry from the early days, when the producers answered to nobody but themselves as they diligently cranked out modest hits for the Intruders. Now as Gamble and Huff worked, Columbia Records looked over their shoulders, anticipating the next gold or platinum album. Ron Alexenburg recalled Gamble working simultaneously on five albums at one point. He just "pressured himself, and we put a lot of pressure on him, because every time we had a hit single we needed a hit album. And Kenny and Huff were just crankin' out the hits left and right." (John Jackson, *A House on Fire*, New York: Oxford University Press, 2004, p. 165)

Gamble had other pressures on him as well, mainly financial. His real estate company was a burden, as was a federal investigation into his involvement in a "payola" scandal, which arose with Clive Davis when the Philly company first struck up a relationship with Columbia. Davis had been fired for financial improprieties, and the investigation was reaching the courts.

Payola

Since the beginning of rock and roll in the mid-1950s, radio airplay became critical to the success of a song or an artist. As more and more time and effort was being spent in the studio developing songs, and more expense arose because of that time, record producers became obsessed with getting their records and artists on the radio. Often, artists traveled from radio station to radio station, record in hand, delivering their music to DJs. When this was not possible, those same record producers and their promotional men would simply send cash, or payola, to those DJs.

Short for a hybrid term combining money "pay" with record spinning machines like "Victrola," payola is the illegal practice of payment or other inducement by record companies for the broadcast of recordings on music radio in which the song is presented as being part of the normal day's broadcast. Under U.S. law, a station can play a specific song in exchange for money, but this must be disclosed on the air as being sponsored airtime.

Many of rock and roll's biggest personalities, including original rock DJ Alan Freed and CBS Records President Clive Davis have had their careers undone by accusations of payola. As recently as 2005, thanks to work done by Eliot Spitzer, the attorney general of New York City, the very biggest record companies in the world, Sony BMG, the Warner Music Group, and the Universal Music Group all settled out of court for a total nearing $30 million. Those funds were distributed to non-profit organizations to fund music education programs.

On June 24, 1975, federal prosecutors in Newark, New Jersey, launched something called Project Sound, an in-depth investigation into payola. After the investigations, they came up with seven payola indictments in four cities and made them public. Kenny Gamble and Leon Huff's organization was one of them. The indictment stated that the defendants went to cities in order to meet with and pay in excess of $25,000 to disc jockeys, music directors, and program directors.

In the specific case of Philadelphia International, the accusations were partially correct. When PIR promotion men Harry Coombs and Lord Gas Richardson received money from their mother corporation CBS for promotional purposes, they turned around and floated it to radio stations and other influential tastemakers in order to secure airplay. It worked. It was also illegal.

Ten months after the indictments Gamble and Huff showed up in court, but the charges had eased significantly since the original accusations. Because of a glitch in their case, the federal government had no leg to stand on, and the charges against Huff were dropped outright. (Bell had never been named in the case.) Gamble's attorney worked out a plea bargain with prosecutors in which he admitted gifting things such as air travel and clothes to other music industry executives, but he did not admit they were intended to compel radio airplay.

As an aside, Project Sound focused almost entirely on the black music industry, just as white payola had presumably gone on without interruption since the 1950s. They were correct in assuming that black payola had been growing into a serious problem. They were also remiss in solely targeting black music. It's only logical to conclude that payola would be endemic to the entire music industry.

In addition, Gamble's marriage to singer Dee Dee Sharp fell on hard times. The couple was so preoccupied with the company they had little time for each other and their marriage suffered. On top of that, Gamble, a deeply spiritual man, felt conflicted about his religious beliefs. He had a hard time reconciling his own growing wealth and financial focus with his devotion to God. The cross-purposes tortured him.

Soon enough, with all these concerns weighing heavily on him, Gamble had a nervous breakdown.

For nine months in 1975, the assembly line at PIR essentially stopped. They issued only one recording during that time, as everybody involved waited for their leader to recover. No one presumed to be able to finish what Gamble had started.

The limbo that resulted threw PIR into a tailspin. During the time Gamble had been in recovery, disco and funk took a firm grip on the music industry. Columbia executives fidgeted while this evolution was taking place, afraid the train was leaving without them. Worse, much of the personnel at the PIR studios had to leave. There was nothing to do, so the staff—including the MFSB rhythm section—began taking advantage of outside opportunities.

In addition to the exodus, another rebellion brewed. The MFSB musicians, the ones who stayed, were starting to grumble. They were unappreciated and under-compensated. From the beginning, the band had plugged in and played backing tracks to all of the Philly projects. But they didn't just play. In many instances, they conceived the songs, or at least the musical underpinnings of them. Gamble didn't read music. He may have had a vision for a song, but he couldn't communicate it to the band musically until the band played it for him. The same with Huff. The two principals were visionary, but they sorely needed the assistance of their talented band to realize those visions.

Despite that fact, Gamble and Huff always took the songwriting credit. They never shared it with the musicians. Even on the MFSB instrumental record, where the band helped to formulate so many of the great grooves, they never received adequate recognition or publishing credit. Gamble and Huff paid them generous session fees. But the big money from publishing credits was off limits. Eventually, given all the money that was made via all those hit recordings, this slight took a toll on the band. They became resentful and began plotting a recourse.

Earl Young, the critically important drummer, went off to form the Trammps. Vince Montana brought some of the musicians with him to record the Salsoul Orchestra.

Gene McFadden and John Whitehead were also complaining about their compensation while with PIR. In fact, no one had told the songwriters about publishing royalties. They were working on salary. They had hit records, but the hefty publishing royalties, went to Gamble, Huff and PIR. As far as the bosses were concerned, what their employees didn't know wouldn't hurt them. When those same people wised up to the situation, Huff soothed them by allowing the duo to record their own album.

Harold Melvin and the Blue Notes began to develop fissures in their structure as well. Melvin, an authoritarian who demanded control of the group's decisions, started grating on Pendergrass, the lead singer. Pendergrass threatened to leave. Attorneys for the band worked out a deal for Pendergrass to record a solo album while the Blue Notes remained together. But Gamble rejected the deal, citing its expense, and to exacerbate the situation, the executives chose not to renew the band's contract at all when it expired at the end of 1975.

Now PIR had only the O'Jays to keep the hits rolling.

These departures and others resulted in a total reshuffling of PIR. Not only was key personnel gone, forcing a change in the label's sound, songwriters and engineers had also left. The camaraderie of the musical experience in the building had long since gone. Gamble's breakdown had changed him as boss; he retreated more, took longer to make critical decisions, and had deepened his spiritual personality, making him more distant and reflective.

The payola scandals arrived in court in the spring of 1976. Gamble and Philadelphia International were indicted but the charges were slight, inconsequential. Charges against Huff were dropped; Gamble was charged with paying radio DJs money to play their recordings. But ultimately, there was much ado about nothing, and Gamble's attorneys worked out a plea bargain agreement. As all of these lengthy legal proceedings were going on, the music scene was flowing like a river past PIR.

In 1976, the label signed Lou Rawls, another veteran of gospel and R&B music. Rawls had been a successful singer throughout the 1960s, but never enjoyed pop crossover until he signed on with Gamble and Huff. His first massive hit, "You'll Never Find a Love Like Mine," hit the top of the charts, and the album, *All Things in Time*, became the biggest of Rawls's career, selling over a million copies and winning numerous awards.

Another veteran group came along next; this one a bit surprising. The Jackson 5 had just experienced an acrimonious dispute with Motown, and they stomped off to look for another deal. They found it when CBS/Columbia, referred them to Philadelphia International. The album, simply called *The Jacksons*, sold a million copies, had a few strong singles, and did well enough to prompt a sophomore effort with the band.

But departures continued. Health problems dogged Thom Bell's wife and the couple was advised to move somewhere quiet. They relocated to Washington state. Linda Creed, Bell's songwriting partner at the label, also took off when G&H decided not to give her new contract a boost. Bobby Martin, the world-class arranger responsible for so many of the label's hits, went to A&M Records. He insisted he had no regrets, but said later that he had "sought light after so much darkness."

Eventually, disco experienced a backlash. In fact, all black music at the time was labeled "disco," and so it became a dirty word at radio.

> It helped to eliminate blacks from mainstream competition and stigmatized black music to an even greater extent. It was stupid. It was racist. It revealed how powerful a force semantics can be in the reception of music. Just as rock and roll came to mean white music, disco came to represent some ugly amalgam of black and gay music. (Nelson George, *The Death of Rhythm and Blues*, p. 181)

In 1978, Elton John came to Bell and asked him to produce his next album. John had enjoyed a prosperous decade with his hit-making and incessant touring, but was understandably exhausted. So when Bell suggested a collaboration, Elton balked. He insisted that Bell do it all. Incredulous, and thrilled with the opportunity, Bell agreed. He worked with John's lyricist Bernie Taupin, and they knocked out six songs in a couple of days. Bell had enlisted the assistance of the Spinners and the Sigma Sweethearts (the studio's backup singers), and banged out the material. Elton John's crew, accustomed to being in the studio for months with the requisite drugs and goofing off, were blown away at the Philly crew's productivity and efficiency.

But when Bell delivered the final mixes, John felt they were too sweet for him, overproduced, too highly orchestrated, and he shelved them. Later that year, a single was eventually released off Elton's so-called *Thom Bell Sessions* EP in 1977. "Mama Can't Buy You Love" became the Elton's biggest hit in three years.

As the decade of the 1980s fast-approached, though, Gamble and Huff were lost amid the changing tides in black music, musically, personally, spiritually, legally, and financially. The two principals, Kenny Gamble and Leon Huff, tried desperately to hold the company together. But both were going through divorces. They began feuding with each other, adding to the gloom around the office. With the original backline band gone, each record became more difficult to make.

In 1982, amid much strife and few hits, they got some terrible news. Their only bankable artist, Teddy Pendergrass, was in a car accident in his Rolls Royce. It was the third or fourth accident for the irresponsible star, but his worst by far. His spine had been crushed. PIR's only surefire star was completely out of commission. The news was tragic on many fronts, a wake-up call for the entire company. The odds were against him ever singing again.

In November 1982, with no prospects on the horizon, CBS Records/Columbia terminated their agreement with PIR after an 11-year run. They had held on to each other for as long as they could, but ultimately, the music industry raced forth without them.

LEGACY

With the entire story of Kenny Gamble, Leon Huff, and Thom Bell written, one thing stands out as we look back over their history: the music. As an entity, these three men had been responsible for a heaping helping of the 1970s' best soul and pop music. Their attention to detail, sonic innovations, and visionary treatment of artists considered past their prime, set them apart from so many others intent on achieving the same success.

For the first several years of their organization, through much of their relationship with Columbia, the songs they created will never be forgotten. In some cases, these songs should be remembered even beyond the material that came out of Motown, widely considered to be soul's most memorable sides. Utilizing the legendary MFSB rhythm section—bassist Ronnie Baker, drummer Earl Young, guitarists Norman Harris and Bobby Eli—the trio conceived and executed the Philly Sound, the sound of a city, the sound of a generation. Were it not for the ever-spinning carousel that is pop, constantly serving up newer possibilities, the trio would still be relevant today. But their inability to change in the end brought them down. It created the unrest that undid the relationships, that unhinged the bands, and that disrupted Philadelphia International's entire creative process. Without harmony—Gamble and Huff most likely knew this—they had nothing; when the harmony left the workplace and the close-knit friendships that formed the basis of the company began to come apart at the seams, Gamble and Huff had no chance of staying on top.

Still, they were responsible for taking the Philly sound to America and the world. They brought pop music to new heights of power and sophistication and history will prove that they constructed an incredible edifice of sound direct from the streets where they lived.

SELECTED DISCOGRAPHY

The Intruders, *Cowboys to Girls: Best of the Intruders* (Epic/Legacy, 1995)

O'Jays, *Backstabbers* (Epic/Legacy, 1972/1996)

Harold Melvin and the Blue Notes, *The Best of Harold Melvin and the Bluenotes* (Epic/Legacy, 2004)

Wilson Pickett, *Wilson Pickett in Philadelphia* (Atlantic, 1970)

The Spinners, *One of a Kind Love Affair* (Rhino, 1991)

The Stylistics, *Best of the Stylistics, Vol. 2* (Amherst, 1976)

The Three Degrees, *Best of the Three Degrees: When Will I See You Again* (Epic/Legacy, 1996)

Various, *The Philly Sound* (Epic/Legacy, 1997)

FURTHER READING

Clarke, William, Jim Cogan, and Quincy Jones. *Temples of Sound: Inside the Great Recording Studios*. New York: Chronicle Books, 2004.

Jackson, John A. *A House on Fire: The Rise and Fall of Philadelphia Soul*. New York: Oxford University Press, 2004.

Various. *The Philly Sound,* liner notes. Epic/Legacy, 1997.

Courtesy of Photofest.

Courtesy of Photofest.

Prince

Jesse Jarnow

THE ARTIST FORMERLY KNOWN AS . . .

It is pouring rain. Lightning shoots from the sky. The 76,500 football fans at Miami's Dolphin Stadium are on their feet and screaming. Millions more are watching at home. The center of their attention takes the stage with no formal introduction, save a volley of fireworks over the upper deck, and the pounding beat of Queen's "We Will Rock You."

The groove fades and a church organ rises. His voice comes first. "Dearly beloved," he intones, as the spotlights come on and the stage is outlined in purple neon. "We are gathered here today to get through this thing called life." The crowd screams again.

He is not who one would expect to find at the 50-yard line on Super Bowl Sunday. For starters, the man is five feet, two inches and tiny. He is dressed in a robin's egg blue suit, an orange shirt, and a do-rag. As he has for his entire career, he looks profoundly androgynous. "Let's go crazy!" he sings, a sheer sexual come-on, and—again—the football fans do.

He steps to the edge of the stage and tears off a devastating guitar solo. He struts across the platform with his wireless instrument, pealing off riffs and leading a sing-along. The song, one of his own hit singles, transitions seamlessly into others. Duetting, he sings verses of John Fogerty's "Proud Mary," his own arrangement of Bob Dylan's "All Along the Watchtower," and "Best of You," a recent song by hard rock band the Foo Fighters.

A marching band—outlined by neon glowsticks—emerges from the end zone and crosses the field. For the grand finale, the band transitions into the man's biggest hit from 20 years earlier. He doesn't tell the crowd to go crazy this time, but they do anyway. In 1984, when the song was number one, it shared its name with the number one album and the number one film in the country. All three were called "Purple Rain."

"Prince does so many things, it's almost like he can do it all," legendary jazz musician Miles Davis wrote in his autobiography. "Plus he plays his ass off as well as sings and writes . . . For me, he can be the new Duke Ellington of our time if he just keeps at it" (Alex Hahn, *Possessed: The Rise and Fall of Prince*, New York: Billboard Books, 2004, p. 99).

A pop songwriter of great renown, with over 20 Top 10 singles and a dozen Top 10 albums to his credit, Prince's talents are legion. He is so proficient on many instruments—including guitar, bass, drums, and keyboards—that he is the sole musician on many of his recordings, and so prolific that he staged a public battle with his record company so that he could release even more music. He is a disciplined bandleader and arranger.

Prince also possesses a quenchless thirst to play music, frequently staging marathon jams at nightclubs following his performances at theaters and arenas. He is a pioneer, as well, introducing drum machines to R&B, and replacing horn sections with banks of synthesizers.

As an entrepreneur, Prince launched the careers of a half-dozen others, penning, producing, and performing everything but the vocals on their albums, often with no credit. In addition to constructing his own recording complex, Prince was also one of the first musicians to sell his music over the Internet, via his New Power Generation Music Club.

But for every grand move Prince has made over his three-decade (and counting) career, he has made an equal number of bizarre choices. Though he reigned over the pop charts definitively in the 1980s, over the next decade he released enormous amounts of subpar music, jettisoned collaborators whose talents threatened him, took songwriting credits away from others, and megalomaniacally directed and acted in half-baked movies.

He sued the record company that nurtured him, as well as devoted fans that published a magazine about him. He scrapped masterpieces on whims, and issued undeveloped recordings on less. At times, Prince seemed plain out of touch, vociferously rejecting the advent of hip-hop and releasing his first CD as one extended track, insisting audiences listen to it straight through. For a time, he changed his name to an unpronounceable symbol before conceding that people could refer to him as "the Artist Formerly Known as Prince" or, if they wished, simply "the Artist."

Through it all, however, Prince remained first and foremost an entertainer. He is a sex symbol like no other, belonging equally to white and black American cultures. Along with Michael Jackson, he was one of the first black artists shown on MTV. In lyrics, Prince mixes lust and religion. In dress and performance, he blurs the lines of sexuality—perhaps shocking to some, but not enough to prevent him from earning a mainstream audience, and being invited to perform at the Super Bowl, perhaps ground zero for the world's machismo.

As if to underscore this, midway through his halftime performance of "Purple Rain," Prince steps behind a billowing white sheet, illuminated in silhouette, and begins another virtuosic guitar solo. It bends and fragments like Jimi Hendrix. Prince turns to his side, and the shadow of his ornately shaped purple guitar distinctly resembles a penis. Prince leads the football fans in another sing-along, and they scream even more.

THE EARLY YEARS

Prince Rogers Nelson was born on June 7, 1958, in Minneapolis, Minnesota. His father, John Nelson, was a jazz and blues pianist originally from Louisiana. Though he worked as a plastics molder for Honeywell Electronics, John had a successful night career as a local musician. He took the stage name Prince Rogers. With his trio, John played bars, clubs, and theaters. At a show on Minneapolis's Northside, John met Mattie Shaw. Mattie was a jazz singer. Two years later, Mattie gave birth to their first son, whom they gave John's nickname: Prince.

As a child, Prince did not like his name. Until he was a teenager, he insisted on being called "Skipper," his mother's nickname for him. Prince took to his father's piano, and played proficiently by the age of seven. When he was five, Prince saw his father perform live at a local theater. Seeing the reception the crowd gave his father, Prince began to understand the allure of being a musician. In the semi-autobiographical film *Purple Rain*, Prince is shown being physically abused by his father. "He had his moments," Prince admitted to Oprah Winfrey in 1996. But several years later, Prince told Larry King that his father was "not rough" with him (Hahn, p. 9). Whether John was abusive or not, Prince's parents, who had never married, separated when Prince was 10.

Prince was also introduced to another musical idol that year: James Brown. His father put him on stage to dance with the Godfather of Soul until a bodyguard removed the young Prince. "He inspired me because of the control he had over his band," Prince said many years later, "and because of the beautiful dancing girls he had. I wanted both" (Serge Simonart, "The Artist," *Guitar World*, October 1998).

When John moved out, Prince spent time playing his father's piano, which had been left behind. Prince quickly showed signs of independence, riding his bicycle to Minneapolis to buy new James Brown singles. Mattie remarried, however, and Prince did not get along with his new stepfather. Prince stayed with his father for a time, though John soon threw him out. Homeless, Prince stayed with acquaintances and relatives until he moved in with his friend André Anderson. Anderson's mother, Bernadette, treated Prince as if he were a member of the family.

With a supportive home life, Prince excelled in school, and played basketball competitively. In high school, he turned his attention to music. A teacher named Jim Hamilton took Prince under his arm. Hamilton gave Prince guitar lessons and designed a special class for the eager student called "The Business of Music." Every day at lunch, Hamilton allowed Prince private access to the band room, where he practiced various instruments. After John Nelson gave Prince a guitar, and André Anderson got a bass, the two jammed regularly in the Anderson basement. Before long, Prince moved out of André's room and into the basement itself. Prince's second cousin, Charles Smith, added a drum set to the clutter.

The three began their musical education together. They listened to Top 40 radio at first, but soon graduated to R&B and psychedelic rock. The trio named themselves Grand Central, and learned songs by Santana, Grand Funk Railroad, and others. One of Prince's heroes was Sly Stone, the leader of Sly and the Family Stone, a multi-racial funk ensemble from San Francisco who blended distorted rock guitars with R&B grooves and a utopian vision of racial harmony. Another hero was the ageless bandleader James Brown, who led his road bands with ruthless discipline. Still another, perhaps surprisingly, was Canadian singer-songwriter Joni Mitchell, whose jazzy confessionals would be a model for Prince's ballads in years to come.

Prince became the undisputed leader and arranger of Grand Central as they gigged on the Minneapolis R&B scene. Drummer Morris Day replaced Charles Smith, and the band changed their name to Champagne. Managed by Day's mother, Prince started to write his own material. In March 1976, Champagne entered the local Moonsound studio to record a demo. The studio's owner, an aspiring British songwriter named Chris Moon, saw Prince's discipline and made an offer. In return for writing music for Moon's lyrics, Prince could have studio time to develop his own material. Prince accepted, though Champagne quickly dissolved.

Moon gave Prince the keys to Moonsound. It became Prince's second home. Every day, after school, he headed to the studio. First he wrote music for Moon's lyrics. Soon, Moon taught him to use the equipment. Now proficient on bass and drums, as well as piano and guitar, Prince began to record songs playing all the instruments himself. When he graduated from Central High in spring 1976, he all but moved in. Though Moon and Prince collaborated on songs like the lascivious "Soft and Wet," Moonsound was Prince's playground. With Moon's encouragement, Prince dropped the "Nelson" from his name, and began to shop his demos to labels.

Audaciously, Prince flew to New York City. Still a teenager, however, no label agreed to meet with him. In Minneapolis, though, Prince found a patron in local promoter Owen Husney. Husney bought new instruments for Prince, and helped produce another demo, and called labels like CBS, Warner Bros., and A&M. Prince was unique, Husney told them: he could write, perform, and produce his own music. Only a few people, such as Stevie Wonder, had that talent.

Husney also sold on them on Prince's shy mystique. Still, he had to resort to lies to create an actual interest. He told each label that the others were flying Prince to Los Angeles for auditions. It worked. Prince auditioned for CBS at Village Recorders by rerecording "Just as Long as We're Together" in front of label executives, instrument by instrument, showing off his virtuosity.

On June 25, 1977, Prince signed a three-album contract with Warner Bros. Records. He was barely 19.

LOOKING FOR THE KEYS TO THE KINGDOM

At first, Warner Bros. wanted Prince to work with an outside producer. Husney balked. Again, Prince rerecorded an entire song, live in the studio, to prove himself worthy. Watching surreptitiously, Warner Bros. president Lenny Waronker agreed to let Prince produce his own debut. He would be the youngest producer in the label's 20-year history.

Prince recorded *For You* at the Record Plant, in Sausalito, near San Francisco. He worked tirelessly and studied the engineers and their equipment carefully. Prince played all the instruments. On an Oberheim synthesizer, he arranged parts ordinarily performed in R&B by a horn section. Though the over-budget album was perhaps too polished, these keyboard arrangements marked the beginnings of an original sound. The album sold modestly, reaching number 21 R&B and number 163 Pop. The single, "Soft and Wet" (co-written with Moon at Moonsound) made it to number 12 R&B.

In Minneapolis, Prince wrote and produced songs for Sue Ann Carwell, an aspiring singer. He suggested she take the stage name "Susie Stone." Though their work never amounted to anything, she was the first of many outside musicians Prince would both use as a creative outlet and attempt to tailor in a new image. Though Champagne had dissolved, Prince remained close with his former roommate, bassist André Anderson, who had taken the stage name André Cymone.

With his old friend, Prince assembled a band he could take on the road. Modeled after Sly and the Family Stone, Prince envisioned a group of different races and genders that would help him reach broader audiences. Drummer Bobby Z. Rivkin, a friend of Tom Moon's, joined, as did keyboardists Gayle Chapman and Matt Fink, and guitarist Dez Dickerson. The latter brought the band a hard-rock edge as they jammed for hours under Prince's authoritarian watch. Prince also broke with manager Owen Husney, replaced by Cavallo and Ruffalo, a high-powered Hollywood team. An ever-growing entourage now saw to Prince's every need.

Though Warner Bros. still believed in him, Prince was in trouble. The label had budgeted $180,000 for the three albums. He spent $170,000 of it recording *For You*. They were happy to loan Prince money to pay his band and record a follow-up, but there was now some pressure to produce a hit. In April 1979, Prince recorded his second album in Los Angeles. Once again, he played all the instruments. Partially because he believed *For You* was overproduced, partially because studio time was at a premium, he moved quicker. The result was more spontaneous. Released in August 1979, the first single, "I Wanna Be Your Lover" hit number 1 R&B and number 11 Pop. The album sold well, too, reaching number 3 R&B, number 22 Pop, and gaining platinum status by early 1980.

After several gigs around Minneapolis, the band toured for the first time in November 1979. The crowds were not large, but Prince gained valuable experience. Though the tour broke prematurely after he suffered a bout of pneumonia in December, they were back on the road by January, opening for funk-pop legend Rick James. Prince continued to create his mystique, as well. During a January appearance on Dick Clark's *American Bandstand*, Prince refused to speak to the veteran host, holding up four fingers when Clark asked how many years he had been a performer.

Prince continued to refine his sound. In Boulder, Colorado, he recorded rock songs with his road band, though the project was scrapped. He absorbed music in nightclubs, and via free records from Warner Bros. He also immersed himself in the bands of rock's dawning new wave, including the Police, Devo, and others.

Just after Prince's 22nd birthday, in a rented house near Minneapolis's Lake Minnetonka, he began to make demos in a 16-track home studio. Instead of keyboards, he wrote many of his new songs on guitar. Some were based on band jams, like "Dirty Mind," but mostly Prince wrote alone. In the lyrics, a new direction emerged: explicit sexuality. Songs explored incest ("Sister") and fellatio ("Head").

When he finished in July, Prince liked the rough-hewn qualities of the demos and decided he did not want to rerecord them in a proper studio. After a brief fight with Warner Bros., the label agreed. Released in October 1980, *Dirty Mind* fared poorly. It reached number 45 Pop, and would only go gold some five years later. Still, *Dirty Mind* received positive reviews. In New York and Detroit, especially, Prince began to sell more concert tickets. His following was starting to take hold.

Like Warner Bros., both guitarist Dez Dickerson and keyboardist Gayle Chapman blanched at the raunchy lyrics. Chapman was the first to depart. Nineteen-year-old keyboardist Lisa Coleman, who would become one of Prince's most important collaborators, replaced her. In Minneapolis, Prince purchased a home big enough to hold his piano. He had the house painted purple, his favorite color, which showed up with increasing frequency in song lyrics.

THE IDOLMAKER

Prince remained a presence on the Twin Cities' R&B scene. After seeing the 1980 film *The Idolmaker*, Prince renewed his interest in developing other artists. The first he chose was Morris Day, former drummer for Champagne. Prince created a gangster persona for his old friend, and, as usual, wrote, performed, and produced the music. Day added vocals and Prince named the project the Time. Released in July 1981, *The Time* reached number 7 R&B and number 50 Pop. The only credits were given to Day and fictional co-producer Jamie Starr. A live version of the band was fashioned from regulars on the scene, who performed in matching suits. Prince oversaw the band's early rehearsals, teaching them to play the songs with precision for five hours a day before practicing with his own band.

Prince and his band continued to tour. In Europe in 1981, he visited more nightclubs, where he learned from the hard synthetic sounds popular in European pop music, such as German minimalists Kraftwerk. Back home, Prince immediately began to make another record. Applying what he had learned, he employed the Linn LM-1 drum machine for the first time on "Private Joy." Its sampled drums became a fixture in Prince's music. Like his use of keyboards to replace horn parts, the drum machine further contributed to his new sound.

Prince also started to insert spiritual themes into his deliberately shocking music. On "Controversy," he recited the Lord's Prayer. The song gave its name to the album. *Controversy* sold better than *Dirty Mind*, reaching number 3 R&B and number 21 Pop. On stage, with increasing confidence, Prince dressed the part. Though he had been a shy performer at first, Prince now reveled in the attention. By fall of 1980, his onstage attire consisted of bikini underwear, leg warmers, and little else.

In December 1981, Rolling Stones singer Mick Jagger invited Prince to open two shows for the legendary British rock band at the Los Angeles Coliseum.

During the first show, homophobic concertgoers pelted Prince and his band with paper cups. Discouraged, Prince flew home to Minneapolis that night. Coaxed back to Los Angeles the following night, the audience was even worse. Knowing what to expect, fans brought food to throw. Prince and his band were hit with everything from a bag of chicken to a grapefruit. After a jug of orange juice shattered on the drum riser, the band retreated.

The tour continued, joined by Morris Day and the Time, who opened. As the Time developed their own identity, they began to fall out of favor with Prince, who went looking for new talent. In a club, Prince met an attractive woman named Denise Matthews. He renamed her Vanity. Originally called the Hookers, Prince settled on Vanity 6 as the name for her accompanying group, who performed in lingerie. *Vanity 6*, released in August 1982, reached number 6 R&B, number 45 Pop. And though their relationship was on the rocks, Prince also found time to record a second album for the Time, *What Time Is It?*, which reached number 2 R&B.

By the time the Time and Vanity 6 albums reached stores, Prince was already knee-deep in his next project. At Sunset Sound in Los Angeles, Prince toiled with engineer Peggy McCreary for days on end. Though known for his image as a lascivious party animal, Prince's off-stage persona was somewhat different. Extraordinarily disciplined, Prince stayed far away from drugs. Though he had many girlfriends, he was frequently shy in conversation. Instead, he focused his energies on music. At Sunset Sound, Prince worked McCreary into the ground, sometimes for over 24 hours straight.

Many of the songs were based around the LM-1 drum machine, which Prince ran through guitar effects pedals. He turned the two-disc set over to his managers, who requested that Prince add another single to it. Though angry, he responded with "1999." Originally sung in three-part harmony by Prince, Dez Dickerson, and Lisa Coleman, Prince mixed the song so each line spotlighted a different singer, an old Sly Stone trick. It became the title track of the new album, released in October 1982. *1999* itself charted at number 9 Pop and number 4 R&B, his first Top 10 Pop album, and yielded three high-charting singles: "1999" (number 12 Pop, number 4 R&B), "Little Red Corvette" (number 6 Pop, number 15 R&B), and "Delirious" (number 8 Pop, number 18 R&B).

It was the first time Prince charted higher on the lucrative white-oriented pop chart. This change in Prince's audience owed largely to MTV, which showed the "1999" video while Prince and his band toured throughout the fall and winter. Audiences swelled to nearly 10,000 people a night. Guitarist Dez Dickerson, however, found it harder and harder to play Prince's explicit music. Early in 1983, he quit, and was quickly replaced by 19-year-old Wendy Melvoin, a childhood friend and lover of Lisa Coleman. She had never played in a band before, but fit in perfectly. Bassist André Cymone, jealous over his former roommate's success, quit too, replaced by Mark Brown.

PURPLE REIGN

In early 1983, Prince gathered his forces. With the lifelong chemistry between Coleman and Melvoin, Prince's group felt even more like a real band. For the first time, he gave it a name: the Revolution. During intensive rehearsals, the band practiced more new material. But Prince had something even bigger planned. The project took shape around one of the new songs, a four-chord sing-along Prince wrote with uncharacteristic simplicity.

Prince worked with television writer William Blinn to create a semi-autobiographical film script. Originally titled *Dreams*, the film was known as *Purple Rain* when shooting began in November 1983. Prince played "the Kid," a Minneapolis musician from an abusive household. Morris Day played a rival bandleader. Both competed for Apollonia, played by Patricia Kotero (a role originally intended for Vanity). Prince and the Revolution took acting lessons, and performed several songs in their garish stage costumes and heavy make-up. They provided the film's soundtrack, too, part of which was recorded during their live debut on August 15, 1983, at First Avenue in Minneapolis, where sequences of the film were shot, too.

Back at Sunset Studio, Prince completed the soundtrack alone, including "When Doves Cry." The song was notable for its lack of bass guitar. "It was just sounding too conventional, like every other song with drums and bass and keyboards," Prince told *Bass Player* in 1998. "So I said, 'if I could have it my way it would sound like this,' and I pulled the bass out of the mix. [My engineer] said 'Why don't you have it your way?' . . . 'When Doves Cry' does have bass in it—the bass is in the kick drum" (Carl Koryat, "His Highness Gets Down!" *Bass Player*, November 1999).

Released in May 1984, the single rose immediately to number one Pop and R&B, and sold a million copies: the year's top seller. *Purple Rain*, the album, was released in June, and followed the same chart path. It stayed at number 1 for nearly six months, selling 16.3 million copies. In July came the movie, which also reached number one, making Prince the first artist since the Beatles to simultaneously have the top song, top album, and top movie. Three more singles followed "When Doves Cry" into the Top 10: "Let's Go Crazy" (number one), "Purple Rain" (number two), and "I Would Die 4 U" (number eight). Prince was the biggest act in the nation. The same summer, a third Time album, *Ice Cream Castle* (number three R&B), and a single by new protégée Sheila E. ("The Glamorous Life," number one Dance) rocketed up the charts.

The tour, of course, was Prince's biggest yet. The stage set cost $300,000. Prince changed costumes five times, and a purple bathtub rose from the stage. Prince now played in arenas for upwards of 20,000 people a night. The band gelled, often closing the show with a jammed-out rendition of "Purple Rain" that featured extended guitar solos by Prince. In addition to being a pop star, Prince's instrumental prowess was a key attraction for his burgeoning audience.

Often, Prince was compared to Jimi Hendrix. "It's only because he's black," Prince said. "That's really the only thing we have in common. He plays different guitar than I do. If they really listened to my stuff, they'd hear more of a [Carlos] Santana influence than Jimi Hendrix. Hendrix played more blues; Santana played prettier" (Neal Karlen, "Prince Talks," *Rolling Stone,* September 12, 1985).

With lyrical references to Prince's favorite color throughout, the shows took a conceptual bent. Midway through, Prince gave a monologue called "God," where he expressed a growing confusion about whether he could reconcile his music's explicit sexuality with his innate sense of spirituality. "I know I said I'd be good, but they dig it when I'm bad," he announced (Prince, *Purple Rain Tour Live in Syracuse,* bootleg).

Indeed, Prince's reputation was now synonymous with the obscene. In late 1984, his notoriety grew even further when Tipper Gore, wife of Senator Albert Gore Jr. (D-TN), discovered her daughter listening to "Darling Nikki," from *Purple Rain.* With its lyrics about the title character "masturbating with a magazine," Gore was outraged. In 1985, with a group of other Washington wives, she co-founded the Parents' Music Resource Center in an effort to mandate that record labels to issue albums with an age-appropriate rating system, similar to films. They held hearings in Washington.

"The PMRC's demands are the equivalent of treating dandruff by decapitation," they were told by iconoclastic guitarist Frank Zappa, who also used profanity in his work. "No one has forced Mrs. Baker or Mrs. Gore to bring Prince or Sheena Easton into their homes. Thanks to the Constitution, they are free to buy other forms of music for their children. Apparently they insist on purchasing the works of contemporary recording artists in order to support a personal illusion of aerobic sophistication" (Frank Zappa with Peter Occiogrosso, *The Real Frank Zappa Book,* New York: Poseidon Press, 1989, p. 268). Though the PMRC's proposed reforms were never formally passed, many labels did begin to brand albums with warnings of explicit content. Though he personally stayed away from Washington, Prince and "Darling Nikki" were a heated topic of conversation in newspapers and magazines.

REBIRTH OF COOL

And though he was undoubtedly a pop star known for suggestive lyrics, Prince began a conscious effort to expand his musical palette. He encouraged his bandmates and associates to expose him to musicians he had never heard before. Wendy and Lisa, who grew up in suburban California, and had rock and roll backgrounds, played him the Beatles and the Rolling Stones. Road manager Alan Leeds—who had worked previously for James Brown—was a jazz aficionado. With his brother Eric, who had joined the band on saxophone during the *Purple Rain* tour, they educated Prince on the catalogs of groundbreaking bandleaders like Miles Davis and Duke Ellington. Lisa's brother, Eric Coleman, was a multi-instrumentalist who introduced Prince to a variety of Arabic instruments.

While the Purple Rain tour continued, Prince began his next album, traveling to Los Angeles and Minneapolis to record between shows. Prince's openness to new music now extended into his approach to songwriting and recording. "Around the World in a Day" was co-written by David Coleman, spiced up with Prince's LM-1, and became the album's title track. Prince taught "The Ladder" to the band during a soundcheck in St. Paul, Minnesota, and recorded it with them the next day. Prince completed *Around the World in a Day* on Christmas Eve 1984, before he returned to the road for the tour's final three months.

A regular topic in the tabloid press, Prince was stung by media coverage that focused on his status as a celebrity instead of as a musician. Prince at first released *Around the World in a Day* in April 1985 with no publicity: no videos, no singles, no advertisements, no interviews. Though the album debuted at number 1 Pop, sales trailed off quickly, and Prince consented to videos and singles. Both "Raspberry Beret" and "Pop Life" made the Top 10, at number 2 and number 4, respectively. Though less successful than *Purple Rain*, *Around the World* still sold some 3 million units domestically.

As was habit, though, Prince was already back at Sunset Sound in Los Angeles. In late April, he and his musicians began several months of feverish work of around-the-clock sessions. At one, Prince recorded the drum tracks for four songs consecutively, leaving the tape running during the short breaks between them. When he was done, one by one, he added additional instruments. The four songs, including "Under the Cherry Moon," appeared in the same order on the album. Wendy, Lisa, Sheila E., and others added their own orchestrations to the songs. Eric Leeds contributed horn arrangements, as well; the first time brass appeared on a Prince album.

As he has been throughout his career, Prince was cavalier about assigning songwriting authorship. Though he credited his father, John L. Nelson, as a co-writer on *Around the World* in order to give him royalties, elsewhere Prince took ideas whole from his collaborators. Mazarati, a group Prince oversaw, reworked a song he had given them titled "Kiss." When Prince heard what they had added, he reclaimed the song and added his own vocals. When it was released on *Parade* in March 1986, it became the album's only Top 10 hit, reaching number 1 Pop.

Before Warner Bros. could release *Parade*, Prince began to shoot the follow-up to *Purple Rain*. Filmed in Nice, Italy, *Under the Cherry Moon* did not fare as well. Conceived as an arty black-and-white romantic/comedy and written by Becky Johnson, there were struggles on the set immediately. Four days into the shoot, director Mary Lambert was fired. Prince himself replaced her. Though disciplined, Prince had trouble with his new role. Worried, Warner Bros. insisted that Prince shoot a different, happier ending for the film. He did, though his original vision was used.

In the meantime, one of Prince's side-projects, the R&B band the Family, fell apart. The band featured both Jerome Benton, Prince's co-star in *Under the Cherry Moon*, as a dancer, as well as Susannah Melvoin on vocals. Melvoin was Wendy's twin sister, and Prince's partner in a tumultuous relationship. Without a tour, the Family's self-titled album was a bomb. When the Family disbanded, Prince simply invited the entire band to join the Revolution, swelling the band's ranks to 11 pieces. Wendy and Lisa were troubled by the addition of new instrumentalists to the already tight band.

END OF A REVOLUTION

In early 1986, before either *Parade* or *Under the Cherry Moon* were released, Prince moved into a new home in the Minneapolis suburb of Chanhassen, replete with a basement studio. Several miles away, work was under way for Paisley Park, Prince's new recording complex. Prince continued his forays into jazz, as well, recording a disc of untitled instrumental collaborations with Eric Leeds released under the name Madhouse. (The single, called "6" reached number five R&B in 1987.) Prince also struck up a relationship with jazz trumpeter Miles Davis. The two collaborated by mail on the unreleased "Can I Play With U," and would remain in touch until Davis's death in September 1991.

Prince's Kingdom

Prince's influence is inestimably diverse, running down a half-dozen branches of popular music's family tree. As a songwriter, others have taken his songs to the upper reaches of the charts, such as Sinead O'Connor's hit with "Nothing Compares 2 U" (number one Pop) in 1990, and the Bangles' iconic 1986 version of "Manic Monday" (number two Pop). Prince has penned songs as well for other pop musicians ranging from late 1980s dance sensation Paula Abdul ("U") to funk legend George Clinton ("The Big Pump") to crooner Kenny Rogers ("You're My Love"). Perhaps more fascinating, though, is how Prince has been interpreted outside the sphere of pop. Jazz pioneer Miles Davis, a friend of Prince's, included "Movie Star" during his live sets. Other jazz musicians have demonstrated the durability of Prince's melodies, including fusion keyboardist Herbie Hancock ("Thieves in the Temple") and old school revivalist trumpeter Steven Bernstein ("Darling Nikki"). In the rock world, Prince's influence has been even more widespread. The Foo Fighters, whom Prince covered himself during his 2007 Super Bowl appearance, put out versions of both "Darling Nikki" and "Drive Me Wild" as B-sides. Recording as Dump, James McNew, the bassist for seminal indie rock band Yo La Tengo, issued a complete Prince covers album. Titled *That Skinny Motherfucker with the High Voice?*, McNew borrowed Prince's recording style as well, playing all the instruments himself. An even more profound devotee of Prince was experimental art-pop-per Beck. On his first albums—1994's *Mellow Gold* and 1996's *Odelay*—Beck played the majority of the instruments himself. On 1999's *Midnite Vultures*, the influence was even greater, as the Los Angeles musician crafted a saucy millennial tribute to Prince's funk era. Though Prince himself has often been insular, working with a small circle of friends and associates, his wish for his music to break down boundaries has succeeded on nearly every conceivable level. It has crossed genres and generations, surviving equally in songs and style, on the dance floor, and in the collections of serious listeners alike.

Parade: Music from Under the Cherry Moon, released on March 31, 1986, charted at number three Pop and number two R&B, selling 2 million copies domestically, as well as 2 million copies abroad. While Prince's sales were down in the United States, he built a new, devoted fanbase in Europe. In July, *Under the Cherry Moon* itself was released, and was panned mercilessly by critics. *The San Jose Mercury News* called the film "an outrageous, unmitigated display of narcissism" (Michelangelo Matos, *Sign 'O' the Times*, New York: Continuum, 2004, p. 53).

Throughout the spring, Prince led sessions for an album to be titled *The Dream Factory*. Though worried about their roles in the Revolution, Wendy and Lisa played a large role in the composition and creation of the new material. When it came time to rehearse for the *Parade* tour, however, tensions came to a head. After Prince replaced several group-written numbers with songs he'd recorded by himself, Wendy and Lisa told Prince that they wanted to quit the Revolution. Tour manager Alan Leeds convinced them to stay for the tour. On October 7, a month after the tour ended, Prince himself fired them, as well as drummer Bobby Z. Rivkin and bassist Mark Brown. Only keyboardist Matt Fink remained in Prince's employ.

With the Revolution over, Prince scrapped the Dream Factory. Over the next months, Prince recorded and threw away three other albums, bits of which, along with *The Dream Factory*, became *Sign "O" the Times*. One was titled *Camille*, with songs based around an androgynous voice Prince developed using a pitch control. Another was a triple-LP set to be titled *The Crystal Ball*, highlighted by the ambitious multi-sectioned title cut, which referenced reggae, jazz, and included a 60-piece orchestra. Warner Bros. was opposed to the length of the release. After intense arguments with the label, Prince stripped the album to two discs. It was the first of many arguments he would have with Warner Bros. in the ensuing years.

Retitled *Sign "O" the Times* and released in March 1987, the set reflected its eclectic origins. It was received rapturously by the press, and charted at number six Pop and number four R&B, with Prince's sales overseas increasing further. Prince hit the road with his new band, which included

Sheila E. on drums, as well as the Family's Miko Weaver on guitar. Without the longtime chemistry shared with the Revolution, he had to build new musical relationships.

Though Prince had always been influenced by the bandleading style of James Brown, he adapted it even further to his own use. Using hand signals and shouts like "greased chicken!" Prince cued his band to play specific parts. With the expanded group, as well as frequent late-night gigs in clubs, the shows became even more like R&B revues. He often led the audience in call-and-response chants and modular sing-alongs, like the winged monkey chant from the *Wizard of Oz*. Though Prince made a concert film of the band's European tour, the footage was too grainy for release. Reshot on a soundstage with the band lip-synching to the original soundtrack, the film was released to theaters just before Christmas 1987 and disappeared. It was just one element of a bizarre holiday season for Prince.

Throughout the fall, Prince worked on *The Black Album*. Recorded mostly by Prince save for overdubbed horns, the album was filled with instrumental jazz experiments and obscene lyrics. There was no single. Prince told Warner Bros. that he wanted to release the album with no cover art or credits, just black on both sides of the jacket. Warner Bros. reluctantly agreed, and the album was readied for a December sale date.

On December 1, 1987, however, Prince visited Rupert's, a dance club in Minneapolis. Acting as a DJ, Prince played *The Black Album* for the crowd and spoke with fans. Sometime during the evening, Prince consumed the drug ecstasy, and had a powerful reaction. During the evening, he made the decision not to release *The Black Album*, set to go to stores in a week. It was too dark, Prince decided, too sexual. Just as he had convinced Warner Bros. to release the album with black covers, Prince now convinced them to recall the album from stores. More than 500,000 copies had to be destroyed.

With 1987 winding to a close, Prince celebrated the New Year at his newly opened Paisley Park Studios with a special concert. During a 30-minute "It's a Beautiful Night," Miles Davis joined the band on trumpet. It was the only time Prince and Davis appeared together on stage. Davis soloed as the band teased versions of James Brown's "In a Cold Sweat" and Duke Ellington's "Take the A-Train." Prince teased the 61-year-old bandleader, "Miles, it's past your bedtime, ain't it?" (Prince, *Ultimate Live Collection,* bootleg).

LOVESEXY AND BEYOND

To replace *The Black Album*, Prince began to record *Lovesexy* in January 1988. A major influence was Ingrid Chavez, a Minneapolis songwriter and poet Prince met while on ecstasy. Prince's new songs, such as "I Wish U Heaven" and the title cut did not eschew sexuality, but embraced even more spiritual themes. Chavez contributed poetry to the album, and was credited in the disc's liner notes as "the spirit child." It was one of Prince's first albums to be released on the new compact disc format. Prince insisted that listeners treat the album as a complete work of art and refused to put track breaks on the CD. He also refused to make videos for the album.

Released on May 10, 1988, it was the first new Prince album in a half-decade to sell less than a million copies. *Lovesexy* charted at number 11 Pop, number 5 R&B, and yielded the single "Alphabet St." (number 8 Pop). It marked a significant change in Prince's career. He now entered a period of decreasing popularity. There were many reasons for this. A large one was the ever-swelling popularity of hip-hop.

Though Prince saw the genre as a novelty, it grew to dominate both the charts and American culture at large. Prince's music started to sound dated, both in arrangement and lyrics. Where rap was built from samples, Prince still emphasized performance (even if he played all the instruments himself). More, after hip-hop, Prince's music no longer sounded shocking to the greater American public. He himself derided rap, even parodying it on "Dead On It," a track from *The Black Album*, which circulated as a bootleg.

Prince was not always absent from the charts. His soundtrack to Tim Burton's *Batman* went number one Pop, and the "Batdance" single did the same. But just as often, Prince's career was marked by questionable decisions. He planned a large tour behind *Lovesexy*. The set included a large fountain, a basketball court, a brass bed (on hydraulics), and a car. A month before the tour was scheduled to begin, Prince abruptly postponed it. He rescheduled it later, though many unsold tickets marked the performances.

He fired his managers when they told him his idea for his next film, to be titled *Graffiti Bridge*, needed work. Prince was ready to shoot it with a 20-page treatment he'd composed. When Madonna and Kim Basinger declined the key role of Aura, Prince drafted Ingrid Chavez, who had little acting experience. Though it was technically a sequel to *Purple Rain* and again co-starred Morris Day, the film fared disastrously. "It was one of the purest, most spiritual, uplifting things I've ever done," Prince argued in an interview. "Maybe it will take people 30 years to get it. They trashed *The Wizard of Oz* at first, too" (Hahn, p. 162).

Prince worked with a variety of other musicians, both within his own band and out. One was Tara Leigh Patrick, whom Prince renamed Carmen Electra. Despite a 1993 album issued on Prince's new Paisley Park Records, she would later have a more successful career as a nude model and actress. Distributed by Warner Bros., Paisley Park never achieved the success many hoped. "[Prince] never displayed the ability to park his own agenda," said Alan Leeds, who became the president of the imprint. "When he produced Patti LaBelle, it sounded like a Prince record. It became his vision, not the artist's" (Hahn, p. 181).

In 1990, Prince gave his band a name: the New Power Generation. The next year, the transition was made complete when he fired keyboardist

Matt Fink, who had joined Prince over a decade before. Prince began to employ the New Power Generation for studio recordings, often making new songs from impromptu jams. He used the distinct LM-1 drum machine only rarely, relying on grooves created by bassist Levi Seacer. The NPG's live shows featured appearances by the Game Boyz, a dance troupe. One of the Boyz, Tony Mosley, was an aspiring rapper. Though inexperienced, Prince gave him many turns in the spotlight, the first time rap became part of Prince's musical vocabulary. "I never said I didn't like rap," he told one reporter. "Anyway, everybody has the right to make mistakes" (Hahn, p. 176).

Prince continued to churn out albums. Co-credited to the NPG, 1991's *Diamonds and Pearls* did well (number three Pop, number one R&B) on the strength of the singles "Cream" (number one Pop), "Insatiable" (number three R&B), and the title track (number three Pop, number one R&B). Despite heavy criticisms of Tony Mosley's rap abilities, the album sold 2.9 million copies in the United States, and another 3.4 million overseas, Prince's biggest seller since *Purple Rain*.

But Prince soon returned to making baffling decisions. In 1992, he released an album whose title was an unpronounceable glyph that was a fusion of the symbols for male and female sexuality. According to Prince, it was a "rock soap opera" (Hahn, p. 187). Narrated by actress Kirstie Alley, the story—which Prince edited heavily in order to fit an extra song onto the album—did not make much sense to listeners. It reached number five Pop, though Prince was angry with Warner Bros. over what he thought was a lack of promotion.

Warner Bros., on the other hand, felt Prince flooded the market with his own albums, as well as those on Paisley Park. In 1993, Prince planned to release *Gold Nigga*, an album that highlighted Tony Mosley. Unimpressed by the music and the talent, Warner Bros. declined. Prince was aghast. He felt that he had too much music to make.

THE ARTIST FORMERLY CONSIDERED IMPORTANT

On April 28, 1993, Prince announced his retirement from recording. He would continue to release albums of leftover material recorded at Paisley Park, but no new songs would be laid to tape. Instead, the press release claimed, Prince would focus on "alternative media projects, including live theater, interactive media, nightclubs and motion pictures" (Hahn, p. 191). A month and change later, on June 7, his 35th birthday, he made an even more puzzling announcement: he was changing his name to the unpronounceable symbol that gave "name" to his last album. He distributed computer discs containing images of the symbol, so magazines could print it. Instead, most publications referred to him as "the Artist Formerly Known as Prince."

Prince gave incomprehensible interviews, including one to *Time Out* magazine. "Prince never used to do interviews," he said. "You'd have to ask Prince why he never used to do interviews, but you're not talking to Prince now. You're talking to me" (Hahn, p. 192). Soon, he was the butt of jokes on late-night television shows like *Saturday Night Live* and morning radio shows, like shock jock Howard Stern, who called him "the Artist People Formerly Cared About." Warner Bros. was not amused. In September 1993, they issued *The Hits*, a best-of collection, and placed an ad in *Billboard* all but making fun of the name change. The following week, Prince placed his own ad.

In August 1993, Prince's first musical-theater production debuted. Titled *Glam Slam Ulysses*, it starred Carmen Electra, and played at Prince's Glam Slam nightclub in Los Angeles, part of a new chain of venues, which also included a spot in Minneapolis. The show closed after only two weeks. In early 1994, Warner Bros. closed Paisley Park Records and gave Prince permission to release a single on his own label, NPG Records. Despite his promise to retire from writing new music, "The Most Beautiful Girl in the World" was released in February. It sold 700,000 copies and charted at number three Pop.

Prince's relationship with Warner Bros. crumbled. He presented the label with an album titled *Come*. With no obvious single, label heads Mo Ostin and Lenny Waronker rejected it. Prince reworked *Come*, and presented the label with a second new album, *The Gold Experience*. He proposed to release the former under the name "Prince," and the latter with his new moniker on the cover. Warner Bros., still wary of too much Prince product, told him they would only release *Come*. From then on, whenever Prince appeared in public, he wrote the word "slave" on his face in eyeliner. He told *Ebony* that Warner Bros.'s "censorship" was racial, and demanded the rights to his recordings. "If you don't own the masters, the master owns you," he claimed (Hahn, p. 196). "Prince, 1958–1993" read the cover of *Come*. The album sold only 345,000 copies.

In interviews, Prince implied that he kept his best material from the label. While he continued his battles with Warner Bros., he staged a massive tour of Europe billed as the Ultimate Live Experience. With a huge and obscene stage set, Prince mixed the sound himself from a soundboard behind the stage. The results were abysmal.

The next two years were marked by a series of back-and-forths between Prince and Warner Bros. In late 1994, Prince agreed to finally release *The Black Album*, in a limited edition. The funk-oriented *Gold Experience* followed in 1995. Though it sold better, was generally received more favorably than *Come*, and reached number six Pop, number two R&B, Prince did not reclaim his status. Finally, in January 1996, Prince reached an agreement with Warner Bros. He delivered two more discs of previously unreleased songs and was free. One, *Chaos and Disorder* only sold 140,000 copies in the United States.

A month after parting ways with Warner Bros., on Valentine's Day, Prince married Mayte Garcia. The two first met backstage at a Prince show in Germany in 1990, when Garcia was only 16. In the ensuing years, Prince had worked with her frequently, producing an album for her, and featuring her as a dancer during his stage shows. Soon after, Mayte became pregnant. In April, Prince was admitted to the emergency room of a local hospital with chest pains and nausea, though he did not make a public acknowledgment of any illness.

On October 16, Mayte gave birth. The child was born with Pfeiffer syndrome, a rare skull disease, and died a week later. Not only did Prince not make any public announcements, he actively made statements implying there was nothing wrong. "There is a rumor out that my baby died," he told *USA Today.* "My skin is so thick now. I care much more about my child than about what anyone says or writes" (Hahn, p. 215). Prince sunk himself into his music. His first post–Warner Bros. album in the form of the triple-disc *Emancipation*, released through a special one-album deal with EMI. While not a smash, it sold over 500,000 copies, and Prince continued to draw between 10,000 and 15,000 fans to most of his concert performances.

The following year, on August 12, Prince met former Sly and the Family Stone bassist Larry Graham at a late night show at Nashville, Tennessee's Music City Mix Factory. The 50-year-old bassist joined Prince and the New Power Generation for extended versions of Stone's "Thank You Falletinme Be Mice Elf Agin" and Al Green's "It Ain't No Fun to Be Me." Immediately, Prince invited Graham and his band, Graham Central Station, to join the tour as an opening act. The two musicians struck up a tight kinship. In April 1998, Graham and his wife relocated to Chanhassen, Minnesota, near Paisley Park, and Graham became Prince's new bassist.

Graham was a Jehovah's Witness, and became Prince's mentor in the faith. "He asked questions, [and] I started answering his questions from the Bible," Graham remembered later. "Not in my own words; I was simply showing what the Bible said. The more I showed him, the more he wanted to know" (Hahn, p. 221). As a result, Prince altered song lyrics to employ less profanity, and even had employees distribute Jehovah's Witnesses material to concertgoers.

THE COLOR PURPLE

Now free of Warner Bros., Prince began a second career as a label head, looking for innovative ways to sell his music. His first project was dubbed *Crystal Ball*, and revived elements of one of the albums he had scrapped for *Sign "O" the Times* in 1987. Prince sold the five-disc set through the 1-800-NEW-FUNK hotline for $60. Over 84,000 people ordered the eclectic package, which included a mostly acoustic disc titled *The Truth*, as well as an instrumental, New Age–like volume titled *Kamasutra*.

While Prince made money by selling albums directly to his fanbase, he also brought lawsuits against some of his biggest supporters. Believing they profited from his image, Prince sued the proprietors of fanzine *Uptown* as well as several Internet Web sites. Many of the sites, which did not have the money to defend themselves legally against the singer's allegations, closed. *Uptown*, whose circulation was not very large to begin with, continued to publish, with some concessions to Prince.

Prince's career continued as a patchwork of collaborations and projects. NPG Records released albums by the New Power Generation, bassist Larry Graham, and soul singer Chaka Khan, none of which sold very well. Prince recorded with folk singer Ani DiFranco ("Eye Love U But Eye Don't Trust U Anymore") and former James Brown saxophonist Maceo Parker ("Prettyman"), and issued a steady stream of projects, including *Rave Un2 the Joy Fantastic* for Arista Records. He continued to battle with Warner Bros., as well. When his former label announced plans to reissue "1999" in honor of the coming millennium, Prince immediately rerecorded it for NPG. In 1999, Prince and Mayte Garcia annulled their marriage.

At the turn of the century, Prince announced that he was once again to be called by his name. He admitted that changing it to the unpronounceable symbol was merely a legal tactic. The next year, Prince founded the New Power Generation Music Club. Each month, Prince posted several new songs to NPGMC site, which subscribers could listen to for $100 a year. With the ability to release music with almost no overhead cost, Prince argued that major labels were now unnecessary. Along with live cuts, Prince issued over three dozen new songs through the NPGMC.

On New Year's Eve 2001, Prince married Manuela Testolini, a longtime Prince fan who became a Paisley Park employee after she posted to a Prince Internet discussion group. Testolini was a Jehovah's Witness, as well. Prince became increasingly involved with the faith. From time to time, he would drive around Minneapolis in his limousine with bodyguards, proselytizing door-to-door.

"There's no more envelope to push," he told *The Mirror*. "I pushed it off the table. It's on the floor. Let's move forward. Back when I made sexy tunes, the sexiest thing on TV was *Dynasty* and if you watch it now, it looks like 'The Brady Bunch.' My song 'Darling Nikki' was considered porn because I said the word 'masturbate.' That's not me anymore" (Nick Webster, "From Sex God to Doorstep Bible Basher," *Mirror*, April 10, 2004).

Prince's new attitude extended to his fans, as well, offering NPGMC members first choice of concert seats. He also held several annual Celebration festivals at Paisley Park, where fans could tour the famed complex, participate in discussions about spirituality with Prince, and see several performances from their host.

In 2004, Prince returned to the spotlight when he included a copy of his newest album, *Musicology*, with all of his concert tickets. Because each counted as a sale, the album rocketed into the Top Five. But it wasn't just a publicity stunt. With the title track hitting number three R&B, the album went double-platinum by early 2005. Prince was nominated for five Grammys, and won two, for Best R&B Vocal Performance and Best Traditional R&B Vocal Performance—his first Grammy wins. The same year, he was inducted into the Rock and Roll Hall of Fame.

As he approached the age of 50, Prince continued to surprise. In 2006, he divorced Manuela Testolini, abruptly closed the New Power Generation Music Club, and opened the 3121 nightclub in Las Vegas. He performed every week at the latter for several months, where he mixed classic songs with spontaneous covers. Just as quickly, Prince moved on from Las Vegas, staging a residency in London, announcing a reunion with Wendy Melvoin and Lisa Coleman, and releasing new songs as ringtones through Verizon.

Prince's reign is far from over. As an idiosyncratic and prolific musician, he still has much to contribute. As an influence, Prince will be heard for many years to come. His songs have been hits for countless others, ranging from Sinead O'Connor to the Bangles, and his style has become the template for others, from pop stars like George Michael and Beck to indie rock muscians like Of Montreal. Everywhere is purple.

SELECTED DISCOGRAPHY

Dirty Mind (Warner Bros., 1980)

Controversy (Warner Bros., 1981)

1999 (Warner Bros., 1983)

Purple Rain (Warner Bros., 1984)

Around the World in a Day (Warner Bros., 1985)

Sign "O" the Times (Warner Bros., 1987)

The Black Album (Warner Bros., 1987, released 1994)

The Gold Experience (Warner Bros., 1995)

Emancipation (NPG/EMI, 1996)

FURTHER READING

Hahn, Alex. *Possessed: The Rise and Fall of Prince*. New York: Billboard Books, 2004.

Jones, Liz. *Slave to the Rhythm*. New York: Warner Brothers Paperback, 1998.

Matos, Michaelangelo. *Sign 'O' the Times*. New York: Continuum, 2004.

Nilsen, Per. *Dance Music Sex Romance: Prince, the First Decade*. London: SAF, 2004.

Bibliography

Bego, Mark. *Aretha Franklin: The Queen of Soul*. New York: Da Capo, 2001.

Bego, Mark. *Tina Turner: Break Every Rule*. New York: Taylor Trade, 2005.

Brown, James, with Tucker, Bruce. *James Brown:The Godfather of Soul*. New York: Macmillan, 1986.

Brown, Ruth with Yule, Andrew. *Miss Rhythm: The Autobiography of Ruth Brown, Rhythm & Blues Legend*. New York: Da Capo Press, 1999.

Burns, Peter. *Curtis Mayfield: People Never Give Up*. London: Sanctuary Publishing, 2001.

Carter, Doug. *Jackie Wilson: The Black Elvis*. New York: Heyday, 1998.

Charles, Ray and Ritz, David. *Brother Ray: Ray Charles Own Story*. New York: Da Capo, 2004.

Clarke, Donald, editor. *The Penguin Encyclopedia of Popular Music*. New York: Penguin, 1990.

Clarke, William, Cogan, Jim, and Jones, Quincy. *Temples of Sound: Inside the Great Recording Studios*. New York: Chronicle Books, 2004.

Collis, Mark. *Ike Turner: King of Rhythm*. New York: Do-Not Press, 2004.

Dalton, David. "Little Richard, Child of God." *Rolling Stone*, May 28, 1970.

Dalton, David, *Rock 100*. New York. Cooper Square Press: 1999.

Davis, Sharon. *Rhythms of Wonder*, London: Robson, 2003

Dobkin, Matt. *I Never Loved a Man the Way I Love You: Aretha Franklin, Respect, and the Making of a Soul Music Masterpiece*. New York: St. Martin's Griffin, 2006.

Douglas, Tony. *Lonely Teardrops*. New York: Routledge, 2005.

Edwards, Wayne, Nathan, David, and Warner, Alan. *People Get Ready! The Curtis Mayfield Story,* liner notes. Rhino, 1996.

Feldman, Jim. *Dusty In Memphis,* liner notes. Atlantic/Rhino, 1999.

Fong-Torres, Ben, and Mitchell, Elvis. *Motown Album: The Sound of Young America*. New York: St. Martin's Press, 1990.

Ford, Glen. "James Brown: The Man Who Named a People." Available online at www.countercurrents.org/for090107.htm.

Franklin, Aretha, and Ritz, David. *Aretha: From These Roots*. New York: Villard, 1999.

Freeman, Scott. *Otis*! New York: St. Martin's Griffin, 2001.

Gaar, Gillian. *She's a Rebel: The History of Women in Rock and Roll.* New York: Seal Press, 2002.

Gaye, Frankie and Basten, Fred. *Marvin Gaye, My Brother.* San Francisco: Backbeat, 2003.

George, Nelson. *Hip Hop America.* New York: Penguin, 2005.

George, Nelson. *Where Did Our Love Go?* New York: St. Martin's, 1983.

Gordon, Robert. *Anthology,* liner notes. Capitol Records, 1997.

Gordy, Berry. *To Be Loved: The Music, the Magic, the Memories of Motown.* New York: Warner Books, 1994.

Guralnick, Peter. *Dream Boogie: The Triumph of Sam Cooke.* New York: Little, Brown, 2005.

Guralnick, Peter. *Sweet Soul Music: Rhythm and Blues and the Southern Dream of Freedom.* New York: Harper Collins, 1986.

Hahn, Alex. *Possessed: The Rise and Fall of Prince.* New York: Billboard Books, 2004.

Hildebrand, Lee. *Etta James: The Chess Box,* liner notes. MCA/Chess 2000.

Hill, Michael. *Sam Cooke: The Man Who Invented Soul,* liner notes. RCA/BMG, 2000.

Hirshey, Gerri. *Nowhere to Run: The Story of Soul Music.* New York: Da Capo, 1994.

Hoskyns, Barney. "Looking at the Devil." *Observer Music Monthly*, March 19, 2006.

Hull, Ted and Stahel, Paula L. *The Wonder Years: My Life and Times with Stevie Wonder.* BookLocker.com.

Irwin, Jim, editor. *The MOJO Collection: The Greatest Albums of All Time.* London: MOJO Books, 2000.

Jackson, John A. *A House on Fire: The Rise and Fall of Philadelphia Soul.* New York: Oxford University Press, 2004.

James, Etta and Ritz, David. *Etta James: Rage to Survive.* New York: Villard 1995.

Jones, Liz. *Slave to the Rhythm.* New York: Warner Brothers Paperback, 1998.

Kempton, Arthur. *Boogaloo: The Quintessence of American Popular Music,* New York: Pantheon Books, 2003.

Kubernik, Harvey. *MOJO.* "Tell 'Em Willie Boy Was Here." London, September 1995.

Larkin, Colin, editor. *The Virgin Encyclopedia of R&B and Soul.* London: Virgin Books, 1998.

Lewis, Miles Marshall. *Sly and the Family Stone's There's a Riot Goin' On.* New York: 33 1/3, 2006.

Love, Dennis, and Brown, Stacy. *Blind Faith: The Miraculous Journey of Lula Hardaway, Stevie Wonder's Mother.* New York: Simon & Schuster, 2002.

Lundy, Zach. *Songs in the Key of Life.* New York: Continuum, 2005.

Lydon, Michael. *Ray Charles: Man and Music.* London: Routledge, 2004.

Marsh, Dave. *The Heart of Rock and Soul: The 1001 Greatest Singles Ever Made.* New York: Plume, 1989.

Matos, Michaelangelo. *Sign 'O' the Times.* New York: Continuum, 2004.

Merlis, Bob, and Seay, Davin. *Heart & Soul: A Celebration of Black Music Style in America 1930–1975.* New York: Stewart, Tabori & Chang, 1997.

Miller, Jim, editor. *The Rolling Stone Illustrated History of Rock & Roll.* New York: Rolling Stone Press, 1976.

Nilsen, Per. *Dance Music Sex Romance: Prince, the First Decade*. London: SAF, 2004.O'Brien, Lucy. *Dusty: The Queen Bee of Pop*. London: Pan, 2000.

Palmer, Robert, *Rock & Roll: An Unruly History*. New York: Crown, 1995.

Pitts, Leonard. *The Temptations Psychedelic Soul,* liner notes. Motown, 2003.

Ritz, David. *Divided Soul: The Life of Marvin Gaye*. New York: Da Capo, 1991.

Ritz, David. *Smokey Robinson and the Miracles: The 35th Anniversary Collection,* liner notes. Motown, 1994.

Robinson, Smokey and Ritz, David. *Inside My Life*. New York: McGraw-Hill, 1989.

Rose, Cynthia. *Living in America:The Soul Saga of James Brown*. London: Serpent's Tail, 1990.

Selvin, Joel. *Sly and the Family Stone: An Oral History*. New York: Avon, 1998.

Shaw, Arnold. *Honkers and Shouters: The Golden Years of Rhythm & Blues*. New York: Collier Books, 1978.

Stewart, Jim. *The Definitive Otis Redding,* liner notes. Rhino/Atco, 1993.

Thompson, David. *Funk: Third Ear Listening Companion Series*. San Francisco: Backbeat Books, 2001.

Turner, Ike and Cawthorne, Nigel. *Takin' Back My Name: The Confessions of Ike Turner*. London: Virgin, 1999.

Turner, Tina with Loder, Kurt. *I, Tina*. New York: Avon, 1986.

Valentine, Penny and Wickham, Vicki. *Dancing with Demons:Dusty Springfield*. New York: St. Martin's Griffin, 2000.

Vincent, Rickey. *Funk: The Music the People and the Rhythm of the One*. New York: St. Martin's Griffin, 1996.

Wade, Dorothy and Picardie, Justine. *Music Man: Ahmet Ertegun, Atlantic Records, and the Triumph of Rock'N'Roll*. New York: Norton, 1990.

Weinger, Harry. *Emperors of Soul,* liner notes. Motown, 1994.

Werner, Craig. *A Change Is Gonna Come: Music, Race, and the Soul of America*. New York: Plume, 1999.

Werner, Craig. *Higher Ground: Stevie Wonder, Aretha Franklin, Curtis Mayfield, and the Rise and Fall of American Soul*. New York: Three Rivers Press, 2005.

Wesley, Fred, Jr. *Hit Me, Fred: Recollections of a Sideman*, Durham: Duke University Press, 2002.

Wexler, Jerry and Ritz, *David. Rhythm and the Blues: A Life in American Music*. New York: St. Martin's Press, 1994.

White, Charles. *The Life and Times of Little Richard: The Quasar of Rock*. New York: Harmony Books, 1984.

Williams, Otis and Romanowski, Patricia. *Temptations*. New York: Cooper Square Press, 2002.

Wolff, Daniel. *Sam Cooke with the Soul Stirrers,* liner notes. Specialty Records, 2002.

Music

Baker, LaVern

LaVern Sings Bessie Smith by Bessie Smith (Atlantic/WEA, 1990)

LaVern Baker Live in Hollywood '91 (Rhino/WEA, 1991)

Soul on Fire: The Best of LaVern Baker (Atlantic/WEA, 1991)

Woke Up This Morning (DRG, 1992)

Brown, James

Star Time (Polydor, 1991)

Roots of a Revolution (Polydor, 1984)

Foundations of Funk: A Brand New Bag, 1964–1969 (Polydor, 1996)

Funk Power 1970: A Brand New Thang (Polydor, 1996)

Make It Funky—The Big Payback: 1971–1975 (Polydor, 1996)

Messin' with the Blues (Polydor, 1990)

Live at the Apollo (Polydor, 1963)

Say It Live and Loud: Live in Dallas 08.26.68 (Polygram, 1998)

Soul Pride: The Instrumentals (1960–69) (Polydor, 1993)

Brown, Ruth

Miss Rhythm: Greatest Hits and More (Atlantic, 1989)

Charles, Ray

Genius & Soul: The 50th Anniversary Collection (Rhino, 1997)

The Complete Country & Western Recordings 1959–1986 (Rhino, 1998)

Modern Sounds in Country & Western Music, Volume 1 & 2 (Rhino, 1998)

Standards (Rhino, 1998)

Cooke, Sam

Sam Cooke: The Man Who Invented Soul (RCA/BMG, 2000)

Live at the Harlem Square Club 1963 (RCA, 1963)

The 2 Sides of Sam Cooke (Specialty, 1970)

Franklin, Aretha

Amazing Grace: The Complete Recordings (Atlantic/Rhino 1972/2006)

Aretha: Live at Fillmore West (Atlantic/Rhino 1971/2006)

I Never Loved a Man (The Way I Love You) (Atlantic/Rhino, 1967/1999)

Lady Soul (Atlantic/Rhino 1968/1999)

Queen of Soul: The Atlantic Recordings (Atlantic/Rhino, 1992)

Funkadelic

Maggot Brain (Westbound, 1971)

The Electric Spanking of War Babies (Priority, 1981)

Free Your Mind . . . And Your Ass Will Follow (Westbound, 1970)

Funkadelic (Westbound, 1970)

One Nation Under a Groove (Priority, 1978)

Gaye, Marvin
Here, My Dear (Motown, 1977)
I Want You (Motown, 1976)
Let's Get It On (Motown, 1974)
The Master: 1961–1984 (Motown, 1995)
Midnight Love (CBS, 1981)
Trouble Man (Motown, 1971)
What's Going On? (Motown, 1971)

Isley Brothers
3 + 3 (T-Neck/Sony, 1973/1997)
Givin' It Back (T-Neck/Sony, 1971/1997)
Harvest for the World (T-Neck 1976)
It's Your Thing: The Story of the Isley Brothers (Epic/Legacy 1999)
Live It Up (Epic/Legacy, 1974/2001)
The Heat Is On (Epic/Legacy, 1975/2001)

James, Etta
At Last! (MCA/Chess, 1961)
Best of the Modern Years (Blue Note, 2005)
Come a Little Closer (MCA/Chess, 1974/1996)
Deep in the Night (Bullseye Blues, 1978/1996)
Her Best: The Chess 50th Anniversary Collection (MCA/Chess, 1997)
Love Songs (MCA/Chess, 2001)
Tell Mama: The Complete Muscle Shoals Sessions (Chess/MCA, 1968/2001)

Little Richard
The Georgia Peach (Specialty, 1991)
Here's Little Richard (Specialty, 1957)
The King of Rock and Roll: The Complete Reprise Recordings (Rhino Hand-made, 2005)
Little Richard (Specialty, 1958)
Little Richard Is Back (Vee-Jay, 1965)
Shag on Down by the Union Hall (Specialty, 1996)
The Specialty Sessions (Specialty, 1990)

Mayfield, Curtis
People Get Ready! The Curtis Mayfield Story (Rhino, 1996)
Curtis
Superfly

Parliament
The Mothership Connection (Casablanca, 1976)
The Clones of Dr. Funkenstein (Casablanca, 1976)
Funkentelechy vs. the Placebo Syndrome (Casablanca, 1977)

Prince
Dirty Mind (Warner Bros., 1980)
Controversy (Warner Bros., 1981)
1999 (Warner Bros., 1983)
Purple Rain (Warner Bros., 1984)
Around the World in a Day (Warner Bros., 1985)
Sign 'O' The Times (Warner Bros., 1987)
The Black Album (Warner Bros., 1987, released 1994)
The Gold Experience (Warner Bros., 1995)
Emancipation (NPG/EMI, 1996)
Ray! Original Soundtrack (Rhino, 2004)

Robinson, Smokey
Pure Smokey (Motown, 1974)
Quiet Storm (Motown, 1975/1991)
Smokey (Motown, 1973)
Smokey Robinson and the Miracles
The 35th Anniversary Collection (Motown, 1994)
Anthology (Motown, 1995)
Going to A Go-Go (Motown, 1965/2002)

Redding, Otis
Otis! The Definitive Otis Redding (Atlantic/Rhino, 1993)
Complete & Unbelievable: The Otis Redding Dictionary of Soul (Atco, 1966)
Otis Blue: Otis Sings Soul Music (Atco 1966)
In Person at the Whiskey A Go-Go (Atco 1968)
Redding, Otis and Carla Thomas
King & Queen (Stax, 1967)

Sly and the Family Stone
A Whole New Thing (Epic/Legacy, 1967/2006)
Dance to the Music (Epic/Legacy, 1968/2006)
Life (Epic/Legacy, 1968/2006)
Stand! (Epic/Legacy, 1969/2006)

There's a Riot Going On (Epic/Legacy, 1971/2006)
Fresh (Epic/Legacy, 1973/2006)
Small Talk (Epic/Legacy, 1974/2006)
The Essential Sly and the Family Stone (Epic/Legacy, 2002)

The Springfields
Anthology: Over the Hills and Far Away (Phillips, 1997)

Springfield, Dusty
The Dusty Springfield Anthology (Mercury/Chronicles, 1997)
In London (Atlantic/Rhino, 1999)
In Memphis (Atlantic/Rhino, 1969/1999)

The Supremes
Diana Ross and the Supremes Join the Temptations (Motown 1968/1991)
The Supremes (Motown, 2000)
The Supremes Sing Holland-Dozier-Holland (Motown, 1967/2007)
Where Did Our Love Go? (Motown, 1964/2007)

The Temptations
Emperors of Soul (Motown, 1994)
Psychedelic Soul (Motown, 2003)
With a Lot O' Soul (Motown, 1967)
A Song for You (Motown, 1975)

Turner, Ike
The Kings of Rhythm featuring Ike Turner: The Sun Sessions (Varese Sarabande, 2001)

Turner, Ike and Tina
The Best of the Blue Thumb Recordings (Hip-O, 1997)
The Great Rhythm & Blues Sessions (Tomato, 1991)
The Kent Years (Ace/Kent Soul, 2000)
Kings of Rhythm Band: Dance (Collectables, 1996)
Proud Mary: The Best of Ike and Tina Turner (EMI/Sue, 1991)
What You Hear Is What You Get: Live at Carnegie Hall (EMI, 1996)

Various Artists
Atlantic Rhythm and Blues 1947–1974 (Atlantic, 1991)
Atlantic Unearthed: Soul Sisters (Atlantic/Rhino, 2006)

Hi Times: The Hi Records R&B Years (Right Stuff/Hi, 1995)

The King R&B Box Set (King/Polygram, 1995)

The Mercury Blues 'N' Rhythm Story (Mercury/Chronicles, 1996)

Specialty Records Greatest Hits (Specialty, 2001)

The Specialty Records Story (Specialty, 1994)

The Sun Records Collection (Rhino, 1994)

Web Sites

All Music Guide: www.allmusic.com
  Authoritative site with discographies and biographies of popular artists.

Atlanta Journal Constitution: www.ajc.com
  Official Web site of the *Atlanta Journal Constitution.*

The Chicago Tribune: metromix.chicagotribune.com
  Official Web site of the Chicago daily newspaper.

The Classic Temptations: www.angelfire.com/stars/classictemptations
  An homage to the Motown greats.

Richard De La Font Agency: www.delafont.com/music_acts
  Blues and R&B booking agents

The Guardian: music.guardian.co.uk
  Music coverage in the London daily newspaper.

The History of R&B: randb.about.com/od/rbhistory/The_History_Of_RB.htm
  A timeline and history of rhythm and blues beginning in the 1930s.

The History of Rock: www.history-of-rock.com
  An exhaustive editorial look at the rock era's significant styles and acts.

The New York Times: www.nytimes.com
  Official Web site of the *New York Times.*

Pop Matters: www.popmatters.com
  Pop music site with a plethora of content, including reviews and analysis.

Rhino Records: www.rhino.com
  Premiere archival reissue specialists.

Rock and Roll Hall of Fame: www.rockhall.com/hof
  A guide to the inductees of the Rock and Roll Hall of Fame.

Rock's Back Pages: www.rocksbackpages.com
  An extensive archive of vintage and contemporary music journalism.

Rolling Stone Immortals: www.rollingstone.com/news/coverstory/the_immortals
  The magazine's selection of music's most influential artists.

Scotland on Sunday: scotlandonsunday.scotsman.com

TMZ: www.tmz.com
  Celebrity gossip, entertainment, and news site.

The *Virginian Pilot:* content.hamptonroads.com/story.cfm?story=114620&ran
=10846
  Virginia newspaper from Ruth Brown's hometown.

WGBH: www.wgbh.org/jazz
  An interview archive of jazz and soul artists.

YouTube: youtube.com
  Video site with hundreds of vintage R&B performances.

Films/DVD/TV

Hail! Hail! Rock 'N' Roll
Taylor Hackford directs Chuck Berry, Little Richard, and other early rock icons in an epic rock and roll film. (Image Entertainment/Universal, 1987)

The Dick Cavett Show: Rock Icons
The talk show of the 1970s hosted many relevant pop music celebrities, including Sly Stone and John Lennon. (Shout Factory, 2005)

Don't Knock the Rock
1957 follow-up to *Rock Around the Clock!* Starring original rock and roll bands and R&B artists. (Sony Pictures, 2007)

Dreamgirls
Oscar-winning feature film roughly based on the Supremes story and directed by Bill Condon. (Dreamsworks/SKG, 2006)

Ray!
Director Taylor Hackford's biopic on Ray Charles stars Oscar winner Jamie Foxx. (Anvil Films, 2004)

Rock Around the Clock!
1956 film featuring many original R&B and rock and roll performers, considered to be one of the first of its kind. (Sony Pictures, 2007)

Rock! Rock! Rock!
1956 film about the birth of rock, featuring many of the genre's original bands. (Passport Video, 2003)

The Temptations
Accurate and well-executed biopic adapted from the book of the same name. (De Passe Entertainment, 1998)

Index

About the Author and Contributors

BOB GULLA is a professional writer and co-author of *The Greenwood Encyclopedia of Rock History* (2005).

JESSE JARNOW has written for the *London Times, Rolling Stone*, the Associated Press, and elsewhere. He blogs about books, b-sides, and baseball at jessejarnow.com.

ANDY SCHWARTZ is the former publisher and editor of punk/new wave music magazine *New York Rocker*. He also served as national director of editorial services for Epic Records (a division of Sony-BMG) and as a consulting researcher and archivist for the Rock & Roll Hall of Fame.